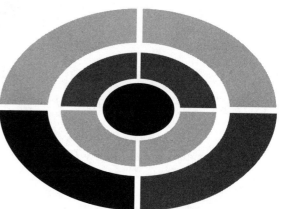

SALES MANAGEMENT

DEMYSTIFIED

Other Titles in the Demystified Series

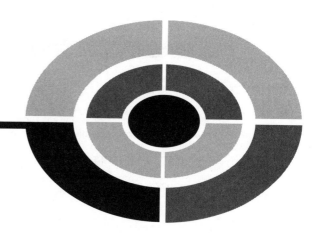

SALES MANAGEMENT
DEMYSTIFIED

A Self-Teaching Guide

Robert J. Calvin

McGRAW-HILL

New York Chicago San Francisco Lisbon London
Madrid Mexico City Milan New Delhi San Juan
Seoul Singapore Sydney Toronto

1 2 3 4 5 6 7 8 9 0   FGR/FGR   0 9 8 7

ISBN-13: 978-0-07-148654-5
ISBN-10:   0-07-148654-2

McGraw-Hill books are available at special discounts to use as premiums and sales promotions, or for use in corporate training programs. For more information, please write to the Director of Special Sales, Professional Publishing, McGraw-Hill, Two Penn Plaza, New York, NY 10121-2298. Or contact your local bookstore.

This book is printed on acid-free paper.

Library of Congress Cataloging-in-Publication Data

Calvin, Robert J.
　　Sales management demystified / Robert Calvin.
　　　　p. cm.
　　Includes index.
　　ISBN 0-07-148654-2 (pbk. : alk. paper) 1. Sales management. I. Title.
HF5438.4.C345 2007
658.8′1–dc22　　　　　　　　　　　　　　　　　　　　　　2006038612

In memory of my father:

Dr. Joseph K. Calvin

my mother:

Pauline H. Calvin

my daughter:

Amy E. Calvin

and my pal:

Father Kim Dreisbach

Dedicated to my wife:

Jane Calvin

my daughter:

Susan Roldan Calvin

and

my granddaughter:

Zoe Miranda Roldan Calvin

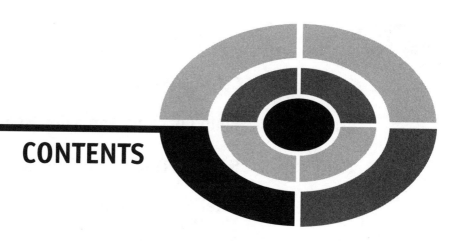

CONTENTS

CONTENTS

PREFACE

Sales Management on Steroids

Sales drive profits and hide many sins. A sales force is no better than its management. This book discusses the strategies, tactics, models, methodologies, theories, and practices that separate the best-of-breed sales managers from the mediocre. The book relies on my 40 years of experience as a salesperson, sales manager, vice president of sales, corporate general manager, company owner, consultant, and marketing professor. Over these years, I have learned from my own painful mistakes and from some very smart experienced professionals. This book attempts to span the gap between theory and practice, strategy and tactics, and the classroom and the marketplace.

The book targets newly promoted sales managers, aspiring sales managers, students of sales management, and all managers who want to improve sales force performance. The ideas in this book represent the proven formula for success that my clients, employees, and students have used for 40 years.

This book does not contain magic formulas or silver bullets. It does contain a lot of important ideas that, when implemented, can increase the probability of sales force success and reduce the risk of sales force failure. The ideas in this book are equally applicable to all types of companies, whether they are offering products or services or consumer or industrial goods or serving old- or new-economy markets.

Many of the ideas contained in this book relate to human resource issues such as hiring, training, motivation, and performance management. You will find these ideas useful not only in sales management but also in managing other business functions.

My goal in writing this book is for you to learn good ideas, to be motivated to use these ideas, and to enjoy reading the material. Learning should be fun.

In business, execution and implementation separate success from failure. Knowledge is power only if we use it. What I do promise you is knowledge, and if you use it, it will empower you.

Another goal is to help you understand more about a possible career in sales management. Let us assume you are a student, a salesperson, or a newly promoted sales manager. Will a career in sales management satisfy your needs and use your skills? Can you succeed as a sales manager, or are you better off in sales, marketing, or operations? The book will provide important insights into that decision.

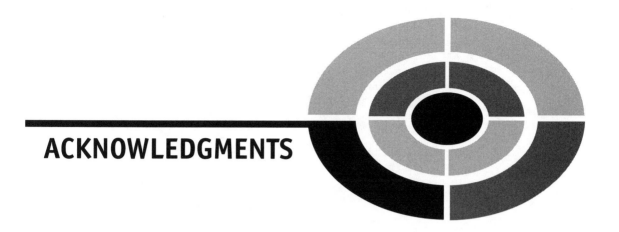

ACKNOWLEDGMENTS

I am grateful to my wife, Jane, who provided quiet time to write this book.

I want to thank my editor, Dianne Wheeler, at McGraw-Hill for her help in organizing this book and my previous editor at McGraw-Hill, Kelli Christiansen for helping me to write my previous book, *Sales Management*, The McGraw-Hill Executive MBA Series.

I also want to thank Angela Tong who assisted me with word processing, formatting, and research.

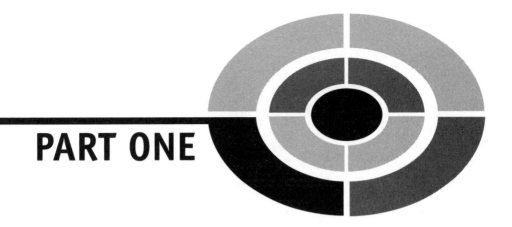

PART ONE

Creating the Sales Force

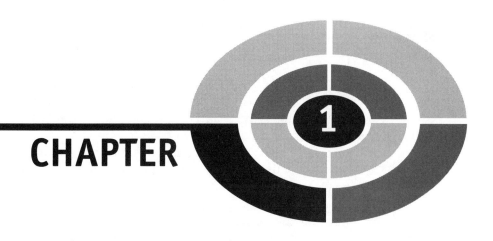

CHAPTER 1

People, Process, Technology, and Performance

The Process

Sales force management is a process—one step logically following another. Control the pieces and you control the whole. In this book we will devote one chapter to each of the pieces in the sales management process. For each piece we will build a model or a methodology, show how marketing and sales management can work together, and how strategy drives tactics.

The marketplace demands that marketing and sales management work together in such areas as quantifying benefits, collecting competitive information, and creating promotional material. However, in most organizations, turf battles and organizational politics prevent such coordination.

To keep sales management and marketing teams working together to improve sales force productivity and implement the steps in the sales management process, upper management must reinforce the need for marketing to devote 20 percent of its time to direct sales force support—for example, by providing market, customer, and competitor knowledge to salespeople. Organizations in which each department or function works in its own silo independently of the others are at a competitive disadvantage in today's commoditized world.

Most sales managers need to spend more time formulating strategies and objectives and less time resolving conflicts within and outside their organization and putting out fires such as filling in for an absent salesperson. If you do not know where you are going, you will never get there.

You must know what the house will look like before you start to build it. And while you are building it, you need to step out on the balcony occasionally to look around and make sure the house is shaping up the way you envisioned it originally. I suggest a sales manager spend an hour a week of quiet time pondering such issues as market-share goals, target markets, and growth objectives. The blueprint for the house is the objective and strategy; the hammers and saws to build the house are the tactics.

As a sales manager or a student of sales management, you must understand not only each step in the process but also the holistic system that these pieces together create. You must understand and master not only the micros but the macros, not only the quantitative but the qualitative. Each step in the process must work in harmony with the other steps. An excellent performance-based compensation system will not motivate salespeople unless they are well trained and have territories of equal potential.

Some sales managers are inspirational motivators but don't understand the process for hiring salespeople. Others excel at coaching but don't understand the necessity for performance evaluations. Few people understand, implement, and coordinate all of the pieces that make up the process as a whole. The resulting weak sales and sales management are the Achilles' heel of most old and new economy businesses. Most sales organizations need to be reengineered as you would a factory to increase capacity and productivity.

The sales management process and/or model involves the following pieces:

- Strategies and objectives

    o Structure follows strategy.
    o Tactics reflect strategy.

- Hiring and recruitment

  - Job descriptions, candidate profiles, sourcing, interviewing, reference checking, and final decisions.

- Training and development

  - Product, competitor, and customer knowledge.
  - Selling skills.
  - Field coaching, sales meetings, and initial training.

- Compensation

  - Total dollar level.
  - Fixed versus performance pay.

- Organization

  - Channel choice: direct or indirect.
  - Geographic, product, customer, or functional architecture.
  - Territory boundaries; deployment and sizing.
  - Time management within territory.

- Forecasts and plans

  - Bubble up versus top down.
  - Format.
  - Sales plan: actions that drive forecast numbers.
  - Measuring productivity.

- Nonmonetary motivation

  - Different sparks light different people's fires.
  - Recognition, usefulness, challenge, achievement, belonging, personal growth, and leadership.
  - Contests and incentive programs.

- Sales force automation

  - Systems applications.
  - E-commerce and the Internet.
  - Implementation.

- Communication

  - Management reports.
  - Techniques and skills.

- Performance management and evaluations

    o Results, activities, skills, knowledge, and personal characteristics.
    o Self-evaluations.
    o Quarterly reviews.
    o Goal setting; development plan.
    o Measuring productivity.

In a 2005 survey, Hewitt Associates asked sales and human resource executives at 63 Fortune 1000 companies to indicate the major sales management issues and/or challenges they will face over the next one to three years. In the 63 responses, retaining high-performing salespeople and improving sales force productivity were cited as the top sales management issues and/or challenges by all the participants, followed closely by restructuring the sales organization and improving communications technology, reporting systems, data access, and sales automation. The other major sales management issues and/or challenges cited were recruiting high-performance salespeople, changing processes or organizational structures to be successful in global sales opportunities, providing salespeople with better training and development, and merging the sales organization with that of another company or business unit.[1]

In an August 2006 survey, MarketBridge asked sales, marketing, and human resource executives at 120 midsized and large companies to identify their most important strategies for growth for the next year. Of those who responded, 74 percent cited new product introduction or product extensions, 59 percent cited changing customer or market segment focus, 50 percent cited integrating the sales and marketing efforts, and 48 percent cited hiring more salespeople.[2]

This Book Makes Three Basic Assumptions

1. *A sales force is no better than its management.* A weak sales force reflects weak management. As a colleague of mine says, "When the fish stinks, it starts at the head." For the multitude of sales managers who complain about their salespeople, this can be a painful concept to accept.
2. *A sales manager's job is to get work done through other people.* His or her success depends on the success of the sales team. Often you can do the job better than any of your people, but you cannot do the job better than the group. A sales manager's job is to make his or her salespeople more successful.

3. ***A manager's job is to make heroes, not be one.*** This applies to other functions besides sales. A sales manager who rides in at the last moment to land a big customer is being a hero, not making one.

Strategic Importance of Sales Force Management

In today's commoditized world, good sales management properly applied is the least expensive and most effective way to increase dollars of revenue and margins, market share, cash flow, returns on investment, and net present value and to beat the competition and make yourself a hero. Effective sales management is a great democrat for smaller firms. As the book shows, it costs little if anything more to properly hire, train, compensate, organize, motivate, and evaluate salespeople. Performing time and territory management, forecasting, planning, budgeting, and good communications and control effectively need cost no more than performing these same functions poorly. Sales drive profits and hide many sins. For public companies, sales growth drives earnings multiples. An annual revenue growth of 20 percent will create a 20 times earnings market valuation.

While good sales management does not guarantee success, poor sales management greatly increases the probability of failure. Also, since sales management deals with human behavior, there are many right answers, and your choice of which one is the best will depend on the nature of your organization.

E-commerce, the Internet, customer relationship management, and sales force automation are not silver bullets for success. They are part of the marketing and sales management process, which, if properly applied, can improve sales force productivity and capacity. Successful e-commerce companies still rely on high-touch telesales and/or telemarketing and field salespeople. Computers don't replace salespeople; they make them more effective.

What the Best Sales Managers Have in Common

I am often asked at cocktail parties and on television talk shows what separates the best sales managers from the not so best. Each year as I journey through corporate America, I meet hundreds of salespeople and sales managers. From those encounters, I have reached the following conclusions:

1. The best sales managers have what I like to call the "will to manage." They are willing to set standards, be critical, and sit in judgment. Since most sales managers were promoted because of their records as salespeople, it is not easy for them to set standards, be critical, and sit in judgment of their peers, even at a different employer. These sales managers need to make the transition from being a salesperson's friend to just being friendly.

2. The best sales managers realize they are agents of change, so they manage change even when it includes changing people's behavior. Rapidly changing competitors, products, technologies, markets, and customers make business a dynamic environment in which the future is a fast-moving target. Sales managers are at the vortex of these changes. The best sales managers may not like change, but they realize that managing change is part of their job. The not-so-best managers constantly complain about change and handle it poorly.

    Similarly, the best sales managers don't whine about their weak salespeople. Instead, they work to change their salespeople's behavior through nonmonetary motivation.

3. In addition, the best sales managers believe in what they are doing—the company, product, and job—which creates strong personal motivation for them, which they pass on to salespeople and customers.

4. The best managers also delegate, set goals, and plan well.

5. The best sales managers can communicate well not only with customers and supervisors but also with peers and the salespeople who work for them. Most sales managers were successful salespeople, and they have excellent communication skills with customers, but few communicate well with the salespeople who report to them. For the latter group to make the transition successfully from sales to sales management, they will need to develop the skills to communicate effectively with those who work for and with them.

6. The ability to execute and implement the sales management process, strategies, and tactics separates the best sales managers from the not so best. Many sales managers could write individual chapters for this book, but few could implement and execute all the tactics, strategies, processes, and methodologies in it.

7. The best sales managers can effectively manage both rookie and veteran salespeople, as well as those older and younger than they are. They can understand the distinct needs, goals, and problems of the individuals within these diverse groups.

8. The best sales managers train or terminate weak performers; they do not try to do their job or put up with mediocre results. If a salesperson underperforms,

the best managers will create a development program to improve performance. If after sufficient time, performance does not improve, the weak salesperson will be replaced.

Key Control Points

Every business and every business function has key control points in all areas of operation. For example, in the financial area these would include dollars of contribution margin, capital expenditures, working capital, sales forecasts, and line item expense budgets. Write down the key control points in the sales management process for your firm or one you are familiar with. Which steps in the process are most important for the success of that business? Knowing where these steps are tells the sales manager where to focus. The key control points will vary by business. They will be different for managing the sales of telecommunications services versus telecommunications equipment. They will be different for managing the sales of bakery products versus refuse-removal services.

There are some control points, however, that exist for almost all businesses. For example, most sales managers would include the following areas in their list of key control points:

1. The company's or organization's strategies and objectives would be included because these drive the business tactics and influence the organization's structure. Is the strategy to target large or small customers, restaurants, or hotels? Is the strategy to increase business from present accounts or open new ones?
2. The job description would be included because it lists the salesperson's anticipated duties. If the manager does not know precisely what a salesperson should do, it will be difficult to hire, train, and evaluate him or her effectively.
3. The candidate profile would be included because it lists the skills, knowledge, experience, and personal characteristics necessary for a salesperson to meet the standards established in the job description. A manager cannot hire appropriate salespeople without knowing what to look for.
4. The training checklist would be included because it covers the topics in which a salesperson must be trained in order to function effectively in the company. What specific knowledge of products, competition, customers, and selling skills produces the best salespeople?
5. Out of the training checklist flows a quarterly development plan for each salesperson. This is a key control point because each salesperson is a revenue, cost, and profit center. To improve revenues, lower costs, and raise dollars of profit, does the salesperson need more training in IT skills, time and territory management, customer knowledge, or closing skills?

6. Accurate targeting of customers and markets is an important key control point. How did each salesperson select his or her top 10 prospects and growth accounts? Salespeople often waste too much time calling on the wrong customers or prospects with the wrong products or services. The sales objective of too many expensive salesperson customer visits is to share a cup of coffee with a friend.

7. Similarly, correctly sizing and deploying the existing sales force can increase revenues without increasing costs, so this is a key control point. How many salespeople does a company need, and how large should each salesperson's territory be? Territory size and boundaries must reflect equal potential, the salesperson's workload (the number of customers and required calls), and the salesperson's daily, weekly, monthly, and annual call capacity. In today's commoditized world, the correct sizing and deployment of a sales force can create a competitive advantage.

8. Sales forecasts and sales plans are also key control points for the sales manager. How many dollars' worth of revenue by customer, product, and service does each salesperson plan to sell next quarter, and what activity (what plan) is necessary to create those sales? How many customer visits, presentations, and plant tours is each salesperson planning?

9. Performance management is another key control point. On a quarterly basis the sales manager should evaluate each salesperson's results and the activities, knowledge, skills, and personal characteristics needed to drive those results. The sales forecast and sales plan contain the standards against which the activities and results are measured.

We manage what we monitor. A sales manager should understand and use key control points to appropriately allocate time. The list presented here represents a good start.

Universal Concepts

The sales management process discussed in this book is equally applicable in telesales and field sales and in retail consumer sales and business-to-business sales. And it works equally well with full-time direct salespeople and indirect representatives, distributors, channel partners, and brokers. Instituting this process will make the salesperson and the manager partners, which will increase the productivity of any type of sales force.

The Changing Landscape

Business is a dynamic environment, and the future is a moving target. Sales managers are agents of change and must manage change. We are paid for managing the future, not the past. The 1990s were turbulent; in the new millennium, the pace of change will accelerate.

As a sales manager or a student of sales management, consider how the following changes will impact the sales management process, strategy, and tactics.

- *Shorter product and service life cycles.* These shorter life cycles quickly commoditize products and services, and make them more difficult to differentiate. In the twenty-first century, this trend will continue and accelerate. Whether you sell semiconductors, medical devices, telephone services, or bakery products, successful services and products are and will be quickly imitated and improved on.

  A company's sales management strategy must address this reality through improved product knowledge and sales skills training, different recruiting requirements, and possibly a hybrid organizational structure. The companies that can reduce the time and steps between a customer's search and purchase will be the winners. You must compensate salespeople to compress the sales-buying cycle, which will be discussed in a later chapter.

- *Longer, more complex sales cycles.* The number of steps from customer search to purchase is expanding. For example, in buying miniature transformers for insertion in a newly designed printed circuit board, customers expect vendors to do a needs assessment, have vendor engineering prepare customized specifications, submit samples that are used for demos and trials (betas), place a trial production order, and submit a final proposal. In selling a new variety of frozen muffin batter to a bakery, the salesperson must submit finished muffin samples for a taste test, deliver a trial batter order, show the baker how to use the batter, and train clerks on point-of-purchase sell-through. As recently as 1997 this was not necessary in either industry. The vendor who can shorten the sales cycle will win the business. So this changing landscape demands a changing sales management strategy that drives new tactics. Sales managers may need to hire people with experience in this type of selling and train them in how to perform each step in the process along with how to track the process. Sales cycles may be long, so performance pay might reflect progress from one step to the next. This might also necessitate organizing the sales force in teams.

- *Buying from experts and friends.* In some industries the people who make buying decisions have become more knowledgeable and experienced;

in others, less knowledgeable and experienced. For example, the people involved in purchasing communications and navigational equipment for aircraft generally have a knowledge level equaling that of any vendor salesperson. Therefore, the salesperson differentiates himself or herself by being more of a friend than an expert, and the candidate hiring profile should emphasize customer knowledge and experience in relationship selling. Hospital personnel purchasing software for measuring efficacy or controlling costs probably will not be experienced or knowledgeable in this area. Such purchases might be a one-time or first-time event, so in this situation the salesperson must be more of an expert than a friend. Therefore, training should emphasize product knowledge over knowledge of competition or customers. The candidate hiring profile should emphasize experience in consultative sales.

- *Group decision making.* In the twenty-first century to spread the risk of major purchases, more decisions are made by groups. For example, when a municipality buys catalytic converters for buses or a telco buys shielded twisted cable for data transmission, the purchasing decision will be made or influenced by engineers, purchasing, finance, and operations. This requires salespeople to be trained in multilevel selling. What are each group's needs and how will each group benefit from the purchase? Who is the decision maker and who are the influencers? Which people can say no and which person can say yes to placing an order? Team selling may be required. Forecasts and plans may become more difficult. The candidate hiring profile might change.

- *Intense competition.* Because of global markets, low barriers to entry, low customer switching costs, and changing technology, competition in the twenty-first century is and will be even more intense. This drives the shorter product and service life cycles and the commoditization mentioned in the first point. The Internet, lower costs, and greater speed of microchips have allowed the proliferation of ants (small start-ups) to compete with the giants. Technology is the great democrat. World markets including the United States are impacted by the low-cost, highly trained and efficient human resources in China, India, Russia, and Eastern Europe. To combat this, sales managers must use competitive grids to train salespeople. Who are the present and potential competitors? What are the competitive issues, and how does a customer choose between vendors?

- *Less customer loyalty.* People who make buying decisions will be increasingly less loyal to a particular vendor in the twenty-first century. The CFO of a major hospital recently told me that unless he lowers the cost per patient day by 10 percent in the year 2007, he will be looking for a new position in 2008. The hospital's managed-care customers demand this cost reduction. Access to the Internet provides instant competitive product and price information, thereby increasing transparency and further reducing customer loyalty.

In the twenty-first century, salespeople must be trained to quantify benefits and alternative costs by demonstrating how much a particular feature can lower a customer's or prospect's costs, increase revenues, and lower capital expenditures or working-capital needs. Whether you are selling paper stock to a printer or hand tools to a dentist, salespeople must be trained to demonstrate, quantify, and prove the value-added benefits for the customer. This makes price less important and allows a customer to rationalize his or her choice of vendors.

The Best Salesperson Is Promoted to Sales Manager

Often the best salesperson does not have the skills, knowledge, experience, or personal characteristics appropriate for a sales manager. However, to motivate and reward the high-performing salesperson, he or she is promoted to sales manager, often without training for the new position. Since a sales force is not better than its management, this creates major problems for the organization. Often the organization loses a good salesperson and gains a mediocre sales manager. This may cause poor performance and increased turnover.

Legacy Issues

In many mature industries such as chemicals and steels, legacy issues influence sales management decisions. We have always paid straight salaries and organized territories by state, so we must continue these traditions. Since the business environment constantly changes, the sales management processes need annual revisions. As new products are introduced and as strategies, competitors, customers, and technology change; the hiring, training, compensation, and organization of salespeople must also change.

Similarly some firms choose their sales management processes by following the competition. I call this "following the loser." The competition may not employ the most productive sales management process, and certainly its business is different from yours. By constantly updating the sales management processes to reflect the changing landscape of your firm, you can create a competitive advantage in a commoditized world.

Quiz for Chapter 1

1. Which of these is *not* part of the sales management process?
    a. Strategies and objectives
    b. Hiring and recruitment
    c. Training and development
    d. Compensation
    e. Forecasts and plans
    f. Product development
    g. Nonmonetary motivation
    h. Performance management and evaluations
    i. Market research

2. Which two of these do not separate the best sales managers from the not-so-best sales managers?
    a. Strong financial skills
    b. The will to manage
    c. Agents of change
    d. Strong communication skills
    e. The ability to execute and implement
    f. Strong selling skills

3. Select from this list the key control points:
    a. Strategies and objectives
    b. Job description
    c. Candidate profile
    d. Training checklist
    e. Product line P&L
    f. Sales contests
    g. Targeting of customers and markets
    h. Sizing and deployment of the sales force

4. Which of these are part of the changing landscape?
    a. Shorter product or service life cycles
    b. Larger, more complex sales cycles
    c. Group decision making
    d. Intense competition
    e. Less customer loyalty

5. True or false?
    Often the best salesperson does not have the skills, knowledge, experience, or personal characteristics appropriate for a sales manager.

6. True or false?
   Since the business environment constantly changes, the sales management process needs annual revision.

7. True or false?
   All the steps in the sales management process must work together to create a holistic system.

8. Which of these are assumptions made throughout this book?
   a. A sales force is no better than its management.
   b. Money is not a universal incentive.
   c. A sales manager's job is to make salespeople successful.
   d. A manager's job is to make heroes, not be one.

9. True or false?
   In today's commoditized world, good sales management properly applied is the least expensive and most effective way to increase dollars of revenue, margin, and market share.

10. True or false?
    The sales management process discussed in this book is equally applicable to telesales, field salespeople, and channel partners.

Notes

1. *Hot Topics in Sales Management and Sales Compensation 2005*. Copyright © 2005 Hewitt Associates LLC. Reprinted by permission of Hewitt Associates.
2. MarketBridge, Mark Donnolo, *Performance-Driven Selling 2006*. Marketbridge Technologies. Copyright © 2006. Reprinted by permission of MarketBridge.

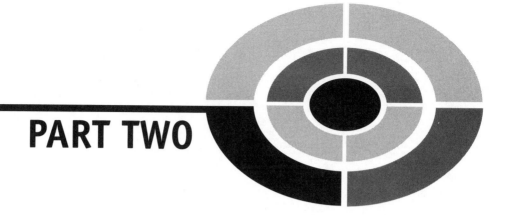

PART TWO

Hiring the Best; Terminating the Rest

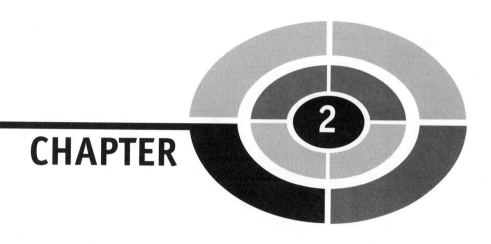

Job Descriptions, Candidate Profiles, and Sourcing

The Hiring Process

What is the most important function a sales manager performs? The answer is hiring. No matter how good you are at training, motivating, evaluating, and planning, all that applied to mediocre salespeople or channel partners produces only mediocre results. Yet hiring is an area many sales managers have never been trained in and often have little experience implementing. Cast the play well and it becomes easier to direct. How many times does a sales manager say, "I just can't improve this person's performance so I must live with below-average results."

In the twenty-first century, you can't afford to live with below-average results because effective sales organizations will create competitive advantages that differentiate one firm from another in a commoditized world.

This chapter and the next talk about a hiring process or filter that will increase the probability of hiring the best person and reduce the risk of hiring the wrong person. The same process should be used to hire inside telesales and outside direct salespeople along with channel partners. As you will see, each step in the process acts as a filter. The more steps you use, the lower your risk of failure, but the longer the process will take. Later in this chapter and the next we will discuss techniques for reducing the time required for hiring a salesperson. In its simplest form the process involves a job description, candidate profile, sourcing, screening, and making the final choice. *Sourcing* is where and how we look for candidates, whether it be competitors, customers, or Web sites. *Screening*, which is covered in Chapter 3, involves phone and personal interviews; reference checking; credit, drug, and driver's license checks; testing; and making a final choice. Each step in a sales manager's hiring process should be driven by strategic corporate issues, such as target markets, revenue goals, and market-share versus customer-share goals.

The vice president for sales of a Fortune 500 company that employs over 1,000 salespeople revealed that 55 percent of his salespeople are wonderful human beings, but they should not be in sales. Their skills, experience, and personal characteristics better suit them for human resources or information technology or operations. He said 25 percent of the salespeople had appropriate skills, experience, and personal characteristics, but they were misapplied. That is, they were good at selling products but were employed to sell services, or they were good at relationship sales but were being used for consultative sales. That left 20 percent of the sales force who produced over 50 percent of the revenues. "Just think," he said, "if we could expand that 20 percent, what our sales would be."

The Role of Human Resources in Hiring

If a firm has a human resources department, the division of hiring duties between the sales manager and HR becomes an important issue. Since the sales manager's success depends on the success of her or his salespeople, she or he must have proper authority and responsibility for key hiring activities and decisions. Human resources can be helpful in sourcing or finding candidates, reviewing job descriptions and candidate profiles, interviewing candidates, and explaining legal issues. The sales manager makes the final hiring decision, but human resources advises and helps.

In some firms the human resources department has the primary responsibility for selecting and training salespeople, who are then assigned to a sales manager. If the salesperson does not perform to expectations in this situation, who assumes responsibility?

The sales manager's job is to make his or her salespeople successful, so the manager must have the proper authority and responsibility to hire the best and terminate the rest.

A Continuous Process

Hiring is a continuous process. You should be looking for outstanding people always, not just when you have a vacancy. The best way to interview candidates is when they don't think it is an interview—at a trade show or casually over lunch, for example. When salespeople call on you to sell a service or product, evaluate them as potential candidates. When a competitor's salesperson contacts you for a position, be sure to meet with him or her. Ask probing questions and be a good listener. Keep a file of qualified candidates. When a position is available, you will have a head start, which will reduce the time required to hire a salesperson.

Getting the Right People on the Bus, the Wrong People Off the Bus, and the Right People in the Right Seats

The president of a medium-sized Omaha-based meat processing firm was losing market share in this competitive industry. The firm employed 10 regional sales managers who each managed 10 salespeople. To improve market share, the company president insisted that each regional manager terminate and replace one of his or her salespeople a year in addition to anyone who retired, voluntarily left, or was terminated for not meeting minimum performance standards.

Two years later market share and revenues were on the rise. Five years later the firm was an industry leader. There might have been many reasons for this, but one stands out. The new policy forced the sales managers to always be looking for better people. Letting 10 percent of the sales force go each year caused continuous improvement. The 10 percent were not top performers, and they were replaced by better people. The salespeople who remained were highly motivated to be part of a select team. They had complained about weak performers, and they hardly

noticed their absence. The lesson: Use hiring to weed the garden, and let the cream rise to the top. Rather than using hiring as a reactive tool, use it as a proactive tool to improve sales force productivity.

Costly Hiring Mistakes

Most sales managers have weak track records in hiring. We make the same mistakes continually and don't take corrective action.

1. Most sales managers prefer salespeople who share their backgrounds, make a nice appearance, are easy to manage, and do not threaten them. Most sales managers hire people they enjoy, but this natural selection does not necessarily result in the best sales force. First-rate managers hire first-rate people. Second-rate managers hire third-rate people. I once attended a sales meeting where 7 of the 20 salespeople were named Randy, 14 were bald, and of those 14, 10 had beards. Randy, the sales manager, was bald and had an attractive beard. I attended another sales meeting where all the salespeople had graduated from the same college as their manager.

2. Being sales types themselves, many sales managers oversell the job when they meet Ms. or Mr. Perfect. They assure the candidate that competition is nominal, customers seldom complain, and "paperwork" remains minimal. Overselling the candidate results in unmet expectations, disappointment, resentment, and high turnover. If the territory requires a great deal of prospecting, or the company culture is highly results oriented or sales are declining, admit it.

3. Occasionally, after you have completed the steps described in this chapter, only a best candidate will emerge, not an excellent candidate. When this happens, don't hire the best of a weak group, because doing so will not solve your problem. A weak salesperson can prove to be more expensive than no salesperson. It is less expensive to continue looking than to hire, fire, and look again.

4. Hiring requires planning, anticipating needs, and working within an appropriate time frame. Many managers hire reactively and under pressure. Customers and management insist that a warm body be put in any open territory and that all territories be fully staffed. The resulting pressure to hire in a hurry increases the risk of failure. The hiring process or filter takes 30 to 90 days. However, having a mobile spare salesperson in training, on the bench, mitigates the time pressure. A study conducted by the International Association of Corporate and Professional Recruitment (IACPR) in 2000 reports an average of 4.13 months to hire a qualified salesperson.

The Cost of Salesperson Turnover

Ask any sales manager how many salespeople he or she has hired in the last four years and how many of those hired are still with the company and of those how many is he or she still happy with. The answers will surprise you. Industry averages are not meaningful because the range has such extremes.

A giftware importer whose business involved selling to retailers had 100 percent turnover in its 350-person sales force, and that represents one extreme. Some of the importer's territories turned over twice. Problems ranged from compensation to hiring to training. The cost of this turnover exceeded $2 million, about equal to the firm's pretax profit.

1. Hiring the wrong salesperson proves expensive because of the loss of potential sales (opportunity cost) and/or the loss and replacement of the person hired. During the absence, the territory productivity suffers, and competitors gain market share. You can easily spend $50,000 in time and out-of-pocket expenses finding, screening, hiring, and training a new salesperson. Losing a new hire for whatever reason represents a nonrecoverable, nonproductive cost similar to a bad debt. Some companies estimate the cost at 150 to 200 percent of a salesperson's annual compensation.
2. Termination results in loss of continuity for the sales force and further reduces sales.
3. Competitors target territories and companies with high sales force turnover.
4. Customers must trust the salespeople they deal with, and continually replacing sales staff destroys this confidence.
5. A company with high salesperson turnover gets a bad reputation with customers, prospects, and potential salespeople, and, of course, it lowers the morale of its current sales organization.
6. In a smaller company, sales force turnover can also have a direct impact on unemployment insurance costs.

Hewitt Associates asked sales and human resources executives at 63 Fortune 1000 companies to supply their actual sales force turnover rates. Of the 60 responses, 12 percent of the participants reported turnover rates of less than 5 percent; 27 percent of the participants reported turnover of 5 to 10 percent; 23 percent of the participants reported turnover of 10 to 15 percent; and 17 percent of the participants reported turnover of 15 to 20 percent. The average turnover rate was reported to be 14 percent. Participants estimated the replacement cost per employee (turnover cost per employee) averaged $67,000.[1] Of the 54 replacement cost responses, 40 percent reported employee replacement costs under $50,000, and 40 percent reported employee replacement costs from $50,000 to $100,000.

The best ways to reduce the risk of making a bad hiring decision and to reduce turnover are to use a realistic job description and candidate profile that reflect a firm's strategy, to contact appropriate sources for attracting candidates, and to skillfully screen and select the best candidates from those who apply. As we move through the first decade of the twenty-first century, more skills and knowledge are demanded of salespeople, and, in return, they are demanding more from the organization, resulting in a more complex hiring process.

Strategic Duties and Issues Involved in Hiring

The job description is a list of anticipated duties. Where do you want the salesperson to concentrate? Does the job description target your most important customers, markets, and products? The candidate profile asks what salesperson experience, skills, knowledge, and personal characteristics are required for success with these target customers, markets, and products.

Exhibit 2.1 lists the strategic duties that should be included in a salesperson's job description. Exhibit 2.2 lists the strategic issues that should be included in a salesperson's candidate profile. (See the end of this chapter for both exhibits.)

1. Allocating the proper amount of time to target accounts, markets, and products is a strategic duty that should be included in a salesperson's job description. Salespeople must be trained in how to determine which customers and markets represent targets.

   Target accounts, markets, and products are determined by dollars of present and potential revenue and income, cost to sell and serve, and probability of success. Some customers have high dollar potential for revenue and gross margin, but they take the margin dollars back by demanding costly free services and/or a long complex sales cycle. *Activity-based accounting* (ABC), which measures the cost of each salesperson's and support person's activities, can help you determine these costs. High-maintenance accounts might require "free" design and engineering support. Export accounts might require special packaging and documentation. Customers and prospects that demand betas, trials, samples, and teams are expensive to sell. Alcatel-Lucent may represent large potential revenue and income dollars for your business, but it has a three-year contract with a competitor. Your probability of success is low.

   Industry publications, associations, and government statistics can be helpful in targeting markets by providing information on potential revenue.

Potential revenue data are often available by SIC (or NAICS) code, region, state, city, and zip code.

Some companies don't have targets or they have incorrect ones. A home-health-care provider thought its target referral customers were physicians when in fact they were discharge social workers at hospitals. You would not hire the same type of salesperson to call on physicians that you would hire to call on social workers. Clearly defining your firm's target customer will help you hire the most appropriate salesperson and help that person correctly allocate his or her time. As you will see in Chapters 8 and 9, salespeople are an expensive human resource, and correctly focusing their activities will increase their productivity and lower the cost per dollar of revenue produced.

2. Another strategic issue to be reflected in the job description and candidate pro-file is whether you want salespeople to concentrate on new accounts (*market share*) or to further penetrate your business with existing customers (*customer share*). Where is the opportunity for growth better? Salespeople need to know this for proper time allocation. Also, opening new accounts versus penetrat-ing existing accounts requires salespeople with different skills, knowledge, experience, and personal characteristics.

    The MarketBridge survey of sales, marketing, and human resource execu-tives from 120 midsized and large firms found that between 2005, 2006, and 2007, respondents showed a shift in priorities toward new customer selling and new market expansion and away from present customer revenue retention. Such a shift must be reflected in the hiring and training of salespeople.[2]

3. How does buyer behavior, a marketing concept, affect your target accounts, job description, and candidate profile? Are your target accounts making one-time or first-time purchases of your product or service (new systems), as with software or medical equipment? If so, salespeople need consultive sales skills, strong product knowledge, and experience in long, complex sales cycles. Or are your target accounts making modified rebuys of the same product or service or existing system (insurance or telco services), in which case your salespeople need strong customer knowledge, relationship sales skills, and experience in negotiations. Or perhaps you sell a commodity (paper to printers) in situations in which salespeople are order takers and time man-agement is most important. On the other hand, your target accounts might be most interested in a continual flow of new products or services (pharmaceu-tical products to physicians), so strong selling skills and the ability to accept rejection are most important for new hires. These issues need to be reflected in the job description and candidate profile. These buyer behavior issues also impact training, compensation, and organization of a sales force, which we will address in later chapters. Exhibit 2.3 at the end of this chapter illustrates the four quadrants of buyer behavior.

4. Similarly, if salespeople have a pricing window and negotiate price, or if delivery and product or service customization is strategically important, it is essential to list this information as a duty in the job description and as a desired experience in the candidate profile. Also include pricing and negotiating skills in the training checklist (see Chapter 4). If telesales is an important salesperson tool, put it in the candidate profile and job description.

5. Strategic management decisions concerning channel choice, team selling, sales force organization, telesales, and national account sales also should be reflected in the job description and candidate profile. If salespeople will be working in a hybrid organization selling through reps, agents, or distributors, this fact certainly influences the anticipated duties as well as the experience, knowledge, and skills you seek. If salespeople will be calling on national accounts in teams, state this as a duty in the job description.

   Strategic decisions concerning deployment will influence territory size and the need for travel. Time away from home might be more appealing to some salespeople than others. If extensive travel is an anticipated duty, it might be helpful to look for people who are accustomed to it.

   Most job descriptions and candidate profiles don't reflect these strategic issues. Your probability of hiring the right salesperson increases if you include strategic issues in the hiring process. Be sure the job description and candidate profile reflect duties and experience related to shorter product or service life cycles; longer, more complex sales cycles; changes in the knowledge, experience, and loyalty of decision makers; group buying decisions; increased competitive pressures; and quantification of benefits.

Job Descriptions

Many companies have job descriptions for everyone in the firm except salespeople. Sales managers need a list of each salesperson's anticipated duties in order to train and evaluate him or her. As with any employee, salespeople need to know what is expected of them. Of course, job descriptions will vary depending on products or services, buyer behaviors, types of selling situations, and the company culture. Within the same company, salespeople handling different products or services, or different types of end users, or different levels of decision makers will have different job descriptions. Some sales managers write slightly different job descriptions for salespeople with the same title but different territory characteristics. A telesales person will quite obviously have a different job description than a national accounts manager. A route grocery store salesperson taking reorders for Mexican-style cheese will have a different job description from a salesperson selling Internet services to major corporations. But in addition, each route grocery store salesperson may have enough variation in customer mix to have somewhat different duties. A new territory you are trying to develop may require more prospecting than a mature territory, where account retention and penetration is the primary task. The current trend is toward more detailed and more customized job descriptions.

When creating the job description, be sure to include sales and servicing duties, planning, reporting, company relations, and administrative chores and housekeeping. Try to keep the job description to one page, two pages at most. Review and revise it each year to reflect rapidly changing products or services, competition, customers, technology, and strategy. The sales manager uses the job description not only for hiring but also for determining topics for training and evaluation of salespeople. (See Exhibit 2.4 at the end of the chapter for an example of a job description.)

Each year ask your salespeople to revise their job description, adding duties not listed and altering duties that have changed. Have them sign the job description, date it, and return it. Some sales managers ask their salespeople to rank each duty as to importance and note what percentage of their time they spend on each activity. The results may surprise you. If salespeople find this difficult, you should probably discuss it further or put it on the agenda for a sales meeting.

I work with 25 salespeople a year, coaching them during customer visits. At some point I ask whether their job description accurately reflects their duties. Eight out of 10 times they reply they have no job description, and so I pull it out of my briefcase. Then they remember seeing it once. The annual review mentioned above prevents this memory loss.

In a worst-case scenario, the job description can offer a defense in a lawsuit based on wrongful termination. The salesperson has acknowledged, by annually signing the job description, that he or she understands the anticipated duties. The lack of a job description and an annual review leaves an employer more vulnerable to litigation.

The job description can also offer a defense in a lawsuit brought for discriminatory hiring. Can you demonstrate that the person you hired has better qualifications for performing the anticipated duties than the people you did not hire?

The job description, candidate profile, and entire hiring process must not discriminate based on race, gender, nationality, age, disability, or veteran status. All the duties must be job related. Have the appropriate person responsible for human resources review your job description but not write it. A sales manager's most important function is hiring the best salespeople. An important part of that process is the job description. It will be the sales manager whose feet are held to the fire for good or bad hiring decisions, not the human resources department.

Candidate Profiles

Once you have developed the job description, it is time to translate it into a written candidate profile. The job description lists duties. The candidate profile describes the skills, experience, knowledge, and personal characteristics necessary for performing those duties. What do your most successful salespeople have in common now and when they were hired? Similarly, what do your least successful salespeople have in common? Which of the skills, experience, knowledge, and personal characteristics are musts, and which are wants? We won't hire any candidate who does not have industry experience or excellent IT skills (a must). A want might be a degree in engineering. The candidate profile creates a disciplined approach to hiring and forces you to learn from experience and not perpetrate the same mistakes.

Some sales managers assign different quantitative weights to different salesperson skills, knowledge, experience, and personal characteristics. Industry experience might carry a numerical weight of 20 out of a total possible score of 100, while selling skills might be 25 and enthusiasm might be 5. After reviewing the candidate's résumé and asking the candidate appropriate interview questions, the sales manager would numerically rate the candidate based on the profile and arrive at a total score. Then the sales manager would compare one candidate's total score to another's to help in making the final hiring decision. I recommend just using musts and wants for the profile in order to eliminate candidates who do not have the musts. Calculating exact scores places too much emphasis on the candidate's profile versus the sales manager's judgment and use of other hiring filters.

Skills might include selling and computer skills, communications, listening, and discerning data. Experience might include type of sales, industry, type of compensation, performance results, prospecting, national accounts, and type of customers. Knowledge might include knowledge of customers, products, competition, and industry. Personal characteristics would include items such as confidence, enthusiasm, persistence, drive, passion, cooperativeness, aggressiveness, empathy, ability to handle rejection, honesty, initiative, and creativity. Most sales managers claim they keep this profile in their heads and never write it down. Write it down and then review and modify it annually to reflect the changing job description. (See Exhibit 2.5 at the end of this chapter for an example of a candidate profile.)

The profile for a salesperson calling on hospitals and physicians with home-health-care services will require very different knowledge, skills, experience, and personal characteristics than will the profile for a salesperson calling on the same customers with medical devices or medications. Both of these sales forces' profiles will be different from the profiles for salespeople calling on tier-two auto firms for contract manufacturing.

Determining whether a candidate has these skills, knowledge, and personal characteristics proves very difficult. For example, what does past compensation tell you about the candidate? Different mixes of fixed versus performance pay attract different types of salespeople. If the candidate was successful in a 100 percent performance pay program, does that mean he or she will be a team player, a self-starter, and confident and successful at your firm? On the other hand, if the candidate was successful in a fixed-pay program, does that mean he or she will be less aggressive, more patient, more loyal, and better able to handle long sales cycles? If a candidate's duties have not changed in five years, does that say something about his or her performance? We discuss techniques for determining this in Chapter 3 on screening and selecting.

Most sales candidates have had many more interviews than you have given, and it is easy to be fooled. The candidate profile is your shopping list.

The most unusual candidate profile I have encountered related to hiring a salesperson of precious gems for a territory in Central America. The position required a knowledge of Spanish, English, Arabic, and rare stones. Skills included self-defense, negotiations, and accuracy with firearms. Experience included taking long trips and carrying large amounts of currency. Personal characteristics included the ability to stay alert on five hours of sleep a night. This profile quickly screened out inappropriate candidates.

Sources for Attracting Candidates

Finding the best candidate can be a challenge and often means looking in many places. The following is a list of alternative sources for attracting candidates:

- Career ladders from within your organization
- Customers, who can be referrals or candidates
- Referrals from your present salespeople in exchange for a bonus
- Suppliers and vendors; industry networking
- Competitors
- The corporate database
- Professional organizations, schools, and military discharge centers
- Recruiters
- The Internet
- Job fairs and outsourcing firms
- Media advertising

Each of these sources has advantages and disadvantages that we will examine. What source or combination of sources you use depends on your job description and candidate profile. The Internet works well when you're looking for salespeople with technical skills. Customers work well when you're looking for salespeople involved in relationship sales. Each job search is different, but if in the past one source has produced better results, start with that.

INTERNAL CAREER LADDERS

Longer, more complex sales cycles and shorter product life have created a need for and scarcity of competent salespeople. A growing number of businesses deal with this by hiring from within and creating a career ladder from other functions or departments into field sales. For example, qualified people can move from engineering, design, or operations to purchasing, telesales, or customer service, and then on to field sales, or some combination of those steps. In distribution companies there is a career ladder from the warehouse to truck driver to route salesperson. Some firms have academies or use outside seminars where nonsalespeople can learn selling and marketing skills as part of the career ladder. Financial institutions like to promote operations people into sales. A Christmas decoration firm finds that its best field salespeople come from the showroom staff. UPS hires mostly salespeople who started as drivers.

The advantages of hiring from within are that management knows the candidates and the candidates know the products, customers, and competition. This saves recruiting and training time and reduces certain risks. The disadvantages are that your firm may become inbred, and candidates may not possess the personal characteristics necessary for success in sales. Candidates may not be confident, enthusiastic, or able to deal with rejection. You may lose a good engineer and hire a mediocre salesperson who must then be replaced. Internal candidates who are rejected may lose their motivation. To avoid the disadvantages, balance external and internal hiring, continually evaluate internal candidates, and quickly take corrective action.

CUSTOMERS

Customers are an excellent source for sales candidates, but they cannot be used if privacy is important. You can hire customers' employees or use them as referrals. Customers understand market needs and have product knowledge, but, again, they may not have sales skills or appropriate personal characteristics. If a customer employee becomes a candidate but is not offered the job, you may have lost a supporter. Unless you wish to lose an account, never hire a customer's employee without first asking permission from the employee's supervisor.

Often a customer's decision makers know of an appropriate salesperson who wishes to change employment. As a sales manager, you should call customers who would be helpful and explain the job's requirements. Choose customers with whom you have a personal relationship and in whom you have confidence. They will be flattered. Tell customers that you are asking for their assistance because they will be dealing with the new salesperson.

The advantages of this source are that customers know salespeople and understand the job requirements. Customer decision makers network with many salespeople. In addition, they understand the job requirements and the skills, knowledge, and characteristics necessary for success. The disadvantages are that customers might recommend a friend or relative who is down on his or her luck but not qualified, or they might want to be considered for the job themselves.

Firms that sell high-tech systems to the military primarily hire salespeople who have worked in government procurement. Food service firms have success hiring food and beverage managers. Many apparel firms hire department store buyers. Many media service firms hire media buyers. These represent examples of using customers as a source for salespeople. For many firms, recruiting salespeople from and through customers is a safe and easy hire.

CURRENT EMPLOYEES

Current employees, especially your present sales force, often know qualified salespeople who might find the available position attractive. Offer a $1,000 bonus for referrals that result in hiring and an additional $1,000 if the candidate stays for 14 months. Your salespeople have a wide network of associates, they understand the job requirements, and they usually want to recommend winners. Be aware though that when an employee's referral is not acceptable, is an unqualified friend, or is hired and then later terminated, the salesperson may blame you and become angry. As with using customers as a source for salespeople, current employees might recommend a friend or relative who needs a job but who is not qualified.

VENDORS AND INDUSTRY NETWORKING

A sales manager always should be looking for qualified candidates. When an impressive vendor sales representative calls on you to sell printing, copy machines, software, laptops, or telephone or Internet services, get to know him or her. Use trade shows and associations as a way of meeting appropriate candidates. You can learn a great deal by watching people work a trade show or sell you their products or services. Keep a file of qualified candidates so that when the need arises, you have people to call. A mobile home manufacturer and a storm

window firm both have great success hiring supplier salespeople because of their industry and customer knowledge. When sourcing through industry networking and vendors, look for industries with customers and sales cycles similar to yours. For example, an industrial gas company has been successful hiring salespeople from the chemical industry.

COMPETITORS

Snatching a salesperson from a competitor may look like a safe hire, but this approach is often risky. The advantages of hiring from the competition are in the salesperson's knowledge of customers, competition, and the product or service. Potential disadvantages are the salesperson's lack of credibility with customers, his or her potential inflexibility with your procedures and culture, his or her potential lack of loyalty to your firm, and the bad habits he or she may have learned at the other firm. If your firm's culture demands a lot of reports from salespeople and is very results oriented, check to see if the salesperson comes from a similar environment.

Make sure you understand why the competitor's salesperson wants to leave, or else you may inherit someone else's troubles. He or she may not be performing or may be having personal difficulties.

Always interview candidates from competitors even if you have no openings. Ask probing questions and listen carefully. This can be a great source of market information. Mergers, reorganizations, territory changes, and new compensation plans make very qualified competitor salespeople open to new opportunities. Often, mature salespeople leave a competitor because their territory faces reduction or because the competitor desires a younger, less experienced, less expensive person. The right competitor candidate can bring captive customers, no bad habits, good product knowledge, and little need for training. Hiring from the competition has been very successful in the pharmaceutical industry. A European conglomerate that sells hand tools to U.S. dentists hires only from the competition, as does a Midwest, family-owned firm that distributes fine papers to printers. Retailers shop the competitors' stores not for product but for salespeople. A large national apparel firm with several thousand retail outlets trains store managers in how to approach competitors' retail salespeople. The chain also insists that managers spend three days a month shopping competitors' stores for the right salespeople.

CORPORATE DATABASE

Larger corporations keep databases of résumés received over the recent past. Generally human resources keeps this underutilized file. Search the database for résumés of salespeople who meet your candidate profile. The corporate database is a larger version of your hiring file. In a large corporation, you may wish to consider a candidate from another division. Corporate human resources can help you find these candidates. At Motorola, Alcatel-Lucent, and General Motors, other divisions within the company remain an important source of sales candidates.

PROFESSIONAL ORGANIZATIONS, SCHOOLS, AND MILITARY DISCHARGE CENTERS

Professional organizations, schools, and armed forces discharge centers are excellent sources for salespeople. Most industries have professional associations, occasionally just for salespeople, that publish lists of available positions for their membership. Many groups have a local chapter in each state or major metropolitan area. Such associations range from the Men's Apparel Clubs in each state to state health-care associations to the Industrial Robot Division of the Society of Manufacturing Engineers. Be sure to list your job opening with the appropriate industry club or association.

Some software, commercial lighting, and pharmaceutical firms have found recent college graduates the best source for sales candidates. These firms require no industry or sales experience, but they do require the right personal characteristics and a strong academic background in engineering, computer, or life sciences. These firms prefer to train and mold younger salespeople. Colleges, universities, and technical schools have placement offices to assist recent and not-so-recent graduates. If appropriate, list sales positions with these placement offices and do on-campus recruiting.

In selecting a college to recruit from, consider the college's academic specialties such as business, marketing, sales, life sciences, computer sciences, design, or engineering. Do these specialties match your candidate profile and job description?

A traditional furniture manufacturer in North Carolina arranges to hire interns every summer from a local junior college. Many of these interns later become permanent salespeople. The junior college has areas of study in interior design and business that fit the furniture company's salesperson profile. Banks and brokerage houses often hire previous summer college interns for sales positions after graduation.

As the armed forces downsize and reorganize, well-trained people are being discharged from the military. An international conglomerate selling emission control devices and particulate scrubbers to utilities worldwide hires only discharged military officers as salespeople. Selling to a public utility requires understanding the decision-making process of large, complex, slow-moving organizations, and ex-military officers can certainly appreciate this. If appropriate, list your sales position with the local discharge office.

RECRUITERS

Recruiters that understand your industry and corporate culture and have a database of salespeople who match your candidate profile can be helpful. Look for recruiters who blend online sourcing with offline screening. Look for recruiters who have Web site job postings, know how to use online job boards, and blend this with e-mail, phone, and in-person interviews. They can save you time in sourcing and screening candidates. Only use recruiters who provide legitimate references from your industry. Also ask to speak with clients who have not been happy with their services. Don't use recruiters who will just make blind calls to your competitors and ask for a salesperson. Ask colleagues for referrals.

Negotiated fees range from 15 to 30 percent of the candidate's annual compensation with a certain dollar amount paid up front and the rest based on performance. Negotiate a holdback to be paid to the recruiter after 14 months of employment. After 14 months you will know whether the salesperson meets your requirements. Put the fee arrangement in writing before the search begins.

Be aware that many recruiters dealing with middle-level salespeople lack professionalism. Their main interest is in making a match, but not necessarily a good fit. If you engage a recruiter, provide him or her with the job description and candidate profile, and agree on a realistic time frame. When candidates emerge, interview them immediately before they lose interest. Recruiters will coach candidates on what you are looking for and how to answer questions. Therefore, when using recruiters, you must vary the interviewing techniques.

A client of mine recently used a recruiter because she was planning to replace an underperforming salesperson, but she did not want the industry to know this. The recruiter, whose references were not checked, mistakenly called the salesperson who was to be terminated. As you can imagine, this resulted in a host of problems. Always check the recruiter's references and give him or her specific instructions on who not to call.

THE INTERNET

The Internet, because of its wide reach, has become a major source for salespeople, and it will only grow in importance. Your company's Web page should list employment opportunities in sales. In addition, employment opportunities should be listed on recruiting Web sites including those of newspapers appropriate for your industry and region. Use a search engine to find the appropriate online candidate employment sites and then key in on candidates who match your profile. General recruiting sites for salespeople include the following:

- www.kforce.com
- www.monster.com
- www.careerexchange.com
- www.bestjobsusa.com
- www.hotjobs.yahoo.com
- www.careerbuilder.com
- www.salesjobs.com
- www.careercentral.com
- www.jobbanksusa.com
- www.salesclassified.com
- www.salesgiant.com
- www.hirequest.com
- www.justsalesandmarketing.net
- www.salesladder.com
- www.rightfish.com
- www.salestalentinc.com
- www.craiglist.com

Online job boards and industry-specific communities of interest list candidates and contain classified ads by employers. They charge a fixed fee to list your firm and search for candidates and then a performance fee based on results. Online job boards such as careerbuilder.com and monster.com produce large numbers of résumés in response to ads, but it requires time to eliminate unqualified candidates. Online job boards now offer software that helps to screen candidates. Also professional recruiters who use online job boards can save their clients' time and money by performing the initial screening.

The Internet provides a particularly appropriate source to look for technically based sales candidates. If you sell telephone services, software, chips, or medical devices the Web is a must. Candidates are listed by specialty. For example, a printed circuit board assembly contractor found, and eventually hired, three salespeople from a two-hour Web search.

JOB FAIRS AND OUTSOURCING FIRMS

Job fairs and outsourcing firms have become important sources for certain types of salespeople. Job fairs are organized by industry associations, sometimes individual firms, to attract less experienced, younger salespeople. Retailers use job fairs as do contract programmers. The fair is an open house to learn more about an industry or a company without actually making an appointment for an interview. A national electronic retailer with 250 stores insists that each store manager have an open house once a quarter. Each open house attracts at least six qualified salespeople, one of whom is hired. If appropriate, consider using job fairs to attract salespeople.

Although unemployment is low in 2007, there is considerable movement from one company and industry to another. As one firm downsizes, for example, General Motors, or one industry contracts, again automobiles, another is hiring and expanding, such as Toyota or mobile phones. Outsourcing firms place professionals who are being downsized, many of them salespeople. List the sales employment opportunities with these firms.

MEDIA ADVERTISING

Media advertising for salespeople can be very effective if used correctly. The first issue is where to advertise; the second is what to say. Studies have shown that retailers, food service firms, and apparel manufacturers obtain the best results from local newspaper ads. The Sunday help-wanted section generally produces better results than other days and sections, but depending on the job, the weekday sports or fashion page also attracts candidates. Most major newspapers also offer online hiring sites.

Business-to-business firms generally obtain the most qualified candidates at the least expense in the classified "lines offered" section of trade or association publications. One day a week, or one week a month, the trade publication will specialize in employment ads or in your market segment. Advertise in the publications and sections that your target candidates read and keep track of which media produce the best results. An agricultural seed firm primarily sources salespeople through its trade publications as do an aluminum die casting firm and a plastic injection molder.

Targeted radio stations can also source candidates. A Chicago-based Hispanic food manufacturer successfully hires salespeople from ads on the local Spanish-speaking radio station. This firm advertises its products on the Hispanic radio station and then adds a line or two concerning available positions.

Copy for print media and online job board employment ads should include company name, address, telephone number, and the person to contact. Ask candidates to write, e-mail, or phone the sales manager directly if they feel qualified for the position. This humanizes the ad.

Blind media ads do not produce qualified applicants. Salespeople hesitate responding to them because they may have been placed by their current employers. Blind ads also cause suspicion: What sort of employer won't divulge its name in an ad? If replacing a salesperson requires secrecy, rather than placing an unsuccessful blind ad, I suggest using other sources. For example, some online job board listings require a company name; some do not.

Your ad must contain an honest description of the position. If too much information is provided, qualified candidates might find something to discourage them from applying. If you include too little information, unqualified candidates are encouraged to apply. Remember that the ad's objective is not to hire and select the salespeople but only to produce qualified applicants. You will do the selecting from those who reply.

An honest description of the position states the product or service to be sold, type of selling, territory available, type of customer, what experience is necessary, and the amount of overnight travel, if any. I would not include a compensation range, since this generally varies greatly depending on the applicant's ability. I would not mention whether the territory contains established volume or requires pioneering. This information changes quickly and can best be handled in a personal discussion.

The ad should contain words accurately describing the job's nonmonetary benefits such as "rewarding," "steady," "interesting," or "challenging." Choose the words honestly. For example, a route salesperson's work is steady; a door-to-door salesperson's work is challenging.

Media ads with creative copy attract attention and pull best. An effective technique for advertising in the Sunday paper involves asking the applicant to call you that Sunday. This requires that you or your administrative assistant devote that day to the project, but it produces results. If the ad is run outside your area code, it must specify a toll-free number or that collect calls will be accepted.

In addition to the copy already suggested, your Sunday ad might state something like this:

> Don't write or e-mail, but pick up your phone now and call me, Tom Brown, at this number. I am the sales manager of FirstNet.com, and I will be at my telephone between 9 and 5 today. I will tell you about the job opportunity, and you can tell me about your qualifications. I will not ask your name unless you wish to tell me.

The personal aspect of this ad plus the easy opportunity it offers for immediate response produces qualified candidates. Also, it allows people who are currently employed to call without fear that their employers will learn of their interest. Most companies have greater success hiring currently employed salespeople than they do unemployed salespeople. A variation of this idea involves asking candidates to call your assistant, having him or her do the initial screening and then turning the most promising candidates over to you. As noted later, describe the job but not the candidate profile. Use probing questions to determine candidate knowledge, skills, experience, and personal characteristics. (See the sample employment ads at the end of this chapter in Exhibit 2.6.)

Certain advertising agencies—NAS Recruitment Communication and Shaker Advertising—specialize in employment ads. In exchange for the 15 percent commission collected from the media, they will advise you on copy and choices of publication.

HELP FROM HUMAN RESOURCES IN SOURCING

Human resources and the sales manager should be working together in finding salespeople through all these sources. Sometimes the sales manager will use certain sources and HR will have responsibility for others. In any case, to cast a wide, efficient net, both must coordinate their activities.

Exhibit 2.1.   Strategic Items to Include on the Salesperson's Job Description.

- Target accounts, markets, and products
- New accounts versus penetration of present accounts
- Territory size and sales force deployment
- National accounts selling
- Telesales involvement
- Sales force organization
- Coordination with other departments
- Type of selling: consultative, relationship, commodity, or new product
- Team selling
- Negotiating with customers
- Available pricing window
- Channel choice; reps and/or distributors

Exhibit 2.2.   Strategic Items to Include on the Salesperson's Candidate Profile.

- Buyer behavior
- Group decisions
- Multilevel sales
- Long sales cycle from search to purchase
- Complex decision-making process; needs assessment, demo, samples, trial, beta, test, and proposal
- Shorter product or service life
- New product or service sales
- Differentiation
- Channel conflicts

Exhibit 2.3. Matching, Business-to-Business Sales, Buyer Behavior.

New Systems Buyer

- Inexperienced but real user. First-time or one-time user.
- Financial services, software, communication systems, consulting, law, computers, big ticket, high tech. Heterogeneous products or services.
- Long sales cycle, group decision, consultative sell, problem solving. Strong product knowledge. Expert image. Partnership sales. Technical and application support. One-time purchase. Risk of failure. Highest total compensation for salespeople. High percentage fixed pay.

Established Systems Buyer

- Experienced real user. Modified rebuy.
- Agriculture, horticulture, security systems, insurance litigation, printed circuits, subcontracting. Homogenous products or services.
- Shorter sales cycle, group decision, relationship sell. Customer knowledge. Friendly image. Purchase and delivery needs. Great patience over a long period of time. Politicking, bargaining. Upper-middle or lower-upper total compensation for salespeople. Fixed versus performance pay 50/50. Increasing percent of customer's business, penetration.

New Product Buyer

- Experienced users.
- Feature and/or benefit selling.
- Good closing skills. Low fear of rejection. Emotional appeal, pressure. Aggressively initiate customer contact. Probing questions.
- Midlevel total dollar compensation.
- High percentage performance pay.

Commodity Buyer

- Experienced users with standardized products or services. Routine functions and rebuy.
- Die castings, hardware, office supplies, injection molding. Homogenous products.
- Route sales. Frequent sales calls.
- Individual decision maker. Often delegated.
- Relationship sale. Price, delivery, availability, customer service, convenience.
- Increasing share of customer's business.
- Maintenance or penetration.
- Order taking. Time management. Electronic data interchange (EDI). IT.
- Small risk of rejection. Little personal involvement. High percentage performance pay. Lowest total compensation.

Complexity of using a product or service and experience or expertise in its use or application. How does this influence hiring, training, compensation, and organization of salespeople?

Exhibit 2.4.   Salesperson Job Description.

Overall Purpose

Meet or exceed sales objectives of assigned territory by promoting and selling tires through professional sales techniques, product service, and long-term customer relationships.

Major Activities

- Meet and exceed sales targets; achieve maximum sales in assigned territory through dealer, affiliate, and other channels.
- Make at least 25 quality sales calls each week on dealers or fleet managers.
- Target A, B, and C accounts by present and potential dollars of revenues or profits, cost to sell and service, and probability of success.
- Allocate time and call frequency based on A, B, and C accounts targeting.
- Make the appropriate number of calls on prospects versus customers. Identify potential growth areas, and open new accounts.
- Increase market share by calling on a large universe of diverse dealers to promote and sell tires, communicate special programs, present marketing and advertising programs and new products, handle and process warranties, prepare and conduct dealer training and educational seminars, collect competitive information. Handle and resolve problems and complaints, and collect overdue receivables. Advise dealers on market conditions and wholesale and end-user accounts.
- Increase market share by calling on a large universe of diverse fleet accounts to sell tires, communicate special programs, conduct fleet inspections, monitor tire mileage, conduct educational seminars, and handle and resolve problems and complaints including credit issues. Advise customers on market conditions and wholesale and end-user accounts.
- Sell all products, but concentrate on high-performance tires and value-added selling.
- Prepare written presentations, reports, and price quotations.
- Sell at transaction price approved for this type customer.
- Negotiate delivery, availability, warranty, advertising, and pricing for discontinued items. Follow up on back orders.
- Maintain accounts receivables in compliance with objectives.
- Conduct customer education and product information meetings.
- Continually learn new product knowledge and acquire better selling skills.
- Keep abreast of competition, competitive issues, products, and markets for tires.
- Attend and participate in sales meetings, product seminars, and trade shows.
- Create customer sales programs.

(Continued on next page.)

Exhibit 2.4. *(Continued from previous page.)*

Time Management

- Work a 50-hour, five-day week.
- Do necessary overnight travel.
- See first customer by 7:30 a.m.
- See last customer at 3 p.m.
- Utilize laptops and cellular phones.
- Maximize percent of time in front of customers.
- Minimize travel time.
- Use customer service reps for follow-up and smaller accounts.
- Call on accounts in clusters. Work one section of territory each day. Use loops and cloverleafs.

Self-Organization

- Plan each day, week, and month.
- Plan each call.
- Keep sales aids in mint condition.
- Dress neatly.
- Maintain a neat automobile.
- Present a professional image.
- After each call, fill in the customer profile and your daily planner.

Administrative

- Maintain customer profiles and customer files.
- Submit the following in a timely manner: daily planner and/or call reports, sales plans, forecasts, and expense reports.
- Communicate competitive information to corporate marketing.
- Complete and submit credit applications for new accounts.
- Use information technology to save time.
- Analyze and monitor data and reports.

Company Relations

- Comply with all company policies, and operate within the expense budget.
- Work with, develop positive relationships with, communicate with, and coordinate activities with other employees in marketing, customer service, distribution, credit, accounting, human resources, engineering, national fleet, and finance departments.
- Communicate effectively; cooperate with your fellow salespeople and management.

Exhibit 2.5. Salesperson Candidate Profile, Musts and Wants.

Skills	Knowledge	Experience	Personal Characteristics
• Listening	• Tire technology	• Success in selling a business-to-business (B2B) product	• Neat appearance
• Written and verbal communication	• High school degree	• Three years of related experience	• Enthusiasm
• Sales	• Customers	• Success in selling a premium product at a premium price	• Self-organization
• Persuasion	• Markets	• Long hours	• Persistence in following up
• Computer	• IT	• A large diverse customer base	• Sense of urgency
• Planning	• Bilingual	• Longevity in previous positions	• Cooperativeness
• Analytical	• Business management	• Industry experience	• Self-confidence
• Conflict resolution			• Assertiveness
• Creativity			• Good business judgment
• Learning			• Consistency
• Presentation			• Ability to develop new ideas
• Negotiation			• Initiative
• Time management			• Ethics and integrity
• Technical aptitude			• Ability to be a high achiever
			• Motivation to make money
			• Ability to handle rejection

Exhibit 2.6.   Sample Employment Ads.

Anyone Can Take an Order

As an industry leader for over 25 years, we are a manufacturer of specialty transformers for the telecommunications and computer industries. Our customers look to us for quality, reliable service, and ideas. We are looking for several people who can make it happen and make a difference. The ideal candidate is a highly motivated career-oriented professional with a successful track record in new account acquisition and maintenance.

Challenging, Rewarding Opportunity:
Electronic Components

Salesperson wanted to sell our extensive line of quality, premium-priced miniature transformer supplies to a broad customer group of telcos, computer manufacturers, instrumentation, and switching firms. Prior selling experience in the territory desirable. Occasional overnight travel. Challenging and rewarding opportunity for the right person.

Are You Stuck in a Rut with No Future
to Expand Your Horizon?

Are you an eager, energetic, and excitable self-starter who is interested in developing a career in sales and marketing? Would you be willing to aggressively pursue new account possibilities, rising an hour earlier each morning?

Are you adequately self-motivated to prove your abilities for an established company promoting and selling the most unique and exciting software of its kind to hospitals and doctors? Are you ready to roll up your sleeves preparing, directing, and participating in field product demonstrations?

If you fit that description and have experience in software sales, we want to talk to you now. We have a special and critical niche to fill with an individual willing to earn his or her wings joining our professional sales organization. Send résumé to:

Industry Leader

Are you an eager, energetic, and excitable self-starter who is interested in developing a career in sales and marketing? Would you be willing to aggressively pursue new account possibilities, even rising an hour earlier each morning to prepare fresh customer samples for the day?

Are you adequately self-motivated to prove your abilities for an established manufacturing and distribution company promoting and selling the most unique and exciting product line of its kind to food service and bakery-related customers?

If you fit that description, we want to talk to you now.

(Continued on next page.)

Exhibit 2.6. *(Continued from previous page.)*

Are You Stuck in a Rut with No Future to Expand Your Horizon?

_____, a leader in B2B e-commerce, is seeking hungry, aggressive sales reps who are currently calling on the plastics industry. Only those sales representatives currently calling on the plastics industry need apply.

Are you looking for a company where you can rise before the sun and be miles ahead of the competition? If you have experience in long complex sales cycles, with a proven track record, we want to talk to you. We offer competitive salary, 401(k)s, stock options, and profit sharing. Please send résumé to:

Sales Representative

_____ has an immediate opening for an experienced financial services representative in this area.

To be considered for this position, you must have a minimum of three years of sales experience in financial services. We are looking for an individual who has built solid customer relationships in the past and is capable of establishing new relationships with our customers. You must demonstrate a proven ability to plan, organize, and execute successful sales presentations.

We offer an extensive benefits package, competitive compensation, and an opportunity to grow with an industry leader. Qualified applicants, please forward your résumé in complete confidence to:

Questions and Exercises for Chapter 2

- Create a job description and a candidate profile for your most recent job, or for a salesperson in your company, or for a full-time salesperson at a company you are familiar with. On the candidate profile, note which items are wants and which are musts. On the job description, state the job title and which anticipated duties relate to strategies versus tactics.
- Where would you look for candidates? What sources would you use? Rank those sources by importance.

Quiz for Chapter 2

1. Why is salesperson turnover expensive and/or costly?
   a. The cost of hiring
   b. The cost of training

c. Unemployment insurance

    d. Loss of customer trust

    e. Potential loss of market share

2. Which of these strategic issues should be included in the job description and candidate profile?

    a. Target accounts, markets, and products

    b. Concentrating on new accounts versus further penetration of existing accounts

    c. Buyer behavior

    d. Negotiating price, delivery, and customization

    e. Channel choice

3. True or false?

    Most sales managers prefer salespeople who share their backgrounds, make a nice appearance, are easy to manage, and do not threaten them.

4. True or false?

    The job description is a list of a salesperson's anticipated duties.

5. Which of the following salesperson's tactical duties should be included in a job description?

    a. Sales and servicing

    b. Planning

    c. Reporting

    d. Company relations

    e. Administrative chores

6. True or false?

    The candidate profile describes the skills, experience, knowledge, and personal characteristics necessary to perform a salesperson's duties.

7. Which of these would not be included under skills in a salesperson's candidate profile?

    a. Computer

    b. Communication

    c. Selling

    d. Listening

    e. Product

8. Which of these would be included under personal characteristics in a salesperson's candidate profile?

    a. Confidence

    b. Enthusiasm

      c. Persistence
      d. Team player
      e. Creativity
      f. Appearance

9. Which of these is not a source for hiring salespeople?
      a. From within the firm
      b. Customers
      c. Referrals from employees
      d. Suppliers
      e. Competition
      f. Recruiters
      g. Media
      h. Internet
      i. Past employees

10. True or false?
    The best source for hiring salespeople is competitors.

Notes

1. *Hot Topics in Sales Management and Sales Compensation 2005*. Copyright © 2005 Hewitt Associates LLC. Reprinted by permission of Hewitt Associates.
2. MarketBridge, Mark Donnolo, *Performance-Driven Selling 2006*. Market-bridge Technologies. Copyright © 2006. Reprinted by permission of Market-Bridge.

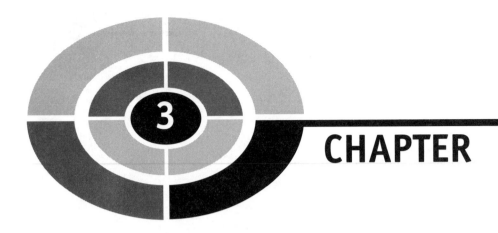

Screening and Selecting

The Screening Process

Choosing the best candidate from a qualified group requires not only intuition and insight but also structure and technique. The probability of success can be enhanced and the risk of a bad hire reduced by following certain procedures. Because of time limitations, the temptation exists to take shortcuts in the selection process, but shortcuts only increase the risk of failure, forcing you to accept a mediocre salesperson or eventually seek a new one. Do it right, or do it again. Human resources, salespeople, and the vice president of sales—all can help a sales manager in the hiring process. However, the sales manager must make the final decision and live with the results.

The techniques and structure employed in successfully narrowing the field include the following:

1. Preliminary screening of résumés
2. Telephone interviews
3. Personal history forms
4. Preliminary personal interviews
5. Continuing interviews for finalists
6. Reference checking and background investigations
7. Testing
8. Making the final choice

Not every job search requires all these steps, but as you can see, the process requires considerable time. The more time you make available to contact sources and screen applicants, the higher your probability of success. As mentioned, to maximize the available time for recruiting and to compress the necessary time for hiring, try to anticipate hiring needs, have a file of qualified candidates, or have a present salesperson in reserve.

The best sales managers set standards, are critical, and sit in judgment. Hiring in general and screening candidates in particular is a test of these skills. Candidates are selling themselves.

RÉSUMÉS

Begin the screening process by reviewing the résumés received and comparing them to the candidate profile. Eliminate those candidates who do not have the experience, knowledge, and skills listed as "musts" on the candidate profile. Look for employment gaps, job-hopping, weak written communication skills, inconsistencies, misspelled words, and lack of completeness or accuracy. Be careful of candidates whose records show no improvements, such as a salesperson whose shipments and compensation have remained unchanged for many years or a salesperson who traded a good line with a top company for an inferior line with a second-rate organization.

Write a cordial letter to those people initially eliminated, expressing appreciation for their interest but informing them their fine backgrounds do not meet the position's requirements. The hiring process represents an opportunity for the company to make friends. Job applicants sometimes become customers, suppliers, politicians, managers, or repeat candidates. I know of many situations in which an applicant originally rejected for one selling position was hired later for another. You should write rejection letters with this in mind, and keep a file for future reference of all résumés received and notes taken from conversations.

TELEPHONE INTERVIEWS

Call each remaining candidate for a telephone interview. Ask factual questions pertaining to background, résumé, experience, knowledge, and skills. Why did he or she leave one employer for another? Does he or she have a formal education in molecular biology? Has he or she called on biotech laboratories? See if the candidate sells and persuades you to arrange an in-person interview. How does the candidate come across over the phone? This is an important part of most sales processes. Salespeople use the phone to sell appointments, take reorders, and resolve customer conflicts. If you are recruiting for a telesales position, give even more weight to the telephone interview.

For the candidate, the goal should be to sell you the value of an in-person interview. If the candidate does not ask for an appointment, this reflects on his or her selling skills. Since the telephone represents an important sales tool, tone of voice can be important. Listen to the music in addition to the words. Does the candidate exude warmth, confidence, and enthusiasm over the phone?

PERSONAL HISTORY FORMS

The telephone interview will eliminate more candidates. Set appointments for an in-person interview with those you still have an interest in. Fax or e-mail these people a short, simple personal history form to fill out and return before the interview. The personal history form asks the applicant for the following information: name and address, educational background, employment history with dates and responsibilities, and outside interests. Although this repeats the résumé material, it often reveals conflicting information or provides more information. You also can see how quickly the candidate responds, whether he or she writes or types, how complete the information is, and whether the response is in digital or snail mail form.

Planning and Preparing for Personal Interviews

VIDEOCONFERENCING

With enhancements in technology, some businesses make videoconferencing part of their recruiting process. Companies such as AT&T, Dell Computer, Shell Oil, and Nike use videoconferencing to initially interview candidates. Dozens of firms,

including some Radisson and Hilton Hotels, and FedEx Kinkos, provide video-conferencing facilities. Some recruiters, candidates, and sales managers have videoconferencing capabilities on their PCs. Some recruiters stream video interviews to their clients via the Internet. A number of managers can watch the video interview. Videoconferencing represents another step in the hiring process that can reduce the time and cost of interviewing.

THE NUMBER OF IN-PERSON INTERVIEWS

Most sales managers interview too many unqualified candidates because they don't do enough prescreening. Time and knowledge are your most valuable resources. I suggest limiting yourself to five candidates for face-to-face interviews. If those five don't produce a finalist, then expand the field.

SIMULATING

Now you begin the art and black magic of in-person interviewing. The interview is an opportunity for the candidate to persuade the sales manager that he or she should be hired. The sales manager's strategy is to create an interview situation that simulates an actual sales call in that particular industry and that reflects the candidate profile requirements.

For example, pharmaceutical salespeople have two or three minutes of face time with physicians to present their firm's medications. Persistent follow-up with physicians proves very important in getting a commitment to prescribe a medication. To reflect these requirements, a regional sales manager for a large pharmaceutical company uses the five-minute interview. After a candidate arrives for an interview, she informs him or her that she has been called into a meeting at the last moment. She apologizes, lets the candidate know the meeting will be only an hour, but asks the candidate in the five minutes before the "meeting" to explain why he or she should be hired for the job. Some candidates do very well in this environment, and some do not. Then she explains why she has done this, and the interview continues. At the end of the interview, if she is interested in hiring a candidate, she asks him or her to call back at a precise time on a specific day. She is never available, but tracks how persistent the candidate is in follow-up calls and what techniques the candidate uses to reach her.

If your salespeople make presentations to groups of customers, have group interviews to see how the candidate reacts. If new product sales and high customer rejection represent important parts of the sales process, have the candidate sell you his or her present product or service and present the salesperson with some objections.

Another example of creating an interview situation that simulates an actual sales call is throwing some rejection at the candidate concerning their backgrounds. The sales manager for an advertising agency tells all candidates she interviews that although their backgrounds are interesting, they are not appropriate for this sales job. Then she listens to their responses. Some candidates agree with her statement, and others get mad, but those she hires try to persuade her she is wrong. On the second interview she takes telephone calls to see how a candidate deals with interruptions. Can he refocus, or does he get angry? This simulates actual sales calls in the advertising industry.

The sales manager for an innovative software firm asks all candidates who are invited back for a second interview to be prepared to sell him a product or service they are familiar with. Then the sales manager evaluates the candidate's ability to establish rapport, to ask probing questions that establish needs, to present features, benefits, and proof, to overcome objections, and to close. The sales manager for a fund-raising telesales organization asks candidates to sell her their previous product or service over the phone.

The sales manager for a money center bank finds her present salespeople lack closing skills. She ends each candidate interview by crossing her arms, remaining silent, and looking the candidate in the eye. Some candidates get anxious and reveal information heretofore not mentioned. Some candidates ask probing questions or remain silent themselves. She looks for a candidate who seizes the moment by saying, "I assume by your silence that you agree I am the best candidate. What is the next step toward my being hired?"

These provide examples of sales managers tailoring the interview to their firm's particular sales process and candidate profile. This proves a powerful screening technique.

If applicants live nearby, you can conduct interviews in your office. If the available territory is out of town, initial interviews should take place at a hotel in that area.

In-Person Interviewing

Interviews prove more productive if the sales manager knows exactly what type of candidate he or she is seeking and if the sales manager has prepared a written list of questions based on matching the candidate's résumé and personal history to the candidate profile and job description. This means using different questions for different candidates. Also use information obtained in the telephone interview to formulate questions for the face-to-face interview. Again, you may seek people similar to your current best performers. Don't waste time asking questions such

as where the candidate went to high school, which have already been answered on the résumé or personal history application.

The most reliable guide to a salesperson's future performance is his or her past record; therefore, obtaining a reliable picture of the past record represents an important aspect of screening. In the telephone and face-to-face interviews, ask the candidate to comment on specific past achievements with each employer.

Compensation history becomes an extremely important indicator of past performance. Has compensation increased each year reflecting improved performance or more responsibility? Was compensation primarily fixed or based on performance, and what does that tell you about the candidate? Do you want people who have succeeded with a high portion of performance pay because that indicates motivation, or with a high portion of fixed pay because that indicates a team player?

Unfortunately people seldom change their bad working habits. The mediocre sales performer continues to perform at mediocre levels. The job-hopper continues to hop. The person with financial problems usually finds new ones. The salesperson who works four days a week seldom switches to five, and in fact often regresses to three. Therefore, know what aspects of past performance you need to concentrate on.

Start the interview by introducing the candidate to other people in your office, perhaps an administrative assistant or an associate, to see how he or she relates. This indicates how he or she might react to a new customer.

To make an applicant comfortable and more willing to talk, immediately establish rapport by discussing some common interests you discovered on the résumé or telephone interview. Don't dive into the interview. Take a few minutes to establish a bond and dissipate nervousness.

Next, state the purpose of the interview and how long it will last. The maximum should be 60 to 90 minutes, especially with multiple interviews. The purpose of the interview is first to learn more about the candidate and then to explain the position and answer any questions. To relax a candidate, make it clear that a hiring decision will not be made that day. To instill a little fear, tell the candidate that you have many applicants.

Just because you happen to be the interviewer, don't assume that you are cleverer than the applicant. Some salespeople have had many more interviews than you have given, and some have read books on interviewing techniques. Some salespeople prove more professional at interviewing than at closing a customer sale. Probing questions, reference checking, and scrutinizing of résumés usually identifies such a person.

Don't show the candidate the job description or the candidate profile or discuss specifics of the position until you have asked all your probing questions. Then, realistically describe the position and truthfully answer all of the candidate's questions. Don't oversell the position; it only leads to disappointment. A good candidate will ask to see the job description and ask probing questions about the position. Acknowledge the questions but defer them until later. If a sales manager tells a candidate the job specifics at the start of an interview, the candidate will just feed back what the sales manager wants to hear. However, handing a qualified candidate the job description toward the end of the initial interview and asking how he or she would prioritize the tasks or allocate time among them can be insightful. Use the job description as a tool to learn more about the candidate. In tight labor markets, waiting to describe the position requires courage, but it produces better hiring results.

WHAT CANDIDATES ARE LOOKING FOR

According to the March 2000 issue of *Sales and Marketing Management* magazine:

> A recent study by Development Dimensions International, a human resource consulting firm in Pittsburgh, shows that job candidates are seeking companies that offer in order of importance: a solid reputation, generous benefits, a positive corporate culture, and potential for advancements. Companies with the best recruiting strategies were nearly 20 percent more likely to offer these advantages, as well as stock options, learning opportunities, and competitive pay.

A study by Towers Perrin in 2003 showed similar results.[1] The Towers Perrin study involved 3,581 sales and marketing employees at midsized and large companies in North America. The top 10 attractors for the sales and marketing function were the following:

1. Competitive health-care benefits
2. Competitive base pay
3. Career advancement opportunities
4. Work-life balance
5. Reputation of the company
6. Bonuses based on performance
7. Raises link to individual performance
8. Challenging work
9. The caliber of coworkers
10. Recognition for work

However, as we will see in later chapters, the order becomes reversed when it involves retaining and then engaging or motivating sales and marketing personnel.

Hewitt Associates asked sales and human resource executives at 55 Fortune 1000 companies to indicate reasons salespeople left their companies.[2] Of the

55 respondents, 31 percent answered better career opportunities, 21 percent greater upside earning potential, 15 percent higher base salary, 12 percent better work environment, and 10 percent for job opportunities outside of sales.

LISTENING TO THE CANDIDATES

Although many sales managers feel they are more interesting than the candidate, the interview's purpose is to learn more about the candidate. That requires the sales manager to listen 80 percent of the time. Display empathy and understanding, but don't talk about yourself. We have two ears and one mouth for good reason. Selling and interviewing require probing questions and good listening skills. What do the answers tell you about the candidate? The more the applicant talks, the more you will learn. Tailor questions to the candidate. Don't use canned questions unless you want canned answers.

If, on the first interview, a sales manager creates a nonthreatening atmosphere in which a candidate feels free to talk, the candidate will volunteer all the information you desire. In the first interview a sales manager can best put the candidate at ease by being punctual, not accepting phone calls, not rushing through the interview, not putting a desk between the two of you, and sitting in chairs of equal status. Don't criticize the candidate, or you will find future responses guarded. When you want more information on a subject, agree with the applicant. When the conversation veers from the subject at hand, subtly steer it back in the desired direction. Once you have established rapport, keep the candidate talking about himself or herself and don't let the conversation lapse into sports, global politics, or the stock market.

If you nod your head or say "u-huh," the candidate senses you are listening and will talk more. By occasionally stopping to summarize a prospect's point or answer, you give feedback to confirm understanding and interest. Don't feel compelled to fill voids caused by silence. Instead, use silence to put pressure on the prospect. You want to know how he or she would react to this in a selling situation. Often applicants bridge a silence with significant information.

ASKING OPEN-ENDED PROBING QUESTIONS

Open-ended probing questions, which cannot be answered with yes or no, are the key to good in-person interviewing. Such questions tell the sales manager a great deal about what is important to the salesperson. A candidate will return to the same subjects in answering these questions; for instance, the importance of family, better serving customers, an unfair boss, superior competition, and weak support services. The amount of time a candidate devotes to each subject reveals a great

deal about his or her personal characteristics and priorities. It may be that questions about the family or customers receive long, detailed answers, while questions about the boss or the competition are dealt with quickly. Some candidates quantify the answers to probing questions; some candidates are analytical, critical, logical, and/or linear thinkers.

Exhibits 3.1 and 3.2 at the end of the chapter list hundreds of probing questions and interview probes to choose from when interviewing highly experienced salespeople or recent college graduates. A sales manager must determine what the answers reveal about the candidate. You can discover a great deal about applicants' skills, motivation, personal characteristics, and experience by asking how they organize their day, what they think of their current employers, and what they like most and least about past positions and through self-analysis questions that elicit their own opinions of personal strengths and weaknesses and areas to change or develop further.

Some sales managers like to ask candidates why they chose sales as a career. Many candidates answer "for the money," others say they like people, some talk about a mother who sold, and still others reply they like to persuade people. Most managers like the last two answers much better than the first two. A candidate who chooses a sales career for the money might be very disappointed in certain industries.

Some sales managers ask candidates for their long- and short-term career goals. A candidate might reply, "My short-term goal is to be the number 1 salesperson; my long-term goal is to move into sales management." This candidate might not be a good fit for a firm with a limited career ladder.

Some sales managers like to ask candidates for examples of their best and worst bosses. If a candidate replies, "My best boss was there when I needed her but otherwise stayed out of my way," and you are a micromanager, it might be a bad fit.

Other managers ask candidates, "How was your performance evaluated, and was it fair?" Many salespeople can't answer this question or just refer to results, but a good salesperson knows the metrics on which he or she was evaluated.

Most managers say, "I plan to ask your previous supervisors for a reference. What do you think they will say about you?" This puts a reality check on the interview and encourages the candidate to speak candidly.

The answers to situational questions are also revealing. "Tell me about your best customer, your worst customer, your most difficult customer, and a customer you lost." Often the best customer was a friend or a captive account. Often the worst customer was a person the candidate could not get along with. Did the candidate sell the most difficult account? Did the candidate try to win the lost customer back? "Tell me about your most successful customer and your least successful and how you helped them."

Don't ask leading questions that signal the response you hope to hear, such as, "Do you like to work with people?" Questions that ask "why," "how," "what," or "tell me" elicit more complete answers.

Behavioral questions can also tell you a great deal about the candidate. A sales manager might ask the candidate, "Whom do you most admire and why?" The candidate can choose a family member, a businessperson, an athlete, a movie star, a politician, or a person from any other category. Which category the "most admired person" is chosen from says something about the candidate's interests. Why this person is most admired tells the interviewer about the candidate's own values and goals. For example, a grandmother is chosen because she was honest, raised a family, and made great personal sacrifices. An athlete is chosen because of skills and achievements.

A sales manager might ask the candidate to describe his or her greatest disappointment, problem, or setback and what he or she did about it. The candidate must choose between a professional or personal disappointment. What he or she did about it indicates the candidate's ability to deal with rejection and adversity, a very important trait for salespeople. The disappointments range from divorce or the sudden death of a loved one to a bad grade or the loss of a job. One candidate told me his greatest disappointment was being terminated last year from a great job. He also admitted he has been unable to overcome this rejection, and he still finds it difficult to take interviews. A sales manager will learn more about the candidate from these two questions than he or she would after years of association.

Occasionally a candidate will give fuzzy replies or no replies to such questions as, "Why did you leave your last job?" or "What was your compensation?" To elicit a more forthright response, drop the questions for a while and go on to something else. Then return later to the subject and probe further by phrasing the questions differently—for example, by asking, "What sort of a person was your boss?" If related questions continue to produce indistinct or weak replies, you have found a problem area, which after the interview will require independent investigation through reference checking.

KEEPING NOTES

When possible, record in writing your impressions and key information immediately after the interview. After six interviews, as after six sales calls, information and impressions merge unless you have made notes. If you wish to take notes during an interview, ask the salesperson's permission, and make your notes at regular intervals, not after revealing statements. Candidates attach importance to what you record, so don't tip your hand.

As you record information, it is a good idea to mark each item with a plus, minus, or zero, depending on its bearing on the candidate's desirability. Try to look for information that helps you reject or accept the applicant. After the interview, organize this information in two columns with plusses on one side and minuses on the other. Human resource professionals tell us not to keep notes on a candidate's résumé. Should there be litigation based on the interview, the placement of these notes is often misunderstood.

I know of one instance in which a sales manager hired the wrong candidate from two finalists because he relied on his memory for the requisite information. When the candidate, now employee, reported for his first day of work, the sales manager realized his mistake, but he decided not to admit it. The story has a happy ending, however, because that salesman proved highly successful. When the sales manager retired, he told the story at his farewell dinner, while his successor, the wrongly hired salesman, listened in astonishment.

LITTLE THINGS MEAN A LOT

In interviewing candidates, salespeople who criticize past employers and bosses signal a problem that requires further investigation. The fault often does lie with the previous employers, but you need more information. Ask whether the previous bosses would rehire them, or what those bosses would say about them.

The rigors of some sales positions require a great deal of energy, which not all people possess. In such a situation, look for active people who channel their energy into work and don't just talk about working hard. A person who works long hours or Saturdays generally meets this requirement. Salespeople at a bakery supply distributor make their calls on independent bakeries from 6 a.m. to 3 p.m., and they end their long day by calling on ice cream and yogurt shops from 3 p.m. to 6 p.m. We are what we do, not what we say.

During the interview, watch for verbal slips or for stories and anecdotes that reveal personal weaknesses. A candidate once told me about a "funny" incident that involved missing an important selling date because he had accidentally walked under a sprinkler and gotten his suit wet. Another candidate told me that every Friday he "got gassed," then corrected himself to say that every Friday he "bought gas."

BODY LANGUAGE

Watch for body language when a candidate answers sensitive questions concerning compensation, advancement, the boss, or company politics. Does the candidate look you in the eye, wet his or her lips, wring his or her hands, sit erect, fidget,

grimace? Most people can't hide anxiety, and anxiety points to problem areas. The salesperson who claims to be sincere but does not look you in the eye or claims to be confident but whose voice shakes raises doubts.

ENDING THE INTERVIEW

To end the initial in-person interview, ask the candidate to summarize why he or she feels qualified for the position and if he or she has any more questions for you. See if and how the candidate asks for the job or asks you to define the next step, or steps, and a timetable. Then tell the candidate what your next step is and when it will occur. "I will arrange for you to meet my boss in two weeks." "Your skills and background are great, but we need someone who has traveled the territory." Don't make false excuses for not hiring someone.

As was mentioned earlier, you might choose to end the interview with a "strategic silence" and see how the candidate reacts. In such a situation, the sales manager closes the interview by crossing his or her arms, looking the candidate in the eye, and saying nothing. This simulates what actually happens in many sales situations. Does the candidate match your silence with his or her own, ask more questions, nervously mention negative aspects of his or her background, or ask for the next action?

PREJUDGING CANDIDATES

Although candidate profiles are essential, don't stereotype the ideal candidate. We have a tendency to hire people we like, who don't threaten us, whom we feel we can manage easily, and who fit the company mold. I recently attended a sales meeting where no one was taller than the sales manager, who was five feet one inch tall.

Many of us make judgments early in an interview and then look for information to support that decision. Public relations professionals claim that lasting personal impressions, often based on appearances, are made in the first 10 seconds of an interview. "I sized him up as a phony the minute he walked in." "I liked her style and confidence the moment I saw her." Use the interview to obtain a complete, well-rounded profile of the candidate. Save your decision until the end. Set standards, be critical, sit in judgment.

Often a single unfavorable or favorable item will warp your judgment. "He is friendly with the purchasing agent at our largest account." "She drives an old car." Look at the whole picture before making a decision.

Often a glib, egocentric, evasive, talky, or argumentative candidate forces us to lose control of the interview. Be direct. Tell the applicant the questions you

want answered. Don't hesitate to end the interview if this disruptive behavior continues. Remember, the interview allows a sales manager to view the candidate on a personal sales call.

Continuing Interviews for Finalists

After the initial face-to-face interviews, a few candidates will be selected for the next round. These candidates should be interviewed by the sales manager (for a second time), his or her supervisor, at least one salesperson, and the manager of a related department (for example, engineering, operations, or customer support). Before these interviews, a sales manager should meet with those doing the interviewing to review the job description and candidate profile and coordinate each person's questions. To ensure uniformity and fairness, some companies require all interviewers to ask all candidates the same standard questions. However, the candidate soon knows what to expect and starts giving standard answers. I suggest each interviewer choose different questions for the candidate in order to explore different aspects of required skills, knowledge, experience, and personal characteristics.

After the interview, each interviewer independently recommends in writing to the sales manager whether or not to hire the candidate and why. Once these recommendations are received, the group meets to discuss the candidate. The sales manager is the decision maker; other members of the group are advisors. If hiring a salesperson becomes a group consensus decision, the dominant personality or highest-ranking member prevails.

Including top salespeople in this decision makes them feel useful, important, and worthwhile. Their involvement has motivational value, and their job knowledge makes them an important filter. Also a candidate may speak more openly with a fellow salesperson than with management. As an example, a Fortune 1000 global manufacturer of long-haul trailer trucks insists that all finalists spend a day calling on customers with a key salesperson. The candidate receives a first-hand look at the job, and the key salesperson can evaluate the candidate at the moment of truth. At this point, some candidates decide the job is not of interest because dealing with small family-owned dealerships proves too frustrating. This self-selection proves less expensive than hiring the wrong person.

Based on reference checking and a reexamination of résumés, personal history forms, and notes from the previous interview, the sales manager prepares a written list of questions to ask on the second and possibly third interview. Differing from the first interview, the questions are specific, not general. If one former boss has reported employment dates and a reason for leaving that differs from what the candidate told you, what explains the inconsistency? Or, although the candidate has a marvelous past record selling established products for large companies, how will he or she adapt to selling a relatively unknown product for a small company? In the second interview, take some phone calls, create some anxiety, challenge the candidate, and see how he or she reacts. Again, simulate a sales call.

Make sure that you have honestly answered all the finalist's questions about the company and the position. Allow the applicant several opportunities to ask questions. When inviting a finalist to a second interview, provide that person with product or service literature, company Web site information, and general company information. End all the interviews by telling the applicant that within a certain time frame you will call or by agreeing on the next action.

Reference Checking and Background Investigations

If you don't check references, you might just as well hire your staff by throwing darts or flipping coins. Don't delegate reference checking to human resources or an outside service. A sales manager needs to reach the right people, ask probing questions, and listen to the words and the music. Most sales managers don't check references because it challenges their infallible judgment; it is time-consuming, burdensome, difficult, and awkward; and they mistrust what the references say. They also misunderstand the legal issues and how to correctly check references.

During the interviews, you asked for professional references and for permission to contact past supervisors, customers, and competitors. If the applicant currently holds a job, you usually cannot contact the present employer. If the applicant asks you not to contact past supervisors, customers, or competitors, ask why. This could be a red flag. What is the applicant hiding? The candidate must give you written permission to call customers, competitors, and previous supervisors for references. You not only do this for legal reasons but to protect the candidate's rights to privacy.

Disregard written references provided by the candidate because obviously these represent a form of advertising. Telephone interviews with past supervisors, customers, and competitors, however, will provide useful information.

CUSTOMERS AS REFERENCES

Customers represent a reliable source of information about a candidate. Few legal restrictions apply here. Often a sales manager knows key decision makers at customers' firms, who will speak freely about the candidate. Sales managers must ask customers, competitors, and previous supervisors appropriate questions to close information gaps. After looking at notes from the previous interviews, the job description, candidate profile, résumé, and personal history, the sales manager might be concerned about a candidate's ability to open new competitive accounts, sell value versus price, sell new highly technical services, travel extensively, or provide in-depth service. A sales manager might ask a candidate's customer, "Did Alex follow up on and solve service problems?" "Did he increase his share of your purchases or sell you new products?" "Was his sales approach based on value or price?" "Was he enthusiastic and confident when faced with rejection?" "Could you suggest other customers I could call who worked with Alex?" "Would you recommend Alex as a salesperson to represent your firm?" Some sales managers ask candidates for permission to call their "worst" customer or a customer they lost. A candidate's reaction to this question makes it worth asking.

If the candidate sold a product or service noncompetitive to yours and you know competitors in that industry, their input could be useful. They can provide information on the applicant's employer and possibly on the applicant as well.

PREVIOUS SUPERVISORS AS REFERENCES

Previous supervisors represent a critical source of information about candidates. As discussed above, decide specifically what you want to know and formulate questions around this. General questions produce unreliable general answers. Ask the candidate for his or her previous supervisor's work, mobile, and home phone numbers. In many cases you cannot call the candidate's present employer.

Some previous supervisors remain with the same firm, but most have moved on to another sales management position, which makes them more agreeable to candidly discuss the candidate and vastly reduces any legal liabilities. I suggest calling these references at home or on their cell phones because they are more relaxed.

Introduce yourself as the sales manager of your firm and establish rapport so that the previous supervisor does not feel you are a telephone solicitor. Refer to a common acquaintance, trade show, or customer. After several minutes of "warm-up," state the purpose of your call. "We have a common acquaintance who worked for your firm, and I am considering hiring him. Sales manager to sales manager, I have a few questions that will take 15 minutes to discuss."

If the sales manager has changed employers since he or she supervised Alex, you will generally receive a positive reception. If the sales manager is still employed by the same firm, you may encounter difficulties. If the sales manager is receptive, have your five questions ready. Besides the five specific questions, you might try a few of these: "What type customer did the candidate have trouble selling?" "Did you try to convince the candidate to stay?" "How does the candidate compare to his or her replacement?" "Have you seen the candidate's résumé?" If so discuss it; if not, possibly fax one and then discuss it. One sales manager at a financial services firm said she faxed a candidate's résumé to a reference and when he read it, there was laughter. If possible, verify dates of employment, salary range, and reason for leaving.

Find out the reference's exact title and past relationship to the applicant. I once discovered the reference was the applicant's ex-brother-in-law. You also may wish to contact the reference's immediate supervisor if he or she also knew the candidate. Some sales managers will ask fellow salespeople who were employed with the candidate for a reference.

If the sales manager you are calling as a reference is still employed by the same firm, he or she may refer you to human resources and refuse to answer questions. "Our company policy is not to discuss previous employees." The previous employer has some legal liability for references, which varies by state. There is little if any legal liability in asking for references, so don't be shy.

Human resource departments often discourage reference checking for legal reasons, even though there is hardly any basis for this. They confuse the legal liabilities in giving references to those in asking for references. According to a study by C. Patrick Fleener, a management professor at the Albers School of Business and Economics at Seattle University, between 1985 and 1990, federal and state court records nationwide showed only 16 defamation cases arising from reference checks. And plaintiffs prevailed in only 4 of the 16. All 16 defamation cases were filed against the previous employer, not against a prospective employer checking references.

In situations in which the sales manager you are calling as a reference refers you to human resources and refuses to answer questions about the candidate, be ready with another set of questions related to the company, not the candidate. You might say to the referring sales manager, "I understand the problem. Our firm has similar rules. May I ask you a few questions about your company?" Generally the answer is yes. You might then ask, "Do you require salespeople to prospect for new accounts or provide technical services to existing accounts? Is overnight travel required? Do your salespeople sell on value or price? Do you provide sales skills training? Who are your target accounts?" The answers to these company-related questions will help you better understand the candidate's skills, knowledge, experience, and personal characteristics and may contradict answers you received directly from the candidate.

Last and most important, ask, "Would you rehire the candidate?" Company policy often prohibits rehiring. In this situation ask, "If company policy allowed rehiring, would you rehire this individual?" This is the moment of truth, when previously withheld information comes tumbling forth. I have encountered reactions such as, "Never," "Only if his father-in-law made me," and "I would, but my boss would not."

As with the candidate interview, listen carefully to the previous employer's responses and tone of voice. Phrases such as "unfortunate circumstances," "personality clashes," or "chose to resign" usually indicate problems.

Be aware that if the previous employer is your competitor, you may receive a false recommendation. The competitor may wish to burden you with one of its previous problems. You may also receive a false recommendation from a previous employer who feels guilty about terminating the candidate.

BACKGROUND INVESTIGATIONS

Background investigations on the finalists are a useful precaution. Contact the secretary of state for a driver's license check. Equifax, TransUnion, and Experian all offer a service that investigates appropriate court and financial records and, if necessary, verifies places of residence and past employers. These reports generally cost $100 each, and large credit agencies offer online computer access to their databases. Through such an investigation, one sales manager discovered that the finalist had just lost his driver's license. The job required extensive use of a car. Knowing how applicants handle bills, loans, and other financial obligations helps predict their responsibility on the job. A salesperson who remains preoccupied with lawsuits or overdue loan payments will be distracted from selling to customers. One company was won over to background checks after a new hire was apprehended stealing from a customer, and it was later learned he had been previously convicted for a similar act.

Under the Federal Fair Credit Reporting Act of 1971, you must advise candidates that credit reports will be used. At that point the candidate might ask you not to use a credit report, and you need to ask the candidate why. Should a credit report provide information possibly leading subsequently to rejection, you must supply the candidate with the source's name and address, and you might also want to leave the door open by asking the candidate to comment on this information.

Verify a candidate's college degrees by contacting the appropriate educational institutions. Did the candidate receive a degree or just attend this school? If the latter is true, such inaccurate résumé information might reflect on a candidate's honesty. We need not only competent but ethical and honest salespeople.

Three of Warren Buffett's favorite interview questions involve ethics and honesty. "What are your three core values?" "Why should I trust you?" "What would you do if your best friend did something illegal?"

Testing

Intelligence, personality, aptitude, and interest tests for salespeople can be administered and scored either by you or by outside services. Such tests provide insight into the subject's learning and reasoning ability, emotional stability, confidence, enthusiasm, and occupational interests. The problem lies in interpreting the results. Which test results can accurately predict positive or negative job results? Have your current sales force take the test, and correlate their individual test results with their individual sales performance. You can then use your best performers' test results as a standard by which to evaluate candidates. If the best performers don't test any differently from the not so best, then testing may not be useful.

A sales manager obtains from testing what he or she puts into it. If you are willing to devote time and energy to this area, you can obtain useful information. These tests, available from distributors for a number of companies, include Caliper Human Strategies, Personality Dynamics, the Strong Vocational Interest Test, the Minnesota Vocational Interest Test, the Martin Bruce Test of Sales Aptitude, the Thematic Apperception Test, the California Personality Test, the Guildford-Zimmerman Temperament Survey, the John G. Geir Personal Profile System, the Otis Quick-Scoring Mental Ability Tests, the Wesman Personnel Classification Test, the Adaptability Test, the Concept Mastery Test, and the Wonderlic Personnel Test.

Some companies test candidates on knowledge of their industries, products, markets, and technology. Generally such domain knowledge tests are created and graded internally.

Testing is a tool to help you hire outstanding candidates, not a crutch to make the decision for you. Don't substitute test results for your judgment. Narrow the field to the three best candidates, test each, and compare results. Use tests to eliminate certain candidates or to better understand strengths and weaknesses, not to choose one candidate over another. Also use tests to customize a training program for the person hired.

Some sales managers give tests to all qualified applicants after the telephone interview. The test is done online by an outside service. In order for a candidate to qualify for an in-person interview, his or her test scores must be above certain thresholds. In this case, testing is used as an initial, not a final, filter. With this approach you miss a lot of good candidates who just don't test well.

Tests cost between $100 and $200 per applicant. Turnaround times vary from a day (using fax, e-mail, or overnight delivery) to a week (using regular mail). Some tests are taken online by the candidate; others use hard copies. Some tests can be taken at home; others only at the office.

CASE STUDIES

Asking sales candidates to write case studies represents a growing trend. The sales manager gives the candidate a case involving a situation such as prospecting, new product placement, customer service, or conflict resolution. Then the candidate is asked to answer the case questions in writing by e-mail.

Case studies ask candidates to solve a problem in writing. This tests their experience, analytical ability, and writing skills. If such skills are important to the success of a salesperson at your company, try using cases.

Making the Final Choice

To assist in making your final choice, classify each item listed on the job description and candidate profile as a "must" or a "want" with a numeric value weighting its importance. For each duty, skill, level of knowledge, or area of experience and for each of several personal characteristics, decide which are the musts, which are the wants, and how each ranks in importance in selecting a salesperson. Any finalist possesses all the musts, so in making your choice review which finalists have the most important wants. Review the weightings of each category, but do not rely on a total score to select the best candidate. Never be rushed into a decision by the need to put a warm body on the street. Remember these same hiring filters should be used not only to recruit outside direct salespeople but also channel partners and inside and/or telesales people. Simply adjust the filters to reflect the appropriate situation.

One last word of caution: Before hiring the final choice, many companies require drug, AIDS, and/or liver testing, especially if the sales job requires driving. In some states this may raise legal issues, so before proceeding with this type of test, consult your human resource department and attorney. After hiring, most firms ask salespeople to take physical exams.

Equal Employment Opportunity (EEO)

In working with the job description, candidate profile, sourcing, interview questions, reference checking, and testing—that is, the entire recruiting process—keep in mind that the 1964 Civil Rights Act and extensive city, state, and federal legislation since then require that minorities, older people, women, and the disabled receive a fair and equal opportunity for employment. All aspects of the hiring process must be justifiable in terms of job performance. Federal legislation prohibits withholding employment on the basis of race or color, gender, religious affiliation, national origin, age, disability, or veteran's status.

Your objective is to identify people who can do the job. EEO legislation does not restrict you from asking any bona fide job-related questions, but when in doubt, consult a knowledgeable attorney. Human resource departments can mislead you with too much caution. However, questions seeking the following information (as well as job descriptions, candidate profiles, and candidate evaluations based on this type of information) are illegal:

- Date of birth
- Maiden name
- Previous married name
- Marital status
- Name of spouse
- Spouse's occupation and length of time on job
- Spouse's place of employment
- Number of children and their ages
- Arrest record
- Ancestry
- Age
- Gender
- Religion
- National origin (race)
- If child care has been arranged for
- Whether wages are garnished

Exhibit 3.3 at the end of the chapter lists specific questions you can and cannot ask. Again, when in doubt, contact a knowledgeable human resource attorney.

As North America becomes more globalized, equal employment laws will assume greater importance. As good corporate citizens, good global citizens, and good human beings, we should not only obey the letter of the law, which we must, but the spirit of the law, which will create a stronger social fabric for business. Recent amendments to the Federal Sentencing Guidelines state that organizations are responsible to train employees on compliance and ethics. The U.S. Sentencing Commission found in 2004 that fines for a criminal conviction can be reduced up to 95 percent when an organization has an ethics program in place.

In the twenty-first century, qualified salespeople will be more difficult to find. In the twenty-first century our customer base, whether business to business or business to consumer, will include many more women, people of color, and the disabled. To satisfy our employment needs and the needs of our customers, we must hire a diverse sales force, which will prove equally rewarding for the salespeople.

International Sales

When hiring salespeople outside North America, some of the filters we ordinarily use inside the United States are inappropriate. For example, it is culturally inappropriate to ask for references in South America or Asia, and throwing rejection at a candidate would be considered impolite. For this reason many North American companies use recruiters to help hire salespeople in South America and Asia.

Hiring the Best

Hiring competent salespeople is a process with a beginning—the job description and candidate profile; an end—the offer; and the steps along the way such as sourcing, interviews, and reference checking. If you view recruiting as a process and consider all appropriate steps, even if you decide against using all of them, the probability of success increases, and the risk of failure decreases. Viewed as a process, you realize that hiring requires 30 to 90 days to recruit the right person. Hiring requires planning and anticipating needs.

Sales Managers' Major Mistakes/Weaknesses in Hiring/Recruiting

- Hiring the best of a bad bunch.
- Hiring under pressure and making snap judgments.
- Hiring people we like; comfortable, nonthreatening, easy-to-manage people.
- Not networking, not keeping files, no continuous process.
- Not continually upgrading the sales force through continuous improvement.
- Not using a variety of sources.
- Not checking references.
- Not asking probing questions at interviews.

- Talking too much at interviews.
- No job description or candidate profile.
- Not matching candidate to type of selling or type of sales process: relationship, consultative, closer, order-taker, partnership, application.
- Termination issues; not weeding the garden.

(Exhibits start on next page.)

Exhibit 3.1.   Sample Probing Questions.

The following are questions that can be asked during an interview. However, whenever possible, your question should relate to the previous response of the interviewee.

Screening Questions

- Tell me about yourself.
- What are your long- and short-term goals?
- What are you doing now?
- Why did you choose selling as a career?
- How do you feel about it?
- Why are you looking for a new position?
- What are you looking for?
- What type of person would you like to work for?
- Would your previous employer hire you back? Why?
- What would your boss say about you if I called?

Work History

- Could you tell me about your work history? How would you compare the companies you worked for?
- The first company you worked for, how did you select it?
- What was the company like? What are you looking for in a company?
- What type of individual was the person you reported to?
- What were your responsibilities?
- What do you feel were some of your major accomplishments? Why?
- What are areas in which you feel you could have been more productive? In what way?
- What type of person do you like to work for?
- What was your best boss like? What was your worst boss like?
- How would you compare them?
- What do you consider to be some of your greatest accomplishments?
- What do you consider to be some of your most disappointing work experiences?
- What type of individuals do you like to have working with you?
- Have you ever had any fellow workers or a boss who did not function at the level you expected? Tell me about it.
- If they did not live up to your expectations, what was your approach?
- What do you think determines a person's progress in a good company?
- What are the advantages and disadvantages of working for a small as compared to a large organization?
- How do you feel your career progress has been to this point?
- What are some examples of important types of decisions you have been called on to make or problems you had to solve?

(Continued on next page.)

Exhibit 3.1.   *(Continued from previous page.)*

- What do you feel contributed to your effectiveness as a salesperson?
- What do you feel may have interfered with your effectiveness as a salesperson?
- In what respects do you feel you have improved most as a salesperson during the past few years?
- How many hours do you feel a person should spend on his or her job?
- What do you see for yourself in the future?
- How do you spend your spare time?
- How do you see yourself in relationships with others?
- What do you feel are some of the greatest motivating forces for your fellow workers?

Educational Background

- Could you tell me about your educational background?
- Why did you select that particular school?
- What were you looking for in the institution you attended?
- What was your major field of study?
- How did you select your major?
- Where did you live on campus?
- What would you consider to be the advantages and disadvantages of living in a fraternity or sorority as compared to private or university housing?
- Were you involved in extracurricular activities?
- If you held an elective office, how did you campaign for the position?
- Did you make any changes while you were in office?
- How would you compare the individuals who lived in your housing unit to those in other units?
- How would you compare your college experience to your high school experience?
- Select the professor that you liked best. What type of individual was he or she?
- What courses did you like best? Why?
- What courses did you like least? Why?
  (If one is asked, the other should always be included as a follow-up question.)
- If you changed majors, why?
- How did you determine what new curriculum to pursue?
- Describe your university. What type of place was it?
- How was the school spirit?
- Were there any changes that could have been made on the campus so as to make it more beneficial?
- How do you feel such changes could have been initiated?
- How were the college administrators?

(Continued on next page.)

Exhibit 3.1.   *(Continued from previous page.)*

- Did you have a roommate?
- What type of individual was he or she?
- What are his or her future plans?
- How did you spend your vacation periods?
- Overall, how did you do from an academic perspective?
- Are there any aspects of your academic background that you wish you could have changed?
- How effective was your academic background in preparing you for the future?
- Considering your accomplishments, what are some of the reasons for your successes?
- What are the advantages and disadvantages of sales as a chosen field of endeavor?
- What personal characteristics do you feel are necessary in order to succeed in sales?
- What do you find to be unique about yourself?

Exhibit 3.2. Interview Probes.

The following probes are phrased in a very direct fashion. During the course of the interview, you will have to rephrase them to suit the topical area and to make them less threatening.

Motivation

- Why did you choose this line of work? Why did you choose sales?
- Which of your characteristics do you think are the most important?
- What do you think most people think is important in achieving success?
- Can you give me some examples of experiences on the job that you felt were satisfying?
- Can you give me some examples of experiences on the job that you felt were dissatisfying?
- What basic factors motivate you and why?

Risk Taking

- Tell us about the biggest risk-taking decision that you have made (present company, previous employment). If the answer is career, follow up with a company risk-taking decision. How did you gather the information to make the decision? How long after that did it take you to make the decision?
- Do you think a big company discourages people from taking risks?

Problem Analysis

- In your opinion, what are the most difficult problems with which a salesperson has to deal? Give an example.
- Describe the biggest problem that you have faced within the last six months. How did you handle it?

Self-Analysis

- All of us have areas that we'd like to change or develop further. What are some of yours?
- As we think back to what we've covered today, what do you think are some of the chief strengths you would bring to the job?
- Based on what we've covered so far, how would you summarize your strengths and qualities, both personal and professional, which make you a good prospect for any employer?

(Continued on next page.)

Exhibit 3.2.   *(Continued from previous page.)*

Salesmanship

- Tell me about your toughest sales experience.
- Give me an example of your ability to sell.
- How would you spend your first 30 days in setting up a new territory?
- What do you think the job of selling takes?
- What do you think makes a good salesperson?
- How do you qualify a prospect?
- Summarize your past sales career.
- How do you feel about working on commission versus salary?

Work Habits

- How many calls do you typically make in a day?
- How many prospects do you think you should handle at any one time?
- Why do you like sales?
- What kind of support are you going to expect from me?
- What types of reporting are you used to?

Independence

- What do you like about your job? Why do you like it?
- Describe an incident when you disagreed with your boss and how it was settled.
- Why did you go to the college you attended?
- How do you want to be managed?

Planning and Organization

- What are your long- and short-term goals?
- Given a new territory, how would you go about setting up time and territory management?

Self and/or Social Confidence (Self-Perception)

- Describe yourself.

(Continued on next page.)

Exhibit 3.2.   *(Continued from previous page.)*

Judgment

- How do you determine where you stand with your fellow workers?
- How do you think your fellow workers would describe you?
- How do you think your boss would describe you?
- What can a manager do that is important in developing salespeople?

Aggressive

- Why do you think you are especially suited to sales?
- If the customer called you and told you he was going to buy from the competition, and you have worked for one year on the account, what would you do?

Killer Instinct

- How do you respond when the customer says no?

Initiative

- How important is friendship in selling?
- If I assigned you to new account sales only, how would you proceed?

Oral Communication Skills

- What different approaches do you employ in talking with different types of customers?
- How do you evaluate the effectiveness of these approaches?

Emotional Adjustment and Control

- What is your reaction when you're late to an appointment and get caught in traffic?
- What kinds of people do you like to work with?
- What kinds of people do you not like to work with?
- What do you do in the case of an extreme personality conflict?

Stability and Maturity

- What do you like to do best?

Exhibit 3.3.   Sample Guidelines for Interviewing Job Applicants.

Unlawful Inquiries

- Do not ask the applicant's age.
- Do not ask an applicant over 40 years old whether he or she can work under or with younger supervisors.
- Do not inquire as to age and relate how it affects health and pension benefits.
- Do not ask if an applicant has children or the age of an applicant's children.
- Do not ask who will care for the children if an applicant is hired.
- Do not ask about the applicant's race, or question directly or indirectly the race or color of an applicant's spouse.
- Do not ask about height or weight when it is not relevant to the job.
- Do not ask about U.S. citizenship or if an applicant intends to become a U.S. citizen.
- Do not ask an applicant if he or she has ever had his or her wages garnished. A credit check is a better method to learn this and other pertinent information. If an applicant is rejected due to the applicant's poor credit rating, you must inform the applicant the reason for the rejection and the credit service used.
- Do not ask an applicant if he or she was ever arrested.
- Do not ask an applicant whether he or she is married, divorced, separated, widowed, or single. (But you may ask how an applicant prefers to be addressed—"Mr., Mrs., Miss, or Ms.").
- Do not ask a female applicant for her maiden name or for her father's surname.
- Do not ask an applicant what church he or she attends or the names of his or her priest, rabbi, or minister.
- If an applicant is divorced, do not ask the reasons why.
- Do not ask for the name or address of any relative of an adult applicant.
- Do not ask about any organizations, clubs, societies, or lodges that the applicant belongs to if this information would indicate through character or name the race, religion, color, or ancestry of the members.
- Do not ask an applicant if anyone resides with the applicant or the identity of any roommate.
- Do not ask a female applicant if she would be comfortable supervising men or a male applicant if he would be comfortable supervising women.
- Do not ask an applicant if he or she owns or rents his or her home.
- Do not ask an applicant about his or her spouse's employment.
- Do not ask female applicants if they would be willing to take turns making coffee unless it is part of the job description or men are also required to make coffee.
- Do not ask about an applicant's union sentiments or membership.
- Do not express any antiunion sentiments.

(Continued on next page.)

Exhibit 3.3.   *(Continued from previous page.)*

- Do not inquire about a name change or ask what the original name was unless it is necessary to enable you to check an applicant's work record.
- Do not ask about the nationality or birthplace of an applicant or an applicant's parents.
- Do not ask for photographs with the employment application or before hiring an applicant.
- Do not ask for the specific years of school attendance or graduation.
- Do not ask an applicant to identify his or her mother tongue or the language used in the applicant's home.
- Do not ask about an applicant's military experience other than whether he or she is in the U.S. armed forces, National Guard, or reserve units.
- Do not ask about any physical characteristics such as scars, burns, or missing limbs.
- Do not ask about the health of an applicant.
- Do not ask if an applicant has ever received counseling or has seen a psychiatrist.
- Do not ask if the applicant has ever had a drug or alcohol problem.
- Do not ask about an applicant's workers' compensation history.
- Do not ask how a disability occurred or if the disability is indicative of an underlying impairment.
- Do not ask the applicant if he or she has any potentially disabling impairments.
- Do not ask an applicant whether he or she will need a leave for treatment.
- If an applicant volunteers information about a medical condition such as cancer or HIV, do not ask about the progress of the illness or whether it is in remission.
- Do not ask if family members have had a history of illness.
- Do not ask if the applicant has any disability or medical condition that will prevent the applicant from performing the job.

Lawful Inquiries

- What language do you speak fluently (only if job related)?
- (To a homemaker or retired person) Why do you want to return to work?
- How many years' experience do you have, and what functions have you performed?
- What do you like to do, or what do you do best?
- Can you travel extensively (only if job related)?
- Who recommended you to us?
- Whom can we notify in case of an emergency?
- What academic, vocational, or professional education programs and/or schools have you attended (if job related)?

(Continued on next page.)

Exhibit 3.3.   *(Continued from previous page.)*

- You can ask about specific skills such as reading, writing, word processing, computers, and public speaking where they are job related.
- You can ask where the applicant resides and how long he or she has lived there.
- You can ask how long an applicant has been a resident of this city or state.
- If we offer you a job, will you be able to furnish us with proof of U.S. citizenship or a visa that permits you to work in the United States?
- Have you had any felony convictions? If so, give us the dates, the nature of the offense, and other relevant details.
- If the applicant appears to be under age, do not ask his or her age; just state that proof of age will be required if he or she is offered a job.
- You can ask about an applicant's military experience in the U.S. armed forces.
- You can inquire about the dates of military service, military occupation, and date and type of discharge.
- You can ask whether the applicant has received any notice to report for duty in the armed forces.
- You can ask an applicant about his or her membership in any professional, trade, or service organization.
- You can ask for the names of persons who can supply professional and character references.
- You can ask for the name of the person who suggested that the applicant apply for a position.
- You can state the attendance requirements and ask whether the applicant can meet them.
- You can ask the applicant if he or she knows of any reason that he or she cannot perform the essential functions of the job.
- You can ask questions relating to an applicant's ability to perform job-related functions and tasks.
- You can describe or demonstrate a job function and ask whether the applicant can perform the function with or without a reasonable accommodation.
- You can ask an applicant to describe or demonstrate how, with or without reasonable accommodation, he or she will be able to perform job-related functions.

Questions and Exercises for Chapter 3

- How would you determine if a sales candidate has the necessary skills and personal characteristics for the job?
- List 10 open-ended probing questions you would ask the sales candidate and what the answers will tell you about him or her.

- What references would you check, and what questions would you ask the references?

Quiz for Chapter 3

1. Which of these screening techniques should a sales manager use in hiring a salesperson?
    a. Telephone interviews
    b. Personal interviews
    c. Reference checking
    d. Testing
    e. Meeting the spouse

2. Which of these open-ended probing questions might violate Equal Employment Opportunity laws?
    a. Have you ever been arrested?
    b. Have you ever been convicted of a crime?
    c. Where were your mother and father born?
    d. Who will care for your daughter during the day?
    e. Where did you go to college, and when did you graduate?

3. True or false?
    Telephone interviews are important because salespeople use the phone to sell appointments, take reorders, and resolve customer conflicts.

4. True or false?
    A salesperson's compensation history becomes an extremely important indication of past performance.

5. True or false?
    The most reliable guide to a salesperson's future performance is his or her past record.

6. True or false?
    Start the interview by showing the candidate the job description.

7. Which of these references can provide reliable information on the candidate?
    a. Customers
    b. Competitors
    c. Previous supervisors
    d. Peers

8. True or false?
   You should receive the candidate's written permission to call references.

9. Which of these background investigations should be checked before hiring a candidate?
   a. Credit
   b. Criminal
   c. Education degrees
   d. Driver's license
   e. Drug use

10. True or false?
    After the telephone interview, a sales manager should use testing to decide which candidates are worth interviewing in person.

Notes

1. *The 2003 Towers Perrin Talent Report.* Copyright © 2003 Towers Perrin. Reprinted by permission of Towers Perrin.
2. *Hot Topics in Sales Management and Sales Compensation 2005.* Copyright © 2005 Hewitt Associates LLC. Reprinted by permission of Hewitt Associates.

PART THREE

Training for Results

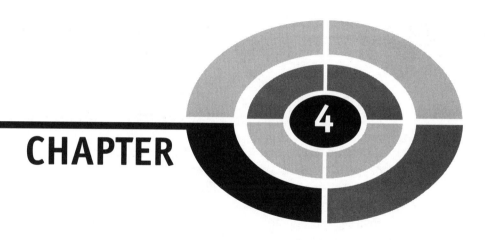

CHAPTER 4

Product, Competitor, and Customer Knowledge

The Model

Pay salespeople more than they are worth. Make them worth more than what you pay them. That is what training is all about. In the twenty-first century's changing landscape, sales force training creates a competitive advantage in an otherwise commoditized marketplace.

Sales force management is a process. One step logically follows another. Control the pieces and you control the whole. Chapters 2 and 3 examined the model and methodology for hiring salespeople; this chapter and the next two

discuss the model and methodology for training these people. Hire the right people, train them well, and you are two-thirds of the way toward a more productive sales force. Hire the wrong people and train them poorly, and you have a self-fulfilling prophecy for failure.

A sales manager's job is to get work done through other people. Your success depends on their success. Therefore, your job as a sales manager is to make the salespeople successful. For salespeople to be successful, they need training in product, competitor, customer knowledge, and sales skills. You provide this training through the continuous process of initial programs, followed by field coaching and sales meetings.

Channel Partners and Telesales

Training makes direct and indirect salespeople plus support personnel more productive. If you sell through channel partners such as distributors, brokers, or independent sales representatives, they are no better than your ability to select the proper organization and train them. A good training program forces channel partners to devote more time and resources to your company's products or services. Since channel partners also represent other products or services, the more training they receive, the more mind share your firm obtains. A good training program makes them more productive, cooperative, and confident partners rather than adversaries. Channel partners spend time where they are comfortable, have a commitment in human and financial resources, and obtain the best return on invested dollars. Companies that use channel partners include a mutual commitment to training in their channel partner contracts. This commitment includes hours and annual number of sales meetings and ride-withs that will be conducted by the principals for their channel partner.

Similarly, a well-conceived training program with proper resources proves equally important to telesales, inside, and customer service people as it does to a direct field sales force. A weak sales force reflects weak management.

Time Logs

Most sales managers do not spend enough time training their sales staff. To see if you are devoting enough time to training, make a list of your duties and activities, and prioritize them by importance in driving revenues. Include hiring, training, organizing, and evaluating salespeople, along with personal selling, management meetings, conflict resolution, motivation, and administrative duties. What percent of your time is devoted to initial training, field coaching, and sales meetings? For sales managers supervising five to seven salespeople, 60 percent of their time should be devoted to training, most of which should be devoted to field coaching. Keep a time log of your activities for a typical month each year. Often an inverse relationship exists between hours spent on each activity and the activity's importance in driving revenues. What action can you take to correct this? Does such action involve delegating administrative work or having top management change your anticipated duties? In Chapter 10 on sizing and deployment, we will look at examples of time logs for salespeople and sales managers.

Strategic Issues

Since strategy drives tactics and structure follows strategy in the same way that form follows function, a sales manager must understand the strategic issues and objectives of training. If you don't know where you are going, you will never get there. Key strategic objectives for training include reducing the time it takes to make a salesperson fully productive, teaching salespeople how to reduce the sales cycle from customer search to purchase, and reflecting buyer behavior in the training program. Strategic training topics include pricing, targeting, change management, group decisions, complex decision-making processes, negotiations, and differentiation.

Depending on your industry and the skill and experience level of salespeople hired, it may take one year for a salesperson to generate revenues or gross margins or net income equal to his or her compensation, benefits, and expenses. It may take two years for the salesperson to reach full productivity and become a profit center. One of the training objectives involves reducing this time. We will look at some specific numbers on a salesperson's breakeven point and profitability in Chapter 9 on channel choice and architecture. In that chapter, we will also explore how to calculate a salesperson's total cost and income contribution. Salespeople represent a revenue, cost, and profit center.

Do you know the breakeven point for a salesperson in your firm? For example, a business selling premium tires to trucking firms compared the cost of putting a salesperson on the road to the revenues and income necessary to break even and become fully productive. It required one year for a salesperson to break even, to move from being a cost center to a profit center, and two years to become fully productive. By using the training techniques described in this chapter and the next two, the time was cut in half. Reducing the company's training cycle changed the paradigm for deployment and staffing. A more effective training program allowed the tire company to hire more salespeople, reduce territory sizes, and increase market share.

A distance learning company that provided MBA courses to top executives at Fortune 500 firms was experiencing a year between initial customer contact and a buying decision. The closing ratios and costs were prohibitive. The sales manager remedied this by training salespeople to track and measure their progress through the many steps in the buying process and to identify each manager's role in the group decision. The sales cycle was reduced to six months, closing ratios increased, and market share doubled. As the distance learning company found, reducing the sales cycle created a competitive advantage and should be considered a strategic objective of training.

Training is an area where marketing and sales management must work together. Buyer behavior, a business-to-business marketing concept discussed in Chapter 2, influences the training process. A firm dealing primarily with new systems buyers or first-time or one-time buyers (telephone or security systems) must emphasize salesperson training in consultative sales and product knowledge. But a firm dealing with existing systems buyers or modified rebuys (semiconductors, frozen doughnut batter, or truck tires) must emphasize training in relationship sales, negotiations, pricing, and customer knowledge. A firm calling on new product buyers (toys, apparel, or consumer electronics) must emphasize training in selling skills. Last, a firm calling on commodity buyers (die castings or plastic injection molding) whose companies often delegate the purchasing task, must emphasize time management and IT training for salespeople.

If your firm expects salespeople to negotiate price, delivery, and product customization, you must train them in negotiating skills and pricing theory. If you don't, your customers will have an advantage. Salespeople will sell at the lowest price unless they are trained to maximize dollars of margin and revenue over time based on their competitive advantage, type of customer, and type of product.

Many of these strategic training topics were mentioned in the previous chapter as strategic hiring issues appearing in the job description and candidate profile. This includes training salespeople in how to identify target customers, markets, and products. A sales manager can increase sales force productivity by teaching salespeople proper call frequency on target customers and prospects with the greatest present and potential revenues and income, the lowest cost to sell and service, and the highest probability of success. Often sales managers train salespeople to identify and concentrate on the top 10 new prospects, top 10 growth accounts, and top 10 present accounts with the largest annual volume. Sales managers refer to this as the "10/10/10 approach." Specifics of implementing the 10/10/10 approach will be dealt with in Chapter 10 on sizing and deployment and in Chapter 11 on sales forecasting and sales planning.

Marketing and sales management must work together in training salespeople on strategic differentiation. Who are your direct and indirect competitors, what are the competitive issues, what product or service features are expected and/or demanded, and how does the customer make a choice? The tactical application of this strategic concept, known as the *competitive grid*, is discussed later in the chapter.

In Chapter 1, we discussed the changing sales landscape that included shorter product or service life cycles, longer and more complex sales cycles, group decisions, less customer loyalty, and global competition. These changes in the landscape require new training strategies and tactics. To deal with less customer loyalty, salespeople require training in quantifying benefits. For example, a dozen B2B e-commerce firms service the paper, pulp, corrugated, and folding box industry. The provider that charges a 3 percent transaction fee has a 50 percent market share. The other 50 percent is divided among the remaining 11 B2B firms, all of which charge a 1 percent transaction fee. The company charging a 3 percent transaction fee with 50 percent of the market trains its salespeople to quantify for each step in the supply chain how its Web site lowers customer costs, increases customer revenues, or reduces inventory and capital expenditures. This quantification justifies the higher price in dollars. (A list of strategic training issues can be found at the end of this chapter in Exhibit 4.1.)

Benefits of a Well-Trained Sales Force

Training provided to a sales force not only increases its productivity and capacity but also improves confidence and enthusiasm, reduces turnover, and makes salespeople feel useful, important, and worthwhile. Failure to provide good training creates another excuse for nonperformance.

Confidence and enthusiasm represent important personal characteristics for a successful salesperson. They are included in the candidate profile. Well-trained salespeople certainly feel more confident and enthusiastic than poorly trained salespeople.

As you know from Chapters 2 and 3 on hiring, sales force turnover proves very costly. Properly trained salespeople earn more compensation and are less likely to change jobs.

A major benefit of a well-trained sales force is motivation. When a sales manager rides with a salesperson or salespeople attend a sales meeting, they feel useful, important, and worthwhile. Salespeople who do not receive proper training feel just the opposite.

Without proper hiring and training, the other pieces in the sales management system will not work properly. In fact, even a well-crafted compensation program, correct sizing and deployment, excellent motivation programs, and good performance management will not improve sales results from a badly hired and poorly trained sales force.

Are Salespeople Made or Born?

Which proves more important: training or hiring? As this chapter and the next two demonstrate, we can train salespeople in product, customer knowledge, competitive knowledge, and selling skills. We can't train salespeople in personal characteristics such as confidence, enthusiasm, the ability to accept rejection, initiative, persistence, passion, or eagerness. However, we can reinforce these traits. When hiring, asking open-ended probing interview questions will help you discover these important personal characteristics. Hopefully, by the end of this book you should know whether salespeople are made or born and whether hiring or training represents a more important part of the sales management process.

Mentoring

Mentoring can help train salespeople and more efficiently use a sales manager's time. The sales manager asks more experienced salespeople to mentor less experienced salespeople. The mentor does field coaching and answers questions on product, competition, customer knowledge, company policy and procedures, and selling skills. One example of a successful mentoring program is provided by a deli products distributor in Cleveland that expanded geographically by buying a similar firm in Toledo. The Cleveland distributor sent its more experienced salespeople to Toledo once a week to work with the less experienced people. The Cleveland salespeople were motivated by being chosen as mentors, and they improved their own knowledge and skills in order to train the Toledo salespeople. The Cleveland salespeople started opening more new accounts and selling more new products than in the past. This worked so well that both team members, Cleveland and Toledo, received a bonus based on joint results.

As you can see, mentoring can create a win-win-win situation. The mentee receives easy access to an expert, the mentors refresh their skills and feel good about being selected, and the sales managers have more time for other duties or for training other salespeople.

To enhance the success of a mentoring program, establish clear goals so that each person knows what to expect from the relationship and track effectiveness of the program to ensure the mentee is learning. Use quarterly performance evaluations as discussed in Chapter 14 and testing to measure results. Some mentoring programs last a month and involve only field coaching. Others last a year and involve continuous training. Some programs involve only new hires; others involve all junior salespeople. Some mentoring programs team one mentor to one mentee; others team groups of mentors to groups of mentees. The group approach prevents spreading bad habits and encourages a multitude of best practices. Make sure mentors are knowledgeable, skilled in training, and interested in helping. Make sure there is positive chemistry between the mentors and mentees. At some firms mentoring represents a stepping-stone into management.

However, as sales manager you must maintain control over the training process. Don't abdicate the ultimate responsibility to other salespeople or human resources. Mentoring represents a training tool for you, not a total solution. If a salesperson succeeds or fails, so does the sales manager.

Testing

Training salespeople involves daily objectives and testing. At the start of each day of initial training, at the start of each ride-with and sales meeting, salespeople need to know the training goals. Goals will range from learning about pricing or closing skills to product knowledge and competitive information. At the end of each day or segment of initial training, at the end of each ride-with and sales meeting, conduct a test related to these goals. Have the salesperson calculate prices for a particular project, or role-play a closing, or answer narrative questions on product knowledge, or create a competitive grid. Knowing that there will be a test to measure understanding creates more attention during training. Salespeople grade themselves using answer sheets. The answer sheets become lasting training tools and sometimes sales aids.

Salespeople object to testing the first few times, but then they become very competitive and start comparing scores. Some sales managers offer a small prize for the best score or scores above a certain level. Some sales managers do pre- and posttraining testing to see exactly what value was provided and to measure the trainer's effectiveness.

Many companies are testing all their salespeople every six months on product, competitor, and customer knowledge and selling skills. These tests are often given online. The results are compared to the scores on previous tests and benchmarked against peers. This represents a reality check for both the salesperson and sales

manager and identifies areas where each salesperson needs more training. It can be a very humbling experience for all parties. Don't assume your salespeople are well trained just because they heard the material. Many companies use these tests as the basis for salesperson advancement in responsibilities, compensation, and title.

Evaluating the Trainer

At the end of each training session, ask salespeople to evaluate the trainer. What was good and not so good and how future sessions can be improved. The evaluations apply to field coaching, sales meetings, and initial training. Based on the evaluation, take corrective action. Evaluations can be anonymous and can be done online.

Face Time with Customers

In an effort to reduce the training cycle, companies place newly hired salespeople in front of customers as soon as possible. The days of spending months at the corporate or regional offices before selling have ended. After a week of orientation, newly hired salespeople make customer calls with another salesperson, a trainer, or their sales manager. This allows them to understand the application of training material. Many firms alternate weeks of inside training on product, customer, and competitive knowledge with weeks of outside training traveling with a salesperson trainer, or sales manager calling on customers.

Customized Training

Newly hired and tenured salespeople need training programs customized differently to reflect each group's knowledge and skills. Training programs also differ from company to company depending on customers' and salespeople's needs. The training program for a belt salesperson calling on department store buyers differs from the training program for a software salesperson calling on hospitals. A belt salesperson and a software salesperson with strong product knowledge who were hired from a competitor need different training than the person hired from another industry or out of college. You cannot mass-produce training.

Your most successful salespeople need customized continuous training because they produce the majority of your firm's revenues. Many companies have separate training programs for top producers. These interactive, experiential programs allow top producers to share best practices, are considered a reward for excellence, and seldom occur in a classroom setting. Topics differ from more basic training and might include major account or multilevel sales.

Web-Based Training

Many companies customize or buy interactive Web-based training programs for certain topics. This allows salespeople to train themselves remotely and to take tests to measure their knowledge. The training can also be done for a group with interactive participant discussions and a leader using a Web conferencing system such as WebEx.

The following are some companies that offer Web-based training services:

- www.webbasedtraining.com
- www.designingwbt.com
- www.bestwebtraining.com
- www.saleshelp.com
- www.intelsalestraining.com
- www.sandler.com/sales_training/alliances.htm

Training Checklist

The training checklist is a universe of topics that a salesperson must understand to be successful at your company. The job description and candidate profile provide sources for these topics. The training checklist represents a key control point for sales management. Out of it flows a quarterly development plan for each salesperson, which represents yet another key control point. You can see how each of the pieces in the sales management process must work together.

The training checklist contains the following general headings down the side:

- Product knowledge
- Competition
- Competitive issues and advantages
- Customer knowledge
- Market and industry knowledge

- Selling skills
- Company policies
- Time and territory management
- Administrative tasks
- Company organization and history
- Conflict resolution

Under each heading the sales manager fills in topics appropriate for his or her company. Across the top of each page appears a heading for the subjects or topics, the date completed, by whom, and comments. Comments would indicate whether training was accomplished by field coaching, sales meetings, or initial training. Exhibit 4.2 at the end of this chapter illustrates a training checklist used by a home-health-care provider.

Most companies have training checklists, but few are comprehensive, and even fewer are used. Execution and implementation separate the best sales managers from the mediocre. If all the regional sales managers in a company use the same training checklist and agenda for all their salespeople, it should provide consistency and uniformity to the training process.

The training agenda presents a daily schedule for initially teaching these topics or subjects to salespeople, the name of the person who has responsibility for each session, and the session's objectives. Salespeople do not want to waste their time in poorly organized, unproductive training sessions. Using a training checklist and agenda to provide structure to a training program will force sales managers to organize the process. Salespeople often complain about wasting time in training, which casts a bad image on your firm. Exhibit 4.3 at the end of this chapter illustrates a training agenda used by a consumer goods health and beauty aids firm.

Ask new salespeople to track their progress on the training checklist and agenda. What did they learn from whom and when? What topics still need to be covered or revisited? Ask more experienced, longer-term salespeople to review the checklist and note areas where they need additional training. From this process flows each salesperson's quarterly development plan, a key control point. For example, this quarter one salesperson needs to work with technical support on product knowledge; last quarter her development plan involved attending a seminar on computer skills. Another salesperson needs field coaching on closing skills; last quarter his development plan involved presenting a competitive analysis at the sales meeting.

Job descriptions and training checklists, agendas, and training records also can prove important from a legal standpoint. You may terminate a salesperson for not performing the duties on the job description or for marginal results. However, the salesperson may claim he or she did not receive the appropriate training. The training checklist, agenda, and records document what training took place, when, and how. The job description, candidate profile, training checklist, and agenda drive the topics included in each salesperson's performance evaluation, which we discuss in Chapter 14.

Product Knowledge

Most companies do an acceptable job of training salespeople in product knowledge. Most sales managers were salespeople in the same industry and/or market, sometimes at the same firm, and because of their strong product knowledge, they feel comfortable in training salespeople on this subject. Often salespeople receive too much product knowledge at the expense of competitive or customer knowledge or sales skills. Product knowledge helps salespeople's confidence, but technology and operationally based firms often overemphasize this area. Too much product knowledge confuses customers and deceives salespeople.

Product knowledge, though, is more than specs. For instance, one leasing firm that specialized in financing used computers taught its salespeople a great deal about the equipment, but little about figuring monthly payments. Customers and prospects were impressed by their knowledge until the discussion turned to numbers.

If your salespeople call on business-to-business new systems buyers making one-time or first-time purchases, product knowledge has more importance than if these salespeople call on managers making modified rebuys or commodity purchases.

Essentially, you must teach salespeople and channel partners whatever product or service knowledge the customer requires in order to make the buying decision. In some situations (such as a modified rebuy) the salesperson's product knowledge will not exceed the customer's; or the customer may have questions the salesperson is not prepared to answer. When required, a salesperson should know where to obtain additional information.

Today, product knowledge can be more effectively taught through hands-on experience—learning by doing. Yes, salespeople need to study the catalog, product manuals, videos, audiotapes, and Web sites, but product knowledge requires application, hands-on, experiential training. Many firms accomplish this by having salespeople work at or tour a customer's location. What better way to understand how a product or service is used, the needs satisfied, and the problems solved. Medical device firms have their salespeople observe operations or procedures where their device is used. They can also talk with the physician doing the operation or procedure.

Other firms teach salespeople product knowledge by having them work in or tour their factory or other departments and/or functions such as dispatch, installation, maintenance, design, the lab, or engineering. Riding on the delivery truck, filling orders in the warehouse, or answering customer service phones also can provide product training. Some firms have salespeople follow an order from entry to shipment or they rotate salespeople through key company functions to provide product knowledge and appreciation for other departments, which are a salesperson's internal customers. At the least, take a salesperson with you to see the product or service in use. If you sell a hospital cleaning service, visit the hospital and watch the service being performed. If you sell garbage disposal, have the trainee ride the garbage truck for a day and visit the landfill. If you sell sweaters, visit some stores that offer your merchandise. If you sell industrial robots, visit some factories that employ them. Every day of product training should start with objectives and end with a test.

If possible, salespeople should use the product. Apparel salespeople wear their product, software and Internet salespeople use it, and food service salespeople taste it. Where possible, have salespeople take the product apart and reassemble it and work with models, prototypes, samples, charts, and graphs.

In an August 2006 survey, MarketBridge asked sales, marketing, and human resource executives at 120 midsized and large companies, "What were your organization's greatest product challenges?" Fifty-six percent replied, "Correctly positioning our product and message to customers." Forty-six percent replied, "Selling a solution [with services and related products] rather than a stand-alone product." Forty-four percent replied, "Training and educating the sales force and channel partners about our products." Forty-three percent replied, "Differentiating a commodity product." All of these issues directly impact sales force training.[1]

Competitive Knowledge and Advantage

Salespeople and channel partners require knowledge, both of their own products or services and of their competitors. To sell effectively, a salesperson must know the competitive advantages or disadvantages of each style, model, or service in the marketplace. Do your company's automatic welding robots cost more than your competitors'; do they work faster, last longer, move up and down as well as sideways? Do your company's wool or nylon sweaters require hand-washing when your competitors' sweaters can be laundered in a machine? Does your service clean hospitals two shifts a day as opposed to your competitor's one shift only? Does your refuse removal company pick up twice a week while the competition picks up only once? Does your firm's life insurance policy offer dividends or dividend reinvestment while others do not?

Most firms do an acceptable job of product knowledge but a weak job of training salespeople in competitor knowledge. Salespeople's understanding of the competition not only allows them to sell more effectively but also to understand strategic issues such as value-added sales, market segments, differentiation, and targeting. The best defense is a good offense. Attack the competition where you are strong and the competition is weak. Ask marketing to help you collect and organize competitive information.

COMPETITIVE GRIDS

Competitive grids for each product, product line, or customer market help train salespeople. They can show salespeople how to make customers more successful or how to wrap a service around a product to further differentiate it. Marketing can assist you in organizing and obtaining information for the competitive grid. Across the top list your competitors. Down the left-hand side list the competitive issues—that is, how the customer makes a choice. List the price last, since we want to train salespeople in selling value. For each competitive issue, show how your product or service compares to that of the competition in features, benefits, and image. Is it better, worse, or the same and why?

Be specific. Don't list quality as an issue. List how the customer defines quality. For example, mean time to failure, natural yarn, or fruit content, handmade, capacity, value-added services, design, speed, all-wood dresser drawers, freeze-to-thaw time, efficacy, or billing accuracy. (Exhibit 4.4 shows a competitive grid for a tire firm selling to trucking fleets. Exhibit 4.5 shows a competitive grid for a waste removal service. Both can be found at the end of this chapter.)

It is essential to be honest in appraising your competition. All companies' products and services have strengths and weaknesses. Accurate knowledge allows the salesperson to target customers with the greatest need for the particular strengths your product or service offers. Accurate competitive knowledge allows the salesperson or channel partner to feel more confident; to present features, benefits, and proof more effectively and forcefully; to make price less of an issue and value more of an issue; and to sell the risk of a bad job. Knowledge increases the probability of success; ignorance increases the probability of failure.

The competitive grid provides a great topic for sales meetings. Ask your sales force to arrive prepared to discuss it. At the meeting ask for a product's, product line's, or market's competitors and the competitive issues on which customers make a choice. For each competitive issue, have salespeople discuss whether your firm is better, worse, or the same as the competition and why. Quantify the differences in units, percentages, or dollars, and place the results at the appropriate spot in the grid. Our frozen batter has 40 percent more fruit, or our Internet site has

20 percent more functionality. Salespeople will not agree but through a meaningful discussion will exchange valuable competitive information.

Do your larger competitors, "the Giants," present more of a threat than the smaller competitors, "the Ants"? Often the flexibility and speed of smaller competitors represent more of a challenge. For example, the competitive grid might convince a salesperson for a company selling consumer electronics, specifically portable media players, that Sling Media, a start-up, posed more of a competitive threat than Samsung. Once you complete the grid, codify it, reproduce it, and make it available to present and future salespeople as a sales aid. Because of the changing business landscape, the competitive grid requires constant updating.

Also discuss by how much these competitive advantages will increase customer sales, reduce customer costs, or lower the customer's working capital needs and capital expenditures. How will these competitive issues impact the customer's return on investment or payback period for a piece of capital equipment? A competitive grid can help salespeople understand the total cost of your product or service compared to a competitor's rather than just the selling price.

Salespeople must understand that some competitive issues are expected and demanded while others represent differentiators. You cannot sell digital cable unless it is ISO 9005. You cannot sell tier-two automotive manufacturers unless you offer next-day, just-in-time deliveries. These are table stakes necessary to enter these markets. But the ability to deliver ISO 9005 products on time in China and Russia would be a real competitive advantage to global customers. These would represent important differentiators.

COMPETITIVE DATABASES

Some sales managers and marketing departments keep a library or database of material, catalogs, and articles on each competitor. Salespeople and channel partners access it online or by visiting the file. Some sales managers assign one or several salespeople to collect and/or present information on a particular competitor. A sales meeting might include a presentation about the competitor, disassembling a competitor's product and comparing it to yours, or having a recently hired salesperson who worked for a competitor present the competitive product or service. These same techniques should be used to train channel partners in competitive knowledge.

Some sales managers ask salespeople to submit fresh competitive information at the end of each day. Most sales managers will reserve a portion of each sales meeting for salespeople to share newly acquired competitive knowledge.

Sources for collecting competitive information include customers, interviewing competitive salespeople, trade shows, vendors, trade publications, competitors' annual reports and catalogs, consultants, and the Internet. Salespeople and marketing should carefully examine each competitor's Web site, just as competitors examine yours. Competitors' Web sites contain a wealth of information. A Google search of the Internet may turn up competitors you were unaware of. Knowledge is power. Know the competitor as you do your own firm. In collecting competitive information, emphasize ethics and the spirit and letter of the law.

STAYING OUT OF THE COMMODITY BOX

People who make buying decisions, whether purchasing agents, chefs, or factory managers, are taught to segment all vendors into one of four categories: must haves, like to haves, somewhat differentiated, and commodities. People who make buying decisions will attempt to put your product or service in the commodity box, where price represents the primary competitive issue. Salespeople trained with a competitive grid can better persuade buyers to place their product or service in the like-to-have box where value is more important than price, allowing them to sell at a higher price and generate greater profits.

STRATEGIC COMPETITIVE ADVANTAGES

For a business to be successful, it must have at least one of the following three competitive advantages:

1. *Operational excellence.* An example would be Dell.
2. *New product development.* An example would be Intel or Apple.
3. *Customer intimacy.* An example would be Southwest Airlines or Lexus.

To sell effectively, salespeople need to understand which represents their firm's strategic competitive advantage and how to present it. Be sure to include this in your training program.

If none of these represents a competitive advantage for your firm, then rethink your product or service offering and your marketing program.

In the MarketBridge 2006 survey referred to earlier in this chapter, 54 percent of the sales, marketing, and human resource executives at 120 midsized and large companies said that "greater competition" had the most impact on their organization's present and future performance.[2]

Customer Knowledge and Profiles

Customers represent the most important asset of any organization, the most important stakeholders in the value chain. Salespeople and channel partners need training in how to collect, organize, and use customer information. Often the vendor with the best product or service does not get the order, but usually the salesperson who knows the most about the customer does. Do your salespeople know more about their customers or prospects than the competition knows? Remember: Knowledge is power.

Your salespeople and channel partners will have better customer knowledge if they maintain appropriate customer profiles. The sales manager should meet with the salespeople to design a customer profile. Determine what customer profile information provides your salespeople with a competitive advantage. A well-designed customer profile forces salespeople to ask the right probing questions that identify customer needs, budgets, time frames, opportunities, decision makers, and decision-making processes. Obtaining personal information on the decision maker allows the salesperson to establish rapport and build the relationship. We buy from experts, which requires product knowledge and company information, and from friends, which requires personal information on decision makers.

Contact management software allows salespeople to record this information digitally and allows the sales manager to access and aggregate it easily. It also allows salespeople to share information on common customers. Available software programs include Act, Saratoga Systems, Goldmine, Clarify, Salesforce.com, NetSuite CRM, Sage CRM, SalesLogix CRM, and Siebel. Generally, contact management is embedded in more comprehensive customer-relationship software. However, many companies continue to record customer profiles with pen and paper.

The important customer profile issues are what information to include, how to collect it, and how to motivate salespeople to use it. The required customer information can be divided into company information and personal information. Companies write the checks, but people make the decisions. Customer profile formats will differ from one company and market segment to another. A company selling surgical instruments to hospitals, outpatient surgical centers, and physicians will need three different formats.

Most customer profile formats contain business information on the following:

- The decision makers
- Decision-making processes
- Budgets
- Time frames
- The relationship of purchasing to other departments
- Needs

- Opportunities
- Problems
- Competitors
- History with your firm
- Credit
- Past usage
- Potential dollars of purchases
- Whether to sell at corporate or division levels
- Buying groups
- Type of products or services used
- Key drivers of customer's business
- Sales history
- The customer's competitors and customers
- Key metrics (number of)
- Locations
- Attitude toward your company

Most customer profile formats contain personal information on the decision makers and influencers including education, past positions, hot buttons, "don't talk about," hobbies, interests, families, important dates (for example, birthday), decision-making styles, relationships with other employees, best time and way to reach them, e-mail address, and phone and fax number. When a new or different salesperson is assigned to the customer, and when a salesperson leaves the company, this information proves critical. Customers appreciate the continuity. Again, we buy from experts (business information) and friends (personal information). (Exhibit 4.6 is an example of a physician profile used by a pharmaceutical firm. Exhibit 4.7 is an example of a company profile used by a B2B Internet firm. Both can be found at the end of the chapter.)

HOW CUSTOMERS MAKE DECISIONS

How customers use and filter information and make decisions represents an important training area for salespeople. Customers are not a homogeneous group. Some customers require a great deal of data to make concrete, logical decisions. They spend a lot of time analyzing information, and they get bogged down in detail and have difficulty making a final decision: aim, aim, aim. Other customers prefer concepts to data and make fast decisions: ready, fire, aim. A third group requires assurances concerning the positive or negative impact of any buying decisions on other people in their organization. This ready, ready, ready group resists change. The last group not only prefers concepts to data but also thinks globally and makes fast gut decisions: fire, fire, fire. Most salespeople attempt to persuade customers based on the salesperson's decision-making mode, not the customer's. When selling to group decision makers, this becomes more complicated. Exhibit 4.8 at the end of this chapter illustrates the four quadrants of decision making.

The best salespeople obtain customer information on every call. After each visit salespeople should write at least two new things they learned about the business and the decision maker. Salespeople and marketing can find important customer information from Web sites, catalogs, trade publications, trade shows, annual reports, customer surveys, vendors, and other salespeople inside and outside your company.

As with competitive data, ask marketing to help collect customer data. A November 2005 study by the Chief Marketing Officer Council (CMO Council) found that "know thy customer" represented a major responsibility and unfilled challenge for the marketing function. The CMO Council found that most marketing executives included in the survey felt there was room for improvement in determining how their customers want to be served and in developing customer-centric solutions.

KEEPING ACCURATE CUSTOMER PROFILES

We motivate salespeople and channel partners with love and fear, rewards and punishments. Maintaining accurate and complete profiles represents an important competitive advantage for your firm. Salespeople and especially channel partners resist keeping customer profiles because easy access to this information makes them less valuable to their employer. Does the salesperson or the company own the customer? Many salespeople insist they have perfect memories. Often sales managers include accuracy of customer profiles on the salesperson's performance evaluations and include it as an element in his or her bonus.

The key to persuading salespeople and channel partners to keep accurate and complete customer profiles is to sell the benefits of using them. The sales manager should refer to information on the customer profile when reviewing account information with a salesperson. The salesperson needs to know you read the profiles.

Also point out to the salesperson how knowledge of a buyer's hobbies and customer's competition can help to close a sale. This can best be accomplished during field coaching when you visit a customer together.

Many firms make customer profiles a part of their channel partner agreement. The channel partner is required in the agreement to keep complete profiles on all customers and prospects and to make them available to the principal. Such an arrangement requires trust, but it should be beneficial to both parties.

When customer profiles are kept digitally, a sales manager can easily access and even aggregate certain information from the company database. For example, the sales manager can analyze the average number of prospecting calls required to open a new account. Also operations people and customer service people can access information important to satisfying customer needs.

Whether kept in hard copy form or digital form, a sales manager should examine the customer profiles and files during field coaching ride-withs. Do all customers and prospects have a complete profile?

A newly hired software salesperson from Chicago calls on a business prospect in North Carolina. To establish rapport, since it is October, he asks whether the decision maker hunts or fishes, only to find out that he is a vegetarian and president of the Animal Rights Association. A refuse removal salesperson calls on a large Asian automaker in Ohio to sell recycling equipment. The salesperson refers to "associates" as employees and is reprimanded. The plant manager puts a 12-minute sand clock on his desk and announces the call will end when the sand runs out. All of this information was on the customer profile, but neither salesperson reviewed it before the call. The lesson is, customer profiles create a competitive advantage; not using profiles creates a competitive disadvantage.

CUSTOMER SATISFACTION SURVEYS

Once a year perform a customer satisfaction survey and compare it to the past year's results. Using either online or snail-mail communication, ask customer decision makers to evaluate your company's products, services, deliveries, prices, invoicing, support functions, and the sales force. This survey provides useful information for evaluating the salesperson and also helpful information for the customer profile. Have a friendly customer work with your marketing department to assist you in developing the survey questions.

You might offer a merchandise credit for completing the survey. Most customers enjoy doing surveys if later the firm answers their questions and addresses their concerns. From the survey you will find out what factors most influence the customer's buying decision and how the salesperson can better serve the customer.

(Exhibits start on next page.)

Exhibit 4.1.   Strategic Training Issues: Structure Follows Strategy; Sales Management Integrates with Marketing.

- Getting people from 0 to full productivity faster. Reducing the training cycle. Salesperson's contribution margin and breakeven point. Paradigm busting.
- Reducing the sales cycle from search to purchase. Selling a premium product for a premium price. Creates winners.
- Buyer behavior and type of selling. Consultative versus relationship selling.
- Pricing to maximize dollars of margin or revenue over time based on competitive advantage, type of customer, and type of product. Value-added pricing. Alternative costs. Pricing window.
- Target market segments, accounts, and products. How to determine.
- Group decisions. Multilevel selling. Correctly identifying decision maker, influencer, and gatekeeper. Who can say yes and who can say no?
- Complex decision-making process. Tracking and measuring the process.
- Negotiations.
- Change management. Changing landscape. Managing the future.
- Strategic differentiation.

Exhibit 4.2. Training Checklist.

Account Representative _____ Date Hired _____

Subjects	Date Completed	By Whom	Comments

1. **Referral Sources**

Physicians
- GP/FP/Internists _____
- Hem/Onc _____
- Neurologists _____
- Cardiologists _____
- Infectious Disease _____
- Gastroenterologists _____
- Orthopedists _____
- Pulmonologists _____
- Endocrinologists _____
- Gerontologists _____
- HIV/AIDS _____
- Pediatricians _____
- Neonatologists _____
- OB/GYN _____
- Other _____

Payors
- HMO/PPOs _____
- Physician practices _____
- Self-insureds _____
- State/county _____
- Other _____

Facilities
- Hospitals _____
- Extended care _____
- Subacute _____
- Surgery centers _____
- Rehabilitation _____
- Infusion suites _____
- Other _____

(Continued on next page.)

Exhibit 4.2. *(Continued from previous page.)*

Subjects	Date Completed	By Whom	Comments
2. Product Knowledge			
General nursing			
Traditional IV			
Diabetes			
• Type I			
• Type II			
Asthma			
• Pediatric			
• Adult			
Hip and knee			
Pressure ulcer			
Cardiac			
Hemophilia			
Pediatrics			
Rehabilitation			
3. Competition			
Apna			
Corum			
Columbia			
Local hospitals			
Local home-health-care firms			
Nurse finders			
Chartwell			
Staff builders			
Interim			
4. Competitive Issues and Advantages			
Pricing			
Availability			
Comprehensive care			
Holistic approach			
Number of caregivers			
Disease-state management			

(Continued on next page.)

Exhibit 4.2. *(Continued from previous page.)*

Subjects	Date Completed	By Whom	Comments
Rare chronic-care management			
Partnership with drug company			
Cost control with quality outcomes			
Efficient organization model			
Training/screening of caregivers			
Nursing at core			
Continuity of caregiver			
Reliable			
Large pool of caregivers			
Name recognition			
Market share			
Image reputation			
Breadth/variety of services			
Specialty programs			
Key customers			
Strategic partners			
Size; years in business			
Market share no. 1 in 4 categories			
Financial strength, reliability			
600 locations in United States			
Strengths and weaknesses			
Market philosophy			

(Continued on next page.)

Exhibit 4.2.   *(Continued from previous page.)*

Subjects	Date Completed	By Whom	Comments
5. Customer/Referral Source Profiles			
Competition and competitive issues			
Decision makers			
Expectations			
History			
Personnel: Their habits, interests, tastes, concerns			
Needs, problems, opportunities			
Customer and decision maker's priorities			
Strategy			
Objectives			
Demographics and key drivers of referral source			
Profile			
6. Paperwork/Administrative			
Contracts			
Territory manual			
Monthly and weekly planners			
Writing skills			
Daily call reports			
Expense reports			
Quarterly sales plans			
Customer/prospect profiles			
Customer files			
Phone/fax/voice mail			

(Continued on next page.)

Exhibit 4.2.   *(Continued from previous page.)*

Subjects	Date Completed	By Whom	Comments
Collateral review ordering			
Presentation binder reviews			
ACT			
Weekly activity reports			
7. **Time and Territory Management**			
Number and type of calls per week			
Clustering accounts, quadrants, clover leaf			
Daily planners			
Weekly call schedules			
Daily goals			
Managing time with customers			
Managing time between calls			
Time wasters/traps			
Car/trunk organization system			
8. **Company Policies**			
Pricing			
Entertainment			
Automobiles			
Expenses			
Code of conduct			
Operations			
Human resources			
Evaluations			

(Continued on next page.)

Exhibit 4.2. *(Continued from previous page.)*

Subjects	Date Completed	By Whom	Comments
9. **Selling Skills**			
Prospecting			
Making appointments			
Precall planning			
Research on each account			
Objective for each call and account			
Using customer/prospect profiles			
Building rapport			
Finding problems to solve			
Showing empathy			
Questions that uncover needs/problems			
Competition and competitive advantage			
Long complex sales cycles			
Decision-making process			
Budget			
Time frame			
Value-added proposition			
Strategic sales			
Using benefit statements			
Building interest			
Asking questions to obtain agreement			
Using referrals and the reference sell			
Overcoming objections			
Closing commitments			
Negotiating skills			

(Continued on next page.)

Exhibit 4.2.   *(Continued from previous page.)*

Subjects	Date Completed	By Whom	Comments
Listening	_____		
Self-analysis	_____		
Postcall analysis	_____		
10. **Customer Complaints, Service Problems, Conflict Resolution**	_____		
11. **Company Organization and History** Names of key people	_____		

Indicate by Each Item How Training Was Given:
IT: Initial training
FT: Field training
SM: Sales meeting

Exhibit 4.3.   Training Agenda: Health and Beauty Aids Firm.

Sales Representative _____   Date Hired _____

Territory _____

Activity and Date	Objective	Where	Responsible Person
Week 1			
Day 1: With trainer, call on customers.	Sales process	Field	Trainer
Day 2: Review competitive grid and competitive catalogues.	Competitive knowledge	Office	Sales manager
Day 3: Work on assembly line.	Product knowledge	Factory	Foreman
Day 4: Work in new product laboratory.	Research and development	Lab	Chemist
Day 5: Work in order processing.	Accurate orders and pricing	Office	Customer service manager
Week 2			
Day 1: With senior salesperson, call on customers.	Selling skills	Field	Senior salesperson
Day 2: Review customer profiles.	Customer knowledge	Office	Sales manager
Day 3: Ride on delivery truck.	Learn distribution	Field	Transportation manager
Day 4: Complete online activity reports.	Computer software	Office	Information systems manager
Day 5: With junior salesperson, call on customers.	Sales skills	Field	Junior salesperson

Exhibit 4.4. Competitive Grid: Commercial Tire Manufacturer Selling to Trucking Fleets.

Competitive Issues	Bfca	General	Goodyear	Toyo	Michelin	Yokohoma
Cost per mile						
Retreadability						
Availability/delivery						
Warranties						
Relationship						
Accessibility						
Expert advice on choice and use						
Training						
Tire tracking: Use, miles						
Casing resale value						
Road service: National fleet program						
Transaction price						
Terms						

Exhibit 4.5.   Competitor Comparison: Waste Removal.

Competitive Issues	Competitor A	Competitor B	Competitor C	Competitor D
Length of contract				
Condition of containers				
Type of equipment				
Number of trucks and containers				
Number of salespeople and drivers				
CSR, dispatch, telemarketing staff				
Years in business				
Variety of services				
Landfill access and ownership				
Disposal costs				
Markets serviced				
Policy concerning ethics				
Safety				
Credit and collection				
Financial stability				
Reliability				
Image, reputation				
Specialization				
Number of customers				
Key accounts				
Strengths and weaknesses				
Thinks and acts				
Price				

Exhibit 4.6.   Physician Profile.

- Name
- Nickname
- Primary and secondary office addresses; home address

    ○ Phone
    ○ Fax

- Office manager or nurse
- Receptionist
- Primary decision maker
- Schedule
- Best time to call and/or see
- Directions to office
- Hospital affiliations

    ○ Title and responsibilities
    ○ Privileges
    ○ Location of hospital
    ○ When is he or she there?

- HMO affiliation
- Nursing home affiliation
- Which other physicians refer to him or her?
- Which physicians does he or she refer to?
- Our primary competitors
- Patient demographics

    ○ Age
    ○ Income level
    ○ Type of problems

- Background and special interests

    ○ Previous locations and employment
    ○ Status symbols in office
    ○ Professional associations
    ○ Honors
    ○ Mentors
    ○ Research interests
    ○ Articles published

(Continued on next page.)

Exhibit 4.6.   *(Continued from previous page.)*

- Education

    - College
    - Medical school
    - Residency
    - Honors
    - Extracurricular activities
    - Internship
    - Fellowship
    - Board certification
    - Military service; rank

- Communication style
- How he or she makes decisions
- Prescribing habits
- Products used and how
- Knowledge of our products
- Appropriate to ask out for a meal

    - Breakfast
    - Lunch
    - Dinner
    - Cocktails
    - Restaurant preference
    - Food preference

- Professional goals
- Business goals
- Physician's competitors
- What are the physician's professional and personal priorities?
- What are the physician's professional and personal problems and/or needs?
- Family

    - Home address
    - Phone
    - Appropriate time to call
    - Birth date and place
    - Hometown
    - Marital status
    - Wedding anniversary
    - Spouse's name
    - Spouse's birthday

(Continued on next page.)

Exhibit 4.6.   *(Continued from previous page.)*

- o   Spouse's interests, activities, affiliations
- o   Spouse's education
- o   Children's name, birth date, education, and hobbies

- Hobbies, interests, lifestyles

  - o   Clubs
  - o   Community activities
  - o   Leisure-time recreational activities
  - o   Vacations
  - o   Sports
  - o   Personal goals
  - o   Product achievement

- What not to talk about

Exhibit 4.7.　Customer Profile for Packaging Industry: Business-to-Business Internet Exchange.

Business name:

Headquarters location:

Decision maker:

Influencers:

Gatekeepers:

Users:

Decision-making process:

Time frame:

Budget:

Technical proficiency:

Systems staff:

Platform:

Operating system:

Hardware:

Software:

Products manufacturer:

Products purchased:

Products sold:

Plant locations:

Their competitors:

Their customers:

Their suppliers:

Ownership:

Needs and problems:

Opportunities:

Our competitors:

Our competitive advantage:

Critical risks:

Barriers:

Exhibit 4.8.   How We Use and Filter Information and Make Decisions.

	Concrete	Abstract
Logic	Logical, organized, action oriented. Sell the facts. Thinker and sensor; wants a lot of data; practical. Reality based, likes information and research. Aim, aim, aim. Make appointment; be on time. Wants proof; gets bogged down in detail.	Likes ideas, concepts, theories, Intuitive thinker. Sell the options. A little preparation, test it, then see if it works. Bold, takes action, Ready, fire, aim. Innovator. Enjoys change and risk. Provide direct, brief answers.
People Oriented	Concerned with impact on people. Feeling, sensing, emotional, sincere. Wants to please and serve people. Harmonizer. Ready, ready, ready. Likes status quo; resists change. Emphasize benefits that reduce risk.	Dreamer, Big picture, Global, Concerned with impact on people. Intuitive, feeling. Sell idea. Innovator; action, no preparation. Quick start; gut decisions. Fire, fire, fire. Likes brainstorming. Acts impulsively. Offer expert testimonial.

Questions and Exercises for Chapter 4

- Prepare a training checklist and a training agenda for your sales force or a sales force you are familiar with.
- Prepare competitive grids for your various product lines and markets or for product lines and markets you are familiar with.
- Prepare the format for a customer profile.

Quiz for Chapter 4

1. Which of these are strategic training issues?
   a. Getting people from "0" to full productivity faster
   b. Reducing the sales cycle
   c. Increasing revenues
   d. Decreasing costs

2. Which topic should *not* be on the training checklist?
   a. Product knowledge
   b. Customer knowledge
   c. Salesperson motivation
   d. Selling skills

3. Which of these items should be on a customer profile?
   a. Decision maker
   b. Decision-making process
   c. Customer's markets
   d. Decision maker's hobbies
   e. Decision maker's favorite restaurant

4. Which of these are benefits of having a well-trained sales force?
   a. Increases in sales force productivity
   b. Improved confidence and enthusiasm
   c. Motivated salespeople
   d. Allows the sales manager to put less emphasis on hiring
   e. Lower turnover

5. True or false?
   General annual knowledge testing of salespeople has few benefits and should be discouraged.

6. The most effective ways to teach product knowledge include which of the following?
   a. Studying catalogs
   b. Working for a customer
   c. Working in the factory or lab
   d. Rotating through departments of your business

7. Which of these items should be listed on a competitive grid as competitive issues?
   a. Price
   b. Quality
   c. Service
   d. Features
   e. Benefits

8. To be successful, a firm must have a competitive advantage in which of the following categories?
   a. New product innovation
   b. Customer intimacy
   c. Operational efficiency
   d. Sales force organization

9. Customers make decisions in which of the following ways?
   a. Logical and concrete
   b. Conceptual
   c. Impact on other people
   d. Global ideas
   e. Features and benefits

10. Channel partners require training in which of the following areas?
    a. Product knowledge
    b. Customer knowledge
    c. Competition knowledge
    d. Selling skills

Notes

1. MarketBridge, Mark Donnolo, *Performance-Driven Selling 2006*. Marketbridge Technologies. Copyright © 2006. Reprinted by permission of MarketBridge.
2. Ibid.

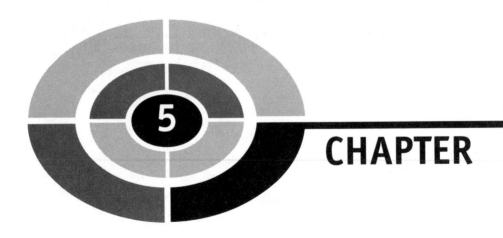

CHAPTER

Selling Skills

Now that the salespeople understand the products, competitors, and customers, we must reinforce their selling skills. Many sales managers assume their salespeople can sell. After riding with and coaching hundreds of salespeople, my experience indicates most need improvement in sales skills. A sales force that understands strategic and tactical sales skills provides a strong competitive advantage in a commoditized world. In today's competitive, commoditized markets, it's how you sell, not what you sell, that differentiates your company from another. Superior selling skills represent an important competitive advantage.

Today a salesperson's job is not just to discover needs by asking customers probing questions but also to discover needs the customer does not recognize yet. On each visit the customer expects a salesperson to provide value-added free advice. During each call, salespeople should offer content and advice that a customer would pay for. This represents yet another way to stay out of the commodity box.

Outside trainers, seminars, video and audio cassettes, and books on sales skills are the place to start. Tom Hopkins, Brian Tracy, Miller Hyman, Xerox, Wilson Learning, Asher Training, and Productive Strategies are just a few resources.

Ask your peers for references, read trade publications, visit trade shows, and search the Web.

The sales manager's job involves reinforcing and customizing these basic strategic and tactical sales skills. Knowledge is power only if we use it. Every industry, product, or service involves the individual use of certain broad selling techniques. Training salespeople in selling skills involves deaggregating these skills and then prioritizing the pieces most important for success in your industry and at your company. Long, complex sales cycles involving group decisions require different training than shorter, less complicated sales cycles with an individual decision maker. Selling one-time or first-time new systems buyers requires different skills than selling a modified rebuy, existing systems buyer; or new product buyers or commodity buyers. Some salespeople call on multiple types of buyers and need to understand both strategic and tactical sales skills.

Strategic sales skills primarily used in longer more complex sales cycles involve the following:

- Understanding the customer's decision-making process
- Understanding organizational issues
- Understanding the value-added proposition
- Quantifying benefits
- Understanding the decision maker's motives

Tactical, more basic sales skills include these:

- Qualifying customers
- Precall planning
- Obtaining an appointment
- Using probing questions to find needs and problems
- Presenting features, benefits, and proof
- Overcoming objections
- Obtaining a commitment

Exhibits 5.1 and 5.2 at the end of this chapter outline training topics for complex longer sales cycles involving groups and the more tactical basic topics included in the selling pyramid.

Longer, More Complex Sales Cycles Involving Group Decisions

Big-ticket items, one-time or first-time purchases, new systems buys, such as a security or telephone system, enterprisewide software, consulting or legal services,

navigational equipment for aircraft, B2B Internet services, complex financial services require salespeople be trained in strategic sales skills as well as the basics.

In such industries with long sales cycles, salespeople must understand the decision-making process: time frame, budget, decision makers, and influencers and the steps from search to purchase. A salesperson selling enterprisewide software who obtains this knowledge has a competitive advantage over a salesperson who does not have this knowledge. How does a salesperson obtain information about the customer's or prospect's time frame for purchase, budget, decision makers, and decision-making process?

IDENTIFYING KEY PLAYERS

The salesperson needs a fox and a champion. The fox is not a decision maker but probably a knowledgeable mid-level influencer. The fox prefers your enterprisewide software program over competitors'. Because of this, he or she reliably and accurately answers a salesperson's probing questions on time frame, budget, decision makers, and process.

The salesperson also needs a champion. Generally, the champion is not a decision maker but a high-level influencer who prefers your enterprisewide software and will support a decision to buy it. Your salesperson needs to supply the champion with information to help persuade colleagues and make the champion a hero. Some salespeople supply their champion with a list of possible objections that colleagues might raise and how to overcome them. Sales managers train salespeople how to identify the fox and the champion and make clear that without their support, the probability of failure is high. In working with a fox and a champion, your salespeople must not only observe the letter but the spirit of the law. Salespeople must also understand and respect company policies on ethics.

The enterprisewide software salesperson must be trained to identify the key players in the decision-making process. Many people can say no; only one can say yes. Is this key decision maker the CEO, CFO, COO, CIO, or VP of purchasing? Who influences the decision and how? The CIO can say no because the software does not integrate well with the company operating system. A plant manager, who might be a software user, can say no because of features and functions.

FUNNEL MANAGEMENT

The salesperson must be trained to identify, track, and monitor the steps from search to purchase in the sales cycle, sometimes called *funnel management*. Steps for the enterprisewide software might include a needs analysis, a customer referral,

a plant visit to a satisfied user, a demonstration, a presentation to the decision makers, entertainment, a beta trial, an alpha test, analysis of results, a final presentation to decision makers, and a written proposal. The salesperson assigns a time frame, cost, and probability to each step. Success is defined by moving from one step to another within the time frame and cost budget. Each month the salesperson and sales manager discuss the status of the sales process, which might be shown as a diagram. Failure to move to the next step requires analysis and corrective action. Training salespeople in this process prevents unexpected disappointments late in the sales cycle.

Ask your salespeople to identify not only the steps they must perform to move from search to purchase but also those the customer must perform. Many steps are common to both, but the customer's decision-making process might also include evaluation by an outside consultant and consultation with other company divisions.

As sales manager, you might wish to aggregate each salesperson's results as he or she moves through a long sales cycle. For all your salespeople, how many needs analyses were performed in a year, and how many of those needs analyses resulted in a demonstration, a beta trial, a final presentation, and an order? What was the closing ratio? At which steps was business lost, and what is the corrective action?

For example, let's say your seven salespeople conducted 350 needs analyses last year, but those 350 resulted in only 14 contracts. Were prospects lost equally at each step in the funnel, or were most prospects lost after the demo or after the beta trial, or after the final presentation?

If most prospects were lost after the demo, maybe you need to do a better job of needs analysis. If most prospects were lost after the final presentation, maybe you need to improve closing and presentation skills.

BUYER BEHAVIOR AND BUYING CENTER ISSUES

In long complex sales cycles, a salesperson must understand buyer behavior and when to use consultive selling versus relationship selling, buying center issues such as the level at which to enter a prospect's organization, the relationship between various people in the prospect's organization, and the competitor's history there. A high-tech miniature transformer sales manager teaches her salespeople to qualify prospects by first calling a design engineer at the plant level and not working with corporate purchasing until designs are submitted. She has found that starting at corporate purchasing wastes months of a salesperson's time.

In approaching large organizations, salespeople are taught to look for conflicts or alliances between key decision-making personnel. Who wants whose job? Understanding this prevents costly mistakes and builds relationships.

During long complex sales cycles, the competitive grid provides basic knowledge. However, salespeople must understand as much about their competition as they do about their own firm. Salespeople partner with customers or prospects in solving problems.

QUANTIFYING BENEFITS

In the long complex sales cycle you must train salespeople how to quantify benefits. The enterprisewide software salesperson presents her customer a program with a price of $2 million, twice that, $1 million more, of the competitor's program. However, the salesperson has spreadsheets proving that this program can increase the customer's annual sales by 3 percent, or $9 million, reduce material and labor costs by $1,400,000, and reduce inventory by $500,000.

The competition does not have such a spreadsheet. The higher-priced, higher-value software vendor wins the job because it proved value-added benefits, lower payback period, lower total costs, favorable alternative costs and higher return on investment. The buyer was able to take this information to the purchasing committee, which persuaded the company to choose the higher-priced vendor. Marketing and sales management cooperate in producing these spreadsheets. Preparing these spreadsheets also requires cooperation and data from the prospects, which helps to make them customers.

To prepare these spreadsheets, the salesperson must ask the prospect questions concerning customers, competitors, costs, problems, needs, and opportunities. In addition, the salesperson must understand the prospect's competitive advantage, markets, customers, expenses, and key drivers. All this information increases the probability of converting a prospect into a customer.

MARKET SEGMENTATION

You must also train salespeople to customize their presentation of features, benefits, and proof to different market segments. In presenting a medical device to physicians, the salesperson might emphasize efficacy, but when presenting the same device to hospitals, the salesperson might emphasize cost savings.

In the August 2006 MarketBridge survey, sales, marketing, and human resource executives at 120 midsized and large companies were asked, "What is the greatest challenge faced by your sales force?" Sixty-four percent of the respondents replied, "Increasing productivity." Sixty-one percent of the respondents replied, "Conducting solution selling rather than transactional selling." Fifty-six percent replied, "Recruiting the right talent."[1] Those are some of the important issues we are dealing with in this book.

Basic, Tactical Sales Skills

Salesperson training in long complex group decisions reduces the sales cycle and separates winners from losers. All salespeople, in both short and long sales cycles, need training in the basic or more tactical sales skills outlined in Exhibit 5.2, which presents the selling pyramid. Constant reinforcement of this training is the sales manager's job.

Deaggregate the items listed in the selling pyramid. Pick those pieces in the sales process most important to the success of a salesperson in your firm. Concentrate your training on those areas.

Previously, we discussed the marketing issues, customer profiles, and competitive grids. Chapter 9 on channel choice and architecture and Chapter 10 on sizing and deployment will discuss call frequency. Also, salespeople must understand that if they do not have an objective and a strategy for the call, they should not make the call. Leave coffee calls for Sundays. A legitimate objective might be to introduce a new product that requires a demonstration as the strategy.

For many salespeople the entire area of precall planning needs more attention. Some sales managers have a conference call each Monday during which they ask each salesperson to review the precall planning for each customer that week.

In moving from qualifying customers and obtaining an appointment to obtaining a commitment or closing, generally the most common areas for reinforcement include asking probing questions to find needs and opportunities, presenting features, benefits, and proof, and overcoming objections.

PROSPECTING

To drive growth in some businesses, the salesperson must know how to efficiently find additional prospects with greater-than-average needs for the product or service. In such situations the sales manager must teach the proven techniques that have produced qualified leads for successful salespeople, or he or she must develop and test new techniques. Ask your more successful salespeople to share such information with their peers at a sales meeting. Test these skills and techniques by role-playing.

Prospecting creates growth, but the time required and risks involved are not worth the reward unless leads are qualified. The sales manager must teach salespeople efficient ways to prospect for new customers. Track the closing ratio from prospecting. How can you train salespeople to improve it?

The sales manager for a distributor of ice-making machines instructed salespeople to prospect by following an ice delivery truck. The sales manager for a distributor of solar heat-reflecting shades and glass instructed salespeople

to prospect by calling on offices with large windows and southern exposures. Remind salespeople that referrals from satisfied customers represent an excellent introduction to qualified prospects.

SELLING THE APPOINTMENT

New product salespeople, new systems salespeople calling on first-time or one-time customers, and salespeople who depend on a constant stream of new customers must be taught proven techniques for selling the appointment. For example, in the giftware industry, a modified rebuy, having an appointment can double the size of your order. On the other hand, salespeople with delivery routes selling commodities don't require appointments, and salespeople calling on repeat customers for reorders—that is, modified rebuys—have little difficulty arranging them.

Salespeople need training on how to use e-mail and faxes to help set appointments or create interest in appointments. Faxing or e-mailing short articles of interest proves effective.

Salespeople need training on how to deal with voice mail. Pressing zero to reach a gatekeeper who will find the person you are trying to reach represents one way to penetrate voice mail. Also, unless you know the prospect, voice mail messages must be short.

Calling early or late in the day, when you know the decision maker picks up her phone is another idea for contacting hard-to-reach people and avoiding voice mail. Salespeople must be trained to sell the appointment, not the product or service over the phone. People who make buying decisions lure salespeople into selling the product by phone so that they can say no to an appointment. Train salespeople to sell the benefits of an appointment. For example, "I can offer you some knowledge that will help your firm increase its market share." Offering alternative times to meet with a customer, especially at 15 minutes before or after a particular hour, works well. Set limits on the length of an appointment. For example, "I will leave after 30 minutes unless you invite me to stay."

PROBING QUESTIONS

You must continually remind the salespeople on your team that selling is listening, not talking. Salespeople should not present features, benefits, and proof until the customer and salesperson have agreed on the need, problem, or opportunity. In longer sales cycles, salespeople must continually reconfirm the customer's need, problem, or opportunity. The answers to probing questions, customized to your industry, identify customer needs, problems, and opportunities. In the corrugated box industry, questions center on yields and equipment utilization. In the semiconductor industry, a salesperson is trained to ask about failure rates and quality control. Empathetic listening and a knowledge of potential problems and opportunities helps in identifying customer needs.

Many sales managers ask salespeople to submit their favorite probing questions annotated to say what the customer's answers reveal. These often are listed on a board at the sales meeting and discussed. After the meeting, this list of probing questions, along with notes on what the answers tell a salesperson concerning customer problems, needs, and opportunities, is reproduced as a training aid and placed in the training manual.

PRESENTATION SKILLS

In addition to identifying the best probing questions, presentation skills need continual refinement. Generally, salespeople know the product or service features, and sometimes they mention benefits, but they seldom give proof. In surveys of people who make buying decisions, results show that the salespeople who obtain the orders know how the product or service features benefit the customer and can offer proof of these benefits. The features of a B2B Internet site are the ability to transact purchases and sales efficiently, and the benefit of that feature is an increase in revenues or a decrease in cost and inventory for the participants, and the proof is found in the actual trades made by other customers.

Sales managers test salespeople at sales meetings by going around the room asking each person to give a feature, benefit, and proof for a particular product or service. No one can repeat what already has been said. This forces salespeople to think on their feet in front of their peers, which, hopefully, they will be able to repeat in front of their customers. When doing this exercise, if salespeople quickly run out of complete features, benefits, and proof, the sales manager will realize there is a need for more training.

OVERCOMING OBJECTIVES

To help the sales force close or move to the next step in the sales cycle, sales managers must continually reinforce salespeople's training in overcoming objections. Salespeople must understand that objections show interest. If there are no objections, there is no interest and probably a credit problem. Salespeople should smile when customers raise objectiions. The objection needs to be restated in a positive manner and then overcome. If the objection is, "Your cable is too thick," the salesperson might reply, "Oh, you would like a thinner cable." This shows the

customer that the salesperson heard the objection correctly, and it also gives the salesperson more time to think about how to overcome it.

Many sales managers ask salespeople to submit the most common customer objections. Then, at a sales meeting, the objections are presented, listed, and prioritized. Salespeople are asked to share how they overcome the objection. A meaningful dialogue ensues, great ideas evolve, everyone learns; and the objections and ideas on how to overcome them are recorded and used as a sales aid.

Objections range from price to why make a change to sizing, features, delivery issues, or a bad past experience. A good means of testing salespeople on this topic is the objection game. At a sales meeting, each salesperson throws out an objection at another salesperson. He or she must restate the objection and quickly overcome it. If someone fails to do this, he or she is out. The last person in is the winner. One salesperson may ask another, "Why make a change? I am happy with my present situation." The other salesperson might restate the objection by saying, "Oh, you feel there is no reason to change?" Then follow with, "Whom did you deal with before your present vendor, and why did you switch?" This might produce the rationale for the customer to consider a new vendor.

CLOSING

Another key part of the selling process that requires constant reinforcement is closing, obtaining a commitment, or moving to the next step. Salespeople who make great presentations and ask good probing questions often forget to close. Often the fear of failure, of a no, of a rejection, prevents salespeople from attempting to obtain a commitment.

Salespeople must be trained that no is only no today and that it takes a certain number of nos to get a yes. The salesperson can always go back next week with another idea or product. Closing ratios vary by product or service and industry. The sales manager should measure the closing ratio for each salesperson quarterly and discuss means of improving it, such as qualifying customers or more quickly identifying needs. For longer, more complex sales cycles, the closing ratio may not be reflected in an order but rather in moving to the next step in the sales cycle.

Many sales managers believe that the key to closing is for both the salesperson and the customer to feel more comfortable. To create this comfort, they suggest the salesperson review what was agreed on. For a temporary help service, for example, the salesperson might say, "Well, we agreed you need more people in your shipping department at the holidays. We agreed we did a good job for you last year and that our fees are within your budget." The word *agree* makes all parties more comfortable.

Next the salesperson requires a partnership statement: "I know this is an important decision. I will drop by the first day you use our people. Here is my beeper number if you have questions." A partnership statement helps alleviate concerns that the salesperson will disappear after receiving an order. Last, the salesperson must offer a choice, "Should we start Monday or Tuesday? Do you need 10 or 12 people?" Video-recorded role-playing provides the best way to test closing skills.

Lateral Selling

Salespeople also need to understand *lateral selling*—that is, how to ask a present satisfied buyer within a customer organization for the name of another buyer in another department who might benefit from her product or service. If you are successfully selling marketing services to one product manager at a pharmaceutical firm, why not ask him or her for an introduction to another product manager who might benefit from your firm's services. What questions should the salesperson ask and what statement should he or she make to obtain the referral? Lateral sales skills represent an important training issue for many firms.

For other firms, the sales manager might train salespeople in the questions and statements necessary to obtain referrals to potential buyers outside the customer's organization. This represents an effective, inexpensive means of obtaining leads.

The success of a sales call is determined by meeting the salesperson's objectives and obtaining customer agreement on the next step. The objective may be an order or a meeting with a key decision maker. The next step may be the date for a trial run. The key point is that as sales manager, you must reinforce sales skill training or it will quickly be lost.

(Exhibits start on next page.)

Exhibit 5.1. Training Topics: Complex Sales Processes, Long Sales Cycles, and Group Decisions.

Understanding the Decision-Making Process

- Time frames. Sales cycles.
- Budgets.
- Influencers. Decision makers. Committees.
- New systems buyer; established systems buyer; new product buyer; or commodity buyer.
- Steps in decision-making process. Definition of a successful call.
- Measuring the process.

Strategic and Organizational Issues

- Relationships of customer personnel.
- Organizational issues. Sell at what level.
- Identifying the fox.
- Identifying the champion.
- Consultative versus relationship sell.
- Competitor's history and relationship with customer.

Value-Added Propositions

- Understand customers' problems, needs, and opportunities.
- Ask probing questions.
- Study customers' competitors, competitive advantage, markets, customers, and key drivers.
- Quantify in dollars how you will increase sales, reduce costs, lower capital investment, and/or increase dollars of margins. Benefit realization.
- Features, benefits, and proof.
- Dealing with fragmentation.

Understanding the People/Players and the Profiles

- How they use and filter information to make decisions.
- Their hobbies and interests.
- Their decision-making motives.
- Their comfortable level of risk.

Exhibit 5.2. The Selling Pyramid: Tactical Sales Skills and Training Topics.

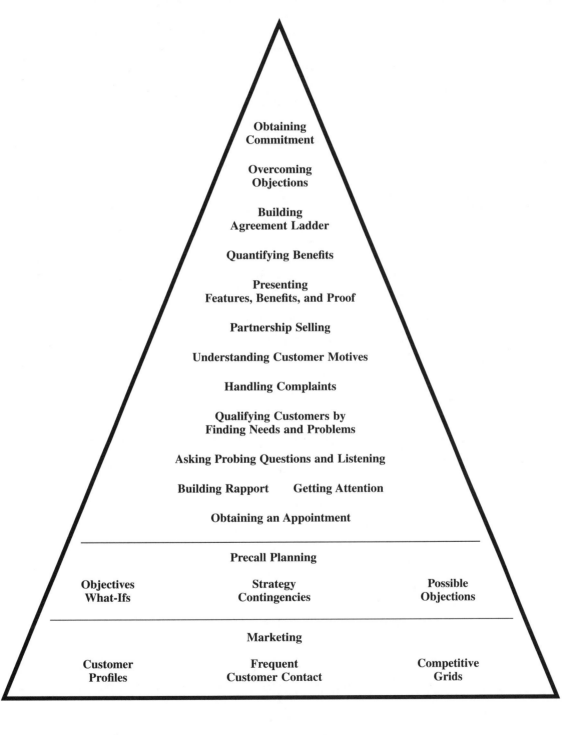

Obtaining
Commitment

Overcoming
Objections

Building
Agreement Ladder

Quantifying Benefits

Presenting
Features, Benefits, and Proof

Partnership Selling

Understanding Customer Motives

Handling Complaints

Qualifying Customers by
Finding Needs and Problems

Asking Probing Questions and Listening

Building Rapport   Getting Attention

Obtaining an Appointment

Precall Planning

Objectives What-Ifs	Strategy Contingencies	Possible Objections

Marketing

Customer Profiles	Frequent Customer Contact	Competitive Grids

Questions and Exercises for Chapter 5

- Quantify the benefits for a product or service you are familiar with.
- Prepare a list of probing questions you would ask to sell a product or service you are familiar with. Which needs, problems, or opportunities would these probing questions identify?
- Outline the steps in the sales funnel for a product or service you are familiar with.

Quiz for Chapter 5

1. True or false?
   Today a salesperson's job is not just to discover needs by asking customers probing questions but also to discover needs the customer does not even recognize.

2. Strategic sales skills involve understanding which of the following?
   a. Decision-making processes
   b. Obtaining an appointment
   c. Probing questions
   d. Value-added propositions
   e. Quantifying benefits

3. Tactical sales skills involve understanding which of the following?
   a. Qualifying customers
   b. Precall planning
   c. Obtaining an appointment
   d. Decision-making processes
   e. Probing questions
   f. Overcoming objectives
   g. Closing

4. True or false?
   A fox is someone in the customer's organization who will support the choice of your product or service in a group decision.

5. True or false?
   A champion is someone in the customer organization who will provide a vendor salesperson reliable information on the decision-making process.

6. Quantifying benefits involves proving which of the following?
   a. How your product or service can increase customer revenues
   b. How your product or service can lower customer expenses
   c. How your product or service can lower customer working-capital and capital expenditure needs
   d. How your product or service can improve customer's employee morale and the customer's company image

7. Salespeople obtain in-person appointments in which of the following ways?
   a. By presenting the features of their product or service over the phone
   b. By offering the prospect a variety of times for the appointments
   c. By selling the benefits of the appointment
   d. By limiting the amount of time for the appointment

8. True or false?
   Selling is talking first and listening to the customer second.

9. In training salespeople to overcome customer objections, the sales manager should use which of the following?
   a. Emphasize that objections show interest.
   b. Ask salespeople to restate the customer objections in front of the customer.
   c. At sales meetings, have salespeople present a list of their most common objections and how to overcome them.
   d. Have salespeople move on to another customer if the same objection surfaces twice.

10. In training salespeople to close, the sales manager should use which of the following?
    a. Emphasize that "no is only no today."
    b. Have salespeople summarize what the customer and the salesperson have agreed on.
    c. Have salespeople make partnership statements.
    d. Have salespeople ask a question offering the customer a choice.
    e. Have salespeople ask for the order before overcoming objections.

Note

1. MarketBridge, Mark Donnolo, *Performance-Driven Selling 2006*. Marketbridge Technologies. Copyright © 2006. Reprinted by permission of MarketBridge.

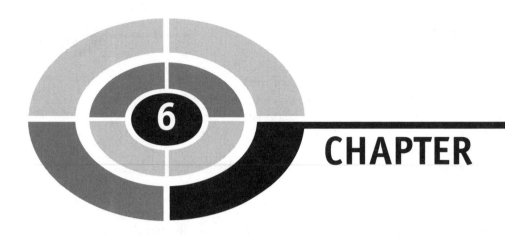

CHAPTER

Field Coaching and Sales Meetings

Field Coaching

Clearly, salespeople require knowledge of products, competition, customers and selling skills. The sales manager delivers this knowledge through initial training, field coaching (ride-withs, work-withs), and sales meetings.

Because of its many benefits, field coaching represents a regional sales manager's most important responsibility. Field coaching allows a sales manager to train, evaluate, and motivate salespeople, share best practices, and establish rapport with customers.

BENEFITS

Field coaching allows sales managers to observe salespeople in planning and critiquing a customer visit along with observing their knowledge of customers, competitors, products, and sales skills. You cannot accurately evaluate salespeople's skills and knowledge unless you observe them with customers. Sales results tell you the outcomes; field coaching gives you insight into the causes of outcomes. In critiquing salespeople's performances, sales managers reinforce positive skills, knowledge, activities, and personal characteristics and train salespeople in areas of weakness. Salespeople often complain that sales managers don't reinforce initial training and sales meetings with field visits, and because of this, they have no evidence for performance evaluations.

Sales manager field visits make salespeople feel useful, important, and worthwhile, and satisfy their need to belong. For this reason, plus establishing rapport with customers, you must work with both weak and strong salespeople. Your best salespeople can develop bad habits, and only riding with the underperformers creates an image of remedial training. Often the best salespeople or their customers will teach you a best practice that can be passed on to the entire sales force. After all, our best performers produce most of our sales volume, so any suggestions for improvement, such as proper targeting, can have a major impact on revenues. Field training and supervision give salespeople confidence in you as a sales manager.

Furthermore, field visits give you a firsthand chance to learn more about problems and opportunities with customers, with products or services, with salespeople, and with competitors. When a customer complains to you in person about late deliveries or weak product performance, it has more impact than when a salesperson complains over the phone. Customers appreciate your time and interest. Also, should a salesperson leave, you have the customer profile, and with field visits, you have personal rapport. Some sales managers make it a point to meet and know the top customers and decision makers in each territory.

Occasionally ask your boss to travel with your salespeople. This reinforces all the benefits, allows your supervisor some insight to the moment of truth, and allows her or him to suggest how you can improve sales force performance. However, unless there is a compelling reason, only one management person should ride with a salesperson at any time. Customers and salespeople feel uncomfortable when more than three people are present.

FREQUENCY OF FIELD COACHING

If the sales force resides locally and you have up to seven reports, spend at least 2 days a week, 100 days a year, riding with salespeople. If the sales force is national or if you have more than seven reports, 3 to 4 days a week may be required.

If the sales force resides locally, shorter but more frequent ride-withs prove most productive. This gives you an opportunity to observe change and reinforce best practices. If the sales force is national, economies of scale usually dictate longer, less frequent ride-withs.

As mentioned in Chapter 4, look at your job description, make a list of all your activities, prioritize them by importance in driving revenues, and then track the time you spend on training in general and field training in particular. As a regional sales manager with five or more reports, field training requires 40 to 60 percent of your time because of its importance in driving revenue. If you find that training does not receive enough of your time, ask yourself the following questions:

- Are there non-sales-related activities that require too much of my time?
- Can these be eliminated or delegated?
- Are the reasons I don't spend more time on training really excuses?

OBJECTIVES

Field coaching is more effective if you and the salesperson have an objective. Focused ride-withs that alternatively concentrate on new products, new accounts, or a particular product line or market segment prove most effective. The focus may involve training the salespeople on selling a major account. Ask the salesperson for his or her input on the work-with goal or objective and have a different focus for each ride-with.

UNANNOUNCED RIDE-WITHS

Occasionally do an unannounced ride-with. Call a salesperson, announce that your schedule has changed unexpectedly, and you would like to ride with him or her tomorrow. If that is not practical in your longer-sales-cycle business or if salespeople work long distances from your office, make a date for early next week. You will experience a more typical salesperson's day: fewer calls, shorter hours, a trip to the bank or day-care center; plus a customer mix that includes fewer friends and more cell phone time. Salespeople quickly communicate the unannounced ride-with to their peers, which results in more attention to planning highly productive days. A salesperson who tells you he or she can't do a ride-with on short notice raises a warning flag. We manage with fear and love.

CHANNEL PARTNERS

Field coaching proves especially important for managing channel partners. If you use indirect sales representative organizations, distributors, or brokers, field coaching not only trains and motivates but obtains a time commitment. An indirect sales force that you ride with will devote more time and resources to your products or services. The obstacle may be getting channel partners to accept field training. Training makes an indirect sales force more comfortable and competent with your products or services. Many firms have contracts that require their indirect sales force to spend a certain amount of time at sales meetings and in field coaching related to the principal firm's products.

ORGANIZING FIELD COACHING

Generally, we divide field coaching, ride-withs, or work-withs into five parts:

- Your phone call to arrange time with the salesperson
- In the field precall planning
- The sales call itself
- Postcall critique
- End-of-the-day summary

Many sales managers spend the necessary time in the field, but they don't implement the correct process and thus don't improve their salespeople's productivity.

PRECALL PLANNING

In planning each field coaching day, whether with a channel partner or direct field person, agree with the salesperson on the objectives: management selling of major accounts, new product placement, learning customer or competitive knowledge, or refining selling skills. At the end of your work-with day, were those objectives met? Some managers ask their salespeople for lists of what they would like help with, and in turn they send the salesperson a list of customers or market segments to be called on.

Before each customer call, review with the salesperson the precall planning—that is, what he or she should do when you are not there. What is the call's objective and strategy for reaching that objective? No objective, no call. As mentioned previously, too many salespeople engage in coffee calls. "I always call on my friends at Imperial on Tuesday morning." With shorter sales cycles and modified rebuys, such as bakery products, tires, or hosiery, the objective may be a reorder. The strategy may be sampling or discussing delivery dates. With longer sales cycles of first-time or one-time purchases, such as telephone systems, consulting services, or software, the objective may be moving to the next step in the sales process—that is, meeting a key decision maker, agreeing on a trial, and obtaining information on budgets and timetables. The strategy may involve quantifying benefits and referring to industry leaders who use your services.

Before each call, discuss competition at this account with the salesperson. What items are bought from the competition and why? Are competitors ants (start-ups) or gorillas (the phone company) or both? What percent of this customer's business does your firm have? What are this account's problems, needs, and opportunities? Has the competition made a mistake? Does the customer need better deliveries or customized products? How can your firm help solve the problems and satisfy the needs of customers and still take advantage of competitor mistakes?

For longer more complex sales cycles, discuss the decisions making process with salespeople. What are the steps from search to purchase? Who is the decision maker, influencers, fox, and champion? What is the timetable for moving from one step to the next?

What probing questions do you or will you ask to determine needs? What customer objections will we hear on this call, and how will we overcome them? Will there be an objection on price, delivery, space, content, a bad past experience, or no budget?

I ride with 25 salespeople a year from many different industries. I always ask, "Tell me about the personal interests of the people we are calling on." I always ask for last and first names of key contacts. We buy from experts and friends. Despite the importance of this information, however, too many salespeople cannot answer these questions.

As a sales manager, always look at the customer profile and file, whether hard copy, digital, or hybrid. Is the salesperson accumulating appropriate customer information on usage, history, needs, opportunities, long-term goals, weekly activities, decision makers, and decision-making processes?

End your field training precall planning by discussing what happened on the last call, how long this visit should take (30 minutes or all day), long-term goals for this account, what role you as the sales manager will play, and how you will be introduced. For a new salesperson, you may wish to make the sales presentation with a few customers, then allow the salesperson the opportunity to do it. The new salesperson will learn from watching you in action, from critiquing your approach, and from your analysis of his or her performance.

With seasoned salespeople, let them make the presentations unless otherwise agreed upon, but define your role. You may occasionally help or be a silent partner. An experienced salesperson may ask you for specialized assistance selling a particular product or service or type of account. In this case, you would make the call as an expert, but allow the salesperson to show what he or she has learned by making the presentation on a similar account.

Because your presence could make your salespeople uncomfortable, before the call express confidence in their ability. This puts them at ease. One sales manager found that her salespeople often locked keys in their cars when they traveled together because they were so nervous.

Sometimes major customers or prospects prefer to be sold by management. Similarly, when you call on management rather than on the buyer, purchasing agent, or design engineer; a presentation by sales management or a dual presentation by you and your salesperson may be preferred. Dual presentations allow you and the salesperson to share the responsibility so that no customer need or benefit is missed. Discuss with your salesperson before the call who will make the presentation and what your role will be. Discuss how you will be introduced—as the sales manager or as some other type of associate. Customers are complimented by the sales manager's presence, but then sometimes the conversation is directed toward you rather than toward the salesperson.

DURING THE CALL

During the sales call, when the salesperson makes the presentation, try not to interfere; but if you must inject something, be gentle. You accompany the salesperson on this call primarily for training purposes, not necessarily to write an order or to move to the next step in the decision-making process. Salespeople learn from failures as well as from successes. If you interfere, the buyer becomes confused and the salesperson embarrassed, which strains the relationship. You may gain an order but lose a customer and a salesperson. You may travel with a particular salesperson for 4 days annually, but on the other 236, he or she travels alone. When the sales manager sells for the sales force, the sales force stops selling.

Often, salespeople prefer that you take over on a field trip. It takes them off the hook. However, keep in mind that while your instinct in front of a customer is to sell, the purpose of this trip is training.

When you must interrupt, use a question to make the point indirectly. For example, if the salesperson suggests the wrong model, ask if the customer might also be interested in the correct model. If the salesperson concentrates on price when another benefit should be emphasized, ask if the customer might wish to have the other benefit explained.

If the customer directs questions to you, turn them over to the salesperson. Sit farther away from the buyer than your salesperson does. Take yourself out of the conversation. Lean back rather than forward in your chair. During a joint sales call never speak to the customer or prospect as "executive to executive" or do anything else to make the salesperson feel less than equal in the customer's presence. Maintain the selling chain of command or customers may start contacting you directly for concessions. Don't volunteer concessions to a prospect or customer simply because you have the authority. Avoid "piling on" when the salesperson is trying to close.

When sales managers ride with salespeople for the purpose of field coaching, they should be looking for some of the following:

- Does the salesperson establish rapport with the customer by discussing personal interests from the profile before asking probing questions about the business?
- Does the salesperson demonstrate knowledge of the decision makers, the influencers, and the decision-making process?
- Does the salesperson demonstrate knowledge of the customer's business, operations, competitors, key drivers, and use of his or her product or service?
- Does the salesperson ask probing questions to identify key problems, needs, and opportunities?
- Does the salesperson suggest solutions, products, and services?
- Does he or she properly present features, benefits, and proof?
- Does he or she quantify benefits in dollars?
- Does the salesperson actively listen?
- Does he or she overcome objections?
- Does he or she appear well organized by using sales aids?
- Does the salesperson use a reference sell?
- Does he or she act like a consultant but think like a customer?
- Does he or she properly ask for the desired action (possibly an order or a trial)?
- Does the salesperson establish the next action (another meeting or samples)?

As a sales manager, know what you are looking for, set standards, be critical, and sit in judgment.

POSTCALL CRITIQUE

After each field-coaching sales call, do a postcall critique or analysis before driving to the next customer. A good salesperson will eventually employ self-analysis after each sales call, but to help develop this faculty, ask the salesperson how he or she felt about the call. What went well? What went poorly? Were the call objectives met? The salesperson will do most of the work for you. Agree on follow-up action and objectives for the next call on this customer.

After this self-analysis, share your thoughts on the strengths and weaknesses of the presentation. If you first tell the salesperson what was done right, it will be easier to accept criticism on what was done wrong. Reinforce skills used effectively. Review the extent to which call objectives were met. Give the salesperson credit for any positive accomplishments, including writing the order or agreeing to the next step. Your comments should be logically organized, easy to understand, and action oriented so that corrective steps can be taken on the next call. You will obtain better results from analyzing major issues than you will from offering blanket criticisms or trying to cover too many areas. The fewer the messages, the better they will be understood. Use questions to make points: "Do you think you emphasized our lease plan enough?" To emphasize points, conduct some role-playing before the next call. Salespeople are self-conscious and often not at their best when accompanied by their sales manager. You must factor this into your evaluation.

After the call, what information, if any, did the salesperson add to the customer's profile? Ask the salesperson, "What did you learn about the business and the person?" Generally the salesperson's response is less than adequate. Then you can add your own list of items, discuss the list, and ask for agreement. Hopefully, the salesperson will observe and note such information when you are not there.

AT THE END OF EACH DAY

At the end of each field coaching day, summarize key issues with the salesperson. Ask the salesperson how many hours and what percent of the time was spent in front of the customers. On a work-with, "eyeball time" versus "windshield time" drives results. Generally, salespeople overestimate the actual customer or selling hours. For each account or call, keep track of actual time spent toe to toe. Point out the actual hours versus the salesperson's perception. This creates self-awareness of how few hours, and how small a percent, of a salesperson's time is actually spent with customers. This allows you an opportunity to summarize the day's activities in terms of number of calls; markets, customers, and products focused on. This also gives you an opportunity to discuss which of the agreed-on work-with objectives were met.

Next, ask the salesperson how far you drove today and for the odometer reading. You casually read the odometer at the beginning of the day. Generally, salespeople grossly underestimate driving miles. You point out the importance of customer face time versus car windshield time. For some sales jobs this represents a key issue; for others it is less appropriate.

Next, have salespeople evaluate themselves using the field coaching salesperson evaluation in Exhibit 6.1 at the end of this chapter. Then, using the same format, evaluate the salesperson, and together agree on goals, objectives, and a development plan. Include this in your follow-up letter. Be sure to review this before the next ride-with. Put this information in the salesperson's quarterly performance evaluation file.

Last, ask, "What did you get out of our time together?" This question asks salespeople to evaluate the field training, plus it allows you another opportunity to summarize key issues. Most likely, the answer will be similar to, "I learned about my need for more probing questions, better product knowledge, and more accurate customer profiles." To which you might answer, "Did you also get a better understanding of overcoming objections and competitor knowledge?" However, be prepared for candid answers such as, "Not very much, but I enjoyed your company and the free lunch."

When you return to the home office and write to the salesperson, you can both acknowledge certain strengths and remind him or her of specific weaknesses. Make sure the memo includes agreed-on action, objectives, and a time frame for correcting these weaknesses.

The sales manager for a seed company uses a "Work-With Checklist" to assist in properly performing field coaching. That checklist appears at the end of this chapter as Exhibit 6.2.

Some sales managers who have many salespeople reporting to them conduct remote ride-withs. In such a situation, on certain days the salesperson calls the sales manager before each customer call to have a precall conversation. Then after each call, the sales person calls the manager again, this time to have a postcall critique. The sales manager of course does not observe the salesperson in front of the customer. This process is acceptable as a supplement to in-person ride-withs but it is not a substitute.

If you manage a telesales organization or one that primarily sells over the phone from an office, you might want to listen to salespeoples' outbound customer calls. You might do this with or without their knowledge. In such situations the sales manager would also conduct precall planning and postcall critiques with the salespeople.

Sales Meetings

Periodic, well-planned sales meetings provide a productive format for communication, motivation, and training. The basic purposes of sales meetings are these:

- To provide continuing training to sales personnel
- To offer a forum for salespeople, management, and other departments for sharing problems and successes
- To make salespeople feel useful, important, and part of something larger
- To give salespeople recognition for their achievements or motivation through peer pressure to perform

- To allow salespeople personally to meet management and other department personnel
- To give management a chance to disseminate policy to the sales force
- To provide an opportunity for management to visit salespeople with minimum travel

Contrary to popular belief, being a field salesperson is a lonely job full of disappointments and rejections. The sales meeting helps to assure salespeople that someone cares. They arrive dusty and tired from the commercial battlefield, and with luck and intelligent planning, they leave refreshed, enthusiastic, and ready for new challenges.

Sales meetings strongly influence salespeople's image of the company, which they pass on to customers. It is therefore very important that they leave feeling up. Have you ever had an unsuccessful sales meeting? What effect did it have on your short-term sales?

OBJECTIVES

To justify the cost, time, and energy involved, the specific objectives of your sales meeting must be well thought out. These objectives must reinforce your marketing plan. Holding a meeting because you had one last week, last month, or last year does not constitute a justifiable objective. You need a more concrete reason. Decide in advance what you specifically hope to achieve and then carefully plan toward those goals. The objectives might include a combination of the following:

- Introducing a new product or service
- Alleviating tensions between the sales force, other departments, and management
- Explaining a sales contest, forecast form, appraisal form, or new compensation plan (see Chapter 7 on introducing new compensation plans)
- Convincing the sales force that the company can stay in business
- Analyzing the competition
- Opening new accounts
- Retaining or expanding old accounts
- Discussing sales force automation
- Improving selling techniques
- Improving collections
- Obtaining leads
- Managing time better
- Defining new territory boundaries
- Discussing safety or legal issues

Open-ended sales meetings don't work. If you don't have an objective and an agenda, don't have a sales meeting. Many sales managers have weekly or even daily sales meetings to review each person's results. In my opinion, this type of review is better done in individual meetings. Ask salespeople what they would like to discuss at their sales meetings. They know what is needed.

Sometimes, even with proper objectives, these functions become stale and monotonous. At that point everyone needs a rest. If you feel the meetings no longer achieve their goals, change the format, or stop convening them for a while.

Time is limited, so the objectives and subject matter must be applicable to the entire group. Group training loses its effectiveness unless all participants share a similar level of proficiency. Training the most experienced salesperson with the least experienced and the strong performer with the weak often dilutes results. The material may be too challenging for the least experienced and weaker salespeople and not challenging enough for the most experienced and stronger salespeople. For certain training, you may remedy this problem by forming subgroups at the sales meeting.

COMPLAINTS AND CRITICISMS

Many sales managers strongly dislike sales meetings because in these settings they can't control the salespeople, who outnumber them. Also, they must listen to salespeople's complaints and accept criticism in front of the entire group. A good sales manager, however, will be sensitive to complaints and criticisms and welcome them because they generally contain important messages.

Turn this potential disruptive problem into an opportunity by devoting limited time in the middle of your meeting to complaints and criticisms that concern the entire group. Salespeople need a forum in which to express their frustrations, and if they know their "day in court" will arrive, the rest of the meeting will be more productive. A salesperson who presents a problem must also present a possible solution. Criticisms and problems raised by salespeople require a management response now or in the future. Criticisms or problems that don't involve all the salespeople can be handled at individual meetings.

The sales manager for a steel service center has salespeople submit anonymously written complaints and criticisms that apply to the entire sales force. Then after the formal sales meeting in a more social setting, she blindly selects several of these criticisms and/or complaints from a hat and discusses them. This relaxed approach takes the discussion out of valuable sales meeting time and makes it more lighthearted.

Making Sales Meetings More Interesting

PARTICIPATION OF SALESPEOPLE

Sales meetings can be made more interesting by having salespeople present certain topics and even run the meeting. Salespeople learn best through proactive, interactive group discussion and sharing best practices, successes, and problems; they do not learn as much through lecture-type PowerPoint presentations by management. They believe each other a lot more readily than they believe management. Encourage all salespeople to participate in the discussion by asking questions.

The sales manager for a dental equipment firm assigns one salesperson to manage each sales meeting, which represents the ultimate of salesperson participation. That salesperson suggests the agenda and presenters for the manager's review. Once approved, the salesperson is responsible for content and delivery. At this company, salespeople pay special attention to sales meetings because responsibility for the meeting rotates among salespeople and they may run the next one. Salespeople who present at or run sales meetings feel useful, important, and worthwhile. Rewarding high performers with responsibility for sales meetings motivates them to achieve even greater results.

Similarly, the sales manager for a financial services software firm runs the sales meetings, but he has salespeople present topics on selling skills, prospecting, or product, customer, and competitor knowledge. Often he chooses the salesperson with the best performance record to present a topic, but sometimes he chooses weaker salespeople in an effort to improve their skills.

INVITING CUSTOMERS

To make its sales meetings more interesting, an aircraft navigational instrumentation firm invites a customer to each sales meeting. The customer speaks for 20 minutes on how he or she selects a vendor in that industry and on the salesperson's role in influencing that selection. The next 40 minutes consists of questions and answers from the sales force, which allows salespeople to have a candid nonthreatening discussion about their job with a customer. This company invites customers from various market segments; invites a variety of decision makers, engineers, and controllers; invites firms not sold by them; and invites previous customers who no longer buy. Careful selection of customers proves important. Most customers are complimented by the opportunity. One year the sales meeting was held at its largest customer's facility. The agenda included a plant tour and

presentations by many customer decision makers and influencers. Major customers may have interest in this type of partnering.

SUCCESS STORIES

To begin on a positive note, the sales vice president for an independent regional telephone firm starts her sales meetings by asking salespeople to tell a success story or a problem-solving story. The stories might involve opening a difficult new account, saving a problem customer, resolving a conflict, adding an additional service to a major customer, or beating out a major competitor. Salespeople compete to tell their success stories in front of their peers, and meetings start on an upbeat note.

SCOREBOARDING

To create competition, the sales vice president for a giftware firm uses sales meetings for scoreboarding. Each month she ranks the 50 salespeople from 1 to 50 based on attainment of their year-to-date revenue forecast. The salesperson most above forecast is number 1, and the salesperson most below forecast is number 50. The rankings are changed monthly and posted on the firm's intranet. Number 1 runs faster to stay ahead of number 2. Salespeople work hard to avoid remaining in the bottom 10. At each sales meeting, salespeople sit according to their ranking. At lunch all salespeople above the forecast get fish or meat and those below forecast get franks and beans. Everyone has fun with the concept.

BALANCING THE TOPICS

The regional sales managers for a semiconductor equipment firm organize their agendas so that they can devote a portion of each quarterly sales meeting to product knowledge, selling skills, current customer issues, changes at competition, administration, and territory management. In January each regional manager announces the dates and agendas for the next four quarterly meetings. This procedure forces the sales managers to plan in advance and have a balanced agenda.

The sales manager for a reform math textbook firm reinforces some aspect of selling skills at each meeting. For example, she will devote a portion of one meeting to discussing probing questions, another portion at another meeting to best practices for obtaining an appointment, another to presentation skills, another to overcoming objections, and another to closing. She uses the techniques discussed in Chapter 5 on selling skills.

COMPETITORS' PRODUCTS

Having competitors' products, product lines, service brochures, or service agreements at a meeting generates a lively and informative discussion. You might assign each salesperson or a team one competitive product or service to analyze for the group. In such a discussion, be sure the sales force understands both the firm's competitive strengths and its weaknesses. Just concentrating on strengths does not prepare a salesperson for the realities of the marketplace. In Chapter 4 we showed how competitive grids could be used at a sales meeting to teach competitive knowledge. If you employ a salesperson who has worked for a competitor, he or she might volunteer to present that competitor's products or services.

SUPPLIERS' PRESENTATIONS

To create a variety of presenters and control costs, a food service distributor asked a different supplier to present its line at each sales meeting. Your suppliers and vendors represent inexpensive trainers for sales meetings and field coaching. Be sure to limit their time at sales meetings and give them a list of topics to be covered. Suppliers and vendors emphasize product knowledge, but they often forget how this helps to make a sale. Topics should include target customers, competition, features, benefits, and proof. For example, are the frozen desserts targeted at country clubs or company cafeterias? Who is the competition? And why should customers buy the product?

You might also take your salespeople to visit a vendor facility. A furniture retailer took her salespeople to visit a different company supplier each month. Often this included touring the manufacturing facility.

As mentioned in Chapter 4, be sure to present your products, target customers, competition, features, benefits, and proof at your channel partners' sales meetings or invite them to attend your meetings. Have your channel partners include these activities in their annual business plans, which they submit to your firm.

ROLE-PLAYING

Skits and role-playing that enact customer-salesperson interchanges represent powerful, realistic, nonthreatening learning techniques at sales meetings. One salesperson takes the role of the customer, while the other plays himself or herself. Use a script to describe the particulars of the situation. For example, you have neglected to call on this account regularly, or the purchasing agent has recently been approached by a particular competitor. Pick two people who will take the

task seriously, and allow them to rehearse. Use a tape recorder or videocamera, and occasionally stop, critique, and replay the action. Then, after the role-play or during the playback, ask for analysis and comments from the group.

A variation of this role-play is to assign three people to each group. One person plays the customer, another the salesperson, and the third observes and comments. Roles are rotated. After each of three role-plays, each with a different scenario, the participants view the video and discuss what went well and what went poorly.

An electronic subcontractor assembler of computers has its purchasing agent play the customer. Occasionally this firm asks a customer design engineer to act as the customer. Videotapes of their role-play are given to salespeople for review.

Salespeople often dislike role-play because they must perform in front of their peers, but it represents the best nonthreatening way to simulate an actual sales situation. Furthermore, when salespeople know role-play is part of the agenda, their attention level increases. The techniques described above make role-play fun, which lowers the resistance to it and forces the salespeople to take it seriously, thus making it more valuable.

With a group of senior salespeople, brainstorming can produce creative ideas and motivate high performers. You see an unfilled need in the marketplace for small business or medical waste disposal services. You ask your waste disposal salespeople if they perceive the same need. If so, how could it be structured, presented, and priced?

CASES AND SIMULATED SALES SITUATIONS

A new trend in sales meetings involves the use of cases and computer software-generated games that simulate sales situations. The computer plays the customer asking for, evaluating, and responding to different combinations of prices, product mix, delivery, and customization. Customized board games can also provide this experience. Salespeople can see the impact of their decisions on their customer's and their own firm's revenues, costs, and margins.

Often salespeople are given written cases to analyze and discuss. The cases might involve targeting customers, deciding how frequently to call on large accounts, negotiating pricing or delivery issues, or opening a major new account.

A continuing trend at sales meetings is for salespeople to solve case problems in groups to promote team building. Both these techniques make sales meetings more interesting for the participants.

Films, videotapes, or guest speakers discussing such topics as selling techniques, motivation, collections, good listening, time management, or prospecting can spice up your meetings. Video Arts, Xerox Educational Publications, and

John Cleese all rent and sell such films and videotapes. Most local telephone companies and utilities offer free guest speakers for sales meetings.

SALES SUPPORT

A salesperson's customers are both inside and outside the company. So, at each meeting, devote some time to a presentation and discussion of company functions outside of selling: quality, operations, manufacturing, human resources, credit, transportation, and/or deliveries. Use other members of your company's management team to present appropriate topics. For instance, invite the credit manager or controller to talk about collections, the manufacturing or operations manager to discuss quality, your boss to talk about pricing, a supplier to talk about features and benefits, and a channel partner to talk about target markets. These outside speakers often offer a fresh perspective.

Many sales managers invite inside sales and customer support personnel to attend all or some of the sales meeting. For companies with career ladders into sales, this is especially appropriate and inexpensive.

INVITING CHANNEL PARTNERS

If your firm uses channel partners, invite them to the direct sales force sales meeting, hold a separate meeting for them, or participate in their sales meetings. As mentioned earlier, well-trained channel partners have many benefits. Specify in the channel partner agreement the number of sales meetings involving your products or services that their salespeople must attend. If you hold separate sales meetings for channel partners, include the same topics and techniques as mentioned above. Make sure you train the channel partners' salespeople directly and do not rely on their management to do this.

ENDING SALES MEETINGS

An upbeat way to end a sales meeting is to recognize certain salespeople for their outstanding performance and/or to present awards. You might present the salesperson-of-the-month award, announce contest results, present bonus checks, or thank a salesperson in front of the group for opening a major new account. Often at multiday national sales meetings, this is done at an awards dinner.

Often sales managers use workbooks or CDs to highlight key topics. The workbooks and CDs become reference material when the salespeople return to their offices.

TESTING AND EVALUATIONS

At the end of each sales meeting or topic, hand salespeople a short test on the subject matter. After completing the test, hand them the answers and ask for their scores. The best score receives a small prize. The answers codify what was learned. The test reminds salespeople what the meeting's objectives were and rewards them for paying attention. The test informs the presenters whether the material was understood, and, if not understood, what topics need more attention. Some managers use pre- and postpresentation testing to measure improvement.

Also, at the end of each sales meeting or topic, have people anonymously evaluate what went well and what went poorly, and solicit their ideas for improvement. Ask salespeople to rate the subject, the presenter, and what they learned. Evaluations and testing can be humbling but informative exercises. Salespeople usually do not learn as much as you expected, so corrective action proves necessary. The corrective action might involve the content or teaching techniques.

Why Sales Meetings Fail

Sales meetings fail when administrative matters receive more time than selling matters, when one or more salespeople dominate the meeting, when trivial matters encroach on more important subjects, when management threatens and criticizes salespeople rather than training them, when the format consists of lectures rather than discussion, when participants do not share a similar level of proficiency, when there is no agenda, and when the meeting takes too long. Do not devote more than 25 percent of a meeting to administrative matters such as proper order writing, credit and collection, sales reports, expense reports, or putting enough postage on order envelopes. Use sales meetings for training, not for a group review of results. You can best review results individually.

Do not allow any salesperson, whether superstar or laggard, to turn the meeting into a personal speaking platform. Remind these people that you have scheduled individual meetings to discuss individual problems. Also, involve people who have not participated by asking them questions. You must run the meeting and not let the meeting run you.

Do not let the discussion digress into unimportant aspects of important matters. When a salesperson notes that the welding seam in your new ultrasonic cleaning tank rises one-half inch rather than one-quarter inch, remind this person that the new tank degreases customer components at half the cost in half the time of any competitive product.

Sometimes sales meetings fail because they contain previously unannounced surprises, such as a new compensation plan or territory changes. Such matters are best communicated at individual meetings.

Criticize in private; praise in public. Some sales managers feel obligated to start a sales meeting by telling their salespeople how bad they are. This creates a real turn-off and does not support the purpose of the meeting. You are blaming both the strong and the weak performers and at the same time limiting the meeting's training and motivational benefits. Instead, start the meeting by asking a salesperson to share a success story.

As mentioned earlier, group meetings can also lose their effectiveness when all participants do not share a similar level of proficiency. Mixing the most experienced salespeople with the least experienced and training the strong performers with the weak can dilute the results. For certain subjects, you can remedy this problem by forming subgroups at the sales meeting.

Frequency of Sales Meetings

When the entire sales force or the regional sales force resides locally and overnight accommodations are not necessary, meetings can be held frequently, but for short periods of time. For example, meetings could be held on the first Saturday of every other month, or the last Friday afternoon of each month, or every Monday morning. For local sales forces, sales meetings should be held no more frequently than once a week and no less frequently than once a month, and they should last two to six hours. If most customers can't be seen Friday afternoons, have your meetings then. If each week you offer new services, have a meeting on Monday mornings.

When most members of a national or international sales force live a plane trip away, economics necessitates less frequent but longer meetings. In such instances, two- to three-day gatherings once or twice a year, or possibly every other year, generally provide the best use of time and money. Teleconferencing via phones, WebEx, and video can supplement in-person sales meetings for the national or international sales force. Many sales managers use weekly conference calls for discussing best practices, which, again, supplements formal sales meetings. WebEx Communications can help the sales manager make visual presentations at a remote sales meeting. WebEx continually introduces new features that make remote sales meetings more productive.

Some companies have regional sales meetings quarterly and a national sales meeting annually. This hybrid approach allows regional sales managers to organize their own meetings and customize topics for their salespeople and customers. Regional sales meetings might be two days, but the national meeting might be three or four days. Such a hybrid approach can save money and improve training.

Annual, semiannual, quarterly, or biennial sales meetings requiring several days should be scheduled during slack periods or at the start of a selling cycle. You don't want to remove a salesperson from his or her territory during a peak selling period. For example, many menswear manufacturers and book publishers schedule annual sales meetings in early December because at this time of the year, retailers are too busy to see salespeople and January begins a new wholesale selling season.

Agendas

Sales meetings can consist of formal group meetings, formal individual meetings, informal social gatherings, official social functions, or some combination of these. Participants should receive an agenda before they arrive so that everyone will know where to be, when to be there, what material is going to be covered, the objectives, and what preparation is necessary. The agenda might state that once a formal group meeting has begun, cell phones, Blackberries, and other electronic devices must be turned off, and that you will lock the doors until break time. This eliminates a tendency for people to use the phones, straggle in late, or otherwise interrupt the gathering. Actually, once you initiate the locked-door policy, no one arrives late.

Whether you conduct three-day sales meetings twice a year, two-day sales meetings quarterly, one-day sales meetings six times a year, half-day sales meetings monthly, or two-hour meetings weekly, you should allocate from 60 to 80 percent of your time to all formal group matters. The company president and other top management should attend some of these formal group meetings.

In these sessions, management and senior salespeople introduce and everyone discusses subjects such as these:

- New or problematic products, services, markets, or programs
- Opening new accounts or retaining existing accounts
- Target customers and territory business plans
- Price increases
- Collections
- Company policies and organization
- Selling techniques
- Overcoming objections
- Time management
- Software, sales force automation, laptops, and/or customer-relationship management
- Obtaining qualified leads and appointments

- Sales promotions
- Advertising
- Competition and competitive issues
- Sales contests and compensation plans
- Evaluation forms, forecasts, and budget procedures

The subject matter must be applicable to the entire group and capable of being meaningfully presented in the time allotted. For example, a discussion of individual customer issues might not involve the entire group and would therefore be an inappropriate subject. Instead, that topic should be discussed at individual meetings. Likewise, selling in general represents too broad a topic, whereas selling benefits or opening new accounts or qualifying leads could be handled in 90 minutes.

Meeting Formats

If you manage a far-flung national or international sales force and meetings are held annually or biannually, you may want to schedule individual meetings with each salesperson or at least some salespeople. Especially with an international sales force, you will want to take advantage of their presence. Here you share concerns that do not affect the entire group. Have a list of items you wish to discuss, and don't let the meeting digress into trivia or small talk.

At such an individual meeting, you may wish to discuss a change in personnel at a customer's or a prospect's company that requires a visit. You may have brought for discussion expense reports, call reports, or a customer analysis containing puzzling information. The salesperson may wish to discuss fears that a competitor has added more service people in the territory.

Do not use these individual conferences at sales meetings for formal compensation reviews or formal performance evaluations. Such procedures require more than an hour and considerable preparation, and they conflict with the learning and social atmosphere of a sales meeting. Compensation reviews and performance evaluations deserve separate handling in a different setting.

If your sales force resides locally and you have sales meetings weekly or monthly, you may wish to schedule one or two salesperson meetings around the group event. With a local sales force, individual meetings can be arranged any time.

Salespeople probably learn more from casual conversations with each other than they do from presenters in formal gatherings. So at annual or semiannual national sales force meetings, afternoons (between formal individual meetings) and evenings should allow opportunities for socializing that might include golf

or spas. When salespeople get together, they do not discuss sports or politics; they discuss their jobs. "Whom did you sell what, and how?" Although order sizes inflate by a third, the participants share valuable information. Maintaining a casual atmosphere even with tight scheduling promotes socializing.

Don't overschedule the formal meetings. Salespeople have just so much capacity for learning. Allow for breaks every 90 minutes. Morning and afternoon sessions should not last more then three hours.

Don't jam too much material into too little time because salespeople will not retain it. Be realistic and selective about what you want to achieve. Concentrate on quality, not quantity.

Even at its most social moments, the gathering revolves around shoptalk, and for this reason—not to mention the additional costs involved—sales meetings work best without spouses or significant others. Also, some spouses resent and feel uncomfortable in the commercial atmosphere of a sales meeting. With younger sales forces most of the salespeople may be single and prefer to separate their work from their personal lives. Some spouses and significant others may have important, time-consuming jobs, including taking care of their families.

After weekly or monthly local sales force meetings, occasionally invite the group to lunch, dinner, golf, bowling, a social hour, or a team-building event. Even local sales forces benefit from the opportunity to socialize.

Official social gatherings range from casual breakfasts or lunches to more formal dinners at which speeches are made and awards presented to team-building exercises where people learn to work together. Generally, at a multiday national meeting, participants arrive in time for an opening dinner at which acquaintances are renewed, management delivers a welcoming address, and everyone unwinds. During dinner on the second evening, the president presents a state-of-the-company address, and this becomes another opportunity for management and the sales force to socialize. The state-of-the-company address gives some insight into the "big picture," enlightening the sale force as to overall corporate strategy, performance, and plans for the future.

A sales force that knows management on a personal basis becomes more involved. "I had dinner with the president of my company. He knew who I was. He is a pleasant fellow, and certainly has his hands full." A management team that knows the sales organization on a personal basis has more empathy. The company president might comment, "After spending several evenings with the sales force, I more fully appreciate their problems in reopening accounts we have lost because of late shipments. The salespeople are a noisy bunch, but they work hard at a difficult job." One of a sales meeting's many purposes is to allow management and the sales force to mingle. Be sure to allow time for this.

After dinner on the second evening, the company president presents awards for outstanding performance and prizes to winners of the sales contests. Outstanding performers should be officially recognized by management in front of their peers. If possible, have an employee take photographs of these events and e-mail copies to the participants.

Several times a year, after local sales force meetings, invite participants to a formal social gathering, usually lunch or dinner, with upper management. The benefits and format are the same as those for national sales meetings.

Consider having an official team-building exercise at your sales meeting. You organize the salespeople into groups that can compete against each other in everything from bowling to snowmobiling to problem solving.

Hopefully, everyone returns home from the sales meeting with new knowledge, skills, renewed vigor, and pleasant feelings. The sales force has learned, participated, and enjoyed. The company has said, "Thank you for doing a fine job" by attending to their needs and showing them a good time. A successful sales meeting is a celebration that strongly influences the salespeople's motivation and image of their company, which they pass on to your customers.

Sales Managers' Major Weaknesses/Mistakes in Training

- No checklist or agenda.
- Not devoting enough time; overdelegating.
- Using ride-withs to do personal selling, not training.
- Using sales meetings for results and administrative matters, not training.
- Not customizing training to each salesperson's needs.
- Not enough hands-on training and outside training.
- Too much product training; not enough customer, competitor, or sales skills training.

(Exhibits start on next page.)

Exhibit 6.1.   Field Coaching Salesperson Evaluation.

Name: _____

Date: _____

Success Profile

This report gives an overview of the major factors associated with good sales performance. Each factor is evaluated on the Performance Scale from poor to excellent on the graph below. Additional information and personal recommendations for improvement are provided in the paragraphs that follow.

Performance Scale

	Poor	Fair to Average	Good	Excellent
Product knowledge				
Account knowledge				
Presentation				
Preparation for calls				
Knowledge of customers' needs				
Visits have purpose				
Proposal was made: ☐ Yes ☐ No				
Personal rapport with customer				
Questioning technique				
Reporting				
Records				
Call frequency				
Appearance				
Closing skills				
Comfort level				
Attitude				
Working with others				
Gross sales				
Gross margins				
Overall performance				

Evaluation and Personal Recommendations

Primary areas needing improvement are listed below. Refer to the following pages of this report for more specific information and recommendations for improving your job performance.

☐ _____

☐ _____

☐ _____

☐ _____

☐ _____

☐ _____

Exhibit 6.2.   Seed Company Work-With Checklist.

Before Each Call—Precall Planning

- Establish objectives—for example, to write an order for a new variety of cuttings or seeds or sell a seasonal product such as poinsettias.
- Discuss what items the competition sells to this customer and why. What percentage of their business does our firm have?
- Agree on a strategy for reaching the objective—for example, sampling, discussing markups, merchandising, and techniques for closing.
- Discuss customer problems and needs.
- Discuss possible customer objections (for example, no production space) and how to overcome them (what is your slowest-selling variety). The what-ifs. What could go wrong?
- Agree on which of the customer's personal interests to open the conversation with and which probing questions to ask to discover needs.
- Review customer file, account history, usage sheet, and *profile*.
- Establish what role regional sales manager will play.
- Discuss what happened on the last visit and how long this call should take.
- Discuss long-term goals for this account.

During Each Call—Did the Sales Representative

- Establish rapport with a few minutes of nonbusiness personal interest conversation? Build relationship? Use information from profile?
- Know the names of decision makers and influencers?
- Review the usage sheet and what happened on the last visit?
- Look at what is being grown (production space) and bought (competitors)?
- Suggest items?
- Properly show a new product, a new variety of a present product, a seasonal product, or an existing product not presently carried by the customer?
- Ask questions to get the customer talking and discover needs, problems, and opportunities? What percentage of the time did the salesperson talk versus listen?
- Make benefit statements about the product (our product can save you time, waste, or money and it can increase margins, customer satisfaction, or shelf life)? Use power words?
- Quantify benefits in dollars?
- Answer any technical questions?
- Answer objections?

(Continued on next page.)

Exhibit 6.2.   *(Continued from previous page.)*

- Appear well organized? Focus on strengths?
- Use a reference sell and sales aids?
- Act as a consultant? Think like the customer?
- Properly ask for new business?

  o Review what was agreed on
  o Make partnership statement
  o Offer a choice, and so on

- Establish next action: "I will bring a sample or picture next week"?
- Work on growing our products with greenhouse supervisor? Retail sell-through?
- If appropriate, discuss overdue invoices or credit application?

After Each Call—Postcall Analysis

- Ask each sales representative what went well and what went poorly.
- Did he or she achieve his or her objective?
- What did he or she find out about the customer to add to the profile?
- Add your observations of what went well, what went poorly, and what to add to the profile.
- Ask for the salesperson's objectives and strategies for the next call on this customer. What are the long-range goals and future opportunities?
- What follow-up action is needed with customer? What corrective action is needed for sales representative?
- Estimate the actual amount of time spent with customer.

At the End of Each Ride-With Day

- Estimate how many hours you and the sales representative spent in front of customers versus in the car versus on the phone. Discuss how time in front of customers might be increased and made more productive. Compare mileage out in morning to final mileage at end of day.
- Evaluate the sales representative 1, 2, 3, 4 (1 is best) on each area of this checklist. Have the sales representative evaluate himself or herself. Discuss each area.
- Summarize the day—number of calls, number of cold calls, and markets and products focused on.
- Review with the sales representative any corrective action that needs to be taken based on your discussion of this checklist and a timetable for implementation.
- Send a follow-up letter putting this in writing.
- Ask how you were helpful.

Questions and Exercises for Chapter 6

- Prepare the agendas for your next four sales meetings or the agendas for the next four sales meetings of a company you are familiar with.
- Prepare a field coaching salesperson evaluation form for your firm or a firm you are familiar with.
- Prepare a work-with checklist for your firm or a firm you are familiar with.

Quiz for Chapter 6

1. Which of these statements is incorrect?
   a. The sales manager should ride with a salesperson only when asked.
   b. On joint sales calls, the sales manager's job is to get the order.
   c. After the call, the sales manager should give his or her critique first.

2. Which of these statements is correct? Sales meetings often fail when
   a. The attendees don't share the same skill level.
   b. The salespeople participate in presentations.
   c. The customers present some topics.
   d. The main purpose is to present results from the last quarter.

3. True or false?
   Occasionally the sales manager should conduct unannounced ride-withs.

4. True or false?
   Occasionally the sales manager's boss should ride with salespeople.

5. True or false?
   The sales manager should not only ride with direct field salespeople but also with channel partners.

6. Which of these are correct? After each customer visit on a ride-with, the sales manager should
   a. Ask the salesperson what went well and what went poorly.
   b. Tell the salesperson what went well and what went poorly.
   c. Review the objectives.
   d. Agree on follow–up.
   e. See if the salesperson adds new information to the customer profile.

7. Which of these are correct? At the end of each field coaching day, the sales manager should
   a. Ask the salesperson how many hours and what percent of the time was spent in front of customers.
   b. Ask the salesperson how many miles you drove that day.
   c. Ask the salesperson how much his or her expenses were for the day.
   d. Ask the salesperson, "What did you get out of our time together?"

8. Which of the following are benefits of sales meetings?
   a. They make salespeople feel useful, important, and worthwhile.
   b. They provide continual training.
   c. They allow salespeople to meet management.
   d. They create a setting in which to give salespeople recognition for achievement.
   e. They give salespeople a chance to complain.

9. Which of the following make sales meetings more interesting and productive?
   a. Salespeople presenting certain topics
   b. Inviting a customer to present certain topics
   c. Inviting channel partners to attend
   d. Inviting sales support personnel to attend
   e. Presenting administrative issues and sales results

10. True or false?
    At the end of the sales meeting and at the end of each topic at the sales meeting, salespeople should take a test on the subject matter and also evaluate the presenter.

PART FOUR

Sales Force Compensation

CHAPTER 7

Total Salesperson Compensation; The Mix Between Fixed and Performance Pay

To attract, retain, and motivate the best salespeople, pay them more than they are worth. Then, using proper techniques for hiring, training, organization, deployment, forecasting, planning, nonmonetary motivation, evaluations, and automation, make these well-paid salespeople worth more than what you pay them. The sales manager's job is to make the salespeople successful.

However, remember that money is not a universal incentive. Salespeople reach complacency plateaus and comfort zones. Even a commission-based compensation plan that rewards recurring revenue can create a phantom base salary. Today, salespeople have two-income families and other income-producing assets such as real estate, stocks, and bonds. Also, a salesperson might have satisfied his or her need for compensation or be approaching retirement. In addition, career salespeople who have no interest in management or no opportunity for management require nonmonetary motivation. In Chapters 12 and 13 on motivation, we will discuss how to engage salespeople and maximize their productivity by satisfying their nonmonetary needs for recognition, growth, challenge and achievement, usefulness, belonging, and leadership.

Sales force compensation involves deciding how much your successful salespeople should earn in total dollars, the target compensation, and then what portion of that total should be fixed versus performance pay. Total compensation depends on the complexity of the salesperson's selling tasks. The mix between performance and fixed pay depends on (1) balancing salesperson and company needs; (2) the type of salesperson you wish to attract; (3) the salesperson's influence on the sale; (4) the type of product or service sold; and (5) rewarding the salesperson's specific actions or results most important to the company's success. Sales force compensation involves not only salary, commission, and bonus but also fringe benefits and reimbursed expenses.

A company's sales force compensation plan communicates to salespeople where management wants them to focus, but this compensation plan may not change salespeople's behavior. For example, a nonresidential, commercial security service offered customers smoke and motion detectors plus door and window sensors. The firm changed its compensation system to pay salespeople a higher commission and bonus for leases rather than for outright purchases, for renewal of central monitoring contracts, and for new accounts, because these results and activities drove profits. However, salespeople did little prospecting for new accounts, contract renewals remained low, and leases were seldom offered. This firm did not properly hire and train salespeople for these tasks, and although the compensation program gave a strong message on where to concentrate, the salespeople did not alter their behavior. A good compensation plan loses its effectiveness when applied to a weak or improperly trained sales force or when territories do not contain equal potential. Each piece in the sales management process impacts the other pieces and affects the total system.

Some managers abdicate their sales management responsibility by rationalizing that the compensation system will direct all salespeople's behavior. The ultimate example of this type of thinking is the company that compensates salespeople on 100 percent performance pay, which may be a commission based on revenue or margins. In such a situation, the manager often does not spend enough time and thought hiring, training, planning, motivating, or evaluating salespeople, claiming that 100 percent commission will self-select the right people and self-direct them to work hard or smart, train, and evaluate themselves. These are dangerous assumptions.

Each year successful sales managers reevaluate the sales force compensation program. Business is a dynamic process. The future is a moving target. In the twenty-first century the landscape changes quickly and often. As an agent of change, the sales manager must expect and manage change. If you were to totally reconstruct the compensation program using the model in this chapter would it look the same? In the last year, how have your products, customers, competitors, technology, salespeople, strategy, goals, the sales cycle, customer decision-making process, and prices changed? Does the compensation program reflect these changes? Since a compensation system acts as a natural filter in attracting and retaining salespeople, annual changes should be modest rather than dramatic. Increasing compensation for a new product or revenue growth while decreasing it on matured products or previous revenue levels represent acceptable adjustments. Going from 100 percent salary to 100 percent commission will create confusion and salesperson turnover. Admitting the mistake by changing back to the original program proves difficult like putting toothpaste back in the tube. Compensation changes represent a very emotional issue for salespeople, which we discuss later in the chapter when we talk about implementation.

The compensation system is often a legacy issue, inherited from a predecessor and continued year after year, or it follows industry tradition or it is copied from a competitor. But a follow-the-loser or why-make-a-change strategy does not work in the type of dynamic business environment described in the previous paragraph. A sales manager, like a factory manager, must strive for continuous improvement.

To achieve continuous improvement and a best-of-breed compensation program, test it annually by using the models discussed in this chapter. Does your compensation program reward positive action and superior results important to the success of your company? Does the mix between fixed and performance pay reflect the type salesperson you wish to attract and the salesperson's influence on the sale? Does the total level of compensation reflect the complexity of the sale? What action can you take to correct any disconnects?

The compensation models and methodologies discussed in this chapter and the next apply to field salespeople, in-house salespeople, and telesales people. Use the same criteria for each group in deciding on total compensation and the mix between fixed and performance pay.

Types of Sales Force Compensation

Salespeople receive direct compensation, fringe benefits, and reimbursed expenses as part of their total pay package. Direct compensation consists of fixed pay (salary), performance pay (commission), and deferred performance pay (bonus). Fringe benefits range from mandatory Social Security, Medicare, and unemployment insurance to expected medical and health plans to optional profit sharing, stock options, and tuition reimbursement. Reimbursed expenses range from salespeople paying their own expenses, to employers' sharing of these costs, to total salesperson reimbursement on all travel, entertainment, communication, and office expenses. The key is giving salespeople an economic incentive to spend wisely. This chapter and the next deal with all these alternatives in some detail.

Total Compensation

In constructing a compensation program, you first decide on the total dollars of compensation for a successful or top salesperson, the target compensation. Your next decision is dividing those dollars between fixed and performance pay. The total compensation appropriate for a successful salesperson is determined by the complexity of the sale and type of selling. You define a successful salesperson as someone who ranks in the top 25 percent of your sales force in terms of results (annual dollars of sales or margin and growth).

A successful or top salesperson involved in a long, complex, multistep, consultative, partnership sales process should receive over $100,000 annually in total direct compensation regardless of the mix between fixed and performance pay. These salespeople generally hunt "big game" and have titles such as "territory consultant" or "key account executive."

As previously mentioned in Chapter 2 under buyer behavior, salespeople selling enterprisewide supply chain software and services, complex medical devices or procedures, B2B e-commerce sites, complex financial services, or telephone systems, all of which involve long complex sales cycles of big-ticket items, generally receive total annual direct compensation in excess of $100,000. Such a salesperson often sells a product or service to a one-time, first-time, new systems buyer.

A successful salesperson involved in multilevel relationship sales, which includes modified rebuys of existing systems, which may require some postsale service, generally receives $60,000 to $100,000 annually in total direct compensation regardless of the mix between fixed and performance pay. These salespeople use more transactional sales to hunt or harvest "smaller game" and have titles such as "territory rep" or "account manager." For example, modified rebuy, multilevel relationship salespeople selling equipment and supplies to dentists, tires to truck fleet managers, semiconductors to consumer electronic firms, contract programming to IT managers, home health care to hospitals, or pharmaceuticals to doctors generally receive annual direct compensation between $60,000 and $100,000.

A successful salesperson involved in route sales of homogeneous products or services, requiring a multitude of daily customer visits and feature selling and order taking from a person delegated by the buyer's decision maker generally receives under $60,000 a year in total direct compensation, regardless of the mix between fixed and performance pay. Salespeople selling and servicing grocery stores with food products, drugstores with giftware, midsized businesses with temporary help services, and manufacturers with die casting or injecting molding products generally receive annual direct compensation under $60,000.

Where does your firm fit, and does total direct compensation reflect these criteria? Is there a disconnect? If so, why? Can it be corrected?

Most firms have salespeople in at least two of these classifications. Should they be paid differently depending on the type of selling and complexity of the sale? Most firms also have salespeople whose duties include several levels of complexity, but one remains more dominant. If your firm has hunters and farmers and consultative, relationship, and transactional salespeople, consider different levels of total compensation and different mixtures of fixed and performance pay for each group.

Salesperson Loyalty and Control

Some managers claim that the higher the total dollars of direct compensation, the more control they exercise over their salespeople's behavior in such areas as changing territory boundaries or sales policies. Other managers claim that the higher the fixed pay as a percent of total compensation, the more control they exercise over their salespeople. Many managers who should pay more performance compensation to reward specific results important to the success of their firms rationalize not doing this by claiming such actions would reduce their influence over the salesperson. Is salesperson loyalty and control a function of dollars of total compensation or fixed versus performance pay? Will salesperson turnover decrease with a larger percent of fixed pay or more total pay? My experience points to total dollars of compensation as allowing the manager to more easily direct a salesperson.

SALES FORCE COMPENSATION DATA AND SOURCES

The *Watson Wyatt Worldwide Report on Sales and Marketing Personnel Compensation, 2005/2006*, published by Watson Wyatt Data Services, Rochelle Park, New Jersey, surveyed 5,315 U.S. organizations in 103 industry classifications and collected data on 58,135 incumbents. The report is 1,000 pages long.

The report found that total annual cash compensation (salary, commission, and bonus) for consumer goods sales representatives averaged $59,000, had a median of $55,300, and a weighted average of $72,000. Consumer goods categories included manufacturing, durable, nondurable, utilities and energy, retail and wholesale, services, health care, and insurance. On the other hand, total annual cash compensation for industrial products and services averaged $69,500, had a median of $63,600, and a weighted average of $65,500. Senior sales representatives for consumer products had an average total annual cash compensation of $89,700, median of $87,500, and a weighted average of $156,400. Senior sales representatives for industrial products had an average total annual cash compensation of $88,100, median of $77,600, and a weighted average of $78,400. Sales trainees for consumer and industrial products averaged total annual cash compensation of $40,700, median of $41,300, and a weighted average of $38,100. National accounts managers for consumer and industrial products averaged total annual cash compensation of $104,900, median of $104,200, and a weighted average of $110,600.[1]

Exhibits 7.1 and 7.2, at the end of this chapter, contain 2004 and 2005 salesperson compensation data for the consumer products industry and the high-technology industry. The data were collected and analyzed by Western Management Group of Los Gatos, California (www.wmgnet.com). The data reflect information from 55 large and midsized consumer products firms and 85 large and midsized high-technology firms. As you can see from the data, total compensation rises as the complexity of the sale rises. As you can also see from the data, high-technology salespeople at all levels earn greater compensation than those in comparable positions selling consumer products. And also, as you can see from the data, high-technology salespeople receive a higher percentage of their total compensation as performance or incentive pay than salespeople in the consumer products industry. Base pay for the two industries are quite similar.

Sales and Marketing Management magazine reported on a 3,000-respondent 2005 sales compensation survey performed by Equation Research. The survey further confirms the numbers from Watson Wyatt Data Services and Western Management Group. The average total compensation for top sales staffers in 2005 was $157,234, for midlevel performers $94,872, and for low performers $64,844. Fifty to 60 percent of the total compensation was fixed pay for all three groups.[2]

Choosing the Correct Mix of Performance and Fixed Pay

The mix between performance and fixed pay depends on (1) balancing the company's and salespeople's needs; (2) the type of salesperson you wish to attract; (3) the salesperson's influence on the sale; (4) the type of product or service sold; and (5) rewarding the salesperson's specific actions or results most important to the company's success.

COMPANY'S AND SALESPEOPLE'S NEEDS

The correct mix between performance and fixed direct compensation must reflect the company's and salespeople's needs. Basically, the company needs to attract, retain, and motivate salespeople who produce a desired level of sales at a cost that generates profits and allows necessary percentage returns on sales and invested capital. Good salespeople need a compensation plan that relieves them of basic financial worries, gives them pride in what they earn, reflects their qualifications and experience, and equals or betters that of the competition. Compensating salespeople on the basis of the cost of replacing them—or just the cost of keeping them from leaving—does not satisfy these needs. Generally, you will obtain better results with fewer but more qualified and more highly paid salespeople than you will with a larger sales force that includes less qualified, lower-paid people.

Satisfying the company's and salespeople's needs also requires the compensation plan to embody simplicity, fairness, and stability, and must reflect the company culture, strategy, and position on the growth curve.

Simplicity and Fairness

A universal objective for all sales compensation plans ought to be simplicity. Often salespeople do not understand or remember complicated plans, and companies have difficulty administering them. A compensation plan that pays different commission rates and bonuses for different products or services in different months based on various prices would be difficult for a salesperson to understand and difficult for the accounting department to administer.

A good sales compensation plan must have fairness and equity built into it. For example, orders that a salesperson's customers phone, fax, or e-mail directly to the office should be credited to the salespeople's account just as if they had been written in the field. Also, nothing dulls a salesperson's enthusiasm more than "house accounts." Taking lucrative accounts out of a territory for handling by management or family members hurts morale.

Channel conflicts challenge many firms' ability to provide fairness. Today most firms will reach their customers through multiple, hybrid sales channels, including a direct field sales force, telesales, e-commerce and Web sites, distributors, brokers, and independent sales representative organizations. Does the direct field salesperson receive credit and full performance pay for e-commerce, telesales, and distributor orders placed by his or her assigned customers? In such a situation, is performance pay split or reduced? The present trend is to pay full performance pay to both parties, but you must still establish detailed guidelines on channel conflicts. Most firms accept but do not encourage channel conflict because though inevitable, it hurts salespeople's morale. When Hewitt Associates surveyed 120 Fortune 1000 firms, 61 percent reported using multiple channels.[3]

Stability

A good compensation plan provides a certain level of stability so that salespeople have some downside protection for their incomes. The income of a salesperson who loses a large account might decline by 25 percent, but not by 50 percent or to a level that threatens his or her ability to meet mortgage payments. Such a salesperson requires time to obtain another major account. The income of salespeople selling to cyclical industries such as the auto, aircraft, steel, and farm equipment industries should be less in bad times than in good, but not so much less as to threaten their ability to put food on the table. These salespeople must survive the bad times in order to write orders when business improves. Rewards must reflect results, but a certain minimum level must be assured.

Company Culture and Strategy

In selecting the mix between fixed and performance pay for salespeople, consider your company culture and strategy. Is the company culture driven by efficient operations, cost reduction, or market or customer needs? Market- and customer-driven firms often choose a higher mix of fixed pay, while operations- and cost-driven firms choose a higher mix of variable or performance pay.

If your company strategy is to maximize market share or customer share, profit or revenue growth, these results and the activities that create these results must be rewarded. If your company strategy is to reduce customer turnover or employee turnover, your salesperson's compensation plan must reflect this.

Sales force compensation plans that do not reflect company culture and strategy eventually create conflicts between management and the salespeople. Take some time to understand the culture and strategy.

Position on the Growth Curve

In selecting the mix between fixed and performance pay for salespeople, consider your company's or business unit's position on the growth curve. Start-ups generally have a volume-driven, uniform, commission compensation plan. High-growth and early-stage firms rely more on a bonus tied to revenue, profit, and product mix that differentiates between one type of sale and one type of salesperson and another. Mature companies also rely more on a bonus, but one that is tied to market share. As firms mature and move from start-up to growth, the changing compensation plan attracts different types of salespeople, which can cause turnover. Start-ups must keep this in mind.

TYPE OF SALESPERSON YOU WISH TO ATTRACT

The mix of performance versus fixed pay acts as a natural filter in attracting certain types of salespeople. Review the candidate profile you prepared for hiring the sales force (see Exhibit 2.5, Chapter 2). Pay particular attention to the desired personal characteristics. Fixed-pay-oriented compensation plans generally attract salespeople who are team players, ambitious to climb the executive ladder, steady rather than top performers, farmers rather than hunters, more professional than commercial, and more comfortable selling presold products. Once hired, salaried salespeople often develop rigid but comfortable routines and often expect considerable sales assistance from management.

Performance-pay-weighted compensation plans generally attract aggressive career salespeople, hunters rather than farmers, and those with little or no ambition for promotion into management. These salespeople are lone wolves, top producers but erratic, who are more interested in the sale than the selling technique. Sometimes these characteristics strain customer and company relations or result in a salesperson who prefers to highlight a large territory rather than saturate a smaller one. Channel partners primarily use performance pay and thus attract this type of salesperson. Does your firm's compensation plan attract the type of salesperson described in the candidate profile? If not, should you change the compensation plan or the candidate profile?

SALESPERSON'S INFLUENCE ON THE SALE

The more influence the salesperson has on the sale, the more performance pay should represent as a percent of total direct compensation. Closed bidding; requests for quotes (RFQs), branded presold, heavily advertised goods or services; team selling; rigid product or service specifications; the importance of price—all these things lessen the salesperson's influence on the sale. Also, people selling to government agencies or other businesses that require bids operate in conditions with no adequate measure of performance. Was the salesperson or the bid responsible for the sale? Here again, salary proves most appropriate. On the other hand, in certain situations the salesperson's persuasion and creativity strongly influence the customer's choice between vendors. In such a situation commission and bonus prove most appropriate. How much influence do your salespeople have on the sale, and does your compensation plan—fixed versus performance pay—reflect this?

A branded men's shirt company with heavily advertised products that are presold by management and are given a large share of each department store's shelf space pays its salespeople 80 percent salary. Its unbranded competitors, who fight for shelf space and orders, pay salespeople primarily on commission and bonus.

A company with all fixed pay means the salesperson has little or no influence on the sale. A company with all performance pay means the salespeople have a great deal or total influence on the sale. Often these two extremes represent industry tradition or company legacy issues rather than the salesperson's true influence on the sale.

TYPE OF PRODUCT OR SERVICE SOLD

Certain types of products and selling lend themselves to a higher weighting of performance pay, while others lend themselves to more fixed pay. Presold, branded, heavily advertised products or services; cyclical, long, complex sales cycles, higher-ticket items; team selling, postsale service—all lend themselves to more fixed pay. Nontechnical, unsophisticated products or services, with lower unit prices, modified rebuys that require constant customer revisits for reorders—all lend themselves to a higher weighting of performance pay. The type of product also reflects the salesperson's influence on the sale. For example, sales of durable goods—such as machine tools or equipment for utilities, which fluctuate dramatically with business cycles, require considerable time working with customer engineers, purchasing agents, and plant managers to make a sale, and often require the salesperson to be accompanied by a sales engineer and involve the salesperson's assistance with installation—lend themselves to fixed pay. Machine tools or equipment for public utilities, like many big-ticket technical products or new systems that involve few orders but many dollars and long complex sales cycles—those situations lend themselves to a large portion of salaried sales compensation. Items presold through national advertising such as pharmaceuticals, soap, toothpaste, liquor, and petroleum lend themselves to a large portion of salaried sales compensation. In these situations the salesperson functions as order-taker, not active seller, and he or she has less influence on the sale. Does your compensation system reflect the type product or service being sold?

Some new salespeople require salaries during their training period because they could not survive financially on the basis of their performance. Salespeople assigned to new territories with no established business require a salary until they can build up the volume.

Sometimes in considering the type of salesperson, the amount of the salesperson's influence, and the type of product, this gives you conflicting signals to use in designing the mix between performance pay and fixed salaries. For example, the product has a long complex sales cycle, but the salesperson must do value-added selling. You need a team player to coordinate sales with engineering, but you need an aggressive person to pursue new business. In such a situation, analyze what factors are most important in driving revenues and profits. Give those factors the most weight in determining the mix between fixed and performance pay.

REWARDING POSITIVE ACTION AND RESULTS

As mentioned, the total dollars of direct compensation must reflect the complexity of the sales process. The mix between performance pay and fixed pay must reflect the general corporate strategy and objectives, company and salespeople's needs, the type of salesperson you wish to attract, the salesperson's influence on the sale, and the type product sold. However, most important, the sales force compensation plan must reward actions and results on the part of salespeople that are most important to the company's success. Salespeople with better results in these key areas must receive superior pay. Most companies' sales force compensation plans do not meet these criteria. Often a disconnect exists between strategic corporate objectives and the activities or results that salespeople are rewarded for. To prevent this type of disconnect, once a year review your firm's sales force compensation plan: Does it meet the criteria stated above? If not, why not? What can you change to better align it?

What positive actions and results on the part of your salespeople are most important to your firm's success? Refer to the job description that contains a list of a salesperson's duties. If you plan to reward people for these activities and results, you require metrics to measure them. Generally a commission is used to reward results, and a bonus is used to reward activities or exceeding goals. A group bonus might also be used to reward teamwork.

In September 2005, Hewitt Associates asked sales and human resource executives at 59 Fortune 1000 firms what positive action and results they rewarded salespeople for. Twenty-four percent said revenue, 15 percent revenue growth,

10 percent each said profit, volume in units, new customer revenue, and new or strategic product revenue.[4]

Pharmaceutical firms reward salespeople for market share gain in particular medications. Several market research services track prescriptions written by doctors and filled by pharmacists. A bonus is paid for reaching specified levels of market share.

In another example, a reform math K-6 textbook firm rewards salespeople for opening new school districts and for further penetrating existing customers. The company pays a bonus on the opening order and a progressive commission rate on revenues generated within a district. As revenues within each district increase, so does the commission rate.

A distributor that sells a broad line of containers to a wide variety of manufacturers rewards salespeople for account and territory profitability. For each customer and territory, all direct manufacturing (product costs) and sales expenses are subtracted from revenue to arrive at dollars of margin. A commission is paid on these margin dollars. Salespeople are rewarded for selling higher margin products at list price and for controlling sales expenses.

A food distributor pays its salespeople a progressive commission rate to reward growth. The rate on this year's sales until they meet last year's total is 6 percent. Once a salesperson exceeds this threshold, the commission rate jumps to 8 percent. The food distributor also pays a bonus for collecting overdue accounts receivable. For salespeople with established business, commission often loses its motivational impact. The established business functions like an annuity or phantom salary, so you require a progressive rate to reward growth.

Utilities that have difficulty rewarding salespeople based on results pay a bonus for customer satisfaction as measured by customer surveys. Firms selling to mass merchants often reward salespeople for in-service training of retailers, amount of shelf space, stock taking, or proper merchandising. All these activities lead to a sale.

If salespeople have a pricing window and/or discretion to give discounts, allowances, and promotions, a portion of their compensation should be based on dollars of gross margin rather than revenue for their territory. Similarly, if you wish to reward the sale of higher-margin items, you might want a compensation system that pays a commission on dollars of gross margin or pays a higher commission rate on revenues of one product line versus another. A semiconductor equipment manufacturer pays a different commission rate for equipment and spare parts sales. It pays a bonus for selling postsale service contracts. A women's apparel manufacturer pays a commission rate on gross margin dollars because salespeople have some discretion to negotiate price.

If your firm has a long, complex sales cycle with many steps from search to purchase, consider paying a bonus for activities that lead to a sale or for moving

major customers or prospects from one step to the next. Salespeople selling big-ticket items involving long complex sales cycles don't necessarily respond to rewards based on revenues because it may take years to make a sale. A financial software firm, which sells real-time data, gives bonuses to salespeople based on the number of demos, trials, and presentations. A management consulting firm gives bonuses to salespeople for identifying decision makers, making presentations to CEOs, CFOs, and CIOs, and obtaining requests for proposals.

A home-health-care provider wanted its compensation plan to reward teamwork. Major branches had a salesperson calling on physicians, another calling on third-party payers, and a third calling on hospitals. All three salespeople received 25 percent of their compensation based on the branch's results using metrics that included the number of patients, product mix, margins, and customer satisfaction.

A marketing services firm selling to pharmaceutical companies rewards salespeople for lateral selling and customer share. The more product managers a salesperson sells within each pharma, firm, the higher their commission rate and dollars of bonus. Similarly the wider the variety of services sold to each pharma customer, the higher the commission rate and dollars of bonus. This rewards salespeople for action and results important to the firm's success.

To prevent making your compensation plan too complicated, limit the performance pay metrics to three actions or results, all of which are controllable by the individual.

NEW PRODUCT PLACEMENT

Many firms reward new product placement through their compensation plans. A salesperson exerts the most influence on a customer's decision during a product or service's introduction and the least during a product or service's decline. Some firms pay a higher level and rate of performance pay on new products and a lesser level and rate of performance pay on mature or declining products or markets. For new products or systems sales, a business-to-business software firm rewards salespeople with higher-than-normal commission rates. With growing or maturing software, salespeople receive a commission based on volume and also a bonus based on gross margin dollars. On declining, older software, a small bonus is paid for maintaining gross margin dollars. This compensation system reflects a product or service's life cycle but could get overly complicated. This software firm has a 60/40 overall mix between fixed salary and performance pay.

If new product placement represents an important corporate objective, consider rewarding superior results with special compensation. A cruise line continually offers new destinations and tours. Salespeople call on travel agents and receive a commission based on revenue generated from their territory. On their new cruise offerings, the sales manager gives salespeople a "placement" quota based on past history with each travel agent. A certain number of agents must send a certain number of travelers on these new cruises to meet the quota. Once that threshold occurs, commission rates increase dramatically on additional revenue over the threshold for these new cruises.

A major high-energy candy bar manufacturer pays salespeople no commission on the initial placement of new products. However, they pay a double commission on all repeat orders within the next 90 days. This compensation program recognizes the salesperson's impact on retail sell-through.

TRANSACTIONAL VERSUS CONSULTATIVE SELLING

Using the criteria discussed earlier for selecting between fixed and performance pay, results for salespeople involved in consultative selling and new account acquisition received a high commission- or bonus-oriented variable pay mix. Salespeople involved in transactional sales will receive rewards in fewer performance areas than those involved in the more complex consultative sales. Salespeople involved in farming or maintenance will receive less variable pay than those involved in hunting or new account acquisition. Depending on their roles, salespeople within the same firm may have compensation plans with different mixes of fixed and performance pay.

SUPPORT PERSONNEL

A sales manager must be concerned not only about proper compensation for direct salespeople but also for sales support personnel. If your firm supports direct salespeople with product specialists, sales engineers, or customer service representatives, consider performance pay for these support people. A miniature high-tech transformer firm pays sales support people 25 percent of their total compensation based on performance. Each product specialist, sales engineer, and customer service representative is assigned to specific direct salespeople and accounts. Twenty-five percent of their total compensation is based on the total revenue, new accounts and present account growth of the salespeople he or she supports. When Hewitt Associates surveyed sales and human resource executives at 61 Fortune 1000 firms in 2005, 66 percent reported having a variable or performance pay plan for sales support positions up from 30 percent in 1998. However, 80 percent reported that the variable pay was part of an all-employee incentive pay plan.[5]

CHANNEL PARTNERS

Brokers, distributors, and outside sales representative organizations generally receive 100 percent performance pay (discounts on commissions) from the firms whose products they sell. However, channel partners need specific rewards for positive action and results important to the success of your firm. For your indirect sales force to become partners rather than adversaries, they require training and correct monetary incentives. Apply the same criteria for your indirect sales force that you did for the direct people. A storm window manufacturer pays its stocking distributors a year-end bonus based on maintaining certain levels of inventory in key items, selling a certain product mix, and exceeding their revenue goals. An electronic component manufacturer pays its indirect independent sales representatives a commission based on gross margin rather than revenue to encourage selling higher-margin products and then a higher commission rate for growth. Generally your channel partners compensate their salespeople with a plan similar to the one you use to compensate the channel partners.

Running the Numbers and Obtaining Sales Force Agreement

Before deciding on annual alterations to your compensation program, prepare spreadsheets of what each salesperson earned last year compared to various new scenarios for this year. If this year's company results mirror last year's, how much will the new altered compensation plan cost in total dollars compared to last year? What will be the mix between fixed and variable costs compared to last year? Run the same analysis for each salesperson. Then run a best- and worst-case revenue scenario for the firm and each salesperson. Which salespeople earn more, which less, and what percent of revenue does total salesperson compensation represent? Which plan maximizes dollars of contribution margin over time? How will you handle the salespeople whose earnings decline? Will guarantees be necessary? Do the right salespeople who perform activities and results you want to reward receive more compensation? Does this plan meet company objectives? These spreadsheets represent a reality check. Share these spreadsheets with human resources and top management. Ask for their agreement on the changes to prevent surprises during the year. Do this analysis for each of the alternative sales force compensation plans you are considering.

In running the numbers, analyze what percent of the sales force earns the targeted compensation and what percent exceeds it. Targeted compensation depends on the complexity of the sale, a concept discussed earlier in this chapter. Compare actual compensation for your salespeople to industry competition. Generally you want 50 to 60 percent of the sales force at or above the targeted compensation and 10 percent clearly above it. In other words, 50 to 60 percent should reach the expected level of performance or 100 percent of goal.

As mentioned earlier in this chapter, in order to minimize fixed expenses and emphasize volume growth, start-up firms and early-stage firms often choose plans that emphasize performance or variable pay over fixed pay. However, often this mix does not reflect the type salesperson they need, the specific action and results that require rewarding, or the salesperson's influence on the sale. So after a few years, they find themselves with the wrong type of salesperson pursuing inappropriate activities to support future growth.

Change Management and Implementation

One way to sell compensation changes to the sales force involves including them in the decision-making process. Select a representative group to participate in the analysis, suggest changes, and anticipate problems. The salespeople must understand their role is advisory but important. Management must understand that the salesperson committee does not guarantee acceptance of compensation changes by the salespeople.

In changing salesperson compensation, you require a steering committee composed of senior business, sales and marketing executives, and a design team with members from sales, marketing, human resources, finance, sales administrative, and information technology. The design team makes critical incentive program decisions and champions implementation and communication efforts.

Most salespeople resist changes in compensation and territory boundaries because they fear the unknown. As managers, we can expect resistance, denial, immobilization, bargaining, depression, and anger from the salespeople. As managers, we must be sensitive to these very emotional concerns and sell the benefits of change through communication, education, and motivation. Changes to the compensation plan should never surprise the sales force and never be sprung on them at a sales meeting.

One additional way to address these fears is for the sales manager to show each salesperson how the new compensation plan can increase annual pay. Under the new compensation plan, what activities and results on the salesperson's part will increase his or her compensation? Consider sharing the individual salesperson's spreadsheets showing the potential earnings with the new plan based on last year's results. If appropriate, you may want to test the new program in a few territories.

Annual performance pay changes must be announced before the year begins so that salespeople have time to adjust their thinking and activities. Many companies do not announce changes until well into the first quarter. This lowers morale and makes any changes more difficult to sell. Changes in the compensation plan should be discussed with each salesperson individually.

Performance pay that rewards positive action and results can create windfall earnings for salespeople. Be aware that additional compensation usually upsets fellow nonsales employees, who feel entitled to more money. In some years, top salespeople earn more than their sales manager or top management. To prevent this, some firms cap earnings, raise future quotas, or create declining rewards as salespeople move into windfall levels. However, such action negates the positive communication and motivation of performance pay. Salespeople lose their trust of such firms, and top performers may leave. Estimate the probability of a windfall and discuss this with top management to prevent surprises. Establish a plan for dealing with it. If necessary, use thresholds rather than regressive performance pay. A tier-two supplier of automotive electronics allows salespeople to earn windfalls, but it defers payments over a certain dollar amount to next year and the year after. This often lowers the salesperson's income tax rate, lowers the firm's turnover of top performers, and prevents complacency and disappointment the following year. A steel service center allows salespeople to earn windfalls but pays part of the windfall with stock options or places part of the windfall in the salesperson's retirement plan. Because the steel industry often experiences business cycles, this program satisfies the salesperson's and the company's needs.

Windfall salesperson earnings can produce unexpected outcomes. A commission salesperson from a small industrial gear company increased his income 10-fold on one order from a conveyor concern. He used the six-figure commission check to buy out the family that owned the small gear company.

(Exhibits start on next page.)

Exhibit 7.1.   Median Annual Pay for Sales Professionals in the Consumer Products Industry.

Position	Base 2005	Percent of Total	Base 2004	Percent of Total	Incentive 2005	Percent of Total	Incentive 2004	Percent of Total	Total Compensation	
									2005	2004
Account manager/sales representative, consultant	$87,000	85%	$68,338	81%	$17,446	17%	$14,861	18%	$102,026	$84,160
Account manager/sales representative, specialist	$70,385	83%	$67,039	81%	$13,356	16%	$13,356	16%	$84,826	$82,506
Account manager/sales representative, midlevel	$54,400	84%	$54,500	85%	$10,700	16%	$9,113	14%	$64,859	$64,397

Source: "2005 Consumer Products Sales Compensation Survey" and "2004 Consumer Products Sales Compensation Survey." Copyright © 2005 and © 2004 Western Management Group. Reprinted by permission of Western Management Group, Los Gatos, California.

Exhibit 7.2.   Median Annual Pay for Sales Professionals in the High-Technology Industry.

Position	Base 2005	Percent of Total	Base 2004	Percent of Total	Incentive 2005	Percent of Total	Incentive 2004	Percent of Total	Total Compensation	
									2005	2004
Account manager/sales representative, consultant	$102,959	57%	$92,808	61%	$81,526	45%	$57,341	38%	$181,489	$152,770
Account manager/sales representative, specialist	$84,035	53%	$67,039	52%	$78,727	49%	$51,946	40%	$159,988	$129,300
Account manager/sales representative, midlevel	$72,574	52%	$78,816	73%	$73,121	52%	$41,984	39%	$139,777	$108,183
Account manager/sales representative, intermediate	$52,724	60%	$46,700	57%	$38,229	44%	$34,454	42%	$87,770	$82,211

Source: "2006 High-Technology Sales and Service Compensation Survey" and "2005 High-Technology Sales and Service Compensation Survey." Copyright © 2006 and © 2005 Western Management Group. Reprinted with permission of Western Management Group, Los Gatos, California.

Questions and Exercises for Chapter 7

- What positive action and superior result on the part of salespeople are important to the success of your firm or a firm you are familiar with? How does the compensation system reward salespeople for this?
- How much influence do your salespeople or salespeople in a firm you are familiar with have on making the sale? Is this reflected in the amount of performance pay versus fixed pay?
- How complex is the sales process for your product or service or a product or service you are familiar with? Does total salesperson compensation reflect this?
- Why does your product or service or one you are familiar with lend itself to performance pay versus fixed pay?
- What type salesperson is most successful at your firm or a firm you are familiar with? Review the candidate profile. How does the compensation program attract these people?
- When was the last time you revised your firm's sales force compensation program?

Quiz for Chapter 7

1. Which of these factors influence the level of sales force compensation?
   a. Complexity of sale
   b. Type of salesperson you wish to attract
   c. Salesperson's influence on the sale
   d. Type of product or service you sell

2. Which of these factors influence the mix between fixed and performance pay for salespeople?
   a. Complexity of sale
   b. Type of salesperson you wish to attract
   c. Salesperson's influence on the sale
   d. Type of product or service you sell

3. True or false?
   A company's sales force compensation plan communicates to salespeople where management wants them to focus, but this compensation plan may not change salespeople's behavior.

4. True or false?
    Each year successful sales managers reevaluate the sales force compensation program.

5. Which of these are part of a salesperson's direct compensation?
    a. Salary
    b. Commission
    c. Bonus
    d. Reimbursed expenses
    e. Fringe benefits

6. A salesperson's prominence in the sale is influenced by which of these factors?
    a. Team selling
    b. Closed bids
    c. Branding
    d. Selling skills

7. Which of these positive actions and results should salesperson compensation reward?
    a. Revenue growth
    b. Profit growth
    c. Number of new accounts
    d. Customer satisfaction
    e. Teamwork

8. True or false?
    A salesperson exerts the most influence on a customer's decision during a product or service introduction.

9. When sales force compensation is changed, you should run spreadsheets for each salesperson to analyze which of these factors?
    a. Which salespeople will earn more and which less under the new program
    b. What percent of the sales force will earn the targeted compensation or reach 100 percent of quota
    c. The total sales force compensation costs in dollars and as a percent of sales
    d. Which salespeople to terminate

10. The sales manager sells changes in the compensation program to the salespeople by performing which of these actions?
    a. Testing the new program in one territory
    b. Including some salespeople in the decision-making process

c. Having top management announce the changes
d. Selling the benefits for each salesperson

Notes

1. *Sales and Marketing Personnel Compensation 2005/2006.* Copyright © Watson Wyatt Data Services. Reprinted by Permission.
2. "2005 High Technology Sales and Services Compensation Survey," Copyright © 2005 Western Management Group, Los Gatos, California. Reprinted by permission of Western Management Group.
3. *Hot Topics in Sales Management and Sales Compensation 2005.* Copyright © 2005 Hewitt Associates LLC. Reprinted by permission of Hewitt Associates.
4. Ibid.
5. Ibid.

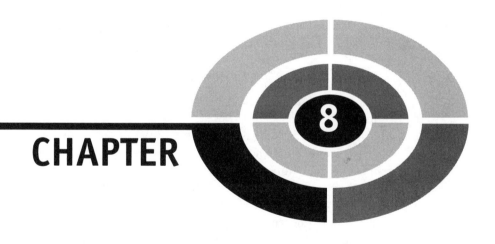

CHAPTER 8

Salary, Commission, and Bonus Plans and Reimbursed Expenses

Salary Plans

Salary provides salespeople with a fixed amount of pay per period regardless of their recent activities or results. Nonetheless, when results exceed or fall short of expectations, you can adjust the salary accordingly. However, the reward for good performance or penalty for weak results is not immediate or direct.

For a national sales force, salary will reflect not only past results and longevity with a firm but possibly skills and experience also, as well as where the salesperson lives. Within the same firm all other factors being equal, a salesperson located in a high cost of living area such as New York or San Francisco will receive a higher salary than a person with a similar job and experience who is living in Omaha.

Straight salary or heavily weighted salary plans provide the salesperson with a steady income but do not stress the immediate importance of writing orders. Salary emphasizes the importance of nonselling activities and encourages the salesperson to engage in these activities. Often a salesperson must perform services after the sale that will not necessarily result in a reorder. For example, the salesperson for a small concern renting expensive tropical plants to offices may be required under the rental agreement to check and treat the plants monthly. A salesperson selling software might be required to train customer employees how to use the software.

Because payments are the same each period, salary is easy to administer and dollars of direct selling expenses remain fixed regardless of volume. Before each month begins, you know the exact amount required for your salespeople's compensation.

Commission Plans

A commission provides an immediate reward for successful performance. If sales increase, your people make more money; if sales decrease, they make less. Commission emphasizes the importance of writing orders and encourages the salesperson to engage in activities that culminate in order writing. Increased sales often require the salesperson to perform many tasks besides writing orders, including prospecting for new accounts, setting up display fixtures, counting stock, calibrating equipment, training, programming, analyzing the prospect's operations, or solving a data entry problem. Commission provides the sales force with an incentive to work hard and earn a great deal of money. Only time, energy, and territory restraints limit the salesperson's compensation.

However, for commission plans to motivate all your salespeople, the sales territories must have equal potential and the salespeople must have moderate to high influence on the sales. Commission plans are often used where setting goals for bonuses proves difficult and keeping sales costs at a constant percent of revenues has importance, which often occurs in immature businesses or industries.

In modified rebuys, the salesperson must visit the same customers frequently for reorders. Commission represents an incentive to return, so firms involved in this type of sales use a heavy dose of commission in their compensation.

Generally, commission plans are easy to understand and to compute. You multiply a fixed percentage times the dollar amount of sales, or a fixed dollar amount times the units of sales. Each day your salespeople know their earnings.

Each month the payroll department performs simple multiplication to arrive at each person's compensation.

However, commissions paid on recurring revenue can create a phantom base salary that does not motivate a salesperson to higher performance. In such situations you require a plan that pays more commission on growth than maintenance or has a threshold under which less or no commission is paid. If 80 percent of a salesperson's revenue is recurring, this will create a phantom salary. Another solution involves paying a slightly lower commission rate and then paying a bonus based on exceeding last year's revenues.

Where commissions have to be split because the sale involves channel conflicts, team selling, or more than one person's efforts or because different rates are used for different products, administration proves more difficult. To prevent arguments, details of commission splits must be decided before a sale, not afterward. In surveying sales and human resource executives at 26 Fortune 1000 firms, Hewitt Associates found that 44 percent used predefined criteria for splitting commission, while for 34 percent sales management determined the split after the sale.[1]

With commission plans, sales compensation costs remain a fixed percentage of your revenues whether they rise or fall, thereby protecting profit margins and helping cash flow.

For smaller and early-stage companies and start-ups with limited capital, this feature is very important. New ventures especially benefit from commission plans because initial sales costs are lower, reflecting the low sales volume. As mentioned earlier, sometimes new ventures and early-stage firms use high-performance pay compensation plans that do not properly reflect the salesperson's influence on the sale, type of service or product sold, type of salesperson required, or the specific actions or results most important to reward. Sometimes these start-ups never mature because sales force compensation plans were poorly designed to begin with. As the business matures, legacy issues can prevent changing to a more appropriate plan.

Because no career ladder exists for salespeople in many organizations, the opportunity to earn large sums from commission takes on added importance. In some small and medium-size concerns, top salespeople regularly earn more than the sales manager or president. Commission also proves more appropriate for businesses in which the sales forces are often smaller but the territories are larger and have unlimited potential.

The major disadvantages of straight commission or heavily weighted commission plans are that they lack emphasis on nonselling activities and encourage *highlighting*, or calling on a small number of large accounts at the expense of a large number of smaller ones. They can also result in high sales force turnover during weak sales periods, in excessive income from large nonrecurring sales, and in salespeople overselling unneeded features in addition to overloading customers with inventory. Commission compensation stresses the benefits (immediate orders) of shorter-term customer relations rather than the longer-term benefits of a growing relationship. However, proper sales training and supervision can overcome many of these disadvantages.

It is difficult to convince commissioned salespeople to collect past-due accounts unless their commissions are penalized for bad debts. It requires more salesmanship on the part of management to obtain weekly call reports from commissioned people than it does from salaried; the salespeople must believe that call reports help their performance. Commission attracts salespeople with a need for freedom and independence, people who feel they are in business for themselves.

Because large accounts generate more sales and commission dollars, a non-salaried salesperson often concentrates his or her efforts on the majors and neglects small accounts. Through proper training and supervision, management must convince the sales force that smaller accounts also have virtues. For example, small accounts often buy at list price, take less time to sell, tend to remain loyal, and require less service.

Some commission salespeople sell customers unneeded features and overload inventory. Again proper sales training can prevent this. Commission people must understand that there will be less commission next year if they mistreat customers this year—because their sales will be lower. Over the long term the salesperson must satisfy customer needs.

If a compensation plan allows commission people to earn a good living that reflects the complexity of the sale, then management can obtain their cooperation in correcting some of these disadvantages. A salesperson earning a good living does not wish to lose his or her job. A commission sales force that trusts and respects management will modify its behavior. On the other hand, if the commission plan merely results in a mediocre level of total compensation that does not reflect the complexity of the sale, it will be more difficult to take meaningful corrective action.

The rate of commission must allow a salesperson to earn a competitive and living wage from average results, but a superior wage from superior results. Also, the rate of commission must allow your company to maintain necessary profit margins and return on capital. Commission rates vary from 3 percent on sales of commodity food products and lumber to 20 percent on software, medical supplies, and scientific research equipment. Again management must understand and the rate of commission must reflect the target compensation for a commission salesperson based on the complexity of the sale.

As prices rise for a product or service, so do commission dollars. A salesperson gets paid more dollars for selling the same units this year than last if the unit price increases. However, a decrease in unit volume because of the price increase can offset this gain. Commission rates require annual review to measure the effects of inflation and unit sales.

Commissions can cause frustration when territories do not contain equal potential. When small territories or realigned territories limit or decrease sales volume, you may have to consider guarantees. Commission compensation plans require territories of equal potential, which is discussed in Chapter 10.

As mentioned in Chapter 7, commissions can be used to reward different sales and margin results important to your company's success. The commission might be paid on total sales, sales growth, net sales after returns and discounts, paid invoices, dollars of gross margin, or dollars of territory profit. To encourage sales and/or reflect profitability, a higher commission rate might be paid on target products, target customers, new products or services, and new customers. Some companies use progressive commission rates that increase with higher results; others use regressive rates that decrease with results. Flexibility represents another advantage of commission compensation programs.

Bonus Plans

Goal-based bonuses represent an excellent means of using performance pay to reward positive action and superior results. Many firms defer bonuses to year-end because the bonus is paid on cumulative results. Some firms defer bonuses to next year to help with tax planning and to lower turnover. Often a bonus provides an extra, deferred reward for some form of outstanding performance over and above forecast or goal. Often bonuses increase with seniority and as salespeople exceed goals. Some firms use a goal-based bonus as their primary means of performance pay; others combine it with a commission plan. Goal-based bonuses often prove effective when territories have unequal potential, when goal setting proves reliable, and in mature businesses and industries.

Many salespeople feel quotas used for bonuses do not fairly reflect market potential or accurate forecasts. Often this results from a lack of reliable data. Better historical tracking systems and knowledge of buyer behavior is improving accuracy. To obtain salesperson buy-in, include them in the quota-setting process.

Some companies that pay bonuses based on meeting or exceeding sales goals or quotas also have an announced policy of terminating salespeople who miss quotas two years in a row. This represents a means of weeding the garden. We motivate salespeople with fear and love. Between 50 and 75 percent of salespeople who are told they will receive a bonus based on their exceeding specified goals do exceed those goals.

If possible, pay part or all of a bonus quarterly to bring the reward closer to the action and results. For example, a portion of the annual bonus can be paid quarterly if the previous quarter's year-to-date performance exceeds a proration of the annual goal. If this is not possible, inform salespeople monthly about their performance progress toward goals and remind them of the resulting annual bonus.

In September 2005, Hewitt Associates asked sales and human resource executives at 61 Fortune 1000 companies "if they have a quota-based component in their sales plan and how effective they feel their quota-setting process is." Eighty percent of participants reported having a quota-based component in their sales incentive plan, and of these 71 percent felt they are moderately effective in their quota-setting process. Sixty-three percent of participants with a quota-based component use a top-down quota-setting process. Sales management projections (69 percent) and territory potential and opportunity (67 percent) are the most prevalent factors for setting quotas.[2]

Goal-based bonuses can be used to reward salespeople for new accounts, new product placements, product mix, gross margin, revenue growth, team results, computer skills, product knowledge, call reports, or customer profiles. Bonuses can be used to reward salespeople for superior results and the activities that drive those results such as plant tours, presentations, identifying decision makers, or moving to the next step in a long complex sales cycle. Decide what positive action and superior results can be best rewarded by commission and which by bonuses. The more a salesperson exceeds his or her goal, the greater the dollars of bonus. Bonuses provide the manager with additional flexibility for compensating salespeople.

A pharmaceutical firm switched from a bonus that was based on exceeding individual quotas to a bonus based on group goals. A companywide bonus pool was based on meeting or exceeding company earnings and revenue goals. The bonus pool was divided among the sales force depending on individuals' absolute dollar sales and percentage growth of certain products. Salespeople who generated the most absolute dollars and the largest percentage growth received more of the bonus pool than lesser performers.

As noted in the last chapter, group bonuses can help promote teamwork within each region. If sales growth depends on salespeople working together, reward that behavior with a team bonus. The team bonus can be in addition to other performance pay or replace it.

In an August 2006 survey, MarketBridge asked sales, marketing, and human resource executives at 120 midsized and large companies to list their organization's greatest sales compensation challenges. Fifty-seven percent of the respondents cited setting achievable quotas, 46 percent cited differentiating top performers, 45 percent cited minimizing plan complexity, 36 percent cited offering attractive pay levels, 31 percent cited compensating the entire sales team, and 30 percent cited managing compensation cost of sales.

In the same survey respondents said their companies had increased targeted total sales force pay levels (salary, commission, and bonus) on average by 4.4 percent over the coming year. However, on average these same companies said they plan to increase quotas by 7.3 percent, or 70 percent more than the total pay increase, providing an anticipated greater return to the company. On average, respondents had a 73 percent confidence level (on a scale of 0 to 100 percent) that their company would reach its growth goal.[3]

A start-up consumer electronics firm allows salespeople to take part of their bonus in stock options. To reduce turnover, this same firm increases possible bonus dollars for similar results based on years of employment. The longer a person has sold for this firm, the larger their bonus opportunity.

In September 2005, Hewitt Associates surveyed sales and human resource executives at 60 Fortune 1000 firms concerning long-term incentives such as stock options for salespeople. Forty-five percent said national and key account salespeople receive stock options, and 27 percent said sales representatives also receive stock options.[4]

Combination Plans

Some combination of salary, commission, and bonus represents the most widely used form of sales compensation. Because the objectives of a compensation plan usually involve quickly and effectively rewarding a combination of actions, results, and behaviors, rather than one simple action or result, combination plans prove most appropriate. Combination plans can be targeted to encourage the specific behaviors, actions, and results most beneficial to your sales effort and to eliminate the disadvantages of straight commission or straight salary.

Combination plans lack the simplicity of straight commission or straight salary plans, however, and this makes them more difficult for the company to administer and for the salespeople to understand. A common mistake of combination plans involves offering a specific compensation for too many activities or results rather than emphasizing the most important ones—for example, paying a bonus for new accounts and new product placement, a commission on sales increases and gross margin, plus a base salary for retention. Because of their complexity, combination plans can require more frequent revision than either straight salary or straight commission.

Because of their complexity, combination plans require the sales manager to spend more time explaining to each salesperson how his or her actions and results will impact total compensation.

In September 2005, Hewitt Associates asked sales and human resource executives at 55 Fortune 1000 companies what is "the percentage of total compensation which is delivered as base salary?" Seventy-five percent of participants have incentive plans where base salary accounts for over 50 percent of total cash compensation. High-tech and telecom reported the least proportion of base pay.[5]

Sales and Marketing Management magazine reported on a 3,000-respondent 2005 sales compensation survey performed by Equation Research. The survey found that 62 percent of the respondents thought their sales compensation plan was "somewhat successful," only 20 percent believed their sales compensation plan was very successful, and the remaining 18 percent rated the plan as less than successful. This survey provides evidence of the difficulty that exists in creating successful compensation plans.

Expense Reimbursement

In addition to direct compensation, the sales force is also rewarded through reimbursed expenses and fringe benefits. Salespeople may be reimbursed for all, part, or none of their travel, entertainment, telecommunication, and office expenses.

Regardless of product or service, any expense reimbursement plan should be fair, controllable, fast, simple, easy to understand and administer, and flexible. Salespeople should have an economic incentive for controlling their expenses and for using expense money productively and efficiently. If no economic incentive exists and if expenses are open ended, salespeople use them as an additional form of compensation. Similarly, management cannot ask its salespeople to pay for expenses when this would lower their total compensation to an unacceptable level that does not reflect the complexity of the sale.

Salespeople should be paid and expenses reimbursed promptly. Many smaller companies finance themselves by remaining months behind in paying portions of their sales force's expenses and performance pay. Many larger companies with weak back-office administrative systems do the same. Such behavior increases turnover of salespeople and certainly hurts morale and productivity. Salespeople must thoroughly understand what is included in the expense plan so they can act accordingly. Make your expense plan as simple as possible to facilitate its administration. Put the expense plan in writing and have salespeople sign and return a copy to you each year.

A good expense plan requires a certain amount of flexibility for exceptions. Your Denver salesperson receives a call from a hot prospect asking him to be in her Salt Lake City office at ten o'clock the next morning. The salesperson flies both ways to save time since he also has appointments in Denver the day following the Salt Lake City visit. Your company policy reimburses auto expenses but not airfare. You might consider making an exception in this case.

Salespeople can be asked to pay all their own expenses out of their basic compensation, the firm and the sales force can split expenses, or the company can reimburse the salespeople for all their expenses. Many variations exist within each of these possibilities. Expense policies, like salespeople compensation plans, require annual review and constant updating to reflect changing conditions.

Salespeople can be asked to pay all their own expenses if the level of compensation takes this into account. Commissioned salespeople in the apparel business, for example, receive a rate of commission high enough to pay all their own expenses. The rate of commission varies according to the level of anticipated expenses. The New York salesperson who travels between customers by subway might receive a lower commission rate than does the Iowa-Nebraska salesperson who drives 50 miles between accounts.

If possible, making the salesperson responsible for all or most of his or her expenses proves best for the smaller, early-stage, or start-up business. Under such a plan, the salesperson, who has the most to gain or lose and is the best judge, has total responsibility for expenses. Money will not be wasted on unnecessary trips or entertainment. If salespeople feel that money spent on travel or entertainment will result in orders, they will spend it. However, if it is their money, some salespeople have a tendency to underspend, which might not maximize dollars of revenue. Certainly this arrangement is the easiest to administer and understand. Smaller businesses and start-ups often use channel partners to reach their target customers because compensation is variable and reimbursed expenses transparent.

A similar but more complicated arrangement involves the salesperson submitting reports and receipts for certain designated expenses, which the company reimburses until the total reaches a specified percentage of sales volume. Anything over that percentage becomes the salesperson's responsibility. At year's end the salesperson receives a portion of the amount saved should expenses total less than the agreed percentage. Here again the salesperson has an economic incentive to spend wisely. The percentage rate varies accordingly to the territory, volume, and expense requirements. The sales volume figure against which you apply the percentage rate to arrive at a dollar expense limit may be last year's actual, this year's forecast, or this year's actual cumulative to date.

Some companies agree to pay a predetermined percentage of allowable expense items. For example, they may agree to pay 65 percent of all the salesperson's entertainment, travel, and telephone expenses. Salespeople submit invoices, receipts, and reports verifying their expenses, and the company then reimburses only 65 percent. The company and salespeople thus share the expenses.

Some companies merely give salespeople a flat monthly expense allowance to use as they see fit. Others allow a flat amount for certain expenses—for example, $60 a night for lodging, $40 a day for food, and 30 cents a mile for auto expenses. Both arrangements must vary dollar amounts to accommodate different expenses in different territories. A hotel room in Omaha will not cost as much as a hotel room in San Francisco. For example, in 2005 the average overnight per diem cost of a salesperson in New York City was $532 versus $351 for Houston. The flat monthly allowance allows you to accurately forecast this expense item. Both these plans are easy to understand and administer.

Some capital goods and financial services companies, for whom salespeople are encouraged to travel and entertain extensively, allow salespeople unlimited expense accounts but require a detailed annual budget for planning cash flow. The budget asks for expenses by type, customer, and month. Salespeople receive a bonus based on meeting the sales forecast and expense budget. A good expense plan gives the salesperson an incentive to spend wisely and limit expenses.

Some expense plans involve combinations of the above choices. For instance, airfare might be 100 percent reimbursable, but lodging and meals are paid for with a flat allowance.

Expense reports represent a mixed blessing for the salespeople and sales manager. Although laptops prove helpful, expense plans that require vouchers, receipts, invoices, and reports involve a great deal of administrative time on the part of salespeople and the sales manager. The salesperson must submit accurate information, and you or your administrative assistant must verify its correctness. This is necessary not only for internal controls but for reporting to the Internal Revenue Service as well. However, expense reports provide important information both on costs and on where the salesperson travels and who the salesperson calls on. Therefore, even if you have an administrative assistant to match vouchers to expense items, review all expense reports before turning them over to the payroll department. If submitted digitally, aggregate material and look for trends.

Credit card companies and outside services can use software to provide the sales manager with detailed information on salespeople's expenses. Some firms require salespeople to submit expense reports, receipts, and vouchers to an outside service, which does all the paperwork and actually reimburses the salespeople. Your company then deposits funds to cover reimbursed expenses with the service firm and pays the service firm a fee. Such firms submit summary expense information on each salesperson to the sales manager.

Unless salespeople pay their own expenses or you pay a flat monthly allowance, these costs are difficult to forecast. It is difficult to estimate in November what travel expenses might be incurred during the following year. For cash-constrained concerns, this can prove especially problematic.

Contact management and customized software programs for salespeople's laptop computers can reduce the time required for reporting and transmitting expenses. These same programs can aggregate expense data for the entire sales force by category and by salesperson, compare actual to forecast, and create budgets based on historical data.

Channel partners such as distributors, brokers, and independent sales representatives generally pay their own expenses out of their commission, discounts, or margins. Occasionally companies do provide channel partners with a travel, entertainment, sample, or trade show allowance.

For many firms reimbursed expenses equal 25 percent of a salesperson's total direct compensation (salary, commission, and bonus) and require constant cost reduction analysis. For some industries such as financial services, capital goods, medical devices, or complex software, reimbursed expenses may equal a salesperson's total direct compensation. Airfare, auto expenses, telecommunications, lodging, meals, and entertainment easily get out of control. Use part of a sales meeting to discuss the relationship between salespeople's time management and expense control. When possible, salespeople should use the telephone rather than a personal visit to qualify prospects, arrange appointments, handle service items, answer specific questions, or write small orders. Salespeople should plan the day and month ahead so as to see more customers and travel fewer miles. They should travel only economy class by air and, where possible, stay at budget-class lodgings. If the same city is frequently visited by air, consult a travel agent or use a Web site to purchase discount tickets. Some discount tickets can't be canceled and others involve penalties. Last, salespeople should make fewer but longer trips. Also, management should negotiate special corporate lodging, auto lease or rental, airline, and telecommunication rates for the sales force.

Fringe Benefits

As mentioned, in addition to direct compensation, sales force costs include reimbursed expenses, which often equal 25 percent or more of direct compensation and fringe benefits, which often equal another 25 to 35 percent. Fringe benefits include mandatory items such as Social Security, Medicare, and unemployment insurance, plus expected items such as health, life, and disability insurance, vacations, retirement plans, and optional items such as profit sharing, stock options, education reimbursement, clubs, dental or vision insurance, and moving expenses. Depending on the circumstances, fringe benefits vary from 15 to 40 percent of direct compensation, and this represents a significant expense item. In established firms, long-term incentives, such as stock options, are reserved for senior salespeople, national account managers, and sales managers. However, younger companies often offer stock options to lure salespeople away from established firms.

In Chapter 3 on hiring salespeople, we referred to a 2003 study by Towers Perrin on the factors that attract salespeople to a particular firm. Providing competitive health-care benefits represented number 1 and providing a competitive base pay represented number 2. However, this study also showed that the factors most important in attracting salespeople were not the same as the most important factors for retaining and motivating them. We will deal with that in Part 7 on motivating salespeople.

Channel partners such as distributors, brokers, and independent sales representatives pay their own fringe benefits. However, if a channel partner devotes over 50 percent of its time to selling your firm's products or services, your firm may be liable for their fringe benefits. Discuss this with the firm's legal counsel. Responsibility for travel expenses and fringe benefits should be clearly defined in the channel partner's contract.

Some employers offer salespeople a choice of fringe benefits and plans. They can choose reimbursed education expenses up to a certain dollar amount or dental and/or vision insurance. Deductibles can be chosen along with coinsurance amounts on health plans. Employees may be asked to share the cost of certain fringe benefits with their employer. The employer pays 80 percent of health insurance and moving expenses. Because salespeople's needs are different, these cafeteria plans prove popular.

Retirement plans and stock options are deferred fringe benefits that increase in value based on years of employment. Such plans help reduce sales force turnover.

Individual Written Compensation Plans

Each salesperson should receive, sign, and return their annual compensation plan. This prevents misunderstandings, and it allows the sales manager and salesperson to discuss the total annual cost of putting the salesperson on the road. The compensation plan includes specifics on dollars of salary, rates of commission, and dollars of bonus, plus details of the expense reimbursements and fringe benefits. Because plans and fringe benefits change annually, can be individually customized, and involve combinations of salary, commission, and bonus, ask salespeople to show their understanding and agreement by signing their plan. Misunderstandings of direct compensation, reimbursed expenses, and fringe benefits waste time, demotivate a sales force, and lower productivity.

Salespeople often misunderstand their compensation program and do not understand how their actions and results drive their total compensation. Therefore, once a year, the sales manager should ask each salesperson what he or she wishes to earn in the next 12 months. The salesperson might say $100,000. Then the sales manager would reply that since salary is $50,000, the salesperson must earn another $50,000 in commission and bonuses. The sales manager would continue by asking what revenues, margins, and other results are necessary to produce $50,000 in commission and bonus? And equally important, what actions and activities on the salesperson's part are necessary to create these revenues, margins, and other results? How many new accounts must be opened, and/or what existing business must be increased? How many customer calls will be required? How much time must be spent on prospecting?

Sample Compensation Plan

Name: Bill Locke

Time Period: Calendar 2007

Salary: $4,000 a month payable every two weeks.

Commission: Two percent of sales when shipped, less uncollectible accounts receivables, returns, samples, and advertising allowances. Four percent of resulting gross margin. Commissions paid on the 20th of each month for the preceding month.

Bonus: Up to $3,000 based on exceeding forecast.

Expense Reimbursement: Up to $2,000 a month cumulative for travel and communication expenses payable two weeks after expense reports are received. The difference between 12 months' actual expenses and $24,000 to be split 50/50 if actual is under $24,000.

Fringe Benefits: Social Security, unemployment insurance, Medicare, health, life, and disability insurance; pension plan, and stock options; reimbursed educational expenses. These fringe benefits would be spelled out in more detail.

These written individual expense plans also allow a sales manager the opportunity to discuss with her or his salespeople their total cost. Most salespeople perceive their total cost as their take-home pay. Most sales managers never explain or fully understand how much more than direct compensation a salesperson costs the firm.

Once a year the sales manager should review and document with each salesperson the cost of putting him or her on the road. Use both historic and forecasted numbers. Show past and projected earnings; salary, commission, and bonus; then total all reimbursed expenses, and add the dollar cost of all appropriate fringe benefits. Compare this total for various years. To make this total number even more meaningful, you may wish to show it as a percentage of the salesperson's territory's revenues. To make this total number even more meaningful, divide it by the number of days a salesperson works each year and the number of hours worked each day. Show the salesperson's cost per day and per hour. If appropriate, divide it by the number of customer calls a salesperson makes each year or the number of prospecting calls or the number of new accounts. Have salespeople keep a time log on what percent of their time is spent in activities that drive sales—that is, in front of customers or on the phone with customers, preparing bids or proposals, or working with engineering on specifications. Most salespeople spend 20 to 40 percent of their time in these activities. Show the cost per hour of that customer sales-related time.

You and the salesperson will benefit from reviewing these numbers. Salespeople are an expensive, important human resource. Discuss with the salesperson how to increase his or her productivity. What additional inputs will increase outputs. Ask the salesperson how she or he can spend more time on sales-related activities, specifically with targeted customers. In the next part on sales force organization, we will discuss using these costs to determine a salesperson's breakeven point and dollars of contribution margin.

The Annual Cost of Putting a Salesperson on the Road

Name: Bill Locke   **Time Period:** Calendar 2007
Direct Compensation
  Salary: $ 48,000
  Commission: 2% of sales $ 30,000
             4% of gross margin $ 20,000
  Bonus: $ 3,000
Total Direct Compensation: $101,000
  Medicare, Unemployment Insurance, Social Security: $ 14,000
  Health, Life and Disability Insurance: $ 10,000
  Pension, Stock Options, Education: $ 6,000
Total Fringe Benefits: $ 30,000
Total Reimbursed Expenses: $ 24,000
Total Direct Cost Bill Locke: $155,000
  Percent of Sales: 10.3%
  Cost per Day Using 240 Days a Year: $ 646
  Cost per Hour Using 8 Hours a Day: $ 81
  Cost per Customer Visit Using 2 a Day or 480 a Year: $ 322
  Percentage of Time in Sales-Driving Activities: 33%
  Cost Per Hour of Sales-Driving Activities: $ 243

Measuring the Results

If you alter sales force compensation, you must measure whether the changes produced the desired results. At the end of one sales cycle, what metrics will you use to determine if the new compensation program is an improvement? Will you use performance standards such as increased revenues and margins per account or per territory? Or will you be more concerned about lowering sales force and customer turnover? In changing sales force compensation, what problem did you wish to solve: higher sales of higher-margin services or salesperson retention?

Every time you change compensation, you must measure the results. If the change did not produce the desired results, consider alternatives for next year.

To make good decisions, the sales manager must define the problem, opportunity, or need; the cause of any problem whether compensation, hiring or training; alternative solutions; and performance standards to measure whether the changes produced the desired results.

Sales Managers' Major Weaknesses and/or Mistakes

SALES FORCE COMPENSATION

- Not rewarding specific actions or results important to company's success, such as selling strategic accounts and products.
- Not rewarding superior results.
- Not analyzing compensation each year.
- Not reflecting the complexity of the sale in the level of compensation.
- Not reflecting the salesperson's influence on the sale and the type salesperson you wish to attract in deciding on the mix between fixed versus performance pay.

Questions and Exercises for Chapter 8

- Create a hybrid compensation plan for your sales force or a sales force you are familiar with.
- Create an individual written compensation plan for a salesperson in your organization or a salesperson you are familiar with.

Quiz for Chapter 8

1. A bonus differs from commission in that
   a. A bonus is a deferred reward for exceeding a goal.
   b. A commission is expressed as a rate or percentage and a bonus is expressed as a dollar amount.
   c. Sometimes a portion of a bonus is deferred until the next year while commissions are paid immediately.
   d. Commissions reward positive action and results on the part of salespeople that are important to the company's success, but bonuses do not.

2. Which statement is correct?
   a. Most sales force compensation plans are primarily fixed pay.
   b. Most sales force compensation plans are primarily performance pay.
   c. Most sales force compensation plans are a combination of fixed and performance pay.

3. For commission plans to motivate salespeople, which of the following conditions must exist?
   a. Territories must have unequal potential.
   b. Territories must have equal potential.
   c. There must be high salesperson influence on the sale.
   d. There must be low salesperson influence on the sale.

4. Goal-based bonus plans prove most effective when
   a. Territories have equal potential.
   b. When goal setting proves difficult.
   c. When businesses are just starting.

5. The major disadvantages of commission plans include which of the following?
   a. They lack emphasis on nonselling activities.
   b. They encourage salespeople to call on a small number of large accounts.
   c. They encourage high sales force turnover.
   d. They encourage salespeople to oversell customers into buying unwanted products or services.

6. Bonuses should be paid at which of the following times?
   a. The end of the year
   b. The end of the quarter
   c. The end of the month
   d. Closest to the period in which the activities or results on which they are based occur

7. True or false?
   Salespeople should have an economic incentive for controlling their expenses.

8. Fringe benefits include which of the following?
   a. Salary
   b. Social Security
   c. Bonus
   d. Insurance
   e. Vacations

9. The annual cost of putting a salesperson on the road includes which of the following?
   a. Salary, commission, and bonus
   b. Fringe benefits
   c. Reimbursed expenses

10. After altering sales force compensation, when should you measure whether changes produced the desired results?
    a. After one month
    b. After one quarter
    c. After one year
    d. After one sales cycle

Notes

1. *Hot Topics in Sales Management and Sales Compensation 2005.* Copyright © 2005 Hewitt Associates LLC. Reprinted by permission of Hewitt Associates.
2. Ibid.
3. MarketBridge, Mark Donnolo, *Performance-Driving Selling 2006.* Marketbridge Technologies. Copyright © 2006. Reprinted by permission of MarketBridge.
4. *Hot Topics in Sales Management and Sales Compensation 2005.*
5. Ibid.

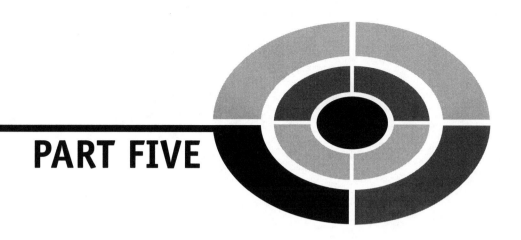

PART FIVE

Sales Force Organization

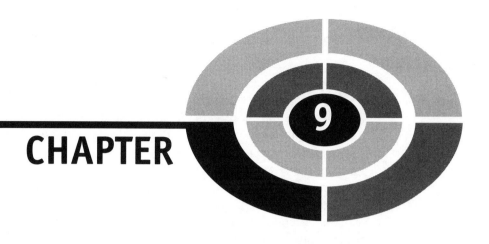

CHAPTER 9

Channel Choice and Architecture

The sales manager must pay considerable attention to the structure of the sales force, and the structure should reflect strategy. A strategy to open new accounts versus one to expand existing accounts requires different types of sales organizations. The model for organizing a sales force progresses from the more general to the more specific, from the more strategic to the more tactical, from macros to micros. A firm's first decision is what channels are most efficient for reaching and serving the target customers; your own direct salespeople or some combination of indirect sales organizations or channel partners? Will you use a combination of distributors, brokers, sales representative organizations, tele-sales or telemarketing, e-commerce, home-shopping television channels, systems integrators, value-added distributors, or retailers?

Once you choose the appropriate combination of sales channels, the second decision is how to organize these channels: by product line, major customer or market segment, function, geography, or no restrictions. We refer to this as *sales force architecture*.

Moving from the more general to the more specific, next decide how many salespeople you need and the boundaries of each person's territory. We refer to this as *deployment and sizing*.

Last and most tactical, a sales manager must assist salespeople in time and territory management. How can a salesperson best allocate his or her time in the territory between prospecting for new customers and further penetration of existing accounts? How frequently should top accounts be visited versus less important customers? How can a salesperson most efficiently travel the territory?

Channel choice, architecture, deployment, and territory management can dramatically impact revenues and costs. As this chapter shows, correct use of channel choice, architecture, sizing, deployment, and territory management can allow a sales manager to increase revenues without increasing costs, or it can allow a sales manager to reduce costs without reducing revenues. As with compensation, the rapidly changing twenty-first-century landscape dictates an annual evaluation of these issues. As products, customers, competitors, technology, markets, personnel, and strategy change, so must your channel choice, architecture, deployment, and territory management. Business is a dynamic process, and the future is a moving target. Each year wipe the slate clean. If you were starting again, what changes would you make? This chapter deals with models and methodologies to help you evaluate and implement such changes.

Most sales managers inherited and continue their channel, organizational, and deployment structure, or they follow competition and industry tradition. Be careful of legacy issues and following the losers. Proper staffing, organization, deployment, channel choice, and territory management provide an opportunity to differentiate your firm in a commoditized marketplace. No matter how well you hire, train, and compensate salespeople, inefficient distribution channels, architecture, deployment, and territory management will prevent a sales force from reaching full productivity. Salespeople represent an expensive and important human resource, just as plant and equipment represent expensive and important capital expenditures. Both require full productivity to be competitive. Full productivity requires reaching the target market in the most effective and efficient way.

Salesperson Breakeven Point

In previous chapters we discussed the strategic importance of reducing the sales cycle from search to purchase, reducing the training cycle, and more rapidly taking salespeople from "0" to full productivity or at least to a breakeven point.

To accomplish these strategic objectives requires metrics and models to measure a salesperson's marginal costs versus marginal revenues.

In the previous chapter on compensation, we discussed the annual cost of putting a salesperson on the road. This represents a salesperson's marginal costs that now must be compared to marginal revenues to establish a breakeven point. Subtract these annual costs from a salesperson's annual revenues to determine a territory's *dollars of contribution margin.*

A salesperson's breakeven point varies depending on whether he or she works in a new territory or an existing territory. For example, a newly started B2B e-commerce exchange for specialty chemicals hires a new salesperson for an undeveloped territory in Louisiana, Texas, and Oklahoma. Using the format discussed in the previous chapter on compensation, you add the salesperson's salary, commission, bonus, fringe benefits, reimbursed expenses, and any variable costs directly related to that salesperson or territory (such as samples, freight in, bad debt, promotions, or advertising). Let's assume the total is $150,000. Let's assume the gross margin after manufacturing costs, or after costs of providing a service, or in this case cost of goods sold, is 50 percent. The breakeven point for this new salesperson in a new territory is $300,000 of new revenue, which will result in $150,000 of contribution margin after the 50 percent cost of goods sold. Existing selling, marketing, and general and administrative expenses are fixed and will not vary because of this new salesperson.

On the other hand, the breakeven point for a salesperson in an established territory will be much higher. Let's assume our new salesperson, who costs $150,000 to put on the road, takes over an existing territory. The cost of goods sold remains 50 percent, but this existing territory must absorb a portion of existing fixed selling, marketing, and general and administrative costs that are allocated at 30 percent of revenues. After allocating the fixed selling, marketing, and general and administrative expenses, but before the costs of putting this salesperson on the road, the company generates a 20 percent operating profit from each matured territory. The breakeven point for this same salesperson in an existing territory is $750,000 of revenue, which will result in an operating profit of 20 percent, or $150,000, equal to the cost of putting the salesperson on the road. Some more sophisticated firms include the cost of capital for account receivables and inventory in the fixed or variable expenses.

B2B Chemical Exchange

($000)	New Territory	Existing Territory
Cost to Put Salesperson on Road	150	150
Breakeven Revenue	300	750
Gross Margin after Cost of Goods Sold	50%	50%
Operating Profit before Cost of Putting Salesperson on Road	20%	20%

Many sales managers and controllers do not realize the breakeven point for a new salesperson in a new territory varies from the breakeven point for an existing territory and underhire for new territories.

In order to determine how much market potential a new territory requires to reach the breakeven revenue, the sales manager needs to know her or his firm's expected market share in the territory. If the expected market share is 5 percent and the salesperson's breakeven point is $300,000, as in the above example, then the territory requires a minimum $6 million market potential to justify a salesperson. In order to generate a substantial profit, the territory possibly requires a market potential of $10 million. We discuss the various metrics to determine market potential in the next chapter.

Salesperson's Contribution Margin

We manage what we monitor. Knowing a salesperson's breakeven point will assist you in staffing and deployment decisions. For example, when should you hire an additional salesperson for a new territory? Knowing each salesperson's territory's contribution margin will assist you in evaluating territory boundaries, product mix, pricing, the salesperson's compensation, and reimbursed expenses. The regional manager of a pharmaceutical firm has seven salespeople reporting to her. For each salesperson or territory, the company provides the following quarterly and cumulative year-to-date data.

Net revenues after discounts and returns for company products sold in the territory, less:

- Salesperson's total direct compensation (salary, commission, and bonus)
- Fringe benefits (Social Security, insurance, pension plan, and so on)
- Reimbursed travel, entertainment, communication, and office expenses
- Cost of samples dispersed to physicians and any UPS freight charges related to physicians in the territory
- Cost of in-service training sessions
- Bad debts
- Local advertising, promotion, marketing expenses, and trade shows

Resulting in a salesperson's gross contribution margin in dollars, less:

- Manufacturing costs for company product shipments sold in the territory, usually sold through a distributor to hospitals and pharmacies, but prescribed by the physicians the salesperson calls on.

Resulting in a salesperson's net contribution margin in dollars.

The pharmaceutical company regional sales manager compares revenues, each line item expense, and dollars of margin for each salesperson or territory. She also notes for each salesperson or territory what percentage of revenue each expense or margin item represents. Once a year she shares the results for each territory with the appropriate salesperson. Once a quarter she compares the results for each territory to each of the others. She has noted large dollar and percentage of revenue variations from one territory to another. Based on these variations, she has realigned territory boundaries, exited some unprofitable territories, increased the number of salespeople in more profitable territories, changed compensation and expense reimbursement plans, and reduced spending on samples and marketing. The difference between the salesperson's gross contribution margin and the salesperson's net contribution margin is the territory's cost of goods sold and/or manufacturing costs for the products delivered to the territory. Salespeople impact this latter margin through their pricing decisions, customer targeting, and product mix sales. Weak results in this area might require a sales manager to use targeted field coaching and sales meetings to reinforce product, competitive and customer knowledge, selling and pricing skills.

As noted in the previous chapter, compensation may be partially based on these dollars of margin and expense control. You might pay a commission on margins or a bonus for expense control. Most firms capture the data necessary to construct a territory contribution margin analysis. The sales manager must know what format he or she wants and work with the controller to obtain reliable figures. There are many variations of these formats. Effective sales managers, use one of them.

Channel Choice

Choosing the proper distribution channels depends on the type customers called on, the type of selling performed by the sales force, operating issues, type of products or services sold, areas requiring control, and capital or costs. Review these each year to see what has changed and if these changes require an adjustment in your choice of distribution channels. Many of these issues are interrelated and repetitive. Using this model or methodology involves looking at many issues. To make the proper channel choice, you must prioritize or rank the issues as to importance for your firm. Based on each issue's importance does this suggest a direct or indirect sales force (your own salespeople or a channel partner). After you have finished looking at all the issues, make your final decision.

TYPES OF CUSTOMERS

Certain customer characteristics lend themselves more to company direct salespeople, others to an independent sales organization. A large number of widely dispersed customers, frequently ordering small quantities, may be more efficiently reached by several outside indirect sales organizations than by your own company-employed direct sales force. If your firm's target customers are leaders (Wal-Mart, Cisco) or innovators rather than followers, they may insist on a company direct sales force. To enter new market segments where you do not have customer contacts or knowledge, you may need a channel partner who does have these contacts.

Credit and hazardous material (for example, toxic chemicals) issues may sway you toward a channel partner who can more efficiently handle these risks. Consider how competition handles all these factors. Can you create a competitive advantage by doing it differently?

For example, companies selling giftware to retail card shops use channel partners to absorb the credit risks of handling many small retail accounts. The channel partner, sales rep organization, or distributor holds the inventory, ships the products, and invoices the small retailer. The channel partner, who probably sells the retailer other items, can make a better-informed decision on credit risks, potential customers, and, if necessary, how to collect delinquent accounts. Also the channel partner may have more appropriate financing for giving necessary credit to small retailers and a lower cost to sell them.

Customer needs and channel function requirements must be analyzed to determine the proper channel choice. This could vary by market segment, which means you may use a company direct sales force for selling to original equipment manufacturers but use stocking distributors for the replacement market. Customers who require one-stop shopping for a basket of products or services or small-lot sizes when you provide only large-lot sizes or a few products or services dictates that you choose a channel partner who better meets the customer's requirements. Similarly, customers may insist on certain after-sale services—engineering, warranty, training, installation, logistics, or transportation—which can be more efficiently provided by a channel partner.

As in hiring and training salespeople, it is imperative for proper channel choice, architecture, deployment, sizing, and time management that your firm has correctly targeted customers based on dollars of present and potential revenue and margin, cost to sell and service, and probability of success. You need proper metrics for determining each of these. Based on these metrics, present and potential accounts become designated A, B, or C. An A account requires more frequent calls than a C account and may require a different channel choice. You may use telesales people or e-commerce for C accounts and account representatives for B accounts.

TYPES OF SELLING

Certain types of selling lend themselves to company direct salespeople, others to an indirect sales organization or a channel partner. Long sales cycles with a great deal of consultative selling to first-time or one-time systems buyers lend themselves to a direct sales organization. A channel partner may not have the patience for a long complex sale. The more influence a salesperson has on the sale, the more important is a company direct sales force. Team selling and partnership selling lend themselves to the company direct model. In contrast, relationship selling to repeat customers, modified rebuyers, display, commodity, and order taking lends itself to using channel partners.

Most sales managers choose hybrid sales organizations by deaggregating the demand generation tasks. For example, lead generation might be most efficiently performed by an outside direct mail house or a Web site, and qualifying these leads might lend itself to an independent telesales organization. However, once you identify qualified leads, those with major potential require a visit from a direct company salesperson, while those with less potential can be seen by an indirect channel partner salesperson. In both cases the salesperson will do a needs analysis, quantify benefits, demonstrate the product or service, offer a free trial, overcome objections, and attempt to close. Postsale service, installation, and ongoing account management might be best performed by a distributor. Look at the sales funnel, the demand generation tasks from search to purchase. What type selling and sales channels will be most efficient for each task or step?

OPERATING ISSUES

Operating issues—such as inventory, spare parts, service, maintenance, repair, customization, engineering, design, installation, programming, customer training, just-in-time delivery, safety, and credit issues—influence channel choice and may be related to previously mentioned items. Who can more efficiently provide each of these services, your firm or a channel partner? Which of these services does the customer value, and which can be deleted? You must do value engineering on each service offered by your firm and your channel partners. A sales contact management software firm used value-added distributors to sell and provide postsale service. Half of the product's cost and price involved training customers on proper use and installation. As the software or contact management market matured, these services were no longer necessary because customers developed internal resources to provide them. The software company and its value-added distributors offered customers a choice between full or partial service with significant price differences. Most customers chose the less-service-oriented package, and the software firm's unit sales and dollars of margin improved significantly.

Eventually the software firm eliminated its value-added distributors with a company direct sales force.

TYPES OF PRODUCTS OR SERVICES

Certain types of products or services lend themselves to company direct sales-people, others to indirect channel partners. Heterogeneous products that can be more easily differentiated, such as biotech or consulting services or semiconductor fabricating equipment, lend themselves to a direct company sales force. Homogeneous products or services that are more difficult to differentiate, like die-castings or injection molding, lend themselves to channel partners. A well-recognized brand can differentiate a homogeneous product or service and make it heterogeneous.

In reaching customers, higher gross margin products or services generally use a direct company sales force, while lower gross margin products or services generally use channel partners, whose costs are lower and less fixed. New products or services, where the salesperson has a strong influence on the sale, do best with a company direct sales force, while products or services toward the end of their life cycle are more efficiently handled by channel partners, telesales, e-commerce, or customer service people. If you require tight control over pricing and limited customer selection or you need feedback and good communication from the field; a company direct sales force will better satisfy these needs.

CHANNEL CONFLICTS

Because most sales organizations require more than one type of selling; have multiple types of products, customers, and markets; various operating issues and control needs, most sales organizations require hybrid channels of distribution. Often these hybrid channels of distribution conflict and compete with each other in certain market segments. Your own salespeople call on major supermarkets with a line of deli products. You use distributors for smaller grocery stores and brokers for hotels and restaurants. One of the distributor's salespeople opens a large supermarket where she has excellent contacts and your salespeople have had no success. Your salesperson is furious. Do you refuse the new business, or try and arrange a compromise? As discussed in Chapter 8 on compensation, many firms will share or split performance pay in such situations. Be prepared for channel conflicts, and have a plan for dealing with them. In the twenty-first century, e-commerce will become a more important distribution channel creating a new set of channel conflicts. Use e-commerce to enable your sales force and channel partners not compete with them.

PERFORMANCE PAY

As mentioned in Chapter 7, channel partners require performance pay that rewards positive action and superior results important for the success of your firm. To prevent channel partners from skimming the best accounts and low-hanging fruit but not pursuing the middle market and smaller accounts; create performance pay that rewards the proper actions and results. You can pay a higher commission rate for one type of sale, customer, or product than another. You can give bonuses, discounts, and rebates for product mix, number of new accounts, postsale services, and inventory levels. Use proper training and compensation to prevent your channel partners from becoming adversaries.

RUNNING THE NUMBERS

The last item in determining channel choice is to run the numbers for various alternatives. If you use a 100 percent direct company sales force, what will it cost (fixed versus variable expenses), how much revenue and gross margin will it generate and what operating income, earnings before income taxes (EBIT) or earnings before income taxes, depreciation, and amortization (EBITDA) will result? Do the same analysis using channel partners or a hybrid channel choice. Run spreadsheets using various assumptions at different revenue levels for different channel choices. What combination produces the most dollars of contribution margin over time? For each alternative, what percent of sales do selling costs and salesperson compensation represent? This is the reality check. What is your market share and number of customers? Is the channel or combination of channels supported by the model or methodology discussed in this chapter or by the other previously discussed criteria?

Generally, channel partners create variable expenses that remain constant as a percentage of revenues. You pay for performance. A company direct sales force has a higher fixed portion of cost. Many start-ups and early-stage firms use channel partners when their own salespeople would prove more appropriate because with channel partners selling costs are variable—and there are no fringe benefits or reimbursed expenses. But then as the start-up moves into a growth stage or maturity, it proves difficult to change to a hybrid or company direct channel. Each year, use the model described in this section to analyze channel choice but think long term.

The August 2006 MarketBridge survey of sales, marketing, and human resource executives at 120 large and midsized firms found that respondents felt on a scale from 0, completely ineffective, to 100, completely effective, that their direct sales force was 77 percent effective, inside sales (inbound and outbound) was 61 percent effective, and dealers and resellers 60 percent effective. The least effective channels were contract sales (third parties), 40 percent effective; third-party Internet, 46 percent; and company-owned Internet, 49 percent effective. As a result, these companies plan to increase their focus on higher-performing channels and slightly decrease their focus on lower-performing channels.[1]

Sales Force Architecture

Once you have decided on what channel or combination of channels you will use to most efficiently reach the targeted marketplace, you must decide whether to organize these channels by major products or services, product or service lines, market segments, key accounts or customers, geography, functions (two tiers), no restrictions, or some combination of those. The choice depends on your particular products or services, size and types of customers, target accounts, markets, market segments, type of selling, core competencies, channel choices, and objectives. Choose whatever type of organization or architecture best meets customer needs and best uses your sales force's human resources, one that maximizes dollars of contribution margin over time by properly balancing expenses with revenues. Use the models or methodologies described in this chapter to assist in this choice. Evaluate the sales force architecture annually and make changes as needed.

PRODUCT OR SERVICE LINE ORGANIZATION

If your company offers a wide variety of dissimilar or unrelated products or services—especially if they are complex—or if your company's products or services are sold to totally different markets, you should consider a sales force organized by product line. A product line sales organization allows each of the various markets and each of the diverse or complex product lines to receive a high degree of specialized attention. It is difficult for one salesperson to effectively sell cost-and-activity-tracking software to hospitals, human resource software to airlines, and supply-chain-consulting software to tier 3 auto firms.

A regional men's belt manufacturer sold a line of better designer merchandise for department and specialty stores as well as a low-end private-label line for chain and discount stores. The company employed 10 salespeople who were organized geographically and who called on both department and specialty stores and chain and discounters. Some salespeople showed unit growth with chains and discounters but declines with department or specialty stores. Other salespeople showed unit growth with department and specialty stores but declines with chain or discounters. The same salesperson had a difficult time selling price to chain and discounters and brand name, quality, and service to department or specialty stores.

Opening a new store account was a complex, long sales cycle, with many steps. Monitoring and penetrating an existing account was a modified rebuy requiring monthly visits for fill-in orders. The department and specialty store sale required a salesperson with strong consultative sales skills; the chain and discount store sale required a salesperson with good contacts and relationship-building skills. This situation resulted in no growth for the company.

The sales manager reorganized the sales force by product line, market, and function. The five best chain or discount store salespeople received larger territories, but they carried just the private-label, lower-end line and called just on chain and discount stores. The five best department or specialty store salespeople received larger territories but they carried just the designer-label better line and called just on department and specialty stores. The best new account salesperson for department and specialty stores and the best new account salesperson for chain and discount stores concentrated on opening new accounts for their group. Territories overlapped, but customers did not; travel expenses doubled, but unit sales of both lines grew at 20 percent annually. Customers accepted having a change in their sales representative after the initial order.

Organization of the sales force by product or service line does not always have positive results. A rapidly growing institutional cleaning service had a sales force that called on restaurants, factories, and hospitals. The sales manager felt even more rapid growth would result from having salespeople specialize in one of three types of sales: food services, commercial services, or medical services. He reasoned that each type of customer had different needs and that a specialized sales force could better meet those needs. Somewhat different products and services were sold to each market. He also reasoned that because salespeople were located in major metropolitan centers, there would be only nominal increases in travel expenses.

Under the new arrangement, growth rates slowed; both customers and salespeople expressed unhappiness. All three salespeople were calling on the same hospital purchasing agent: one to clean the halls, one to clean the operating rooms, and one to clean the kitchen. Both the food services and commercial cleaning salespeople called on the same factory and office building purchasing agents, causing similar overlap.

The sales manager thought that two salespeople calling on the same account would result in a larger share of the customer's business. Two salespeople would get more of the buyer's time and would more aggressively push their particular service. One salesperson might be satisfied to get $10,000 of business, but two or even three could do much better.

In this case, however, two or three salespeople from one company calling on the same buyer caused confusion and frustration on both ends. Purchasing agents resented spending extra time with multiple salespeople from the same company. Salespeople resented competing against each other for the same sales dollar.

As these two companies illustrate, a sales force organized by product line can increase effectiveness for businesses with diverse or complex products or services or markets because each product or service or each market segment receives a higher degree of specialized attention. However, this often results in greater travel expense and sometimes requires you to add more salespeople. When more than one salesperson from a company calls on the same buyer or purchasing agent, confusion, resentment, and frustration can result. Within a sales force organized by product line, each salesperson is assigned a specific geographic area or customer list to call on.

MAJOR CUSTOMER ORGANIZATION

If your company sells large quantities of products or services to a limited number of major customers, especially customers with many branches, you should consider a sales force organized by account. A sales force organized by account allows each major customer to receive a higher degree of specialization. It allows the salespeople to partner with major accounts, obtain specialized account-specific information, and better understand the decision makers, decision-making process, needs, problems, and culture. Often such key accounts involve long, complex sales cycles, group decisions, and consultative selling that benefit from a major account sales organization.

For example, 80 percent of a ladies' pantyhose mill's production was sold to Sears, Ward's, Penney's, and K-Mart. The central buying offices chose vendors and programs twice a year, but computer-generated reorders were placed by individual stores or regional branches. The pantyhose company assigned one salesperson to handle the central buying office, all regional branches, and all individual stores for each chain. That person had the specialized knowledge, contacts, and experience necessary to produce optimum results.

As another example, 90 percent of all nail-making machines in North America are purchased by various branches of AK Steel, Atlantic Steel Co., International Steel Group, Stanley Bostitch, Continental, Dominion Steel, Keystone Steel & Wire, Mid-States Steel & Wire, U.S. Steel, and Steel Canada. Each machine costs about $75,000, resulting in total annual North American shipments of $7.5 million. Two companies compete in this market; both organize their two-person sales force by customer. One salesperson services the headquarters and all the branches of half the steel companies; the second salesperson performs the same task for the other half.

A third example of a sales force organized by major accounts is a local refuse-removal company in eastern Michigan, which specializes in recycling waste and has three sales and service representatives: one for General Motors plants, one for Ford plants, and one for Daimler Chrysler plants. Each representative knows the specific needs of each company.

As these three examples show, a sales force organized by customer proves best for businesses where a few key accounts or national accounts represent a large percentage of sales. However, as with a sales force organized by product, this often results in greater travel expenses than would be the case for a sales force organized by geographic area. Within a sales force organized by product line, each salesperson might also be assigned specific key customers to call on.

GEOGRAPHIC ORGANIZATIONS

If your company sells similar or closely related products or services to a large number of widely dispersed customers in the same industry, then you should consider a sales force organized by geographic territory. This means that salespeople sell all your products or services to any appropriate customers within their assigned territories. Most smaller businesses use this format because of its simplicity and lower travel costs. Unfortunately, most smaller-business people don't even think about the alternatives.

The geographic organization of territories allows salespeople to cultivate local markets more intensely by becoming more familiar with local problems, people, and conditions. The geographic organization promotes relationship selling. Also, a person living in the territory often finds a more receptive ear than an outsider would. Texans know how to handle Texans, and New Yorkers know how to handle New Yorkers. Similarly, salespeople living in a territory can provide better service at less cost because generally less travel is required.

For example, a bakery supply distributor offers 4,000 items to independent bakeries, restaurants, hotels, hospitals, yogurt shops, and grocery stores. The potential account base is immense. Salespeople often walk from one account to another. They are organized by geographic territory, but management is considering having market specialists.

A national firm offering temporary office and light industrial personnel organizes its sales force geographically. The company targets businesses with seasonal needs or rapid growth. New customers and lateral selling within present accounts are key drivers. The potential account base is immense and the services closely related, so the sales manager organized her sales force geographically.

Products and services sold door-to-door such as fire alarms, books, cable TV, DSL, cosmetics, home repairs, magazines, and political and religious solicitations involve the assignment of salespeople to nonoverlapping specific streets, neighborhoods, or towns. Similarly, route delivery salespeople (beer, bread, industrial fasteners) generally have exclusive geographic territories.

TWO-TIER ORGANIZATIONS

If you offer a product that requires considerable service after the sale and different skills for selling than for servicing, consider a two-tier sales organization with separate functions. A nationally advertised underwear company with a large sales force stopped growing when annual sales reached $100 million. The sales manager asked a representative sampling of salespeople why his or her sales had stopped increasing. All replied that because they were so busy servicing current accounts, they had no time to open new ones. The sales manager hired part-time salespeople to count stock and fill display fixtures for existing accounts. This left the full-time salespeople with enough time both to write reorders at existing customers and to open new accounts. Eventually this grew into a two-tiered sales force with different functions: one concentrating on new account development (hunters) and the other on account maintenance (farmers). The new account salespeople continued receiving a partial commission on customers turned over to the account maintenance sales force.

Hiring hunters required a different candidate profile than hiring farmers, and each group had separate compensation plans. The hunters required a more aggressive, self-starter with experience in opening new accounts. The farmers required a more customer- and service-oriented salesperson with successful experience in relationship sales.

The hunters received 60 percent performance pay based on new account acquisition. The farmers received 40 percent performance pay based on reorders and account revenue growth.

In a functional sales organization, customers sometimes dislike the change of salespeople, and salespeople sometimes dislike the change of customers. However, if your salespeople show superior account development skills but a lack of interest in retaining or maintaining accounts, try the two-tier approach. You can test it in one territory at a time. In a functional or two-tier sales organization, you might have the cost of two salespeople calling on each account, and to justify this, each salesperson must be able to call on more accounts or do more business with each account.

Technology companies often employ product specialists to support a sales force organized geographically or by type of customer or market. This also represents a form of two-tier sales force.

MARKET SEGMENTS

Related to several of the above models are sales forces organized by market segments. Based on dollars of present and potential revenue and income, cost to sell and service, and probability of success, the sales manager has chosen target accounts and target markets. A miniature transformer manufacturer targets the communication, consumer electronics, and auto markets. An avionics navigational instrumentation firm sells to the Department of Defense and to domestic and overseas airlines. In both cases products are similar, but the diversity of markets requires specialists.

NO RESTRICTIONS

Salespeople who sell consumer services often operate without restrictions to products or services, accounts, or geographic territories. Independent insurance agencies allow their agents to write any type of policies without territorial limitations. Securities brokers may sell their services to anyone who cares to buy, and real estate salespeople generally do not have territories or customer limitations. A telesales firm selling gospel music to religious bookstores allows the telesales people to prospect and sell any account that is not presently an active customer.

HYBRID ORGANIZATIONS

The most effective use of a sales force often involves combining elements of product, account, geographic territory, function, and no restrictions. Because of varying market structures, you may wish to use a different type of organization in different geographic areas or a different type of organization for different product lines. Remember, simple but flexible structures work best. Generally, smaller companies are more flexible than larger ones, allowing them more readily to use combinations or hybrids.

A nationally advertised athletic shoe company organizes salespeople by geographic territory in the Midwest, where it primarily sells to specialty stores. However, on the East and West Coasts, where it primarily sells to regional chains, the sales force uses a key account organization.

A branded tire manufacturer has one sales force for retail tire stores, which is organized geographically; another sales force for auto manufacturers, which is organized by key accounts; a third for fleet trucking firms, which is organized geographically; a fourth for mass merchants organized by key account; and a fifth for off-road tires, which is organized by product line and market (racing, farm, forestry, and construction).

A reform math textbook firm has one sales force calling on local school districts in states where annual decision making is decentralized and another sales force calling on state adoption boards where decision making is centralized and textbook adoptions are made only every three years. Should you choose a combination or hybrid, analyze the potential conflicts and clearly state the ground rules.

In a smaller company your most important resources are the human resources, and your decisions concerning sales force organization must recognize this factor. If one of your salespeople has excellent contacts with certain major accounts, you may wish to assign him or her to these customers while organizing the rest of the sales force by geographic territory. If one of your salespeople has a very close relationship with a major customer, you may wish to have him or her sell all your products to that account while organizing the rest of the sales force by product line. If one of your better salespeople does well with smaller accounts but poorly with larger ones, you may wish to place two salespeople in this territory rather than the usual one. Assuming available potential, the second person would call on larger accounts, allowing the original salesperson to continue concentrating on the smaller ones. If one of your better salespeople cannot travel overnight but your sales force is organized by widely dispersed key accounts, you may wish to build a geographic territory of nonkey accounts within a day's drive of this person's home. The flexibility of a smaller business allows you to fully utilize the human resource by combining various types of sales force organizations.

Recently, pharmaceutical and telecommunications firms have created hybrid organizations by hiring part-time, flextime salespeople. Better company sales-people who left to raise a family or care for a parent can return on a part-time, flextime basis. They must work at least 20 hours a week, they receive excellent comparable compensation but no fringe benefits, and they have smaller territories. These territories are often built around their contacts and are close to home. A tight labor market for qualified salespeople has necessitated this.

RUNNING THE NUMBERS

As in channel choice, the last item in determining sales force architecture is to run the numbers for various alternatives. If you use a 100 percent geographic organization, what will it cost (fixed versus variable), and how much revenue and gross margin will it generate? Do the same analysis using a product line or key account organization. Run spreadsheets using various assumptions at different revenue levels for different type organizations. This is a reality check. Based on the model discussed in this section, you may have chosen a sales force organized by major product line or key account, but based on the spreadsheets, a geographical organization maximizes contribution margins over time. Each year use the model described in this section to analyze sales force architecture, but think long term. Anticipate future changes in the business environment.

The August 2006 MarketBridge survey asked sales, marketing, and human resource executives at 120 large and midsized firms, "What are your organization's greatest sales strategy challenges?" and "What are your organization's greatest sales channel challenges?"

Fifty-five percent of the respondents said the greatest sales strategy challenges were these:

- Focusing on the right customer segments or products
- Creating clear direction and strategy
- Translating the strategy to action with the channels and sales organization

The greatest sales channel challenges were:

- Increasing sales productivity (61 percent of respondents)
- Developing an effective channel strategy (47 percent of respondents)
- Managing channel conflicts (28 percent of respondents)[2]

Questions and Exercises for Chapter 9

- Prepare a salesperson or territory breakeven point and profit and loss statement for a territory you are familiar with.
- How often does your firm or one you are familiar with analyze channel choice?
- How often does your firm or one you are familiar with analyze sales force architecture?

Quiz for Chapter 9

1. True or false?
    A salesperson's breakeven point varies depending on whether he or she works in a new territory or an existing territory.

2. In arriving at a salesperson's breakeven point, you must consider which of the following?
    a. The gross margin after costs of goods sold
    b. The cost to put a salesperson on the road
    c. The operating profit before the cost of putting a salesperson on the road
    d. Allocated overhead expenses

3. In arriving at a salesperson's contribution margin, you must consider which of the following?
    a. Net revenue
    b. Cost of putting the salesperson on the road
    c. Bad debts
    d. Local advertising
    e. Allocated general and administrative expenses

4. In choosing between various sales channels (channel choice), you should *not* consider which of the following?
    a. Type of customers
    b. Type of selling
    c. Operating issues
    d. Type of products or services
    e. Sizing and deployment
    f. Channel conflicts
    g. Performance pay
    h. Dollars of contribution margin

5. In choosing whether to organize by major product line, major customer, geography, or function, you should consider which of the following?
    a. Type of customers
    b. Type of products
    c. Type of salespeople
    d. Job description
    e. Candidate profile
    f. Costs

6. Channel partners include which of the following?
    a. Sales rep organizations
    b. Distributors
    c. Brokers
    d. Jobbers
    e. Direct full-time field salespeople

7. A sales force can be organized in which of the following ways?
    a. Geographically
    b. By major accounts
    c. By major product lines
    d. By function
    e. No restrictions
    f. Based on salespeople's relationships

8. True or false?
   Hybrid sales organizations work best because of varying market structures.

9. True or false?
   After deciding on channel choice and architecture, you must do spreadsheets to compare alternative costs and gross margins.

10. True of false?
   The model for organizing a sales force progresses from the more general to the more specific.

Notes

1. MarketBridge, Mark Donnolo, *Performance-Driven Selling 2006*. Market-bridge Technologies. Copyright © 2006. Reprinted by permission of MarketBridge.
2. Ibid.

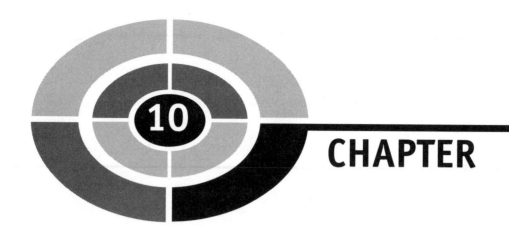

Sizing and Deployment; Time and Territory Management

CHAPTER 10

Sizing and Deployment

How many salespeople do you need, how large should a salesperson's territory be, and how do you determine the territory boundaries? A sales manager's goal is to make his or her salespeople successful by increasing sales force productivity and capacity, reengineering the sales organization as he or she would a factory, being an agent of change, and managing change. He or she must hire the best, terminate the rest, train salespeople, and compensate them properly. However, without proper sizing and deployment, even a well hired, trained, and compensated sales organization will not operate at its full potential.

To maximize the sales organization's productivity, each salesperson's territory must have equal potential based on present and potential revenues and income, present and potential number and type of accounts (call frequency) versus the salesperson's call rate, workload, and capacity. Without equal potential for success, a proper compensation program will not motivate salespeople, and even properly hired and trained salespeople will consider finding other employment. As you can see, each step in the sales management process affects the other steps.

The goal is for salespeople to economically make the optimum number of quality calls on the right customers and prospects. This will maximize dollars of contribution margin over time. Mapping software offered by Salesforce.com, Netsuite.com, Adapt CRM, SAP Business One, Siebel, Saratoga, and Oracle, among others, can assist you in these tasks.

Sizing and deployment involves both strategic and tactical issues. The sales manager must properly identify target accounts and market segments to make sure they receive proper call frequency. He or she must determine whether new customers or a larger share of existing customers' business represents the best opportunities. This will influence how to measure territory potential and how frequently to call on prospects versus customers. He or she must understand the cost of putting a salesperson on the road, a salesperson's breakeven point, a territory's dollars of contribution margin, and how quickly a salesperson can be trained. Lowering the cost of putting a salesperson on the road or lowering his or her breakeven point or faster training for the salesperson may allow the sales manager to hire more salespeople and to create smaller territories that could increase market share.

BENEFITS

The benefits of proper sizing and deployment can give your firm a competitive advantage in a commoditized marketplace. Proper sizing and deployment prevents 70 percent of a firm's revenues coming from 30 percent of the sales force. It levels the playing field and allows total sales to increase. Often salespeople who have the largest territories with the most potential do not have the call capacity to obtain the full potential. Proper sizing and deployment allows the sales manager to allocate some of these accounts to qualified salespeople who are underutilized. Instead of trading dollars each year between new and existing business or between one territory or product line and another, the net dollars of revenue, net dollars of margin, and net number of active accounts actually increases. Proper sizing and deployment will improve market share not only by enabling a salesperson to spend more time in front of customers and on other sales-related efforts but also by increasing the number of customer calls, reducing the cost per call, and matching customer needs with your organizational structure.

PROBLEMS AND OPPORTUNITIES

A major branded manufacturer selling household appliances to retailers analyzed each salesperson's territory relative to present and potential sales, present and potential number of accounts or workload, and the salesperson's call rate or capacity. Out of the 20 regional sales managers, 15 found salesperson territories with major issues of overcapacity or undercapacity. The required workload, number of calls, type of accounts, and frequency of visits did not match the salesperson's call capacity. Each regional manager had 10 salespeople reporting to him or her. Of the 15 regional managers with workload issues, 8 reallocated some accounts, and 7 did not. For the next two years those regional managers who had adjusted territories to equalize workloads and potential had regional sales increases 5 percentage points above those who made no adjustments. Proper territory alignment can significantly increase revenues and market share with little increase in expenses.

Smaller territories maximize market share and minimize travel expenses, but often they cannot produce significant enough revenues to support a salesperson, whether on performance or fixed pay. Larger territories can produce significant enough revenues to support a salesperson, but they can be expensive to travel and may not maximize market share. A key issue is the amount of market potential necessary to support one salesperson and the appropriate metrics needed to measure that potential.

As with compensation, channel choice and architecture, each year you must reanalyze the sizing and deployment of your sales force and make appropriate changes. Each year changes in salespeople, customers, competition, products, technology, markets, and strategy impact deployment and sizing issues. Don't let legacy issues create chronic inertia. Many sales managers inherit and keep their territory structure or just follow competition. As mentioned in previous chapters, competition may not have the proper models or methodologies.

Often territories contain equal physical size, or they have been structured around each major city in the region, or they contain equal past sales and number of accounts. Instead, as an agent of change, let us explore how to create territories of equal potential, based on present and potential sales and the number and type

of accounts (call frequency and workload) versus the salesperson's call rate or capacity.

Creating Territories of Equal Potential

DECIDING ON AND FINDING THE PROPER METRICS

The sales manager's first task in creating territory boundaries and deciding on staffing needs involves deciding on and then finding data for the proper metrics to measure each territory's potential revenues for the company's various product lines. Many industry publications and associations plus appropriate federal, state, and city government agencies (SIC codes) have this information. The pharmaceutical industry has private-market research firms that track prescriptions written for various medications by physician, pharmacy, and zip code. The American Cancer Association has data on new cases of various types of cancer reported annually by state. Firms selling equipment, devices, and medication related to cancer use this data to measure territory potential. Semiconductor equipment manufacturers use geographic data on the annual unit production of semiconductors by type to measure potential. Number of hospital beds, admissions, discharges, and Medicare cases by city provide metrics for hospital supplies and health-care providers. The National Restaurant Association has data on number of restaurants by size and type by zip code, which suppliers use to measure potential.

New home construction and sales in various price ranges by zip code provide territory potential metrics for the furniture and consumer mortgage financing industries. Often the local Chamber of Commerce or newspaper has this data. The Commerce Department and an industry association have data on the number of mattresses sold by zip code. Consumer or industrial buying power indexes are used to measure territory potential for various products. *Sales and Marketing Management* magazine publishes an annual "Survey of Buying Power" (using data provided by Claritas, Inc.) that contains data on population, households, retail sales, and effective buying income (EBI) by region, state, county, and metro markets. Based on the 2005 "Survey of Buying Power," *Sales and Marketing* magazine named the 20 best cities for selling. The top 9 included Dallas-Fort Worth, Houston, Riverside-San Bernardino, Phoenix-Scottsdale, Atlanta, Washington, D.C., Sacramento, Austin, and San Diego.

The number of children in grades K through 6 by district measures potential for selling reform math textbooks. Market potential for tires is measured by the numbers of truck and auto licenses by city and state. Obtaining statistical data is simply a matter of identifying the associations, government agencies, and publications in a specific field and getting the information directly from the source. There are a number of reference books that identify these sources: *Encyclopedia of Associations, National Trade and Professional Associations of the United States, Statistical Abstracts of the United States, The United States Government Manual, Guide to Special Issues and Indexes of Periodicals*, and *Standard Periodical Directory*. Also use the Internet to search for and obtain these data.

Decide which metrics best measure present and potential revenue for your company's products or services. Hire an MBA summer intern to research this project. Ask the student to use historical data to prove the correlation between potential and the metrics. Then using the ideas in this chapter find the best sources for this data.

UNDERSTANDING THE TERRITORY BREAKEVEN POINT

Using the proper metrics for your industry, decide on how much market potential is needed to support a salesperson. If a firm has a 1 percent share of its market segment and the breakeven point for a salesperson, including all fixed overhead expenses, is $2 million of revenue, a territory must contain at least $200 million of market potential to justify this salesperson. If this firm enters a new territory and does not include fixed overhead expenses in calculating the salesperson's breakeven point, considerably less market potential is required. Market potential and territory performance can also be measured in units rather than dollars. If the salesperson sells diverse products or services into many market segments, this calculation becomes more complex. Make sure that each territory contains more than enough potential for a salesperson to break even, and hopefully be profitable.

Assuming an existing sales force, using appropriate metrics, measure the market potential for each salesperson and territory. How can you equalize them? Do you need to hire another salesperson, switch accounts from one territory to another, or change territory boundaries? Assuming your compensation plan contains some performance pay, possibly a commission based on revenues, or a bonus based on meeting sales goals, salespeople require territories of equal or similar potential to earn equitable compensation.

Looking at current and previous years' actual sales by territory, what market share does each represent? Which salespeople have the highest and lowest market share and why? If the top 30 percent of your territories produce 70 percent of the results, ask why. Does it reflect the territory potential, or the salesperson's skills, or both? Research shows that territories of equal potential will increase the total sales of all the territories.

Call Frequency versus Call Capacity

SALESPERSON'S TIME ALLOCATION PLANNER

Next, for each territory, examine current and potential number of and type of accounts, required call frequencies, and the salesperson's in-person call capacity or workload. Refer to Exhibit 10.1, at the end of this chapter.

Using each salesperson's call reports, calculate the annual in-person customer call capacity. A salesperson selling apparel to specialty stores averages five in-person calls a day, but a salesperson at the same firm calling on department stores makes two customer calls a day. The New York City salesperson can make four department store visits a day; the Los Angeles salesperson can reach only three specialty stores a day. Each salesperson's in-person customer call rate varies depending on type of selling, type of customer, industry, and density of accounts. Salespeople involved in modified rebuys will make more customer in-person calls a day than salespeople involved in new system sales. For long complex sales cycles with many steps from search to purchase, a salesperson may call on only one major account a day but visit five decision makers and influencers within the group. If a pharmaceutical salesperson, calling on pediatricians, can make six in-person calls a day and works in the field 200 days a year, her annual call capacity is 1,200.

The salesperson's in-person call capacity is like a factory's production capacity: Physical and time constraints prevent it from varying more than 10 percent from year to year. However, by changing the sales force organization or channels or using automation and more support staff, the call capacity can improve. For example, a salesperson's call capacity could increase by having a customer service or telesales person qualify leads, make appointments, or occasionally handle smaller accounts. A salesperson's call capacity could increase with laptops, contact management software, and cell phones. E-mail, e-commerce, and Web sites increase sales force productivity and call capacity. Technology will not replace salespeople, but it will increase call capacity and lower the cost per call.

Next, compare a salesperson's in-person call capacity to the number of calls required to sell and service present and new accounts, that is, the salesperson's workload in her or his territory. Classify prospects and accounts A, B, and C by present and potential revenues and income, cost to sell and serve, and probability of success. Based on this metric, A accounts need to be called on most frequently and C accounts least frequently.

A salesperson selling real-time database software to petroleum traders calls on brokerage houses, commodity traders, banks, pension plans, and international energy companies. The more users each customer has, the greater the revenue potential. The cost to sell and serve is less and the probability of success is higher at commodity traders. They also eventually need the most copies.

Commodity traders represent the A accounts—that is, the target customers and prospects. Banks represent the other extreme and have a C classification.

Salespeople at this firm call on A accounts and A prospects twice a month (24 times a year), B accounts and B prospects once a month (12 times a year), and C accounts and prospects once every other month (6 times a year). The Texas salesperson can make three in-person calls a day and spends 200 days a year in the field selling, and therefore has an annual call capacity of 600. The Texas salesperson has 15 A accounts and prospects, 30 B accounts and prospects, and 30 C accounts and prospects. Multiplying the number of accounts and prospects by classification times, the required call frequency produces a workload for the Texas salesperson of 900 calls a year versus a call capacity of 600 calls. The salesperson cannot properly service and sell present and potential accounts. Possibly another salesperson is needed, or C accounts should not be called on, or the frequency of in-person calls needs to be reexamined. Possibly a sales support person could handle C accounts. Possibly the salesperson could substitute telephone calls for certain in-person calls.

A seed company sells plugs (small bedding plants), seeds, and supplies to greenhouses, nurseries, and growers for ornamental flowers. The three Illinois salespeople can each make four customer or prospect calls a day. Assuming 220 field selling days a year, each salesperson has an annual capacity of 880 calls. In addition to selling, servicing, and expanding present customers, each salesperson is expected to make two to three prospecting calls a week or 100 a year. The sales manager uses the salesperson's time allocation planner in Exhibit 10.1 to construct each salesperson's workload. A, B, and C accounts are determined by square feet under cultivation, which correlates to dollars of potential sales. One salesperson has 15 A accounts, 30 B accounts, and 45 C accounts. Another salesperson has 20 A accounts, 40 B accounts, and 60 C accounts. The third salesperson has 25 A accounts, 50 B accounts, and 70 C accounts. Salespeople are expected to see A accounts monthly or 12 times a year, B accounts every other month or 6 times a year, and C accounts quarterly or 4 times a year.

Including 100 prospecting calls a year, the first salesperson is expected to make 640 calls a year, the second 820 calls a year, and the third 980. Based on each salesperson's capacity, the first salesperson with 640 required calls has excess capacity, and the third salesperson with 980 required calls is not able to service all existing accounts and also prospect for new accounts. If the close ratio is 10 prospecting calls to obtain one new account, then each salesperson adds 10 new customers annually that need to be serviced as A, B, or Cs. However, this might be balanced by lost customers. The first salesperson is at 73 percent of capacity, the second is at 93 percent of capacity, and the third is overcapacity at 111 percent. Possibly accounts can be switched from the third salesperson to the first, assuming each territory has equal potential sales and number of accounts.

Various software packages can assist you in balancing workloads by preparing and analyzing this data.

Both of these examples represent modified rebuys, where salespeople regularly call on the same customers and prospects. For new system sales that involve long complex sales cycles, the time allocation planner must be used in conjunction with the funnel management techniques discussed in Chapter 5.

The number and type of present and potential accounts in a territory can be obtained from your customer lists plus industry trade associations, trade publications, telephone directories, federal, state, and city government (SIC) data, and the Chamber of Commerce. Use the Internet to help you search for data and possibly download it. Much of this data are available online or on CD-ROMs. The Commerce Department's *Survey of U.S. Industrial and Commercial Buying Power* lists by state and county the number of establishments by major SIC code, their shipments and receipts, and their percent of the U.S. total for their SIC code. *Sales and Marketing Management* magazine aggregates some of these data in their "Annual Survey of Buying Power." Territories may have equal potential revenues, but one may have a large number of small accounts, and another a small number of large accounts. In balancing territory workloads, the sales manager must take this into account. Territories become defined then not only by dollars of equal potential revenue but by classifying accounts as to importance, sales potential, and necessary call frequency, then comparing current and potential accounts with desired market share and the physical call limits of a salesperson.

CHANGE MANAGEMENT

When the sales manager changes the boundaries of a salesperson's territory, generally one person gains revenue, accounts, and potential while another person loses them. Often the person who loses customers and potential is a high performer who has generated more business than he or she can handle. The reward for doing well may be perceived as a penalty causing low morale, loss of enthusiasm, or turnover. Similar to changing compensation, changing territory boundaries represents a highly emotional issue for salespeople. If possible, sell the benefits of change: less travel, more time in front of customers for account development, more leisure, and more new challenges from prospecting. Carefully explain why the change is being made, and massage the salesperson's ego with lunch or a letter from your boss. To smooth the transition, pay a one-year performance pay override to the salesperson on the accounts transferred. If possible, have the existing salesperson introduce the newer salesperson to the accounts being transferred. Insist that the present salesperson transfer all files, customer data, and customer profiles to the new person. Customers belong to the company, not to the salesperson.

If salary represents a large portion of the salesperson's compensation, transferring accounts will prove easier. If salespeople receive performance pay based on growth, market share, or new accounts, the transfer of several accounts might provide an opportunity for more income even for the salesperson who loses accounts. Possibly the salesperson's quota will be reduced.

Try and transfer a mix of large and small accounts. Take into consideration how your salespeople travel the territories, their route analysis, and where they live. Take into consideration customer's needs and personal relationships.

A refuse removal firm in Baltimore that employs five salespeople represents one extreme in changing territory boundaries. The sales manager rotates salespeople's territories every year. The salespeople and customers enjoy it. Salespeople compete to improve on their peers' performance in the territories. Customers enjoy the variety. All the salespeople share best practices and know all the customers, which prevent bad habits and make the manager happy. When a salesperson leaves, there is less trauma. Rotating salespeople prevents complacency and plateauing, but it can interfere with building customer relationships.

Using these analytical, sometimes black-box techniques to establish territory boundaries does not constitute an exact science, but it is a logical approach to improving salespeople's performance. As mentioned, computer software programs exist to assist you in this task.

OTHER CONSIDERATIONS

For a smaller firm, as with channel choice and sales force organization, your salespeople and their needs and contacts also require serious consideration in setting territory boundaries. Flexibility represents a competitive advantage for smaller concerns, allowing the sales manager to temper the analytical approach to territories with important human considerations. Smaller firms take into account where salespeople live, their personalities, personal needs, likes and dislikes, and contacts. One salesperson may prefer a territory with smaller accounts; another might do better with major accounts.

Sizing, deployment, and territory boundaries are also influenced by mountains, bridges, highway systems, and market areas. Although market information on buying power, potential sales, and number of possible accounts is generally available by county, zip code, and city, state, or region, sales territory boundaries may not lend themselves to city, county, or state lines. Highway systems, rivers, bridges, subways, and mountains must be considered. Also, major market and trading areas cross state lines.

For example, the highway system connecting Columbus, Dayton, and Cincinnati with Indianapolis is better and shorter than the highway system connecting Columbus, Dayton, and Cincinnati with northern Ohio. The greater

Cincinnati, Ohio, trading area also includes counties in Kentucky and Indiana. Therefore, many companies create a territory that includes central and southern Ohio, central and southern Indiana, and northern Kentucky.

A WORD OF CAUTION

Before changing territory boundaries, make sure the data you use are accurate. Do you understand which metrics measure potential for your products and services? Do the data you use reflect those metrics? Have you classified A, B, and C accounts correctly? Does the required call frequency reflect historical data? Which data are you using to decide on a salesperson's call capacity? Bad data lead to bad decisions.

Before changing territory boundaries, make sure you consider alternatives and understand the possible problems or opportunities in each territory. Before changing territory boundaries, make sure you also understand each territory's competitive situation, possible past operational problems with delivery or quality, and market dynamics as well as the salespeople's strengths and weaknesses. Look at alternative methods of correcting variances in required call frequency and workloads such as dividing the sales force into hunters and farmers and reorganizing the sales force by markets.

MEASURING RESULTS

Once you change territory boundaries, you must have metrics to measure whether sales force performance has improved. If it has not improved, you need to look at alternative actions. Metrics might include increased revenues, market share and gross margins in all territories, lower customer and salesperson turnover, higher customer and salesperson satisfaction, or more new accounts. Measure these results after salespeople have performed one or two sales cycles, which could vary in length from a month to several years depending on the industry. But do set performance standards and a time frame for measuring the results of your major decisions.

Time Management

Channel choice, sales force architecture, sizing, and deployment have taken us from the macro to the micro of sales force organization. The sales manager's last task in this area involves helping salespeople better plan, use, and track their time within the territory. You must set standards and train and assist salespeople in call frequency, route analysis, allocation of time among various duties, and time wasters. Time and knowledge represent important resources for salespeople. They must learn how to best utilize a finite amount of time within their geographic territory.

Salespeople resist training in and tracking of time management. Most sales managers hesitate to become involved in these very tactical issues, thinking that mature adults don't need assistance in these areas. But poor time management on the part of salespeople reduces productivity, increases the cost per call, and dilutes the positive affects of proper organization and deployment.

As we know, salespeople represent an expensive human resource. Proper time management will allow them to increase their call capacity and lower the cost per call. Proper time management will allow salespeople to economically make quality calls on the right customers and prospects.

TIME LOGS

The use of several techniques can make time management training easier for a sales manager. First, ask your salespeople to list their top 10 daily activities in declining order of importance related to meeting sales goals. Then prepare a time log asking salespeople to track the amount of time they spend at each of those activities each day. Activities might include, in declining order of importance, time in front of customers or prospects, time on the phone with customers or prospects, preparing for sales calls, writing proposals, coordinating activities in-house with other departments, traveling, waiting, training, sales meetings, administrative work, and/or conflict resolution. The list will be different for a modified rebuy versus a long complex new systems sale. Exhibit 10.2, at the end of this chapter, shows an example of a salesperson's time log.

Have the salesperson analyze the amount of time spent in the four most important categories that drive sales versus the four least important. Generally the most important categories will account for less than 30 percent of a salesperson's time. If salespeople receive performance pay, this time log analysis gets their attention. Solicit their suggestions for increasing the time devoted to activities most important to increasing sales. Agree to a course of action. Often internal administrative changes are needed to free up salespeople's time. This also represents an opportunity to discuss the total cost of putting the salesperson on the road (see Chapter 8) and how this impacts time management.

The August 2006 MarketBridge survey of sales, marketing, and human resource executives at 120 midsized and large companies found that on average the sales organization spends 48 percent of its time selling and 40 percent of its time in direct customer contact. My experience with salespeople's time logs shows face time at around 20 to 30 percent depending on the industry.[1]

For one month, do a time log for yourself as sales manager or as a student of sales management. List your daily activities and rank them by importance in driving sales results or college grades. A sales manager's time log might include activities such as field coaching or ride-withs, sales meetings, performance management, motivation, conflict resolution, order expediting, administration, preparing bids, proposals, forecasts, management meetings, and personal selling. How much time do you spend in each of these activities, and how can you spend more time in the most important activities?

The MarketBridge survey showed that sales managers feel time spent training the sales force provides the greatest benefit but does not receive the majority of their time. Similarly sales managers felt they devoted more time to sales force automation (SFA) and customer-relationship marketing (CRM) systems than is reflected by the increased productivity benefits produced by these systems.[2]

TRAVEL TIMES

Second, ask the salesperson to prepare a map of her or his territory with account locations color-coded by frequency of visits. Discuss how the salesperson travels the territory and the most efficient schedule or routes for meeting these call requirements. Can accounts be called on in clusters? What overnight trips are necessary? Discuss efficient highways, public transportation, or airline systems for moving between accounts.

Some sales managers suggest salespeople organize territories into four quadrants, sections, or slices. A salesperson spends a day per week or a week per month in each quadrant, working it in a cloverleaf pattern, or starting at the farthest point and working back, or working in a line between two overnight stops. Usually one day per week remains for cleaning up unplanned events. Some sales managers further refine this technique by gridding each quadrant and assigning it one day of the week or month. Sales managers may also ask their salespeople to make all planned calls before 2 o'clock (prime selling time) and to use the time after 2 o'clock to react to customer calls, missed accounts, and other problems. In other words, act in the morning, react in the afternoon. Every product, service, company, and territory requires a customized approach because the problems, opportunities, needs, and customers are different. Mapping and scheduling software can assist you in this task.

Experienced salespeople don't enjoy being told how to organize their day. So present your map merely as an aid, and let them tell you how they plan to organize their schedule. Provide suggestions and information where you feel they are necessary to accomplish the desired goals.

Some sales managers feel that helping their people schedule calls is not worth their time because it represents a skill possessed by every salesperson. But if your average sales call costs $164, as discussed previously, and if proper scheduling results in one more call a day, or 240 more calls per year per salesperson, then you might be increasing efficiency or lowering expenses per salesperson dramatically. Considered in this light, scheduling deserves and needs your time and attention.

Even the best salespeople sometimes possess poor planning skills or have developed bad scheduling habits. As an objective voice from outside the territory, you can suggest changes.

DAY PARTS AND TIME ALLOCATIONS

Third, ask your salespeople how they use parts of days to organize their time. What are the best times of day or best days of the week to prospect? What are the best hours to call on a physician versus a hospital purchasing agent? Is it better to call on construction sites and restaurants before 8 a.m. but on research labs after lunch? In some industries, Friday afternoons and Monday mornings are prime selling hours.

With each salesperson, share your knowledge of how to allocate time as between prospects and established business. You should suggest a different allocation for mature territories with many established accounts than for newer territories with only a few established customers. Growth occurs not only from opening new accounts but from properly cultivating existing ones.

With each salesperson, share your knowledge of the service versus selling time required for each customer and for each type of customer or territory. What allocation produces the best results?

If your company sells more than one product line or has different or distinct markets or customer groups, share your knowledge with each salesperson on how to allocate time between these products, markets, and customers. What allocation produces the best results?

TIME WASTERS

Exhibit 10.3, at the end of this chapter, lists 41 time-wasting activities or conditions that slow salespeople down. Give it to your salespeople and have them place an X next to those activities that represent time wasters; then ask them to identify and rank the four most important. How many hours a week do these four involve? Discuss with your salespeople ways to eliminate or reduce these

time wasters. And it wouldn't hurt to do the time-waster exercise yourself. You may have a case of memo-itis or be an inefficient do-it-yourselfer. Remember, it's as important for you to properly allocate your precious time as it is to teach others to manage theirs.

Working smart, or efficiently, is as important as working long and hard. You need to do both. Many salespeople attempt to disguise their ineffectiveness by appearing to work hard and long.

Be sure your salespeople plan their calls at least a week in advance and that they put their plans into writing. Who will they see, and what do they wish to accomplish? Be sure your salespeople use available technology to better manage their time. Do all salespeople take full advantage of the contact and calendar management software, cell phones, e-mail, and the Web?

TIME TRAPS

- Be sure your salespeople don't call on unqualified leads that have not been properly screened, analyzed, evaluated, or updated. Selling time is too precious to squander it on low-potential prospects or coffee calls.
- Be sure your salespeople use the telephone and e-mail not only to make appointments but also to answer certain questions and write certain reorders. Salespeople often underutilize the phone and e-mail. You can communicate with a lot more customers each day by phone and e-mail than you can in person.
- Be sure salespeople understand what hours you want worked and how often you want them in the office. Does the day start at 7 or 9 a.m.? Does it end at 4 or 6 p.m.? Is lunch to be used for selling or relaxing? Does Friday end at 2 or 5 p.m.? Set standards, be critical, and sit in judgment.
- Be sure your salespeople don't bury themselves in paperwork and then use that as an excuse for not selling. Analyze their paperwork load and help them to reduce it. Work with top management on reducing administrative work and improving communications with other departments.
- Be sure your salespeople prioritize their day, listing their tasks by importance. Salespeople have a tendency to do the easy work, which may not be the most important work, first.
- Encourage salespeople to use customer support personnel to help make appointments and follow up on service issues. Salespeople often underutilize their support staff.
- Encourage your salespeople to set daily objectives and deadlines, to focus on results, and to develop alternatives. Encourage your salespeople to avoid procrastinating, to concentrate their efforts on one thing at a time, and to consider delegating by using available resources intelligently. Remind them

of their schedules, but when unplanned events occur, encourage them to be flexible. Remind them that to maintain their priorities, they must occasionally say no to customers, fellow employees, and even you. Help them to anticipate problems and to develop contingency plans and to manage the continual flow of daily interruptions. Lack of persistence and poor communication with fellow employees can also be time wasters. These issues apply equally to sales managers.

- Use ride-withs and sales meetings to train salespeople in time management. At the end of each day of field coaching, discuss number of calls, time in front of customers, miles traveled between accounts, and the allocation of time among various markets, activities, and products. At sales meetings, have salespeople discuss best practices and time wasters. Let the salesperson who is the best at time management lead the discussion.

The object of all this information is to have salespeople economically make the optimum number of effective calls on the right customers and prospects. The emphasis is on helping the salesperson work smarter, thus creating a more productive and efficient sales force. Do salespeople control their territories, or do the territories control them? Knowledge is power, and time is money.

GOOD COMMUNICATION

Poor communication between management and the sales force wastes a great deal of time and demotivates all parties. The salespeople are the sales manager's internal customers. Part of making the transition from sales to management is for the sales manager to communicate as well with the salespeople as she or he does with customers.

In communicating with the sales force, remember that all forms of communications have four parts: a sender, a receiver, a message, and feedback. When sending a message, ask for feedback to make sure the receiver understood your meaning. When receiving a message, be sure to offer feedback to show the sender you listened and understand the message. By asking for and giving feedback, you can quickly correct misunderstandings. For example, after sending a message on call frequency, you might ask the receiver, "How many times a quarter will you call on Ashton Machine Works?" Or after receiving a salesperson's message on a prospect, you might reply, "A company with that little potential requires only a quarterly telephone call." Good communication requires many skills, including empathy and listening. As a sales manager you communicate with salespeople in many ways from body language to call reports to phone calls.

In recent surveys of salespeople and sales managers, 80 percent of respondents indicated that the top two sales manager mistakes involve communication: failing to provide feedback and listening poorly. Other mistakes often cited in these surveys involve failing to set clear goals and objectives and failing to train and develop employees.

CALL REPORTS, CALL PLANNERS, AND ROUTE SHEETS

To help salespeople better utilize and track their time, most firms use some type of weekly or monthly reporting. Most firms ask salespeople to inform the sales manager what accounts they plan to visit each week, the objective and strategy of the calls, and after the calls, what was accomplished. These reports come in many different formats.

Some sales managers want to know what accounts and prospects the salespeople plan to call on each day, what they plan to accomplish, how they plan to accomplish it, and what preparation has been done for the call. Some sales managers want this information only for new account prospecting because this activity drives company growth. Other sales managers desire reports organized by major accounts that provide information on what was accomplished during each call. Examples of these reports are included in Exhibits 10.4, 10.5, and 10.6, at the end of this chapter.

For longer, more complex sales cycles, the sales manager will want to know whether the salesperson has moved the customer or prospect to the next step in the decision-making process, sales cycle, or marketing funnel.

Some sales managers help salespeople to manage their time by asking them to report on the status of their 10 largest accounts, 10 accounts with the greatest growth potential, and 10 top prospect accounts. The reports ask for information on competition, products or services to be offered, decision makers, and projected revenue. These are known as the 10/10/10 reports, and we will discuss them more fully in Chapter 11 on sales forecasting and planning.

Salespeople resist providing information in all these reports because as with customer profiles, they feel more secure controlling the information. Also, asking salespeople where they plan to go and what they plan to accomplish each week makes them more accountable, which creates anxiety.

However, some form of these reports proves absolutely essential for helping salespeople to manage and track their time. Show the salespeople that you read the reports, and show them how to use the reports to improve their results and therefore their compensation. In other words, sell the benefits by suggesting more efficient ways for them to travel or a different approach to sell an account. Show them that a record of what happened on the last four calls to an account can help them make the next call more productive.

Sales Managers' Major Mistakes or Weaknesses in Sales Force Organization

- Not measuring salespeople's use of time with time logs and time wasters.
- Creating territories based on equal geography.
- Creating territories based on present sales and actual number of accounts rather than potential sales, number and type accounts, resulting salesperson's workload, versus salesperson's call rate or capacity. Strategic issues.
- Not coaching salespeople on travel routes, time allocation, sequence, frequency of visits to A, B, and C accounts.
- Not realizing and showing the cost of putting a salesperson on the road.
- Not analyzing alternative distribution channels and alternative ways of organizing the sales force. Strategic issues.
- Not reviewing territory boundaries annually.
- Lack of personal organization and time management skills.
- Not understanding the salesperson's breakeven point.
- Not using a territory profit-and-loss statement.

Exhibit 10.1.   Salesperson's Time Allocation Planner.

Salesperson's Name: _____

Territory: _____

No. of Customers in This Category:		No. of Sales Calls per Year on Each Type of Customer:		No. of Calls per Year in This Category:
A _____	×	_____	=	_____
B _____	×	_____	=	_____
C _____	×	_____	=	_____

Plus estimated no. of prospect and cold calls (closing ratio):   _____

Plus service nonselling calls (e.g., deliveries or collections):   _____

Actual no. of required annual calls: _____

Actual daily or weekly calls of salesperson (call rate):   _____

Projected annual calls of salesperson—his or her universe:

Comparison to required annual calls: _____

Exhibit 10.2.   Time Log for Week of _____.

Function/Activity	Sun	Mon	Tue	Wed	Thu	Fri	Sat	Total Actual	Desirable Total
In front of customer:									
On phone with customer:									
In office preparing proposals:									
Working with other departments:									
Traveling:									
Waiting:									
Conflict resolution:									
In office—other:									
Number of prospect in-person calls:									
Number of customer in-person calls:									
TOTAL									

How would you like to allocate your time to improve results?

What needs to be changed to accomplish this? _____

Comments: _____
_____
_____

Exhibit 10.3.   Your Time Wasters.

This checklist will help focus your mind on your greatest time wasters. Place an X next to those that are problems for you. Then identify the four that are the most problematic. Finally, place a 1, 2, 3, or 4 next to these to indicate their importance, using 1 to represent the most important time waster.

☐ 1. Telephone calls and voice mail

☐ 2. Interruptions; drop-in visitors

☐ 3. Meetings, scheduled or unscheduled

☐ 4. Crises; "firefighting"

☐ 5. Lack of objectives, deadlines, or priorities

☐ 6. Cluttered desk and office; personal disorganization

☐ 7. Ineffective delegation

☐ 8. Doing dull tasks

☐ 9. Attempting too much at once

☐ 10. Unrealistic time estimates

☐ 11. Ineffective communication

☐ 12. Inadequate training or development of subordinates

☐ 13. Procrastination, indecision, or daydreaming

☐ 14. Inability to say no

☐ 15. Leaving tasks unfinished; jumping from one task to another

☐ 16. Involved in too much detail; "doing it yourself"

☐ 17. Inadequate staff; poor performance by staff

☐ 18. Socializing; idle conversation

☐ 19. Lack of self-discipline

☐ 20. Constantly switching priorities

☐ 21. Lack of feedback; inadequate information

☐ 22. Failure to listen

☐ 23. Conflict; personal problems

☐ 24. Inadequate planning; not considering alternatives

☐ 25. Worry, fear, or anxiety

☐ 26. Waiting

☐ 27. Memo-itis

☐ 28. Poor memory

☐ 29. Confusing activities with results

☐ 30. Fatigue or boredom

☐ 31. Blaming others

☐ 32. Stress and tension

☐ 33. Inadequate facilities or equipment

☐ 34. Company policies

☐ 35. Poor filing system

☐ 36. Paperwork, mail, reports, or reading

☐ 37. Travel; commuting

☐ 38. Pet projects; outside activities

☐ 39. Impatience or haste

☐ 40. Failure to do first things first

☐ 41. Reading and answering e-mail

Exhibit 10.4.   Daily Planner.

Date: _____

Salesperson: _____

* ** ☑ Customer	Goals, Products, and Programs to be Discussed	Strategy and Call Objectives; Samples Presented	Results and Follow-Up

Place an asterisk (*) next to prospect calls (calling on regularly but no orders yet).
Place two asterisks (**) next to cold calls (first-time visit to prospect).
Place check (☑) if phoned customer instead of visited.
White copy: To be turned in prior to workweek, with plans and goals. Yellow copy: To be turned in after workweek,
with results. Pink copy: Sales rep copy.

Exhibit 10.5.   Account Call Report.

Account Name: _____   Sales Rep: _____   Month: _____

Account Number: _____

VP	Date	GLS	Explanation of Gain or Loss	Programs Introduced	SPR	Action Required for Next Sales Call

*V—Visit   *G—Sales gained   *S—Sold
*P—Phone   *L—Sales lost   *P—Pending
               *S—Sales sustained   *R—Rejected

Exhibit 10.6.　New Prospect Call Report.

Sales Rep: _____

New Prospect Calls Made for Month Ended: _____

Date	*	Account Name and/or Contact and Role	Account Type (Use Attached Key to Type)	Programs Presented	Comments	Sales Results	Follow-up Required
1.							
2.							
3.							
4.							
5.							
6.							
7.							
8.							
9.							
10.							

*Cold Call

Note: If sale is closed, transfer to account call reporting form.

C—Closed
D—Dead
O—Ongoing

Questions and Exercises for Chapter 10

- Have each of your salespeople fill out a time allocation planner (Exhibit 10.1). Based on this information, what deployment action will you take?
- What metrics can your firm or a firm you are familiar with use to measure potential revenues and margins in each territory?
- How often does your firm or a firm you are familiar with analyze channel choice, number of salespeople, and territory boundaries?
- What percentage of your salespeople's time is spent in the activities that drive results? What are those activities? How can more time be spent there?

Quiz for Chapter 10

1. True or false?
   Sales force sizing and deployment depends on creating territories of equal potential, a salesperson's workload, and a salesperson's call capacity.

2. True or false?
   Proper sizing and deployment prevents 70 percent of a firm's revenues coming from 30 percent of the sales force.

3. True or false?
   Proper sizing and deployment create a competitive advantage in a commoditized marketplace.

4. True or false?
   Smaller territories maximize market share and minimize travel time but often cannot produce significant enough revenues to support a salesperson.

5. True or false?
   Larger territories can produce significant enough revenue to support a salesperson but can be expensive to travel and may not maximize market share.

6. A salesperson's time allocation planner contains which of the following items?
   a. The number of A, B, and C accounts in the territory
   b. The frequency of A, B, and C account calls
   c. The number of prospecting and service calls per period
   d. The number of calls a salesperson can make a year
   e. The salesperson's breakeven point

7. Items appearing on a salesperson's time log include time spent in which of the following ways?
   a. With customers
   b. Traveling to see customers
   c. Preparing bids or proposals
   d. Conflict resolution
   e. Personal time
   f. Playing golf with customers

8. Items appearing on a sales manager's time log include time spent in which of the following ways?
   a. Sales meetings
   b. Field coaching
   c. Lunch with salespeople
   d. Performance management
   e. Conflict resolution

9. A sales manager should discuss which of the following items with salespeople?
   a. A map of the territory showing customer locations
   b. The best time of day to call on certain accounts
   c. Travel routes
   d. Call frequency
   e. The cost per call

10. Good communication requires which of the following?
    a. A sender
    b. A receiver
    c. A message
    d. Feedback
    e. Listening
    f. Empathy

Notes

1. MarketBridge, Mark Donnolo, *Performance-Driven Selling 2006*. Market-bridge Technologies. Copyright © 2006. Reprinted by permission of MarketBridge.
2. Ibid.

PART SIX

Goal Setting

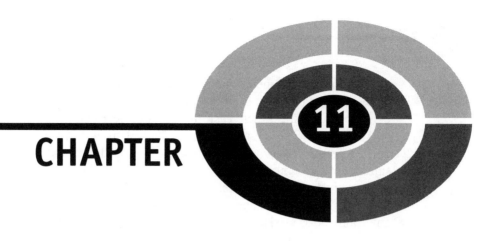

CHAPTER 11

Sales Forecasting and Planning

Planning makes good things happen. Forecasting or planning puts your head in front of your job and creates quiet time. As discussed in Chapter 1, planning, forecasting, job descriptions, candidate profiles, training checklists, development plans, deployment, strategy, targeting, and performance evaluations all represent key control points for sales force management. Using present knowledge, forecasts accurately estimate future sales. Sales plans list the action necessary to generate those future sales and divide the forecast into bit-sized pieces.

All management involves goal setting, measurement, objectives, and strategies. Sales forecasts and plans set the goals. The performance evaluation, Chapter 14, measures and compares actual results and action to these goals. We manage what we monitor.

Financial management and sales management meet each other through the sales forecast. If done correctly, the sales forecast helps operating management schedule

production, procurement, and staffing. If done correctly, the sales forecast helps financial management establish inventory and accounts receivable levels, set expense budgets, estimate cash flow, and project banking requirements.

Accurate, effective sales forecasts and plans involve a blending of objective and subjective material and a balance of top-down and bubble-up input. The salespeople and their manager create a microdriven forecast and plan based on (1) past and present territorial sales trends, (2) changes inside the firm, (3) changes at competitors, (4) changes at customers, and (5) changes in the general business environment or market. Top management creates a macrodriven forecast and plan based on past and present sales trends for the company, market share growth, shareholder value, return on investment, and other market assessment metrics. These will be discussed later in this chapter.

Benefits of a Bubble-Up Sales Forecast or Plan

Asking salespeople to prepare their own sales forecast and plan has many benefits and a few problems. Reaping the benefits and mitigating the problems requires proper structure and process.

Salespeople who prepare and agree to their own forecast or plan have ownership and involvement. If a salesperson's actual results underperform a forecast he or she had little influence on, then the forecast was unrealistic. If a salesperson's actual results underperform a forecast he or she created, it is his or her responsibility. Bubble-up forecasts prepared and agreed to by salespeople make them feel useful, important, and worthwhile. Management cares about them and their input.

Since salespeople are closest to customers and have many data points, their involvement in forecasting should improve accuracy and create more realistic goals. The figures were arrived at through a rational process, not just plucked out of the air. The bubble-up process should not force salespeople to accept unreasonable objectives. Bubble-up forecasts level the playing field by allowing each salesperson to evaluate the factors that drive sales in his or her territory. This prevents management from applying the same percentage or dollar increase to all territories without allowing for individual differences.

Bubble-up forecasts involve collecting a great deal of objective and subjective information on sales trends by territory, customer, and product; changes within the company and at customers and competitors; plus changes in general market conditions that impact sales at the territory level. Using this microapproach, many pieces of information are collected from diverse sources, then aggregated

into modules and models that should result in more accurate, more rational sales forecasts. The totals from these microterritory forecasts are then compared to the macro-level top-down numbers from management, which reflect metrics such as market share and return on investment. If done correctly, these two building blocks produce a near-accurate sales forecast.

Many sales managers claim the major benefit of a bubble-up forecast is that it forces the manager and the salesperson to periodically have a meaningful dialogue about the salesperson's entire job. It forces the salesperson and manager to look at past and present sales trends and to evaluate the factors inside and outside the firm that drive sales. Asking salespeople to forecast their sales without the proper format, discussion process, models, modules, numbers, information, and management input creates frustration and inaccuracy. You can't ask salespeople to forecast from a blank piece of paper.

Many sales managers want to hire salespeople who can not only sell but also act as business managers in their territory. Asking salespeople to participate in the forecasting or planning process helps them manage the business in their territory. It forces them to think about the territory as a sales and profit center. It also forces them to consider all the levers that drive results.

Bubble-up sales forecasts and plans operate as a reality check and early warning system for sales managers and salespeople. If a salesperson cannot discuss changes occurring at customers and competition, the sales manager may have a problem salesperson.

Brokers, distributors, and outside indirect sales representatives (channel partners) should prepare a bubble-up forecast using the same techniques and format as direct full-time salespeople. The sales manager should meet with channel partners to have a meaningful dialogue on inside and outside factors that drive their numbers. By making quarterly or annual sales forecasts and plans part of their contract, you will get more of their commitment and involvement. Channel partners who forecast sales and make commitments give you more of their time and resources. The accuracy of their numbers is also important for the operational and financial management of your company.

Problems with a Bubble-Up Sales Forecast or Plan

Salespeople may intentionally underestimate or overestimate their sales. When a bonus is based on meeting a forecast, when the forecast becomes a quota or budget, or if a salesperson wants to look like a hero by beating a forecast, he or she

may underestimate sales. On the other hand, a salesperson who wants to please her or his sales manager or keep his or her job may overestimate sales. Also, when salespeople don't understand or aren't given the proper forecasting tools, overestimates and underestimates occur.

In Hewitt Associates' 2005 survey of sales and human resource executives at Fortune 1000 firms, of the 63 respondents, 80 percent used a quota-based component in their sales incentive plan. Of these, 71 percent felt their quota-setting process was moderately effective, and 63 percent used a top-down quota-setting process. In another Hewitt survey of 14 companies, with at least 1,000 salespeople each, sales managers ranked their satisfaction with the quota-setting process at 2.3 on a 5-point scale. The most common obstacles cited in setting quotas were inability to obtain market-potential data (64 percent) and inaccurate or insufficient product forecasts (62 percent). Market research available through the Web and databases created through customer-relationship management software may correct some of this.[1]

Often salespeople resist forecasting or planning because it creates a standard against which they can be measured. Some salespeople dislike being held accountable. Also, forecasts can be time-consuming and confusing.

Sometimes salespeople do not have enough data or visibility to prepare a 12-month forecast. In that case, consider forecasting sales for a shorter period such as one quarter.

Many firms include forecasting skills and accuracy on the salesperson's and sales manager's performance evaluation. As mentioned, many firms use sales forecasts to create quotas and pay bonuses to salespeople and sales managers based on reaching or exceeding quotas, although, as noted earlier, many firms are moving away from quota-based compensation.

Sometimes sales managers resist a bubble-up forecast because it requires them to set standards with their salespeople, then sit in judgment and be critical. When a salesperson misses his or her bubble-up forecast, both the salesperson and the manager have responsibility. A sales force is no better than its management.

Many sales managers dislike sales forecasts and plans because they either misunderstand or mistrust the mechanics and because they also fear the results. When a sales manager's forecast or plan turns out to be incorrect, it reflects on his or her ability and performance. Many businesses prepare no forecast, but that is akin to sailing without a rudder—or a map.

Some companies ask salespeople and sales managers to invest a lot of time and energy in preparing forecasts or plans but once prepared, do not use them. On a monthly basis management should compare actual results and actions to the sales forecast and sales plan. Variances should be noted and corrective action discussed. Firms that ask for the sales forecast but never use it demotivate salespeople and sales managers.

BEST- AND WORST-CASE FORECASTS

Some of these problems can be overcome by using the techniques, models, modules, formats, and processes described in this chapter. To improve accuracy and increase the comfort level, many firms ask salespeople to prepare a best- and worst-case forecast, the probability of each, factors that create the variance, critical risks, and contingency plans. For example, let's assume that a salesperson for a computer manufacturing subcontractor forecasts next quarter's best case at $5 million and the worst at $4 million. The $4 million forecast has a 100 percent probability of success; the $5 million forecast an 80 percent probability of success. The salesperson claims she will meet the $5 million forecast if her largest account does not go on a credit hold, if her company can meet its delivery schedule, if another customer successfully launches its new product, and if her friend does not retire as the decision maker at yet another customer. The sales manager asks the salesperson for her contingency plan should these negative events or critical risks occur, and if there are any other circumstances that might prevent her from making the $5 million. Contingency plans allow salespeople to anticipate problems and their solutions. This removes some emotion from disappointing events.

This process allows the manager and the salesperson to discuss all the excuses 30 days before the quarter rather than afterward. Salespeople who are reluctant to forecast generally feel comfortable with the best- or worst-case method. This bracketing process mitigates the fear for forecasting. As the year progresses and more of the what-ifs become reality, as visibility improves, the salesperson can make revisions to produce a more precise forecast.

The use of probability for the best- and worst-case forecasts allows the sales manager to ask for a higher best-case forecast with a lower probability. In the computer manufacturer subcontractor example, the sales manager might ask the salesperson to raise the best-case forecast from $5,000,000 to $5,250,000. The salesperson might agree but lower the probability for meeting the forecast from 80 to 75 percent and possibly add some more what-ifs or critical risks.

MANAGEMENT FORECAST EXCEEDS SALESPERSON FORECAST

Another problem with bubble-up forecasts occurs when management will not accept them or when management's top-down forecast exceeds them. Imagine that your seven salespeople have forecast an 8 percent increase for the region. Some territories will rise substantially above 8 percent, some less.

However, top management also has prepared its sales forecast, and it reflects return on investment and market share metrics. Based on these metrics, top management wants a 12 percent increase from the region.

Salespeople must understand that although management wants and values their bubble-up forecast, that management will prepare its own using different criteria. Salespeople and management must understand there can be differences that may be negotiated.

When differences occur, analyze what caused them. Examine each party's assumptions and resources. Did the salespeople evaluate their individual territorial forecasts against market assessment tools, such as hospital admissions, buying power indexes, or semiconductor purchases? Did management evaluate the effect of a new competitor and also the loss of a major account on their company forecast?

What compromises are possible? Is the top-down forecast doable with more resources such as another customer service person, more advertising, a Web site, cell phones, or laptops? Can territory boundaries be changed or other products or services sold? Top-down management, and bottom-up salespeople or sales management must be willing to negotiate and compromise or the model will not work. If salespeople continually lose, then the bubble-up forecast loses its many benefits. If the forecast becomes a quota on which salespeople receive performance pay, and it is viewed as unrealistic, then salespeople will lose their motivation to exceed quotas.

As a sales manager, the key to avoiding such conflicts lies in anticipating the correct upper management top-down number and then working that number, that increase, into each salesperson's bubble-up territory forecast. The sales manager needs to understand what metrics top management uses to prepare the top-down forecast. Past history can indicate this, or you can just ask. You might have observed that each year upper management takes market growth as reflected in industry publications and adds another 5 percent for desired market share growth to arrive at their figure. Now you can anticipate upper management's top-down number and using the models, modules, and methods described for preparing the bubble-up forecast, work management's number into each salesperson's territory forecast.

Or management might prepare its top-down number based on percentage or dollar growth in corporate revenues or profits, return on investment, shareholder value, appropriate buying power indexes, focus groups, or macro-economic data such as GDP growth. Management might analyze data using regression analysis, time series, adaptive filtering, or moving averages. The important factor is to understand how management arrives at its number to help the salespeople arrive at theirs.

Format and Process for Bubble-Up Sales Forecasts

FORMAT

Thirty to ninety days before the start of your company's accounting year, send by snail mail or e-mail to each salesperson, agent, representative, or distributor who sells your product or service a forecast form for his or her territory. On this form, ask the sales force to forecast orders or shipments or both by month or quarter for each customer or industry as well as for each product or service or style or product or service or style group. You may ask for this information in terms of dollars or units or both. Request information that the sales force finds easiest to work with and that proves most helpful in meeting the forecast's objectives. If the sales force thinks in terms of dollar sales per customer and if the objective of your sales forecast is cash flow projections, not inventory control, then ask each salesperson to forecast dollar sales per appropriate period by customer. Don't ask for unit sales by product or service.

If your company takes orders for future rather than immediate delivery, then the salesperson must identify what months orders are to be shipped. If 90 percent of all orders are shipped within 45 days, you can use a standard factor to translate orders into shipments. Similarly, you can translate any unit forecasts into dollars using standards or averages.

If your industry has selling seasons, as the apparel industry does, you may ask for a forecast by season rather than by month or quarter. You may also ask salespeople to update their forecasts each month or quarter to reflect the changing dynamics of the marketplace.

Once you have established the format for your forecast and sent it to your salespeople, it is important to meet with them to discuss the factors that drive the numbers. With new salespeople or those not familiar with the process, help them prepare the numbers. With established salespeople and those familiar with the process, review the numbers. Issues common to all salespeople may be addressed at a sales meeting. Sales forecasting and planning must be started and completed before the appropriate year, quarter, or season begins. Firms that do not start and complete their quarterly territorial forecasts or plans until the end of the quarter's first month demotivate salespeople and dilute the forecast's or plan's value.

When discussing the forecast, the sales manager has a meaningful dialogue with each salesperson on past and present sales trends in the territory plus changes taking place at competitors and/or customers as well as in general business conditions, and conditions at your firm. The sales forecast can be prepared online, which allows you to quickly aggregate numbers. An example of a possible sales forecast format appears at the end of this chapter as Exhibits 11.1, 11.2, 11.3, and 11.4.

PAST AND PRESENT SALES TRENDS

Each salesperson starts their bottom-up forecast by analyzing past and present sales trends in their territory. This represents the first step, first module, in building the sales forecast. The salesperson may do this in total or by customer or by product, depending on what historical data are available. If next year or next quarter looks like a continuation of trends from past quarters or past years, what will sales be? Obviously, companies that don't prepare customer and product analyses by territory cannot do this; they can work only with territorial totals.

This requires a company to share historical sales data with salespeople. This data become the baseline for a territory forecast so it must be accurate. Sharing this information helps to make the salesperson into a business manager.

A marketing consulting company that provides temporary expert help to Fortune 1000 firms asks its salespeople to prepare quarterly sales forecasts. The San Francisco salesperson looks at her total quarterly sales for the last two years. From the first to the last quarter (eight quarters), total sales doubled from $100,000 to $200,000, an average of $12,500 a quarter, or 12 percent. Price increases accounted for 20 percent of the total increase over this two-year period. More of the unit or hourly sales growth came in year 2 than year 1. She considers just using the last four quarters' growth trend to predict next quarter. Averages computed by removing the oldest period and adding the newest are called moving averages. She notes that growth has accelerated each quarter in the last year and considers giving the last quarter's growth rate more weight. She also notes that growth in web-based services far exceeds growth in direct marketing and media advertising services. Most of last year's growth came from three large accounts.

Based on these past and present quarterly sales trends for the territory, product lines, and customers, assuming no price increases and using moving and weighted averages; she decides on initially forecasting a 20 percent total sales increase from this quarter to next. She then uses these same techniques to forecast sales for next quarter by customer and product line. She assigns a probability of 85 percent to meeting her forecast, lists several events that could cause her to miss it, and notes critical risks and contingency plans.

CHANGES WITHIN THE COMPANY

The forecast process begins with the assumption that the future will look like the past, so we extrapolate next quarter's sales based on past trends. But the future is a moving target and business is a dynamic process, so next the salesperson must analyze how changes within her company, at competitors, customers, and in the marketplace will impact future revenues. To understand these changes, the salesperson again must have a meaningful dialogue with the sales manager. The sales manager presents changes within the company, the salesperson presents changes at customers and competitors, and together they decide on changes in the marketplace and general business conditions. Then they discuss how these changes will affect the territory sales forecast numbers and the sales plan action.

In our example, the sales manager for the marketing consulting firm asks each salesperson to quantify how the following changes within the firm will impact their territorial sales for the next quarter:

1. Prices on all e-commerce services will be raised 10 percent.
2. A strategic sales alliance has been signed with a major e-commerce software provider.
3. The salespeople will receive new laptops and new cell phones.
4. Salespeople will receive a $2,000 bonus for exceeding their revenue goal plus a $1,000 incentive for each new account with revenues exceeding $10,000 in the quarter.
5. More marketing consultants, product specialists, and customer support people are being hired.
6. A new Web design service will be offered.
7. Some territory boundaries are being changed.
8. More participation in trade shows and more trade publication advertising.
9. Payment terms will be changed from net 60 to 2 percent 30, and the minimum size acceptable assignment increased from 40 to 50 hours.

For firms using channel partners rather than direct salespeople, the sales manager shares the same pertinent information. The sales forecast presents an opportunity for the sales manager to discuss, with each salesperson, anticipated changes within the company. Salespeople must understand that these changes require sales increases to justify their cost.

Changes also must include sharing any negative news such as capacity restraints, discontinuing a product or service, tighter credit restrictions, or reduced sales support and marketing. These changes will potentially decrease sales so compensating increases must be found.

CHANGES OUTSIDE THE COMPANY

Next, the salesperson and the sales manager discuss changes outside the company that will impact next quarter's sales. These include changes at competitors,

customers, and in the general business environment over which you have little control.

CHANGES AT COMPETITORS

For instance, does your competitor plan to add or delete products or services, raise or lower prices, hire more salespeople, improve technology, increase or decrease sales support, change terms, change personnel, or change compensation or policy? Essentially, sales managers and salespeople need to know everything about the competitor that they know about their own company. Knowledge is power if you use it.

The marketing consulting firm sales manager and salesperson discuss changes at three competitors and quantify the impact on next quarter's sales. A large brand-name management consulting firm has hired consultants to provide Web-based marketing services. A regional temporary help firm has added marketing personnel to its roster. Several regional marketing consulting firms have lowered prices for database and direct marketing services. All these firms have high turnover among their salespeople.

CHANGES AT CUSTOMERS

The sales manager has the primary responsibility to explain changes within the company, but the salesperson has primary responsibility to explain changes at customers. As mentioned earlier, a salesperson who cannot identify changes at key customers and how these changes impact sales represents a potential problem. Salespeople have received training in obtaining customer knowledge and keeping profiles, and they should be aware of changes that could affect their forecast.

Consider asking your key customers to forecast their purchases or use of your services. Sell the benefits of their partnering with your salesperson to create a forecast. For key accounts a forecast of their needs will allow your firm to better serve them. Deliveries and quality of service should improve. Many large customers insist on participating in their vendors' forecasts. Such partnering creates a barrier to entry for competition.

The San Francisco salesperson feels that her largest customer, a sportswear manufacturer, may be reducing its budget for consulting services and that her key champion may be changing jobs. However, this potential loss may be compensated for by a major computer company in her territory expanding its online sales effort. Some smaller accounts may have credit problems. A potential strike by hourly employees at another customer would reduce its need for direct mail marketing.

Another firm has new ownership and has decided to bring all consulting work inside.

Other changes at customers might include new ownership and more or less capacity, as well as changes at the customers' competitors and customers. How will changes at your customers impact the salesperson's sales in that territory? This represents another module in building a reliable forecast.

The sales manager and salesperson discuss changes at the top 10 accounts that represent 65 percent of the territory's revenues. The salesperson prepares a dollar forecast for each of these top 10 accounts and compares the number to last quarter and last year. The salesperson also notes the percentage of her total quarterly business each of these top accounts represents and what percentage of their business she accounts for (see Exhibit 11.2). This is the first leg of the 10/10/10 analysis: top 10 accounts in volume, top 10 growth accounts, and top 10 prospects.

The salesperson presents a list of her top 10 growth accounts for the quarter (see Exhibit 11.3). These represent present customers with the highest dollar or percentage growth potential. There may be an overlap with the top 10 volume accounts. The list includes some reality checks such as the decision maker's name, the product or service to be added, competitors, strategy, and projected revenue increase.

The salesperson also presents a list of her top 10 prospects, including the decision maker, targeted service, competition, strategy, and potential volume (see Exhibit 11.4). This level of detail separates prospects from suspects and again acts as a reality check.

CHANGES IN BUSINESS CONDITIONS

Next, the sales manager and salesperson discuss changes in market demand trends, government regulations, and business conditions that will impact next quarter's forecasted sales. For some firms such changes might be in such areas as interest rates, new Medicare guidelines, gross domestic product, unemployment, personal income, retail sales, exchange rates, or oil prices. This discussion includes the macros and micros that drive demand for your products or services and your customer's products or services. Your customer's success drives your firm's revenues. You need to quantify how these changes will impact the forecast. In our example, the San Francisco salesperson and her sales manager believe next quarter's revenues will be impacted by a labor scarcity in the Bay area and by increased demand for high-tech products.

After considering past and present sales trends, anticipated changes within the company, and anticipated changes in the competition, customers, and in demand

trends; the San Francisco salesperson arrives at a best- and worst-case sales forecast for the next quarter of $230,000 to $250,000. She assigns a probability of 100 percent to the worst case and 80 percent to the best. Critical risks and contingency plans reflect the changes inside and outside the firm.

After discussing and agreeing to all the salespeople's bubble-up forecasts, the sales manager aggregates them into a company or regional forecast. He or she might want to add or subtract for a new territory, salesperson, acquisition, management accounts, or other factors outside or in addition to the present salespeople.

EVALUATING THE NUMBERS

Now the sales manager must evaluate whether this aggregated national or regional sales forecast meets market assessment and corporate growth requirements. Before the sales manager has a meaningful dialogue with each salesperson, he or she should know what growth rates and market assessment tools will shape the top-down forecast. The sales manager will use the dialogue to help each salesperson arrive at an acceptable number. The sales manager should know what total sales revenue will prove acceptable. This reduces the need to revise individual bubble-up forecasts and forces communication between the sales manager and top management to identify the top down number.

The sales manager also should evaluate each salesperson's forecast against available market assessment tools for that territory and acceptable growth rates for the territory. A smaller, newer territory should grow at a faster percentage rate than a mature one, which may grow at a slower rate but result in larger dollar increases. Apply top management's metrics and market assessment tools to each territory, but also develop your own. How can you measure market potential and market share for each territory? Hopefully, in establishing territories of equal potential, you have decided on proper market assessment metrics. As discussed previously, these will be different for different industries. They can range from buying power indexes by city or region for different SIC codes, to the number of prescriptions written by physician by medication. You may choose also to look at the most recent territorial sales numbers or at trends from past years weighted by a time series.

LONGER, MORE COMPLEX SALES CYCLES

For products or services with longer, more complex sales cycles, you must modify the sales forecast process. For each product or service, the forecast period would be lengthened from a quarter to six months or more, and the forecast format would include not only sales but also the tracking of the steps leading to those sales. Each customer's, prospects, or project's probability of success would depend on moving from one step to another in a timely manner. The meaningful dialogue between sales manager and salesperson continues as does the bubble-up process.

The sales manager would ask salespeople for a list of their customers, new or additional product placements, and prospects ranked by probability of success and organized by potential closing dates and status between search and purchase. The meaningful dialogue would again include changes inside and outside the company; but it also would include where each major customer, project, or prospect is in the sales or buying cycle, issues affecting probability of success, and closing dates. The forecast discussion would include dates, probabilities, and strategies for moving customers from need qualification to benefit quantification to betas and final presentations.

COMPARING ACTUAL TO FORECAST RESULTS

After asking salespeople and channel partners to invest considerable time in the forecasting process, the firm must compare this information to actual results. Actual monthly and year-to-date results by salesperson, distributor, outside sales representative organization, or another channel partner should be compared to the previous year and forecast. Depending on the level of forecast detail, comparisons can be made for each salesperson by account and product line.

The sales manager and salesperson should discuss the causes of variances each month between actual and forecast, corrective action if necessary, and the impact this might have on the forecast for the next month or next quarter. Variances might indicate a salesperson's or channel partner's training needs, which would be included in his or her development plan or stressed on the next ride-with. Variance might lead to changes in the salesperson's or channel partner's 30/60/90 day objectives. Variances that persist quarter after quarter could indicate a need to replace a salesperson or channel partner. Performance evaluations also offer an opportunity to discuss these issues.

Similarly, you must compare the national or regional forecast to actual results. Did the national or regional forecast accurately project actual sales? Was your forecast correct in units but wrong in dollars? Correct as to direction of sales but wrong as to the magnitude of that direction? Accurate for one product line or customer group but inaccurate for another? Analyze the reasons for these variances, and take appropriate corrective action on your next forecast. Perhaps you should put less emphasis on general economic indicators and sales trends and give more emphasis to changes in industry demand, pricing, new accounts, and competitors' new products. Perhaps the variances between actual results and forecast indicate a poor performing product, or more competition, or a shift in customers. What corrective sales, marketing, and operational action does this dictate?

Under what circumstances should a forecast be revised, especially if salespeople receive performance pay based on actual results versus forecast? What if the firm can't provide the product or service, if a major account announces bankruptcy or is acquired, or if customer demand declines due to changes in exchange rates?

Most companies have a sales forecast and a sales budget. One can be changed; the other cannot. One is used for procurement, scheduling, and financial management; it can be changed. The other is used as a benchmark for salespeople, management, and shareholders; it cannot be changed. Circumstances that should have been anticipated do not constitute grounds for changing the salesperson's forecast. These represent the critical risks for which the salesperson should have a contingency plan. However, circumstances that could not have been anticipated constitute grounds for changing the salesperson's forecast.

The Hewitt Associates 2005 survey of sales and human resource executives at 61 Fortune 1000 firms found that 75 percent adjust their forecasts during the year to reflect salesperson changes or reassignments in territories or customer bases, losses of major accounts, or shifts in the businesses, economy, or industry that affect their company or customers.[2]

THE 10/10/10 FORECASTING AND TIME MANAGEMENT TOOL

By asking salespeople to forecast sales for their top 10 accounts in volume, top 10 growth accounts, and top 10 prospects, you have captured 90 percent of the data needed to produce an accurate territorial forecast. By asking for detail on the top 10 prospects and top 10 growth accounts concerning the decision maker, problems, needs, opportunities, products or services to be sold, funnel position, competition, strategy, and revenue goals, you have learned how the salesperson is pursing this opportunity. By asking for detail on the top 10 accounts in volume concerning anticipated changes at those accounts, percent of their business you control, and percent of your territory business they represent, you have made sure the salesperson understands that major customer's business.

Many sales managers ask their salespeople to update the 10/10/10 reports monthly, and the managers then use the reports as a means to monitor the sales force's performance. If after six months a top prospect has not become a customer or has not moved to the next step in the sales funnel, or a top growth account has not grown, that prospect or account is removed from the report and must be replaced by another prospect or growth account. This can be challenging for the salesperson. Similarly, the top 10 accounts in volume are rotated as their volume changes.

Many sales managers total the projected volume for a salesperson's top 10 volume accounts, top 10 growth accounts, and top 10 prospects to see the gap between the grand total and the sales forecast for that territory. The gap is called the *unidentified other,* and salespeople must fill the gap with more opportunities.

In reviewing the 10/10/10, a sales manager will make comments to help the salesperson reach his or her goals and comments on allocation of time among accounts. Exhibits 11.2, 11.3, and 11.4 show examples of the 10/10/10 format.

Top-Down Forecasts

As a sales manager, your total sales force bubble-up forecast must meet the needs of top management and corporate goals. As discussed, one objective of forecasting is to integrate the top-down and bubble-up processes. Understanding the mechanics of top down will help you accomplish this.

Like bubble up, top down uses objective and subjective methods to accumulate and analyze quantitative and qualitative data. However, top down starts with national economic conditions and industry market potential to generate company potential sales and a sales forecast, which becomes allocated by region, district, and territory and then by account. The top-down number must satisfy management, shareholder, and corporate goals for growth, market share, cash flow (EBITDA), and profit (EBIT).

Statistical modeling is used to extrapolate historic data into future forecasts. Regression models rely on information or factors such as the number of calls that "cause" the sale. Time series models rely on observed changes in sales trends, and may use moving averages which average dollars and percentage changes in sales over a number of months, quarters, or years. Time series models may use exponential smoothing, which gives more weight to more recent or older changes in sales over a number of months, quarters, or years. Adoptive filtering and time series extrapolation represent variations and refinements of moving averages and exponential filtering.

The top-down total company forecast must be allocated by region, district, or territory based on the previous year's sales and future potential for that region, district, or territory as a percentage of the total company sales or potential. This macro-allocation will be measured against each region's, district's, or territory's micromarket potential and market share.

To reduce confusion and save time, the sales manager and top management must use the same or similar metrics for measuring market potential, such as

buying power indexes (BPIs) and data by SIC code that correlate to demand for your firm's products or services. The BPI combines consumer income, population, and retail sales to arrive at buying power by zip code, city, county, and state. What data tracks, drives, or matches market potential for your company's products or services: number of employees, number of telephones, number of hospitals (input-output models)? As mentioned, some firms will survey the buying intentions of their top accounts. Many firms use outside consultants to obtain and prepare this top-down information, which may also involve economic models and leading indicators. Of course you have already used some of this data to establish territories of equal potential (see Chapter 10).

The top-down forecast is presented to a management committee for approval. The committee should consist of representatives from operations, finance, sales, and marketing plus the CEO. This same committee will analyze and approve the bubble-up forecast. The key to successful forecasting is using a variety of techniques and data that combine top-down, bubble-up, and objective and subjective approaches and then running the results through a variety of judges.

If your company relies on a constant stream of new products or services to drive sales, then top-down forecasting requires more customer surveys and focus groups. Based on these surveys and focus groups, management estimates the number and type of customers likely to buy and rebuy this new product or service. The number of customers for this new product will be multiplied by their estimated initial order and reorders to arrive at total dollar sales.

The Sales Plan

THE SALESPERSON'S SALES PLAN

The sales forecast is a number; the sales plan is the tactical and strategic action on the part of each salesperson and sales manager to reach that number. The sales forecast says, "I want to get from point A to point B"; the sales plan says, "This is how I am going to do it." The sales forecast may be bubble up, top down, or a combination. The sales plan must be bubble up. The salesperson, with the help of the sales manager, must plan and commit to the action necessary to attain the forecast numbers.

Sales plans and forecasts overlap and interrelate. The top 10 prospect list (Exhibit 11.4) and 10 present accounts with the highest growth potential (Exhibit 11.3) contain both forecast numbers and sales plan action. (Both can be found at the end of this chapter.) The sales plan as the sales forecast represents a joint effort between the salesperson and sales manager involving the meaningful sharing of information. The sales plan as the sales forecast should not only be prepared by direct company-employed salespeople but also by your channel partners (independent distributors, brokers, and sales rep organizations).

The sales plan starts by breaking down each salesperson's sales forecast into bite-size pieces. If a salesperson's annual sales forecast is $1,650,000, he or she must analyze how that breaks down by product line, market, new accounts, old accounts, present account growth, customer group, gross margin contribution, and sales by month and week.

For example, a salesperson at a Midwest wholesale commercial paper distributor would divide the $1,650,000 by 48 selling weeks and 240 working days. The salesperson knows that to meet the forecast, he or she must produce $34,370 of revenue a week, or $6,874 a day. The rule is no lunch until daily revenues reach $6,000. Each day the sales manager posts each salesperson's dollar results and percent of forecast to a secure Web site.

These commercial paper salespeople call on the same customers and prospects each week or each month to show new products and write reorders on existing products, which we call a *modified rebuy*. For longer, more complex sales cycles, the bite-sized pieces also would include measuring the actions necessary to move from one step to the next in each customer's or prospect's sales cycle.

The $34,370 a week or $137,500 a month has product line, customer group, and pricing goals. The dollar forecast and specific goals vary by territory and salesperson. For one salesperson the monthly goal is 50 percent coated paper, 30 percent copy machine paper, and 30 percent fine paper. Her monthly customer group goal is 40 percent commercial printers, 30 percent offices, 15 percent fast print shops, and 15 percent in-house captive company printing departments.

In addition, each salesperson has pricing or gross margin goals because a great deal of negotiation occurs in setting customer prices for each order. One salesperson has a pricing or gross margin goal of 30 percent and another of 20 percent because one territory has far more competitors than the other.

Each salesperson has a dollar goal for generating new business versus maintaining or expanding existing accounts. For example, $200,000 of the $1,650,000 is forecast to come from 20 new accounts. Since the closing ratio is 9 to 1, it will take 180 prospecting or new account calls or 4 a week to open these 20 accounts. Each salesperson's plan includes a list of target accounts ranked by probability of opening them and their potential dollar volume. Each salesperson's plan includes a list of present high-growth accounts ranked by probability of success and potential dollars of volume. Each salesperson's plan includes a list of accounts that were lost or became inactive in the last year and their annual dollar volume. To reach this year's sales forecast, dollar volume from accounts lost in the past year must be made up.

Once the bite-sized pieces are agreed to, the salesperson and manager can agree on the specific action necessary to obtain the sales forecast. Generally, the action involves the number of calls a day, number of prospect calls a week;

allocation of calls and time among various types of customers, activities, product lines, and markets; call frequency for A, B, and C accounts; targeting; training, development programs; customer service issues; accounts receivable collections; call reports; customer profiles; inactive and lost accounts; and time management and reporting requirements (see Exhibits 11.1 and 11.5 at the end of this chapter). The job description lists most of these activities as duties.

The call allocation goals for the wholesale commercial paper distributor we discussed are based on each salesperson's present and potential accounts, their density; the dollar forecast for new business versus retention or penetration; and the dollar forecast by product line and customer group. The wholesale commercial paper distributor assigns the Milwaukee salesperson a daily call goal of 12, broken down into 1 new account call, 1 service call, and 10 penetration or retention calls. Of those 10 daily penetration calls, 5 should be on A accounts, 3 on B accounts, and 2 on C accounts. The call goals might also be broken down by end-user type and product line.

As mentioned, the sales plan for products or services with long, complex sales cycles will be less focused on the number of calls and more focused on strategic and tactical action necessary to move major prospects or customers from one step in the sales cycle to the next. Training, development, time management, and time allocation issues remain important. It is important to determine how this salesperson will allocate her time between the field and the office—that is, between working with customers and working with in-house engineering on proposals.

THE SALES MANAGER'S SALES PLAN

In addition to the salespeople's plans, the sales manager must prepare his or her own sales plan. He or she must determine what strategic and tactical action on his or her part is necessary to make the region's numbers. The sales manager's plan should include action related to hiring, training, compensating, staffing, deploying, motivating, evaluating, and automating the sales force. Proposed dates and agendas for sales meetings, new territory boundaries, field coaching schedules, telemarketing programs, and software for laptops would be included in this plan. For the sales manager, as opposed to the salesperson, the sales plan is a simplified microcosm of the material in this book. The sales manager's plan should include critical risks and contingencies. What is the sales manager's contingency plan if a top salesperson leaves or becomes disabled? How will training change if a new competitor enters the market? How will deployment and staffing change if a major customer chooses a competitor?

Also the sales manager's plan would include strategic topics such as targeting, channel choice, and pricing. Also the sales manager's plan would contain tactical

action related to territory advertising, promotion, and trade shows (see Exhibit 11.5 at the end of this chapter).

Sales Expense Budgeting

Here again, the sales manager should use a combination of bubble-up and top-down analyses to arrive at the most appropriate, most accurate number. In Chapter 8 on compensation, we said salespeople need an economic incentive to spend wisely. The budget should reflect this. The benefits, problems, and procedures with bubble-up expense budgets mirror those of bubble-up sales forecasts and plans.

Preparing sales forecasts, sales plans, and expense budgets forces the sales manager and his or her salespeople to plan the actions that influence sales and expenses. As you can see, sales forecasts, sales plans, and expense budgets are closely interrelated. These forecasts, plans, and budgets become objectives against which actual performance can be measured and controlled. By involving salespeople in the expense budgeting process, you get more accurate budgets as well as the commitment of the salespeople to keep expenses within budget.

Selling expenses can be grouped into *fixed costs*, which do not vary directly with sales volume and cannot easily be changed; *variable costs*, which do vary directly with sales volume; and *discretionary costs*, which management has the ability to change on a short-term basis. Discretionary costs include both those directly related to the salesperson or territory (primarily reimbursed expenses) and those related to the entire district or region. Fixed expenses include such items as salaries, payroll taxes, group insurance, rent, and utilities. Variable expenses include such items as commissions, bonuses, and royalties. Discretionary expenses include such items as travel, entertainment, telephone use, promotion, and advertising. Although it is easier to budget fixed costs than variable or discretionary ones, all expense budgeting requires assumptions, judgment, and planning.

SALESPERSON DISCRETIONARY, REIMBURSABLE EXPENSES

Sixty to ninety days before the start of your company's accounting year, season, or quarter, ask each direct salesperson or channel partner (outside representative, agent, or distributor) to prepare a monthly budget for whatever discretionary, sometimes reimbursable, expenses he or she will incur. If you use straight commission to compensate the sales force and do not reimburse expenses, naturally you do

not need this information. However, a company that does reimburse salespeople's expenses or pay them directly should ask the sales force for a monthly telephone, car, travel, office and entertainment budget, including detailed information on lodging, food, transportation, and planned itineraries. As mentioned in Chapter 8 on compensation, reimbursed expenses can often represent 25 to 50 percent of a salesperson's total compensation, so controlling them becomes important.

In addition to reimbursed expenses, your firm may directly pay for some salespeople's telephone, car, travel, office, and entertainment expenses. Salespeople also must budget other types of non-reimbursable expenses they have control over such as sampling, regional trade shows, sales aids, in-service customer training, advertising or promotion allowances, and possibly freight in. What activities on the part of salespeople drive these expenses? Which activities are not necessary?

Once received, compare each of these salesperson territorial expense budgets with the previous full year's actual, with this year's actual year-to-date territorial expenses or sales, and with next year's territorial sales forecast. Why does the Denver salesperson budget a 50 percent increase in expenses but no increase in forecast sales? Why does the Minneapolis agent budget expenses at 3 percent of next year's forecast sales, when the actual for last year's expenses totaled only 2 percent of sales? Why does the New York City distributor budget lower expenses but forecast higher sales for next year? It is important to discuss these questions with your salespeople and channel partners, reaching agreement and making adjustments where necessary.

Each salesperson must accept his or her final expense budget as a realistic, fair, and attainable objective. By asking the salesperson to prepare and justify his or her own budgets and by having a meaningful dialogue with him or her concerning the actions that drive these expenses, you obtain the salesperson's involvement and commitment to a realistic figure.

Use these territorial salesperson expense budgets to help plan, control, measure, evaluate, and reward actual performance. For instance, some companies pay bonuses to salespeople whose expenses do not exceed budget. The sum of these adjusted territorial expense budgets becomes part of your regional or district budget and eventually part of the total company budget.

BUDGETED FIXED COSTS

Next, start accumulating monthly figures for budgeted fixed costs, such as salaries, group insurance, payroll taxes, warehouse, showrooms, rent, and utilities. Prepare a worksheet listing yourself, all salaried personnel who report to you, and salespeople who receive a portion of their compensation in salary. By each name and under the appropriate month, place a figure equal to the budgeted monthly

gross salary, taking into account any anticipated raises, retirements, replacements or additions. Various sums of these figures then become the monthly totals for the regional, district, or company expense budget. Compare these totals with the previous year's actual expenses and next year's forecasted sales. Have they risen in dollars and as a percentage of sales? Are the increases justified?

Next, ask the controller or accountant to provide budget figures for fringe benefits, such as group insurance and payroll taxes. He or she likely will ask for a schedule of your personnel and their anticipated compensation. Again, compare total budgeted fringe benefits, group insurance, and payroll tax figures with the previous year's actual expenditures, and calculate what percentage of total compensation and sales they represent. Be sure to understand the reasons for variances.

If you rent space for sales offices, warehouses, or showrooms, review the leases and add to the budget the appropriate monthly figures for next year's rental and utility expenses. If you share rented or owned space with other company functions, such as manufacturing or administration or research, ask the controller or accountant to allocate a portion of the anticipated monthly expenses to selling. Compare the total budgeted rental and utility expenses with the previous year's actual expenditures, and calculate what percentage they represent of next year's forecast total sales. Ask questions, and where appropriate, make changes.

BUDGETED VARIABLE EXPENSES

Next, calculate monthly figures for the variable expenses that are a function of sales. Based on the final monthly sales forecast by territory, calculate each salesperson's commission and/or bonus due (if any). Then place the total figure in your company, region, or district budget. Based on the final monthly region or district sales forecast, calculate your bonus or commission, and any royalty or license fees due, and place these figures in the budget. Again, compare these figures with the previous year's actual expenditures, and calculate their percentage relationship to forecast sales. Have budgeted commissions and bonuses risen as a percentage of forecast sales? If so, is it because of a change in product mix or the compensation plan or because changes in territory boundaries have caused a redistribution of sales among salespeople?

BUDGETED DISCRETIONARY EXPENSES

Finally, the sales manager should accumulate monthly figures for the remaining discretionary expenses such as his or her own travel, entertainment, and telephone costs, plus regional- or district-level information technology costs, training, hiring,

marketing, communications, advertising, trade shows, and promotional expenses. Prepare a monthly travel and entertainment expense budget for yourself using the same format previously suggested for the sales force. To arrive at a district or region total for this category, add your figures along with all other management sales-related travel and entertainment expenses to the numbers submitted by the sales force.

Using last year's actual figures and adjusting for rate changes and possible changes in anticipated activity, budget the sales office's and your business-related personal communications expenses, if any, and arrive at a monthly total region, district, or company budget for this category.

Prepare a monthly worksheet listing various categories of sales-related advertising and promotion engaged in by your district, region, or company. This might include trade, consumer, cooperative, classified, employment, institutional, newspaper, Web, or magazine advertising, as well as display fixtures, trade shows, sales aids, press releases, premiums, models, and samples. Next to each category of advertising and promotion, budget the anticipated monthly expense. Then justify these figures with a more detailed plan. In what newspapers, Web sites, or magazines do you plan to run how many column inches of cooperative, consumer, trade, or classified advertising? What product, service, or employment will the ad feature? Which customers require how much cooperative advertising? What will each ad cost? In what months do you plan to purchase which display fixtures, attend what trade shows, send out press releases, or give away samples; and how much will this cost?

The total of these figures becomes your monthly and annual advertising and promotion budget, which you then compare with the previous year's actual expenditures and also calculate its percentage relationship to forecast sales. Are you planning to spend more on advertising next year than last? Is it a higher percentage of sales? Do increased advertising expenditures result in increased sales? Would decreased advertising expenses result in decreased sales? The budget becomes your advertising plan and raises questions that you must answer.

BUDGETED TOTAL SALES EXPENSES

Finally, total all the sales expense categories by month and for the year; then compare these totals to the previous year's actual expenditures. Also calculate the percentage relationship of these budgeted expense totals to forecast total sales, and compare this percentage with actual past percentage figures. Negative variances require questions and answers.

Don't spend a great deal of time debating which sales expenses are fixed, variable, or discretionary. The way in which expenses are categorized varies from one company to another. Do spend time accumulating data and discussing all sales-related costs, whether fixed, variable, or discretionary. Most sales managers don't know what their sales costs are. We manage what we monitor.

Because selling expenses represent a significant percentage of the corporate revenue dollar, top management will prepare a top-down budget to be allocated among regions, districts, and territories. Again, their frame of reference is macro while yours remains micro. The sales manager builds her or his expense budget from modules and bite-sized pieces submitted from a group of salespeople. Each salesperson's activities with each customer drive these budgets. Management's top-down expense budget will reflect necessary return on investment, cash flow (EBITDA), and dollars of income (EBIT) as a percent of revenues. Top management writes budgets for all areas of the business. The total sales budget dollars must correctly relate to the total expense budgets for all functional areas of the business and to the sales forecast. Top management may accept the sales manager's expense budget or ask for revisions. As with the sales forecast, salespeople must realize that their bubble-up expense budget may be altered. Again the sales manager must be prepared to negotiate and justify these expenses.

COMPARING BUDGETED SALES EXPENSES TO ACTUAL EXPENDITURES

Obtaining the most realistic estimate of future selling expenses necessary to profitably generate forecast sales represents an important objective of the budget. At the end of each accounting year, compare actual expenses with those budgeted, and evaluate how well you have met that objective. Were actual selling expenses above budget because actual sales were above forecast? Did advertising expenses exceed budget because a new customer unexpectedly demanded a cooperative ad? Did higher-than-budgeted travel expenses result from an unexpected trip to hire a new salesperson? Analyze the reasons for the variances, and take appropriate corrective action in your next budget. Using this same process, discuss each salesperson's actual versus budgeted expenses.

Each month, for each salesperson and in total, the sales manager should compare line item actual selling expenses to budget, analyze the reasons for variances, and when necessary, take corrective action. If the Ohio salesperson budgeted $500 monthly for reimbursed travel expenses but after five months has submitted receipts for $4,000, a telephone call is required to find out why. You may have him reduce traveling for two months unless his sales are ahead of forecast, thus justifying the budget overrun. After six months, telephone expenses may be several thousand dollars over budget either because of personal use or because of more business activity. You need to find out which. We manage what we monitor.

Salespeople feel better about preparing budgets if they are used. Don't have the sales force waste time by preparing expense budgets that will not be used.

Each quarter you should review expense budgets for future periods, and based on any new information, make the appropriate adjustments. For example, if a salesperson unexpectedly resigns in the second quarter and you decide not to seek a replacement immediately, the third- and fourth-quarter expense budgets will require downward adjustment. As with the sales forecasts, many firms have two expense budgets, one that has some flexibility and one that does not.

Sales Managers' Major Weaknesses and/or Mistakes in Forecasting and Planning

- Using only a top-down forecast versus a bubble-up forecast and sales plan.
- Using an annual forecast versus a quarterly forecast.
- Asking for a number, but not a plan.
- Not using a model and modules to obtain the number.
- No meaningful dialogue with salespeople.
- Not prioritizing necessary action.
- Not using the sales forecast and sales plan. Not comparing actual versus goal.
- Only forecasting based on past trends, not future changes or events.
- Lack of personal planning.

Exhibit 11.1.   Sales Forecast and Sales Plan for the Quarter Ending _____.

Territory: _____

Territory Manager: _____

Dollar Sales by Product Line					
	Month	Chronic	Acute	Staffing	Total	Percent
1.						
2.						
3.						
Total						

Necessary sales per week each month: _____

Necessary sales per day each month: _____

Factors that might prevent you from reaching quarterly forecast or goals:

_____

_____

Effect of lost or inactive customers versus. previous quarter:

_____

_____

Changes you will make in geographic coverage, customer coverage, and/or product line emphasis:

_____

_____

Number of account calls you plan to make a week: _____

Number of prospect calls you plan to make a week: _____

What assistance would you like from your manager in this quarter to reach your goals:
Training: _____
Ride-withs: _____
Accounts: _____
Other: _____

Account Representative: _____   Date: _____

Exhibit 11.2.   Quarterly Top 10 Accounts Ranked by Volume.

Account Name	Estimated Revenues Past Quarter	Estimated Revenues Next Quarter	Percentage of Accounts' Business Given to Us	Percent of Territory Total Revenues	Changes at This Customer Which May or Have Already Positively or Negatively Impacted Dollars of Revenue or Gross Profit
1.					
2.					
3.					
4.					
5.					
6.					
7.					
8.					
9.					
10.					

Exhibit 11.3.   Quarterly Top 10 Present Accounts with the Highest Growth Potential.

Account Representative: _____   Date: _____

Customer Name, Location, Decision Makers	Target Product or Service, Objective and Strategy, Funnel Position, Problems and/or Needs	Competition	Estimated Revenues Next Quarter	Strategy
1.				
2.				
3.				
4.				
5.				
6.				
7.				
8.				
9.				
10.				

Exhibit 11.4. Quarterly Top 10 Prospects in the Territory.

Account Representative: _____ Date: _____

Prospect Name, Location, Decision Makers	Target Product or Service Line, Objective and Strategy, Funnel Position, Problems and/or Needs	Competition	Estimated Revenues Next Quarter	Strategy
1.				
2.				
3.				
4.				
5.				
6.				
7.				
8.				
9.				
10.				

Exhibit 11.5.   Sales Plan Topics: The Action That Drives the Numbers, Tactical and/or Strategic.

Salesperson	Sales Manager

Salesperson

- Bite-size pieces, by day, by month, by product line
- Target accounts or prospects
- Growth accounts
- Top 20
- Number of calls by type:
  - Prospect versus maintenance
  - A, B, and C accounts, frequency
- Allocation of time
  - By customer type
  - By product line
- Collections
- Call reports
- Customer profiles
- Lost accounts
- Inactive accounts
- Time management
- Reporting requirements

Sales Manager

- Telemarketing
- CSR
- Quality prospects
- Create leads
- Promotion or advertising
- SFA or laptops
- Cell phones
- Sales meetings
- Ride-withs
- Training agenda for each salesperson
- Territory boundaries
- Staffing levels
- New hires or terminations
- Compensation changes
- Pricing
- Target customers
- Marketing funnel

Questions and Exercises for Chapter 11

- List specific changes within your company or one you are familiar with, at specific competitors, at specific customers, in demand trends, and in the general business environment that will impact next year's sales forecast. Show how and why these changes will impact the sales forecast.
- List topics you would include in a salesperson's sales plan. List topics you would include in a sales manager's sales plan.

Quiz for Chapter 11

1. Which of these statements are correct? Preparing a sales forecast involves discussing
   a. Past and present sales trends.
   b. Changes at customers.
   c. Changes at competition.

   d. Changes in demand trends and business conditions.
   e. Changes within your company.

2. Which of these statements are correct? Preparing a salesperson's sales plan involves
   a. Breaking the sales forecast into bite-size pieces.
   b. Discussing action necessary to meet the sales forecast number.
   c. Sizing and deployment.
   d. Field coaching.
   e. Sales meetings.

3. True or false?
   Preparing a sales expense budget involves analyzing fixed, variable, and discretionary sales expenses.

4. Which of the following are possible problems with a salesperson's bubble-up sales forecast?
   a. Salespeople may intentionally underestimate their sales.
   b. Salespeople may not take the forecast seriously.
   c. Salespeople may not have enough data to prepare an accurate forecast.
   d. Management may ask for numbers higher than the salesperson's forecast.

5. True or false?
   As a sales manager, the key to avoiding salespeople forecasting sales below upper management expectations is for the sales manager to anticipate the upper management number and then work that number into each salesperson's bubble-up territory forecast.

6. In preparing a sales forecast, the salesperson and sales manager must look at which of the following changes within the company?
   a. Competitors
   b. Past and present sales trends
   c. Market changes
   d. Capacity
   e. Prices
   f. Technology
   g. Strategy
   h. Promotion
   i. Territory boundaries

7. True or false?
   As part of the sales forecast process, do not ask major customers to help by forecasting their sales because they will either forecast too high or too low.

8. The 10/10/10 forecasting and time management tool involves which of the following?
   a. Top 10 competitors
   b. Top 10 growth accounts
   c. Top 10 products or services
   d. Top 10 prospects
   e. Top 10 accounts in dollars of revenue

9. True or false?
   Obtaining the most realistic estimate of future selling expenses necessary to profitably generate forecast sales represents an important objective of the budget.

10. Which of these budgeted selling expenses are variable?
    a. Salaries
    b. Payroll taxes
    c. Rent
    d. Utilities

Notes

1. *Hot Topics in Sales Management and Sales Compensation 2005.* Copyright © 2005 Hewitt Associates LLC. Reprinted by permission of Hewitt Associates.
2. Ibid.

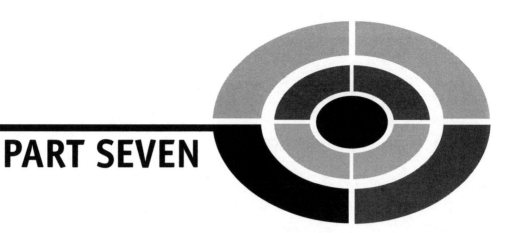

PART SEVEN

Motivating
Salespeople

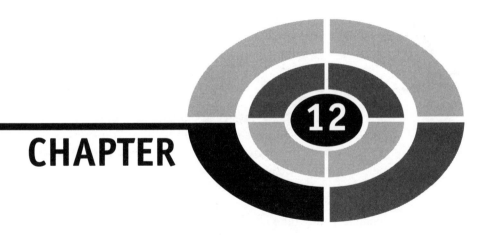

Recognition, Feeling Important, Challenge and Achievement, and Freedom and Authority

Different Sparks Light Different Fires

A sales manager's job is getting work done through other people. His or her success depends on the success of the salespeople. You must hire the best, terminate the rest; train them in product, customer, competitor knowledge, and sales skills; and compensate, deploy, organize, and staff correctly. You have led the horse to water; now you must get the horse to drink. To fully capitalize on a salesperson's potential, you must motivate that person. Successful sales managers are agents of change—they take advantage of change and change or modify people's behavior. A sales manager's job involves making the salespeople successful.

Each salesperson has different needs, goals, aspirations, and problems. The sales manager's job involves uncovering these needs, goals, aspirations, and problems and then helping each salesperson satisfy the needs, solve the problems, and reach the goals. You should have a profile on each salesperson, similar to the one salespeople keep for each customer. The profile might include information on family, interests, hobbies, professional experience, education, strengths, weaknesses, developmental plans, decision-making quadrant (Chapter 4), personal goals, needs, aspirations, problems, and motivational hot buttons. The salespeople are the sales manager's internal customer.

Different sparks light different salespeople's fires. You can't mass produce motivation—overly competitive salespeople want to beat competition and colleagues; high achievers want to better their last year's results; superstars with superegos feel they are the best; service-oriented salespeople use empathy to build lasting relationships with customers and colleagues; and plateauing salespeople reach their "career level" well below their level of competence or may just have stopped learning and growing. The sales manager must create a customized motivational plan or program with time frames for each salesperson and for the group. This motivational plan or program will include a personalized mix of recognition, usefulness, challenge, and achievement, authority and freedom, personal growth, and belonging—all of which are discussed in this and the next chapter.

For example, the sales manager for a regional telecommunications firm offering DSL services to businesses and consumers had six salespeople. One had been a history major in college, had no children, and her husband worked. She had grown up in a small town in Iowa. Her major interest was helping existing customers solve their problems, not opening new accounts, even though financial incentives rewarded new business.

Another salesperson had flunked out of college trying to pursue his father's career as a physician. He had grown up in sumptuous surroundings on Long Island and wanted to maintain that standard of living and social status for himself, his wife, and three children. He needed and wanted to be the best salesperson. Most years he ended up number 1 in new business and total revenue.

A third salesperson had grown up in Eastern Europe under extreme poverty. Each year she worked long, hard, and smart not to be number 1 but to exceed her previous year's figures.

The fourth salesperson was in his midfifties, had grown children, considerable savings, and was in a rut. He had been with his present employer for 15 years in various positions. He had done it all, knew it all, and felt comfortable.

The fifth salesperson wanted to move up the career ladder into management and had all the necessary experience and education. However, the company had no available positions, and so he had turned complacent.

The sixth salesperson, a young college graduate, was still a mystery. As a recent hire, results met standards, but he did not talk about himself.

During field visits, the sales manager developed personal relationships with these people to find out what they most wanted from their job and from their life. At dinner after the ride-with or between calls in the car, he involved the salesperson in some relaxing, self-revealing conversation. He asked each salesperson what working environment promoted the best job satisfaction. What did the salesperson most need to be satisfied in his or her job: security, good wages, appreciation, feeling "in" on things, interesting work, pleasant conditions, growth, tactful discipline, sympathy, or loyalty? Each salesperson ranked these criteria differently, which gave the sales manager insight into his or her needs, goals, and problems. Often, the sales manager's initial ranking of each salesperson's job satisfaction needs was very different from the salesperson's perception. Nevertheless, the dialogue was meaningful, and out of it came each salesperson's monthly motivational program.

That monthly motivational program might involve leading a sales meeting, being named salesperson of the month, attending the new product committee meeting, or going to an outside industry seminar. A sales person's monthly motivational program might involve more responsibility for national accounts, discussions of territorial profit margins, more flexibility in pricing, or a call from the company president.

Most Salespeople Want to Be Successful

Most salespeople want to be successful and enjoy working hard at something, often not their job. The sales managers' challenge involves transferring more of their salespeople's efforts into sales for the company. A salesperson selling B2B e-commerce services produced great results when he worked, but he did not work often or hard enough. On a field visit, the salesperson invited the sales manager to his home for dinner. The sales manager noticed several motorcycles in the garage. At dinner the salesperson spoke about his passion for off-road motorcycle rallies, but he complained about his lack of funds to support this pastime.

The next day, between calls, the sales manager asked how much money the motorcycles required. He then showed the salesperson that by selling one more major contract a month, he would generate sufficient commission income to pay for more off-road rallies. That year, the salesperson's sales increased by one contract a month. In subsequent years, the salesperson and sales manager agreed on a bubble-up sales forecast that met both the salesperson's need for income to support his passion and the manager's need for sales growth.

Why Motivate Employees?

Our objective is to motivate salespeople not just to reach their quotas, goals, or plans but to fully capitalize on their potential. To accomplish this, we must convert a salesperson's complacency, which drives sales managers mad, into the salesperson's elixir, enthusiasm.

MONEY IS NOT A UNIVERSAL INCENTIVE

Money represents an important motivator of salespeople. Hopefully, your compensation system rewards positive salesperson action and superior results important to the success of your firm, and it reflects the salesperson's influence on the sale, the complexity of the sale, the type salesperson you desire, and the type of product your firm sells. But money is not a universal incentive. Salespeople reach comfort zones and complacency plateaus. Older salespeople may retire on the job. Two-income families and outside income make performance pay less important. Also as mentioned in Chapters 7 and 8 on compensation, a steady stream of performance pay can become a phantom salary. At some point a salesperson might perceive his or her income to exceed his or her needs. A salesperson's motivation can depend on factors other than money, including whether he or she is service driven, an achiever, or, maybe, ego driven. The compensation system requires proper structure, but it represents only one factor in driving salesperson behavior.

LACK OF CAREER LADDERS

Most companies employ some career salespeople who have no desire to move into management. Conversely, many companies have no opportunities for salespeople to move into management. In a small firm the career ladder might be closed almost entirely. In both situations, a major motivator of salespeople—the career ladder—has been removed. In these situations nonmonetary motivation must to some extent replace the career ladder. As we will see later in this chapter, research shows that money attracts and retains salespeople, but does not necessarily motivate them to full potential.

LOWER TURNOVER

As discussed in Part 2 on hiring, salesperson turnover proves very expensive. You can reduce turnover with proper hiring and training. Properly hired, trained, and motivated salespeople perform better, earn more, have better job satisfaction, and resign less often.

GREATER PRODUCTIVITY

In earlier chapters, we learned that salespeople represent an expensive and important human resource. The cost of putting a salesperson on the road—direct compensation, fringe benefits, and reimbursed expenses—ranges from $60,000 to several hundred thousand dollars. Highly motivated salespeople increase revenues, productivity, and capacity, which lowers their cost per sales dollar. Motivated salespeople produce more dollars of output for each dollar of input.

INCREASED CONFIDENCE AND ENTHUSIASM

We also discussed how the candidate profile calls for an enthusiastic and confident salesperson. Proper training and motivation maintains and creates enthusiasm and confidence.

EASIER-TO–MANAGE SALES FORCE

An employer deserves a day's work for a day's pay, but motivated salespeople can give you a day and a half's work for a day's pay. A motivated sales force costs no more than an unmotivated sales force, but it does require more of the sales manager's time and energy. Once you have created an environment that encourages self-motivation, it is much easier to sell new ideas to the sales force, whether this involves correcting a salesperson's bad habits or suggesting some new direction.

HAPPY EMPLOYEES CREATE SATISFIED CUSTOMERS

Happy company direct salespeople, channel partners, customer support personnel, and telesales people have a very positive influence on customer's satisfaction. We know this from our own buying experiences in addition to research. A salesperson's positive attitude can overcome many product or service failures. A salesperson's negative attitude can make a very positive product or service experience less satisfying to the customer.

You need a motivational plan or program for each of your salespeople and the group, just as you do a training plan. Many managers consider motivation silly and unnecessary. "My boss doesn't have to motivate me; why should I have to motivate the salespeople working under me?" However, you must employ nonmonetary motivational techniques for the salespeople to achieve the many benefits stated in this section.

The Motivational Process

We can't force salespeople to be successful, but we can help them to solve motivational problems and meet motivational needs. To motivate salespeople, you must first understand the specific needs and desires driving individuals and then find the activities and rewards that satisfy those needs. These activities and rewards become each salesperson's motivational program. Each salesperson has a particular package of needs and goals, and these are not necessarily rational. Most salespeople, for instance, need varying degrees of recognition, a sense of achievement, a feeling of usefulness, and consistent leadership. In addition, some salespeople have a strong need to belong; and many others require job or financial security.

Needs create tensions, and to relieve these tensions, salespeople engage in goal-directed, motivated behavior. When salespeople achieve their goals, the tension is reduced. Other individuals and social groups influence people's needs and the goals they choose to satisfy these needs. A salesperson might desire certain positive results such as leisure, recognition, security, more money, or better use of time. Achieving these results will create a peace of mind and prestige. Not achieving them leads to a sense of failure, humiliation, or rejection and creates anxiety and depression.

As sales manager, your job is both to pinpoint the needs and to encourage the goal-directed actions that lead to the satisfaction of those needs. By using the individual's needs and goals, you thus motivate the salesperson to optimum performance. Of course, the results of this action also increase sales. And, eventually, salespeople obtain enough pleasure from their goal-directed activities to become self-motivated.

Positive incentives produce better results than do negative sanctions such as rank, punishment, and threats. Of course, you must use negative motivation in some situations with certain people, but it tends to lose its effectiveness when used more than once. Before you threaten a salesperson with probation, use up all your positive tools.

The 10 Drivers of Engagement

In the first quarter of 2003, Towers Perrin, a human resources consulting firm, conducted a Web-based quantitative anonymous survey of 40,000 employees in midsize and large companies in North America. The 40,000 employees included 3,581 in sales and marketing. The survey involved questions concerning the drivers of employee attraction (hiring), retention, and engagement (motivation). The results are stated in the lists that follow.

In this survey, why was providing competitive base pay number 2 in attracting or hiring salespeople but only number 7 in retaining employees and omitted entirely from the top 10 drivers for engagement (that is, motivation) of salespeople? Salespeople will not accept or remain in a job unless the compensation meets their expectations. For salespeople who remain with their employer, compensation represents "table stakes."

Most sales managers would choose compensation as number 1 in motivating salespeople because salespeople like to talk about their wages. However, as you can see, challenging work that was number 8 in attracting salespeople is number 1 on the list for engaging them. Challenging work and input on decision making represent important factors for job satisfaction.

Key attraction drivers focus on benefits, pay, and work and life balance. When it comes to retention, the rewards that matter most are about advancement, aligning expectations, and work resources. The top 10 drivers of engagement, or motivation, are about the things that enable salespeople to make a difference.

Generally a disconnect exists between what sales managers perceive as motivating their salespeople and what the salespeople feel motivates and engages them. As a sales manager, you need to discuss the factors that drive job satisfaction with each of your salespeople. This will be different for different people and will change for the same person with seniority as he or she ages.

In this and other studies, Towers Perrin found that only 20 percent of employees are highly engaged, while 66 percent are modestly engaged, and 14 percent are disengaged. Based on this, there is room for improvement.

Towers Perrin also found a correlation between employee engagement and company success as measured by financial results. In their survey, companies with a larger percent of highly engaged employees showed higher revenue growth than those with a lower percentage of highly motivated employees. Although correlation is not causation, this finding makes sense.

The top 10 factors in attracting, retaining, and engaging sales and marketing personnel were the following:[1]

Attracting

1. Providing competitive health-care benefits
2. Providing competitive base pay
3. Career advancement opportunities
4. Work and life balance
5. Reputation of the company
6. Bonus based on performance
7. Pay raises linked to individual performance
8. Challenging work
9. Caliber of coworkers
10. Recognition for work

Retaining

1. Career advancement opportunities
2. Aligning company and employee expectations
3. Resources to get the job done
4. Reputation of the company
5. Challenging work
6. Input on decision making
7. Providing competitive base pay
8. Senior management's communicating a clear vision
9. Developing skills
10. Customer satisfaction

Engaging

1. Challenging work
2. Reputation of company

3. Input on decision making
4. Understanding how performance affects business goals
5. Resources to get job done
6. Senior management's support for new ideas
7. Teamwork between groups
8. Senior management's interest in employee well-being
9. Customer satisfaction
10. Satisfaction with benefits needed for day-to-day life

Primary Motivational Factors

Motivation represents an internal process of need satisfaction. We can't force salespeople to be successful. However, this internal process is very influenced by external factors. You, the boss, represent one of the most important external factors. Consider how you feel when your boss does not return a phone call or congratulates you in front of the president. How does it affect your personal motivation? Your actions, words, and attitudes affect the salespeople who work for you in the same way.

Salespeople's needs, goals, and motivation can be classified as those related to the following:

- Praise and recognition
- Feelings of usefulness
- Challenge and achievement
- Authority and freedom
- Self-realization and fulfillment through personal growth
- Esteem and status
- A sense of belonging
- Pleasant interpersonal relationships with management and peers
- Consistent, competent, motivated leadership
- Fair company policies and administration
- Job security
- Compensation and advancement

These are the external factors that influence internal motivation. No one of these factors alone is terribly important, but taken together they create a powerful interrelated motivational force that requires a delicate, ever-changing balance.

These factors, needs, and goals not only motivate salespeople but any employee. Although this book deals with salespeople, you need to motivate all your employees using these techniques.

The motivational ideas and techniques described in this chapter are not only appropriate for direct full-time salespeople but also for channel partners such as distributors, brokers, independent sales representatives, and value-added resellers (VARs). These same ideas and techniques can be successfully applied to telesales and customer support people.

Recognition

Salespeople want to be noticed, praised, and appreciated for their performance, and as sales manager, you should reinforce and reward positive action and results with recognition. Recognition involves anything from a casual thank-you over the phone to a formal awards dinner. Salespeople possess an insatiable appetite for recognition, which goes with the territory.

Salespeople must understand exactly which positive actions and results will be rewarded with recognition: for example, more new accounts, more calls per day, better retention of existing business, selling price increases, shorter sales cycles, increased net sales, or better collections. The required results and the form of recognition—for example, a plaque, membership in a sales club, or a prize—can be different for different salespeople. Moreover, you must create different levels of recognition for varying levels of performance. The salesperson who visits a customer on Saturday to handle a service complaint deserves your "thank-you." The salesperson who doubles his quarterly new account quota deserves to be nominated for salesperson of the month. Recognition allows the sales manager more flexibility than a compensation program for rewarding salespeople's positive actions and results.

Also, lack of recognition—the silent treatment—can be a powerful tool. Make sure the people you choose not to recognize know why. Otherwise, they will become frustrated and angry. Remember, positive motivation works better than negative.

Recognition becomes a more effective motivational tool when it is sincere, receives publicity, is recorded, and involves top management. Insincere praise has a negative effect on the recipient. Say it as if you mean it or don't say it at all. Save praise for the appropriate occasion or event. You can't praise all the people all the time.

Where appropriate, as when someone has won a sales contest or opened a major new account, publicize the recognition in the company newsletter, in a bulletin, or in an e-mail sent to all salespeople. If the recognition involves an award or civic involvement, consider sending press releases with pictures to the local papers in the salesperson's community. Community, suburban, and small-town newspapers often need this type of material.

When a salesperson opens a major new account or places a new product or service with an important customer, have the other salespeople sign a copy of the order with a congratulatory note and send it to the appropriate sales-person. Peer recognition is a powerful tool and creates peer pressure to emulate the performance.

Where appropriate, record recognition with plaques, sales club memberships, certificates, or annual awards. For example, if a salesperson goes 50 percent over annual quota, issue a plaque or certificate inscribed with his or her name to commemorate the results.

TOP MANAGEMENT INVOLVEMENT

A leading dairy products firm has 10 regional sales managers, each responsible for 10 salespeople. Each month each sales manager must send the company president the name of a salesperson from his or her region who has accomplished something above and beyond the expected. Each month the president sends a letter to the 10 selected salespeople thanking each one for the particular activity or result. The cost is minimal, but the motivational effect is tremendous. The letter goes home so that it can be shared with a spouse, and a copy of the letter goes in the employee's file. Salespeople need to feel that someone at the top knows and cares. Also, this program keeps pressure on the regional managers to create, identify, and track key results and activity for all salespeople. A regional manager who does not have a salesperson with an outstanding accomplishment must answer for it.

SALESPERSON OF THE MONTH

The sales manager of a telecommunications firm inaugurated a salesperson-of-the-month award. The criteria changed from month to month. The sales manager established criteria that fit her marketing or sales plan and that were important to the company's success: calls per day, new accounts per month, net revenue increases, percentage above quota, dollars collected from overdue accounts, gross margin contributions, list price maintenance, new product placements, product mix, number of presentations, number of trials, and closing ratios. The salesperson who did the worst each month got to choose the criterion for the next month. Every fourth month the sales manager chose a winner based on extra effort, improved results, or some outstanding performance related to solving a problem. The goal was for everyone to be a winner at least once a year.

The salesperson of the month used a reserved parking place with gold lines, got a day off (with the sales manager covering the territory), had his or her picture hung in the reception room or put up on the Web site, and received a trophy that rotated each month among winners, as well as a bouquet of flowers. In addition, the sales manager established a salesperson of the year based on her criteria. Winners received a ring, a watch, a clock, or a pin commemorating the award and had their pictures hung in the reception room for the next 12 months. The salesperson-of-the-month award was given at a weekly sales meeting. The salesperson of the year was awarded at the annual sales dinner. Each salesperson of the month and salesperson of the year recorded a 15-minute audiotape on how he or she accomplished his or her results. Copies of the audiotape were sent to the other salespeople to share best practices and further reinforce motivation. The cost of these programs was nominal, but salespeople worked very hard to win the awards.

HONOR SOCIETY

The sales manager for a business-to-business desktop computer accessory manufacturer created an honor society—the Circle of Excellence—for salespeople whose cumulative shipments exceeded $10 million. This generally took three years and required salespeople to have a certain skill level. Members of the Circle of Excellence had a calling card with their picture and the Circle of Excellence emblem. Salespeople's calling cards represent them in the marketplace and influence their self-image. The Circle of Excellence calling card gave salespeople enhanced credibility with customers. The Circle of Excellence members occasionally had dinner with the company president, and all members served on various advisory committees that reviewed new products and services and set agendas for sales meetings. Salespeople worked extra long and hard for this honor, which reduced turnover.

Since this business-to-business desktop computer accessory firm hired many salespeople each year to open new territories, they also had a rookie-of-the-year award. That award was based on actual performance versus goals.

RANKING SALESPEOPLE

As mentioned in Chapter 6 on training, in regard to sales meetings, many companies engage in scoreboarding salespeople on a quarterly, monthly, and sometimes weekly basis. These firms publish salespeople's rankings from best to worst, generally based on percent above or below quota. Depending on the marketing strategy, these firms rank salespeople based on cumulative revenue, gross margin, new business, product mix, or some combination. Rankings appear for each region and the company as a whole. Knowing the status of those salespeople just above and below them makes the top performers run faster. No one wants to be in the bottom 10 percent. Everyone wants to improve. Competitive, ego-driven, and high-achieving salespeople respond more positively to scoreboarding than do

service-oriented salespeople. Some firms that emphasize team selling don't use scoreboarding. Some firms just list those salespeople in the top 50 percent. If you don't scoreboard, consider it. Many successful sales managers recommend it.

In motivation, little things mean a lot. The salespeople for a hospital supply firm deal with an immense amount of conflict resolution because of broad product lines and lack of customer organization. Each month the sales manager presents the Lifesaver award to a salesperson for quickly and economically resolving a customer problem. A pack of three Lifesaver rolls are tied together with fancy ribbon.

A telesales firm asks any salesperson who opens a new account or surpasses the daily quota to ring a bell. People enjoy this, and it creates peer pressure.

CAREER LADDER OF TITLES

A cruise line with a sales force calling on travel agents has created a career ladder of titles. Entry-level salespeople start as "sales representatives." After two years and the attainment of certain sales goals and skills or knowledge levels, they become eligible for the title of "territory manager" and a small increase in compensation. After four years and attainment of higher goals, skills, and knowledge; they become eligible for the title of "senior territory manager" and another small increase in compensation. At each level they receive some managerial responsibilities for interviewing new salespeople, mentoring, or assisting at sales meetings. At each level they also receive responsibility for a few more national accounts. This company has limited management opportunities and attracts career salespeople. So the career ladder of titles has meant reduced turnover. People work extra hard and smart to put that new title on their calling card.

What do you and your firm do to recognize salespeople? Should you do more?

Salespeople often complain that their manager is quick to criticize them, but seldom praises them. We motivate salespeople with love and fear. How well do you balance the two?

Feeling Useful, Important, and Worthwhile

Salespeople need to feel that their work serves a useful purpose and contributes significantly to the company's success and well-being. A salesperson's motivation can be destroyed overnight by a feeling of worthlessness. Training programs, management's attitudes, good communications, appreciation of their work, and sensitivity to their problems all contribute to a feeling of being useful, important, and worthwhile. Each step in the sales management process such as training influences the other steps such as motivation.

Although they hide it, many salespeople approach their jobs with feelings of insecurity and inferiority. They live with customer rejection every day. Their skills are intangible and difficult to describe, and nonselling coworkers, even family members, often don't respect or understand them.

The sales manager's investment of time and the company's investment of money in initial training, field coaching, performance evaluations, development plans, bubble-up sales forecasts, continuing education, and sales meetings make salespeople feel useful, important, and worthwhile. Again, each step in the sales management process such as training, performance evaluations, and bubble-up sales forecasts influences the other steps such as salesperson's motivation.

During the initial training period and in periodic field visits and sales meetings, management should make it clear that the company could not exist without its salespeople. Without a sales force, there would be no orders, shipments, or revenues to employ anyone else. Let salespeople know they serve a useful purpose, that they are important stakeholders in the company, and that you appreciate their work and their contribution to the firm's success. Management's positive attitude will in turn influence that of its nonselling employees, which will further reinforce the salesperson's sense of worth. Management's lead in recognizing the centrality of its sales force proves particularly important in technology- and operations-based firms.

Unfortunately, many manufacturing-, technology-, design-, engineering-, or operations-driven firms look at salespeople as a necessary evil. The salespeople are the turkeys and jokers with company cars and expense accounts. This attitude makes salespeople feel useless, worthless, and unmotivated. Often, this attitude starts at the top and filters down. Such an atmosphere negates other attempts to motivate salespeople and reduces sales force productivity. In a fast-changing world where technology, design, and engineering quickly commoditize products or services, many top managers realize their sales force remains a key differentiator.

When top management travels with salespeople, meets them at sales meetings, and shares their corporate vision, this creates a feeling of usefulness. Words and actions that make salespeople feel part of the team help them to feel important and worthwhile.

GOOD COMMUNICATION, TIMELINESS, AND SALES SUPPORT STAFF

Good communications, especially timeliness in responding to their efforts or to their particular problems, help make salespeople feel useful, important, and worthwhile. For example, when a salesperson has invested effort in opening a new account, placing a new product, or meeting the key decision maker, respond to the situation with the attention it deserves. Follow up on credit approvals, delivery dates, or letters to the decision makers. If a credit or delivery problem develops, get back to the salesperson quickly. Lack of communication, attention, and follow-up tell the salesperson that he or she is useless. It communicates the message that new business, progress in long sales cycles, and the salesperson's efforts don't count. Such instances as well as faulty administration demoralize the sales staff.

In some firms salespeople are the last to know about price increases, management changes, design alterations, new policy, and shipping delays. As a result, they feel useless, worthless, and unimportant.

When you raise prices or a new competitor enters the market, let your salespeople know that you sympathize with the problems this causes them. Help them with your knowledge. Don't say, "That's part of your job; now get it done."

For example, in 2001, when the financial services, steel, and technology markets contracted, smart sales managers in those industries worked with their salespeople to maintain motivation. These sales managers communicated that their markets were cyclical and would rebound as they had in the past. The sales managers suggested the salespeople concentrate on networking, relationship building, increasing market share, and targeting smaller accounts. The sales managers also reduced administrative tasks. In 2004 when these industries rebounded, the companies whose sales managers used these techniques outperformed their competitors.

In-house customer service representatives, sales coordinators, product managers, and engineers who provide sales support can help to motivate salespeople in the field. Similarly, customer-relationship-management software and a 24-hour tech support hotline can help to motivate salespeople. The message is, "We care; you are important."

As sales manager, you should promptly answer all correspondence, e-mails, and phone calls from your people. Make sure they receive samples, catalogs, e-mails, bulletins, sales aids, and software on time. When you wait days or weeks to answer a call, e-mail, or letters from your people, you place their usefulness in question. Always return salespeople's calls, even if only to report, "I am very busy this afternoon but will call back tomorrow." How do you feel when your boss or one of your customers does not return your calls? Similarly, when a salesperson unexpectedly pops into your office and you are swamped, don't say, "I don't have time to see you," but rather, "I am busy right now, but let's set a time to talk tomorrow."

As mentioned earlier, some smaller companies, especially those using commission compensation and/or expense reimbursement, do not pay their salespeople promptly. They may send checks out late or defer payments until the following month. The message conveyed by such action is that the salesperson's work contributes little, and this quickly destroys motivation.

GOOD TRAINING

Lack of training can also destroy motivation. For instance, when the sales manager does the salesperson's job, it makes the salesperson feel useless and unimportant. It also wastes the sales manager's time. If you can't train salespeople to do their job, terminate them. Weak performers are contagious. Admit a hiring mistake and cut your losses.

For instance, the Philadelphia salesman for a men's clothing company called on a number of major accounts who preferred to review his line at the company's New York showroom. The Philadelphia salesman asked his sales manager, who ran the New York showroom, if he could come to New York to work with these major accounts. The sales manager replied that this was not necessary because he, the sales manager, would work with these accounts himself. The sales manager assured the salesman that all commissions on such sales would be credited to the salesperson. The sales manager felt the Philadelphia salesman had plenty to do calling on the many smaller retailers in his territory, but the implication was that the salesman wasn't needed in New York.

These major accounts did purchase clothing through the New York office, and the salesman did receive his commission. He nevertheless continued to complain that he wanted to participate in the selling, even though he received a commission for putting forth no effort. Management refused to let him participate, and after two years this top salesman joined a competitor. At his previous job he had felt useless.

PROPER DECISION-MAKING AUTHORITY

To stay motivated, salespeople need proper authority to make appropriate decisions concerning pricing, delivery, and customization of products or services. A salesperson should have authority to quote prices in a certain range, to set delivery dates after consulting operations, and to approve certain customer-specific product alterations. If management does not give the salespeople proper decision-making authority, management is telling the sales force they are not very useful, important, or worthwhile. The range of this authority depends on the industry and buyer behavior. For example, salespeople need more decision-making authority in selling to new systems buyers than commodity buyers.

CLIMATE OR EMPLOYEE SURVEYS

Climate or employee surveys make salespeople feel useful, important, and worthwhile. They also represent an effective vehicle for communication. Ninety-degree climate surveys allow employees to evaluate those directly above them, upper management, and the firm as a whole. Climate surveys that range 180 degrees allow employees to evaluate those directly above them, upper management, their firm as a whole, and those at their side—their peers; and 360-degree climate surveys allow salespeople to not only evaluate management, their firm, and their peers but also the people below them. In a 180- and 360-degree climate surveys, salespeople and sales managers evaluate each other and are evaluated by their peers. The "degrees" refer to the organization as a circle with peers at your side and management above you.

Exhibit 12.1 at the end of this chapter is an example of a customized sales-function-specific climate survey for salespeople to evaluate management and the firm. The climate survey should be anonymous but coded by region, and it can be filled out in a group or individual setting, in hard-copy form or online. The coding tells you who a particular group of salespeople report to. Human resources or an outside consulting group can administer and score the surveys, aggregate results, accumulate narrative answers, and conduct follow-up meetings. Any question where 25 percent of the respondents are "somewhat" or "very dissatisfied" needs to be discussed with the group for further clarification. Most questions are in multiple-choice form, but they leave room for narrative comments by the salesperson.

Within 30 days of doing a climate survey, a person from human resources or an outside consulting firm should meet with appropriate groups of salespeople. To encourage candid conversations, the sales managers should not be present. Even the best sales managers have trouble remaining neutral during climate surveys. Confidentiality is critical for the success of a climate survey.

The facilitator asks probing questions about areas of salesperson concern. The facilitator first explains why certain changes cannot be made. The facilitator then discusses areas where changes can be made and looks for consensus. "We can use EDI for order entry; we can't accept collect calls from customers." "We can increase the amount of performance pay in salesperson compensation. We cannot increase the amount of fixed pay." After the climate survey, the firm must follow up with agreed-to actions and changes. If changes based on employee input do not result, the climate survey tells salespeople they are not very important or worthwhile.

Few firms customize climate surveys for salespeople. Generally, salespeople become included in a total company generic-format form. Generic formats generate generic results. Customized formats (Exhibit 12.1) allow salespeople to make suggestions on increasing sales, lowering costs, better serving customers, and increasing sales force productivity. After all, they are closest to the customers.

Salesperson climate surveys should contain the following elements:

- The degree to which each salesperson feels his or her sales manager supports or hinders the accomplishment of his or her goals and why.
- Any suggested changes to the compensation package, training program, and performance evaluation.
- Whether job satisfaction has improved or deteriorated in the last year. This benchmarking forces firms to do climate surveys on a continuous basis. Conducting a climate or employee survey once has little value, but conducting surveys on an annual basis provides useful information and improved motivation.
- The level of effective communication between salespeople and other departments. Salespeople stand at the vortex of any organization. The ability to communicate and coordinate with other departments reflects the importance of seamless service.
- How can the salesperson and the firm better serve the customer, increase sales, and lower costs?

As a sales manager, keep in mind that a salesperson must feel useful—that is, he or she must feel a sense of worth in relation to the company. Temper your words and actions with knowledge of this need, and treat salespeople as mature professionals who are performing significant work.

What do you do to make your salespeople feel useful, important, and worthwhile? Equally important, do some of your actions turn salespeople off?

Challenge and Achievement

Different sparks light different salespeople's fires. Most salespeople need recognition, but many salespeople also thrive on the challenge of opening new accounts and increasing the volume of existing ones. They possess a high need to achieve that exceeds any monetary rewards they may gain. Long after they have satisfied their financial needs, these achievers continue going the extra mile to do better. For high-achieving, ego-driven salespeople, money represents the table stakes while beating last year provides the challenge.

Can you pick out the superstars in your organization—the 30 percent who produce 70 percent of your sales? The people with no complacency plateau or comfort level? Often we concentrate on motivating underperformers when in fact motivating the superstars could produce better results. Would you rather obtain a 10 percent increase on 70 percent or 30 percent of your region's sales? The super-stars, who often have superegos, have their own set of needs. Being independent and successful, they appear not to need motivation, training, or management. But without nonmonetary motivation, training, and management their flame can go out.

Generally, the high achievers enjoy taking personal responsibility for problem solving, are willing to take calculated risks, enjoy participating in management decision making, and need constant feedback on their performance. Because they are your best performers, you must continue to motivate them by providing outlets for their achievement-related needs. Assign such people difficult customers, possibly expand their territory, and let them participate in management decisions. These assignments motivate them, and their participation can benefit the company. One note of caution: These people will accept whatever challenge you assign them, so beware of overloading them. They have boundless energy.

A Denver company that erects cellular phone, radio, and television transmission towers knows how to motivate high achievers. Its California salesperson has an insatiable appetite for achievement and challenge. When its largest national customer threatened to take its business elsewhere, the sales manager asked the California salesperson to accompany him on a visit to the customer's national headquarters in Washington. Together they won the business back, and the salesman talked about his participation in this success for the next year.

When a Chicago insurance agency had an opportunity to bid on a large group program in Dallas, it sent its highest-achieving salesperson to make the presentation. He failed to obtain that business, but he enjoyed the opportunity, appreciated the recognition, and worked even harder on his return.

Because many high achievers enjoy participating in management decisions, you should develop vehicles for accommodating this need. For instance, invite these people to participate in the committees that set the agendas for sales meetings, approve new products or services, discuss field problems and new technology with management, or develop new sales techniques and compensation programs. Let them interview, ride with, and evaluate potential new hires. Let them mentor and train new hires. Let them lead sales meetings or make presentations as knowledge experts. Encourage them to make positive suggestions for change. Seek their advice. Let them know you consider their recommendations seriously. When you take a vacation, put them in charge. From this participation they gain a special sense of achievement and self-worth, and you get a job well done. Delegating to high achievers frees your time for other tasks and motivates them to even greater excellence.

Sales managers can also have a negative impact on top performers. For example, reducing a high achiever's territory can severely damage his or her motivation. Such people need to perceive unlimited challenges and opportunities for achievement. Often they outrun their ability to service all the new accounts they open. But by reducing their territory, you are giving a message that can be interpreted only as, "Thanks for the great job; your reward is a demotion, a penalty." The salesperson's time allocation planner, discussed in Chapter 10, might indicate that a high achiever has grown the territory to a point where accounts cannot be called on at the correct frequency. As discussed in Chapter 10, you then need to sell the benefits of a smaller territory to the high achiever.

A large Atlanta conglomerate acquired a storm window manufacturer in Tennessee. The storm window company's New York salesperson also covered Boston and Philadelphia. He worked six days a week, never took a vacation, and produced 25 percent of his company's sales. The conglomerate reduced his territory to New York City so that less traveling would be involved and so that Philadelphia and Boston could each have a resident salesperson. His compensation remained at the same high levels because of overrides on the territories he gave up. His total compensation equaled that of the storm window firm's president.

However, after six months he quit and went to work for a competitor. Because he sold every major account in New York City, no challenge remained, and he lost interest in the job. This unfortunate situation might have been avoided by giving the salesperson part of New Jersey or Connecticut, which were under-developed. He also might have received a title, such as "national accounts sales manager" or "assistant sales manager." Possibly explaining the benefits of a smaller territory—that is, less travel expense and more time off the road for customers and leisure—would have proved helpful.

High achievers want constant feedback on their results. Be sure these people receive weekly, if not daily, comparisons of their results to forecast, quota, and previous year. They respond to and understand territorial gross margin and profit contribution numbers. Discuss this material with them.

Eventually, you may wish to promote the high achiever to assistant manager for the region or to the sales manager for another region. However, sometimes high achievers prefer to remain career salespeople or don't have the appropriate skill set for management.

What are you doing to motivate your superstars with a high need for challenge and achievement?

Freedom and Authority

Many salespeople prize the freedom and authority available to them through selling. They thrive on planning their own day, not going to an office, representing the company to a customer, and making their own decisions. Many salespeople even feel that they are in business for themselves and enjoy managing their own territories. This is why they chose a career in sales to begin with. Can you pick these people out in your organization?

If your firm primarily compensates salespeople with performance pay, you probably attract salespeople with a high need for authority and freedom. If your firm employs channel partners, you will find their salespeople have a high need for authority and freedom. Does your candidate profile list authority, freedom, challenge, and achievement as desired personal characteristics for salespeople? Does your candidate profile look for candidates who have business management skills?

To satisfy such people's needs, you can remove some of the controls, allowing them more freedom and authority. Also, you can allow them to work directly with customers on certain nonselling activities, hold them accountable for performance results, and issue them titles, as discussed in the section on recognition.

You might, for instance, let them make certain decisions on their own that previously had required your approval. As an example, if an account met volume and credit requirements, you might let the salesperson vary prices, terms, freight, and advertising allowances within certain limits. They generally accept this new freedom by pricing at the higher end. If an account met certain operational requirements, you might let the salesperson customize features, within limits, to meet customer needs. If you normally require weekly call and route reporting from your salespeople, you might consider requiring such reports only biweekly. You must measure what impact these changes might have on the morale of other salespeople. Will other salespeople consider these changes playing favorites? You might assign this person more responsibility for forecasting monthly sales and dollars of gross margin in his or her territory and preparing business or sales plans.

A person who greatly values personal autonomy sees himself or herself as a business manager, not a salesperson, and this person often enjoys working directly with the customer on nonselling, service-related projects. Depending on the product or service, this might involve advertising, promotions, recycling, plant layout, design, safety issues, formulas, markups, total quality management, perpetual inventories, estate planning, displays, Web page design, testing, or reengineering. Allow this person the time and authority to get involved with these sorts of activities.

What are you doing to motivate your salespeople with a high need for freedom and authority?

(Exhibits start on next page.)

Exhibit 12.1.   Salesperson Climate Survey.

1. The degree of overall satisfaction with your position as a territory manager.

    Check one:
    ☐ Completely satisfied
    ☐ Mostly satisfied
    ☐ Somewhat dissatisfied
    ☐ Very dissatisfied

2. The degree to which you feel motivated to perform the responsibilities of a territory manager.

    ☐ Completely satisfied
    ☐ Mostly satisfied
    ☐ Somewhat dissatisfied
    ☐ Very dissatisfied

3. Top management's appreciation of your job.

    ☐ Completely satisfied
    ☐ Mostly satisfied
    ☐ Somewhat dissatisfied
    ☐ Very dissatisfied

4. Your regional manager's perception of the importance of your position.

    ☐ Completely satisfied
    ☐ Mostly satisfied
    ☐ Somewhat dissatisfied
    ☐ Very dissatisfied

5. The degree to which you feel that the training needs of your position are being met. Training includes knowledge of products, customers, competition, and selling skills. Training includes ride-withs, sales meetings, and classroom sessions.

    ☐ Completely satisfied
    ☐ Mostly satisfied
    ☐ Somewhat dissatisfied
    ☐ Very dissatisfied

6. What additional training would you like? Please list specific topics and general format (ride-with, sales meeting, classroom session). _____

    _____

7. Your satisfaction with the performance evaluation process and criteria?

    ☐ Completely satisfied
    ☐ Mostly satisfied
    ☐ Somewhat dissatisfied
    ☐ Very dissatisfied

(Continued on next page.)

Exhibit 12.1. *(Continued from previous page.)*

8. The level of your understanding of your goals and performance expectations.

☐ Completely understood
☐ Mostly understood
☐ Somewhat understood
☐ Seldom understood

9. The level of your understanding of corporate philosophy and guaranteed fair treatment policy.

☐ Completely understood
☐ Mostly understood
☐ Somewhat understood
☐ Seldom understood

10. Management's responsiveness to your ideas as to company policy and performance.

Check one:
☐ Completely responsive
☐ Mostly responsive
☐ Often unresponsive
☐ Usually unresponsive

11. Your regional manager's responsiveness to your ideas as to company policy and performance.

☐ Completely responsive
☐ Mostly responsive
☐ Often unresponsive
☐ Usually unresponsive

12. The degree to which you feel your relationship with your regional manager supports or hinders the accomplishment of your goals.

☐ Completely supports
☐ Mostly supports
☐ Often hinders
☐ Usually hinders

13. The level of importance of your compensation package in motivating you to greater accomplishments.

☐ Very important
☐ Somewhat important
☐ Seldom important
☐ Not important

14. Your current compensation package is structured properly.

☐ Completely satisfied
☐ Mostly satisfied
☐ Somewhat dissatisfied
☐ Very dissatisfied

(Continued on next page.)

Exhibit 12.1.   *(Continued from previous page.)*

Why or why not? _____

_____

_____

15. Employee policies are for the most part clearly articulated and fair.

Check one:
☐ Completely satisfied
☐ Mostly satisfied
☐ Somewhat dissatisfied
☐ Very dissatisfied

16. Customer policies are for the most part clearly articulated and fair.

☐ Completely satisfied
☐ Mostly satisfied
☐ Somewhat dissatisfied
☐ Very dissatisfied

17. In the last year has your job satisfaction improved or deteriorated? If you have been with us less than a year, then in the last quarter.

☐ Improved greatly
☐ Improved somewhat
☐ Deteriorated somewhat
☐ Deteriorated greatly

Why? _____

_____

_____

What areas of the company or your region are better? _____

_____

_____

What areas of the company or your region are worse? _____

_____

_____

(Continued on next page.)

Exhibit 12.1.   *(Continued from previous page.)*

18. The people in your region are cooperative and work with a team spirit.

Check one:
☐ Completely satisfied
☐ Mostly satisfied
☐ Somewhat dissatisfied
☐ Very dissatisfied

Any ideas for improvement? _____
_____

19. The people in the company are cooperative and work with a team spirit.

Check one:
☐ Completely satisfied
☐ Mostly satisfied
☐ Somewhat dissatisfied
☐ Very dissatisfied

Any ideas for improvement? _____
_____

20. The level of effective communication between you and the following:

	Completely satisfied	Mostly satisfied	Somewhat dissatisfied	Very dissatisfied
Regional manager	☐	☐	☐	☐
Corporate management	☐	☐	☐	☐
Customer service	☐	☐	☐	☐
Warehouse and/or distribution	☐	☐	☐	☐
Engineering	☐	☐	☐	☐
Telesales	☐	☐	☐	☐
Credit	☐	☐	☐	☐
Marketing	☐	☐	☐	☐
_____	☐	☐	☐	☐

(Continued on next page.)

Exhibit 12.1.   *(Continued from previous page.)*

21. How can our company help you to be more effective and more productive in the future?

_____

_____

_____

_____

_____

22. What constructive criticism would you make of your region's functions?

_____

_____

_____

_____

_____

23. How can communications be improved?

_____

_____

_____

_____

_____

24. Your ideas for better serving customers' needs:

_____

_____

_____

_____

_____

25. Your ideas for reducing costs in any area:

_____

_____

_____

_____

_____

Questions and Exercises for Chapter 12

- What programs does your firm or a firm you are familiar with have to recognize salespeople?
- As sales manager, how do you or would you make salespeople feel useful, important, and worthwhile?
- Do you have a written motivational program for each salesperson?
- How do you or would you motivate top performers?

Quiz for Chapter 12

1. True or false?
   Money is a universal incentive for salespeople.

2. Which of these is *not* a salesperson motivational need?
   a. Praise and recognition
   b. Feeling useful
   c. Challenge and achievement
   d. Sales meetings
   e. Authority and freedom

3. Which of the following are benefits of a highly motivated sales force?
   a. Less total compensation
   b. Lower turnover
   c. Greater productivity
   d. More performance pay
   e. Greater confidence and enthusiasm

4. From the following list, rank the top drivers of engagement:
   a. Competitive health benefits
   b. Competitive base pay
   c. Career advancement opportunities
   d. Work and life balance
   e. Challenging work
   f. Reputation of company
   g. Customer satisfaction
   h. Input in decision making

5. Which of the following represent ways to recognize salespeople?
   a. Salesperson of the month
   b. Top management involvement

c. Honor societies
    d. Ranking salespeople
    e. Career ladder of titles

6. Which of the following represent ways to make salespeople feel useful, important, and worthwhile?
    a. Not returning their phone calls or e-mails
    b. Field coaching
    c. Performance evaluations
    d. Bubble-up sales forecasts
    e. Centralizing decision-making authority

7. Which of the following satisfy high-performing salespeople's needs for challenge and achievement?
    a. Enlarging their territories
    b. Giving them more large accounts
    c. Putting them on the new product committee
    d. Making them a mentor
    e. Discussing their territorial profits
    f. Hiring an assistant to help them

8. Which of the following satisfies certain salespeople's needs for freedom and authority?
    a. Allowing them more pricing flexibility
    b. Allowing them to work with customers on nonselling activities
    c. Sharing territorial margin information with them
    d. Reducing the frequency of their call reports
    e. Making them a mentor

9. True or false?
    Different sparks light different salespeople's fires. You cannot mass produce motivation.

10. True or false?
    a. Most salespeople want to be successful.
    b. Most salespeople are successful at something.

Note

1. "The 2003 Towers Perrin Talent Report." Copyright © 2003 Towers Perrin. Reprinted by permission of Towers Perrin.

Personal Growth, Esteem, Belonging, Leadership, and Sales Contests

Self-Realization and Fulfillment through Personal Growth

Do you have salespeople working for you who are over 40 or have been with the same firm for more than 10 years? These people may require special attention. Older salespeople, especially those who have been with the same firm over

10 years, have a stronger need for self-realization and fulfillment through personal growth. These people enjoy change, fear being in a rut, and want to feel more skilled and knowledgeable this year than last year. If you don't attend to these needs, such salespeople may reach positioning or contribution plateaus, or they may be stagnating in comfort zones.

Your responsibility as sales manager includes creating an environment conducive to productive change and personal growth so that salespeople don't get burned out. Continual training helps to satisfy this need and can take many forms, including sales meetings, field visits, workshops, seminars, continuing education programs, industry conferences, and trade shows. Trained salespeople produce greater sales not only because of improved knowledge but also because of improved motivation.

The sales manager of a successful company selling highway safety devices to various government agencies detected growing dissatisfaction among his three best salespeople. All three individuals were well compensated, received adequate recognition, and were allowed considerable authority. Each had been with the company more than 15 years and was over 50. Their dissatisfaction puzzled the sales manager until he realized that these three salespeople had stopped growing personally and that they felt burned out and had developed negative self-images.

The sales manager decided to send one salesperson to attend a conference in Washington on highway safety; another to participate in a marketing association three-day seminar on selling municipal customers; and the third to view a new European safety system being installed in Mexico City. The next two years he repeated this type of experience, but he rotated each salesperson's activity. The salespeople learned and grew, and a feeling of self-realization and fulfillment replaced that of dissatisfaction. When the salespeople returned from their conference, association, or site visit, they had to present their experience, findings, and conclusions at a sales meeting.

The sales manager for a national giftware company had a plateaued salesperson who had represented the company for 10 years. Paul had long been an above-average performer, had handled the largest territory in terms of dollar sales, and was respected and liked by customers and prospects. But ever since his two children's graduation from college and his wife's promotion at her firm, Paul's attitude and performance had been disappointing. His calls per day fell along with his number of new accounts and total sales dollars.

The final blow came when Paul started losing a significant number of accounts because of a price increase. To make matters worse, the sales manager and Paul had become personal friends. She could not live with the situation, but she wanted to avoid terminating Paul, who had just reached 50. If you haven't had this problem, you will. Only the names will change.

Calling Paul into her office, the sales manager explained how she perceived the problem; declining sales, not properly targeting accounts, less-than-satisfactory calls per day, and a lack of new accounts. She then asked Paul what his goals were, what he would do to solve the problems, and if their roles were reversed, what action would he take. Together, they came up with a specific remedial plan and the time frame for its execution. She reminded Paul of his excellent past performance, but they both agreed that Paul was unmotivated and felt left behind, that he had a bruised ego that needed pumping. She realized Paul was neither angel nor devil and that fear and love were needed to correct the problem. She realized that Paul's problems were really her problems, that if a top-performing salesperson starts to underperform, the manager also bears some responsibility.

They looked at a number of possible causes and alternative situations: changing the territory, providing more training, giving Paul some special projects, making him an inside customer service representative, putting him in charge of trade shows and a national account, and using him for training new people.

The sales manager gave Paul a title, sent him to several seminars, let him represent the company at trade shows, and assigned specific performance goals or metrics. She was careful that the other salespeople did not perceive this as favoritism. They met every two weeks for five months and even discussed the possibility of termination. At one meeting Paul's wife was present; at another the vice president of marketing participated; at a third Paul watched a video on motivation. Slowly Paul started to feel better and once again became an above-average performer.

Many sales managers would prefer to complain about the Pauls in their departments than to confront the issues squarely. Most sales managers procrastinate in dealing with their Pauls. Unfortunately, the problem only gets worse unless you take the bull by the horns and actually offer to help the unmotivated salesperson. The quarterly performance evaluation discussed in Chapter 14 creates early recognition of motivational problems and forces corrective action.

To help in dealing with behavioral problems such as Paul's, meet with the problem salesperson to

- Explain and agree on the problems.
- Discuss what is causing the problems. If you understand the cause, it is easier to find solutions.
- Ask for alternative solutions or corrective action.
- Agree on implementation and put it in a time frame.
- Decide on a carrot (the benefits of change) and a stick (the consequence for not changing).
- Set performance standards. What metrics and time frame will you use to decide whether the salesperson's motivational problems have been solved?
- Have follow-up meetings to monitor progress.

For salespeople to change their behavior, they need a benefit such as a new title, new responsibilities, or a larger territory. They also must understand the consequences of not changing their behavior and performance such as termination, a smaller territory, or a demotion.

Whatever corrective action you decide on, consider the impact this action might have on other people in the organization. Will they see it as rewarding an underperforming or problem salesperson or as helping a colleague to be more successful?

IT TRAINING FOR OLDER SALESPEOPLE

Sometimes older salespeople become intimidated by computers, sales force automation, and customer-relationship-management software. If handled correctly, this offers a wonderful opportunity for personal growth. If handled incorrectly, it can destroy an older salesperson's self-worth. Most sales managers suggest giving salespeople who did not grow up with a computer some special off-site training. They also suggest teaming a computer-proficient salesperson, often younger, with someone who is not as proficient, often older. This represents a nonthreatening way to share best practices for the entire sales process—a form of mentoring. The IT mentor must also be available in the evening, which is when salespeople often have questions. Computer use and skills can be on performance evaluations and part of bonus compensation. Salespeople with weaker computer skills can be asked to present new software features at sales meetings. This forces them to get up to speed.

MANAGING SALESPEOPLE DIFFERENT FROM YOU

Today's sales force is very heterogeneous, containing older and younger people, men and women, and people of different nationalities and races. How should your approach and style vary depending on the type of salesperson? Do you manage women differently than men, older people differently than younger, Chinese nationals differently than Indian nationals? You must treat all people equally but customize your approach based on the salesperson's profile, needs, goals, and problems.

In managing people older than you, give them the proper respect, ask for their opinions, and draw on their experience. In managing people with child- or elder-care responsibility, allow them flextime. In dealing with people from Asia, respect their dietary customs.

Esteem, Status, and Respect

Most salespeople want the esteem of their fellow salespeople and of other company employees, management, customers, friends, and family. This helps build their self-esteem. For some, esteem comes in the shape of praise, recognition, or money. For others, it is associated with status within the organization and is represented by a job title; still others need more direct expressions of esteem.

Little items such as impressive calling cards help establish self-esteem and status every day. When an auto parts distributor stopped issuing embossed calling cards to his salespeople and substituted cheaper offset cards to save money, several of his salespeople paid for the printing of the old personalized embossed cards out of their own pockets.

A successful steel products salesperson did a great deal of customer entertaining with his wife at company expense. They wined and dined customers twice a week, played golf with many, and even took a few on vacations. When industry sales declined because of imports and a recession, the sales manager cut back on these entertainment expenses. The salesperson asked for the expense allowance to be continued even if it meant a decrease in his salary. The lifestyle made available by the expense account was critical to this man's status in the company and to his personal self-esteem.

The salesperson with a high need for self-esteem and status requires special treatment. Special treatment may demotivate other salespeople who feel it is not deserved or warranted. However, budget and performance permitting, consider special privileges such as a company credit card, subscriptions to trade publications, better car, first choice on vacation time, airline or hotel room upgrades, bigger desk, better cellular phone, newer laptop, membership in a private club, entertainment allowance, or fancy calling card. Often, additional expenses can be traded for reductions in other areas, or these perks can be used to reward superior performance or as prizes in a sales contest. Can you identify salespeople within your organization with a high need for esteem, status, and respect? Most important, as sales manager, you should enhance every salesperson's esteem with your respect.

Sense of Belonging

Many salespeople have a strong need to belong and participate in their work organization where they spend 40 or more hours a week. After all, most salespeople belong to a family, a community, some clubs, and probably a religious organization. Within the work organization, any group activities—such as sales meetings, conferences, social events, training seminars, teleconferencing, WebEx conferences, and athletic teams—can satisfy this need to belong. If the sales force lives within a day's drive of your office, scheduling frequent group activities proves more practical than if they live far away. If the sales force sells out of one central office, the everyday personal social contact creates a sense of belonging. In addition, the sales manager's field visits remind salespeople that they belong to an organization. Satisfying the need to belong for a national remote field sales force spread from Boston to Los Angeles proves the most difficult; yet because these people are physically separated from each other, their need is the greatest. A salesperson who works far from the home office can get very lonely.

Newsletters, letters of news, e-mail, and bulletins that contain information about other salespeople or employees remind salespeople that they belong to an organization. Both personal news (concerning births, new houses, birthdays, anniversaries of employment, vacations, graduations, children, illness, and retirement) and business news (concerning contests, competition, customers, programs, products, services, promotions, quotas, results, and new accounts) prove effective. Have salespeople contribute articles and information. Have a contest to name your newsletter. Make it warm and folksy. Many firms use part of the newsletter to scoreboard salespeople as described earlier in Chapter 12. These newsletters or letters of news can be published on a regional, district, divisional, or companywide basis, or some combination. Each regional manager may want to e-mail his or her own letter of news in addition to the company newsletter. Newsletters and letters of news may be sent electronically or by snail mail.

Once or twice a year, resources permitting, a well-planned sales meeting can provide a productive means of communication, motivation, and training. As discussed earlier, the sales meeting is of particular importance because it offers a prime opportunity for one-to-one human interaction within the sales force and between management and the sales organization. Regional companies and regional offices of national firms with local salespeople can hold shorter but more frequent, monthly or even weekly, sales meetings. All this satisfies a salesperson's need to belong.

As good corporate citizens and responsible human beings, the sales manager's sincere expression of concern for salespeople's well-being creates a feeling of belonging. Salespeople want to know that management at all levels cares about them and their families. Congratulate your salespeople on events of joy such as births, graduations, or a marriage. Express your sympathies on events of sorrow such as illness or death. Remember how you felt when your boss and your boss's boss expressed these concerns. People never forget it, which creates bonding and loyalty.

The president of a national software company sends and personally signs birthday cards to all employees. The sales manager of a small garbage disposal company has a birthday cake and brief party for his people. A financial services company gives salespeople a day off on their birthday. Many companies have similar programs to celebrate anniversaries of employment. A wholesale seed company sends flowers to its people on the anniversary of their employment. Many companies send birthday cards to employees' children and spouses. The cost is nominal, and the motivational results are excellent. Salespeople receive a feeling of belonging and a sense that the company cares about them. Once you start such a program, salespeople will remind you should a date be missed.

We send birthday cards to customers. Why not send cards to our internal customers, the salespeople? As mentioned previously, just as salespeople maintain customer profiles, sales managers should maintain profiles on their salespeople. These profiles should include birthdays, anniversaries, children's and spouses' names, events of joy and sorrow, hobbies, education, work experience, training, personal goals, and how the salespeople use and filter information. In order to communicate effectively with the salespeople, you need insight on how each person makes decisions. Again, we ask salespeople to keep this information on customers, and we must maintain such information on them. (See Exhibit 4.8.) Is the salesperson logical and concrete (aim, aim, aim), conceptual (ready, fire, aim), people oriented (how will the decision impact those around me), or big picture (fire, fire, fire).

The sales manager of an international consulting company visited each of 16 field sales representatives twice a year. The first question salespeople asked concerned news of their colleagues in other territories. The company could afford only one international sales meeting a year, but the sales manager sensed a strong feeling for or need for belonging. He decided to have shorter, less expensive regional sales meetings six months after each international meeting. Then between regional meetings each salesperson received videotapes featuring one of their colleagues discussing selling skills and product knowledge. Each month the tapes were rotated.

He also asked his administrative assistant to write an online newsletter for the sales force. Each salesperson submitted information. Each month salespeople received a bouquet with one carnation for every new account opened. A nice spirit developed, and the sales force seemed even more willing to work harder.

Apparel with discrete company logos gives salespeople a feeling of belonging. Use apparel, briefcases, luggage, and golf balls with a discrete company logo as rewards for short incentive programs. And, again, all these techniques prove equally effective for motivating channel partners, telesales people, and inside salespeople.

Last, consider a salesperson and/or channel partner council to advise management on topics for sales meetings, new product ideas, ways to better serve customers, increase revenues, and lower costs. Rotate the membership so all salespeople have an opportunity to serve. This satisfies many motivational needs including belonging.

Can you identify salespeople in your organization who have a high need to belong? How do you help them satisfy that need?

Positive Interpersonal Relationships

Pleasant personal relationships with management and peers represent a positive motivational force for salespeople and also foster a feeling of belonging. Unpleasant relationships represent a negative motivational force, which reduces a salesperson's productivity.

The Los Angeles representative for a data storage company did a satisfactory selling job in his territory, but he had a personality clash with the sales manager. The sales manager was an authoritarian, high-powered generalist, and the salesperson a low-key, detail man. The sales manager recognized their difference in styles as a problem, and he knew that his sales rep would do better if their relationship improved.

Over the next few months, the sales manager showed more flexibility toward, and applied less pressure on, the Los Angeles salesperson. He also provided this salesperson with more detailed information on his territory. The relationship improved, and so did sales in that area.

In dealing with motivational problems, such as plateauing and disruptive behavior, most sales managers procrastinate, which exacerbates the situation. As mentioned previously, have a meeting with the salesperson earlier rather than later. Explain and agree on the problems or issues. You can't solve the problem until you have defined it. Discuss the problem's causes. Ask the salesperson for alternative solutions or corrective action. Agree on implementation and put it in a time frame. What represents the benefit (or carrot) for positive change or results? What represents the consequence (or stick) if positive change and results do not occur? Set performance standards. What metrics will you use to measure change, success, or failure? Have follow-up meetings to monitor progress.

A Detroit automotive after-market company employed five excellent salespeople for the greater metropolitan area. However, one of the people annoyed the other four to the point where sales were affected. This member of the sales organization always had the right answers, told his colleagues what to do and how to do it, monopolized sales meetings, and bragged a great deal. His ideas were right; everyone else's were wrong. He was a superstar with a giant ego.

He consistently told the sales manager how to do her job and seldom listened to her suggestions.

Because this salesperson represented 40 percent of the sales manager's revenues, he felt free to call the vice president of marketing with questions and the district warehouse for inventory information. One action violated the chain of command, the other action violated company policy. The sales manager wondered if the salesperson represented 40 percent of district revenues because of his superior territory or his superior skills. Several saleswomen and female customer service representatives accused him of being abusive. You've probably met this person. If you have not, you will.

The sales manager realized that this dissident salesman's problem probably stemmed from lack of self-esteem and self-discipline. She realized he was neither angel nor devil and that both fear and love were needed to correct the problem. She realized that she bore some responsibility for his bad behavior since they had never discussed it. One day at lunch, the sales manager expressed her respect for the salesman's performance, skills, and judgment, but she noted that the salesman must also respect his colleague's opinions. She explained that he was becoming a problem. They discussed what she considered to be the problems: not respecting fellow workers, plus violating the chain of command and company policy. She asked a number of questions to stimulate self-analysis and discussion. "What do you feel is causing the problem?" "What would you do if you were the sales manager?" "What are your career goals?" She mentioned that he was a role model for younger salespeople.

At that meeting she discovered he wanted her job and had time on his hands. They agreed on a program: If his behavior improved, he would make certain presentations at sales meetings, attend several sales management workshops or seminars, take responsibility for several large inactive accounts, represent the company at several trade shows (the carrots, or benefits), plus read a book on getting along with people. Each month they would meet to discuss progress toward their goal. She was careful not to upset the other four salespeople with her program. The sales manager also stated very firmly that unless his behavior improved, other less pleasant actions would be necessary (the stick, or consequences). She set the metrics for measuring improved behavior. Thereafter, the two had many discussions concerning this matter, and although the problem never disappeared, it subsided. As a result, the performance of all five people improved.

How are you maintaining positive interpersonal relationships with and within the sales organization? What unpleasant relationships exist between salespeople and between management and salespeople? Do these have a negative impact on motivation? If so, what is the corrective action?

Consistent, Motivated, and Competent Leadership

Salespeople and channel partners require consistent, motivated, and competent leadership in order to maintain their own motivation. A sales force or channel partner is seldom more motivated or competent than its sales manager.

Successful sales managers vary greatly in style from autocratic to democratic, from sales or task oriented to employee oriented, from persuasive to consultative. However, successful sales managers do have nine common traits. They realize that their job is getting work done through others, that their success depends on the success of the people who work for them. Their styles, techniques, and policies are consistent. They don't switch between autocratic and democratic, or persuasive and consultative. They believe in what they do, which creates strong contagious personal motivation. They communicate this strong personal motivation to the sales force, who display it to customers. Happy salespeople create satisfied customers. Successful sales managers realize they are agents of change, manage change, take advantage of change, and change or modify people's behavior. Successful sales managers set standards, are critical, and sit in judgment. Successful sales managers can manage a wide variety of salespeople—rookies, veterans, men, women, younger, older, North Americans, Europeans, and Asians. Successful sales managers turn around or terminate weak performers. Successful sales manager can execute and implement company tactics and strategies. Successful sales managers are able to transition from being friends with the sales force to being friendly. All this requires successful sales managers to have excellent communication skills not only with customers but also with the salespeople who work for them.

If asked, most sales managers would say they feel motivated. When asked how they communicate this personal motivation to the sales force, they stumble and hesitate. When these same sales managers' salespeople are asked if their sales managers are motivated, most reply no. Most sales managers do a poor job of communicating strong personal motivation to their sales force.

When asked how they know if a sales manager has strong personal motivation, salespeople reply, because he or she appears organized, prepared, and focused and is a good presenter. This might be observed at sales meetings or on a sales call. Because he or she appears confident, enthusiastic, emotional, passionate, and excitable. Tone of voice, eye contact, hardworking, high energy, asks for more work, volunteers, and loves Mondays are often mentioned.

Ask your salespeople to anonymously evaluate your personal motivation and leadership skills. Each year ask for suggestions for improvement. The answers may enlighten you. At least, evaluate yourself quarterly asking the following questions:

1. How motivated do I appear to the sales force? Do I believe in what I am doing?
2. Am I consistent in my style of management and my techniques or policies? Am I consistent in the use of love and fear? Am I consistent in perceiving a salesperson as angel or devil?
3. Do I attempt to get work done through other people, or do I just do it myself?
4. How much time do I spend training salespeople?
5. Do salespeople have difficulty understanding what I want from them?
6. How often do salespeople turn over in my region or division?
7. Is each salesperson showing net revenue increases?
8. Are the salespeople self-motivated, or must I always prod them?
9. What percent of my time do I spend each month on administrative duties? Personal selling? Time with salespeople? Other responsibilities?

The following are examples of poor sales manager leadership qualities. The sales manager for a DVD company asked his salespeople to call on certain specific retail accounts. If they didn't call on the accounts within 10 days, the sales manager would make an appointment to see the retailer. Soon the sales manager was calling on more accounts, and the sales force fewer. As a result, company sales declined. This sales manager had failed to realize that his job depended on getting work done through other people.

When the U.S. Surgeon General issued his initial warning on smoking, an entrepreneur started marketing no-tobacco lettuce leaf cigarettes. However, the sales manager for this new product continued smoking his old brand, and this contributed to his sales force's lack of motivation. Sales managers must believe in what they are doing.

A regional sales manager for a credit card company told the sales force not to call on smaller restaurants because of credit problems; then, the next month, he introduced a special program just for that market. One week this sales manager would use persuasion to implement policy; the next week, threats. During the credit card company's second busiest month, August, he took a three-week vacation. The salespeople responded by losing their motivation. This sales manager was not competent, consistent, or motivated.

Company Policy and Administration

Company policies and administration that promote an open, constructive, and relaxed environment and embody trust, faith, consistency, and fairness will promote job satisfaction and positive motivation. In contrast, company policies and administration that promote inefficiency, ineffectiveness, and frustration within the organization and do not embody trust, consistency, and fairness will cause job dissatisfaction and damage salespeople's motivation.

For example, a company policy that prohibits salespeople from calling or e-mailing the factory to check on delivery dates or outstanding customer balances can create frustration and job dissatisfaction as can a company policy that prohibits salespeople from communicating directly with engineering and design. A less rigid policy that allowed salespeople to call or communicate once a week would satisfy management's need to limit the time and expense involved and the sales force's need for information. Establishing a real-time Web site with this data would also efficiently satisfy the sales force's need for information.

A company policy that prohibits salespeople from making credit card calls to the sales manager or using the 800 number or asks salespeople to pay their own cell phone charges can cause frustration and unhappiness. A company policy that asked people to share these costs would be more equitable. The latter policy embodies trust but prevents salespeople from abusing a privilege.

An administrative policy requiring a company officer to review each order can unnecessarily delay order processing and thus shipping. Such a policy might cause job dissatisfaction and damage salespeople's motivation. A more moderate policy requiring officer review only of new account orders would be less likely to damage either salespeople's morale or delivery schedules.

In one small family-owned company, salespeople were not allowed to park in the company lot, and the president or owner opened all incoming mail and occasionally listened to phone conversations. Sales force turnover was 50 percent a year.

An information technology policy that does not give salespeople access to customer credit records, EDI, past purchases, gross margin numbers, or certain new product specifications might cause sales force frustration and unhappiness and seriously damage motivation. A company policy giving limited access would be fairer.

A company policy establishing certain national house accounts on which sales-people receive no income certainly dulls motivation. A policy that splits national accounts among a number of salespeople, who then share the income, would improve motivation. A policy that gives salespeople whose territories have been reduced an override on transferred accounts would improve motivation.

In the twenty-first century, company policy concerning channel conflicts and e-commerce will have a major impact on motivation. Create a committee, which includes salespeople, to clearly define how performance pay is to be split on e-commerce or Web-generated orders.

What are you doing at your firm to create company policy and administration that promote an open, constructive, and relaxed environment and embody trust, faith, consistency, and fairness. What are you doing at your firm to eliminate company policy and administration that promote inefficiency, ineffectiveness, and frustration?

Job Security and Compensation

A salesperson who feels underpaid or on the verge of termination will not put forth that extra effort you are looking for. In fact, all other motivational techniques fail when salespeople sense that their jobs are threatened or believe that their remuneration, including expense reimbursements and fringe benefits, is inadequate. Corporate downsizing, right sizing, reorganizations, automation, mergers, acquisitions, liquidity, and personal probation all threaten salespeople's job security and compensation.

As mentioned, money is not a universal incentive for salespeople, because they have many nonmonetary motivational needs. Most salespeople will not be attracted to or continue at jobs that do not meet their compensation requirements. However, sometimes compensation is threatened or changed or a salesperson feels obligated to accept a job with less than satisfactory pay. The following are examples of what might happen in such situations.

A St. Louis regional securities firm employed 40 "retail" brokers to handle its individual investors. When the firm's major partner passed away, the brokers (salespeople) became concerned about their jobs. Unnerved by persistent rumors concerning the firm's imminent liquidation or sale, they became much less aggressive in pursuing new business. To offset this concern, the other partners increased the brokers' commissions, called them account representatives, and held weekly sales meetings—all to no avail. Only after a year did the brokers realize that their fears were unfounded and once again start producing additional business.

Similarly, an international aerospace firm announced a corporate downsizing and reorganization because of reduced government defense spending. It took six months for a group of consultants and management to agree on a downsizing plan. During that period salespeople hung around headquarters and made few customer visits. After 25 percent of the salespeople were terminated, the remaining 75 percent lost their motivation, and the firm lost market share.

In 2006, a specialty European shoe importer lowered its sales force's commission rate from 10 to 6 percent because inflation, duties, tariffs, and exchange rates had raised the price of its line by 40 percent. The sales manager never fully explained the reason for lowering the commission rate to his people. Even though their dollars of commission income rose slightly, because dollars of sales

increased over 40 percent, the salespeople failed to produce that extra effort. They felt underpaid.

A temporary employment agency hired a top salesperson who had lost his previous job, and the agency paid him at a base salary considerably lower than his most recent position had paid. The salesperson arrived at work late, left early, showed little interest in his job, and had to be terminated. He obviously felt underpaid and was not motivated.

Occasionally we must threaten salespeople with termination or put them on probation. Once you do this, the probability of improvement narrows, so start looking for a replacement. A salesperson whose job is threatened generally loses rather than gains personal motivation.

To motivate a salesperson, you must satisfy the many interrelated needs discussed in Chapters 12 and 13, not just one. The sales manager requires a written customized motivational program for each salesperson similar to the training or developmental plan. The customized motivational program might include plans for a salesperson to lead a sales meeting, be a mentor, participate on the new product committee, or prepare a business plan for her territory. Different salespeople have different needs, goals, and problems, so you must motivate them as individuals. Each motivational idea presented in Chapters 12 and 13 represents a spark to light the fire; putting them all together provides the sales manager with a powerful tool.

Sales Contests and Incentive Plans

Sales contests and incentive programs provide fast and frequent reinforcement to a salesperson's needs for recognition, achievement, fulfillment, status, belonging, and additional compensation. As such, they represent a powerful tool for improving sales force motivation and increasing sales without increasing fixed expenses. Thus, sales contests can increase present and future dollars of contribution margin.

A sales organization requires proper compensation; proper use of recognition, feeling useful, challenge, achievement, freedom, authority, personal growth, esteem, status, belonging, and leadership; and layered over this, some appropriate sales contests or incentive programs. These represent the basic pieces most necessary to motivate a sales force.

Sales contests prove most helpful in meeting specific, short-term objectives, such as smoothing out seasonal sales dips, bringing attention to a good product or service that has been neglected, launching a new product, increasing the number of active accounts, or stimulating upgrades and conversions. In longer, more complex sales cycles, contests can be used to reward number of betas, plant visits, or proposals and reduction of time from search to purchase. Sales contests can also revive enthusiasm for meeting longer-term goals, such as improved collections, lower expenses, higher number of cold calls, higher dollar volume, higher number of orders, higher average order size, new prospects, account retention, increased use of displays, revival of inactive accounts, and increased customer satisfaction.

In all cases, these contests attempt to elicit an extra "beyond-the-normal" effort from the sales force by generating enthusiasm and excitement. Selling can become boring and discouraging. A well-thought-out contest generates a continuing momentum even after it has ended because salespeople have experienced the satisfaction of higher sales and earnings. Also, a good incentive program can assist in creating good working habits that will make the sales force more productive on a continuing basis.

Poorly conceived sales contests, by contrast, can lower morale, reduce sales, and lead to resignations. For example, don't use a sales contest to revive an inferior or obsolete product or service that has seen its day. Don't use a sales contest if you can't deliver the product or service being sold. Don't use a sales contest when you already control over 70 percent of the market for that product or service. In all three cases, salespeople become frustrated rather than motivated.

During contests, salespeople have been known to overstock customers, to move orders from one period to another, and even to cheat. You must realize this and set up safeguards.

Contests lose their ability to excite and motivate when they are used too frequently or when the same contest is repeated. Generally, one to three different contests a year satisfy the sales force's appetite.

Types of Contests

There are three basic types of incentive plans: (1) contests in which salespeople compete directly against one another, resulting in prizes going to a winner and several runners-up; (2) contests in which salespeople are divided into teams by region or product line, and each team competes against the others for prizes; and (3) contests in which salespeople win prizes by meeting or exceeding certain individual goals.

DIRECT COMPETITION CONTESTS

Direct competition plans offering prizes to one winner and several runners-up do not motivate or involve the entire sales force. At the beginning, half the participants decide that they don't have a chance to win because the cards are stacked against them, the playing field is not level, and so they do not get involved in the contest.

For example, if the contest rewards the three salespeople who open the most new accounts in April or perform the most demos or arrange the most trial sales, many salespeople immediately lose interest because they know that their territory does not contain the potential for new accounts, demos, or trials that another salesperson's territory does. Then, halfway through the contest, when it becomes evident which three people will win, all but the winners give up. The losers are left unmotivated and with a feeling that management does not care about them.

A contest that does not involve the entire sales force will not achieve its motivational or specific performance goals. Active participation by the entire sales organization is vital. Direct competition proves especially inappropriate for small sales forces because the same person always wins. In a small sales force cooperation is often more important than competition.

TEAM CONTESTS

Team competition plans offering a prize to be shared by the winning group involve more people than direct competition plans but do not rouse your star performers. The stars feel that the group dilutes their individual efforts and results. When the high-achieving, ego-driven performer produces, he or she wants the spotlight. Therefore, in group contests, the highly competitive stars, who may produce most of your sales volume, generally perform under their potential. You can partially offset this by making your star performers team captains.

Team contests do create good group spirit, cooperation, and positive peer pressure. More experienced salespeople help and advise less experienced team members in achieving desired goals. Also, no team member wants the responsibility for causing the team's loss. Therefore, all team members, including service-oriented types, exert some extra effort.

Team contests do not produce resentment against individual winners because a group wins, but they can produce general resentment unless each team has an equal chance to win. When improving group spirit and teamwork is more important than motivating star performers, consider using a group incentive program. Team contests, however, prove inappropriate for small sales forces, which lack the numbers to form teams. Teams may compete against each other to determine a winner or perform against group goals so that all teams can win. For example, each salesperson from any region that exceeds quota by 20 percent can select a weekend trip of his or her choice. A direct competition contest for individuals can be held within each team or integrated into the team contest itself.

INDIVIDUAL GOAL CONTESTS

Contests in which salespeople win prizes by meeting or exceeding certain individual goals produce the best results. In these, salespeople do not compete against each other but rather against an individual target. Everyone becomes interested and involved and participates because everyone can win prizes.

If the contest's objective is opening the most new accounts in April or obtaining the most beta agreements or placing the most new products or services or bundling sales, then the sales manager sets a goal or quota for each salesperson. These individual objectives should reflect each territory's potential, which thus gives everyone an equal opportunity to win by leveling the playing field. A territory with 100 potential new accounts might carry a quota of 10, while a territory with 50 potential new accounts might have a quota of 5. You can obtain information on potential new accounts from the same reference material used to design territories and from field trips. Before setting the quota, discuss your reasoning with the involved salesperson to make sure he or she accepts the quota as realistic, attainable, and fair.

Any salesperson who achieves 95 percent of his or her goal should receive a prize, but a salesperson achieving 120 percent of quota should receive a more valuable prize. Prizes for reaching various percentage levels of quota are the same for each salesperson regardless of territory or quota size.

For example, if the salesperson with a quota of 10 new accounts opens 12, he or she receives the same prize as the salesperson with a quota of 5 new accounts who opens 6. Both achieved 120 percent of quota.

Incentive plans based on individual goals bear a striking resemblance to the goal-based quota or bonus form of compensation discussed in Chapter 8. However, the goal-based quota or bonus form of compensation rewards superior performance spanning from three months to a year with considerable money, whereas the individual goal contest rewards superior performance spanning one to three months with noncash prizes. The sales contest provides a more immediate reward for superior performance. Also, while bonus plans might reward one salesperson for new accounts and another for dollar sales increase, sales contests reward all salespeople for one type of performance. In addition, winners of sales contests receive publicity, no matter how many reach their objectives, while quota-based or bonus compensation rewards remain private information.

A variation of this individual goal plan involves a point system. A salesperson receives points for achieving 90 percent of his or her target in the sales contest and receives an increasing number of points as the percentage of or over target increases. When the contest ends, the salesperson uses these points to buy prizes.

Another variation involves adding overall winners to the individual goal plan. For example, the three people who achieve the largest percentage gain over quota receive a prize in addition to their other awards. Everyone continues to have individual goals and individual awards, but you add additional awards for overall winners. This creates some element of direct competition among salespeople and provides an added incentive for the ego-driven, competitive high performers.

Setting targets for these individual goal plans can be time-consuming because past sales records and market potential require studying, plus each salesperson requires a meeting. Administration of these contests is also time-consuming considering that just about everyone wins something. However, the results generally justify the extra time required. Individual goal plans prove especially suitable for small sales forces in that they can be used with any number of people, even one lone salesperson.

Contest Formats

Regardless of which plan you use—direct competition, teams, or individual goals—properly handled sales contests require objectives, budgets, time frames, appropriate prizes, adequate promotion, and simple, clearly explained rules.

OBJECTIVES

A sales contest without specific short-term objectives and without more general longer-term goals as well wastes time and money. Generally, sales contests without specific objectives fail. Company policy mandating at least one sales contest a year hardly qualifies as an objective. You need a reason for such a project, and the reason must support your basic marketing plan.

The objectives of a sales contest might include increased sales of a particular product or system, upgrades to more service, increased overall unit or dollar sales during a certain period, conversions to a particular raw material, increased average order size, increased number of customers, improved collections, reduced selling expenses, better use of selling aids, better retention of present accounts, lateral selling within an account, or more prospecting. For longer, more complex sales cycles, objectives might include reducing the steps and time necessary from search to purchase, improving closing ratios, obtaining more betas or trials, identifying decision makers, or increasing the number of proposals.

Using one of these specific objectives, you assign each activity or result a time frame and each territory a goal. For example, how many additional units of a particular product, how many additional dollars of sales, or what percentage increase in sales do you want from each salesperson during the contest period? How many new customers do you want each salesperson to add? If improved collections are a goal, how many days' accounts receivable do you want in each territory? If reduced selling expenses are a goal, how many dollars or what percentage decrease do you want from each salesperson? For longer, more complex sales cycles, how many additional proposals or trials do you want from each salesperson, or what closing ratios do you expect from each step in the process?

All sales contests should have as long-range goals the reinforcement of salespeople's motivational needs for recognition, achievement, fulfillment, status, belonging, and additional compensation. The contests should also seek to generate continuing momentum by establishing good work habits, for example prospecting, and exposing salespeople to higher income levels. An incentive plan's objectives naturally influence your choice among the three types of contests.

BUDGET

If properly structured, sales contests can increase sales and profits from existing personnel with minimum increases in overhead. To achieve this, you must understand the economics of your objectives and have a budget. For example, if the contest increases sales by 5 percent, or $100,000, how much marginal or additional dollars of contribution margin or profits will be generated before contest costs? Look at the profit or margin potential for the best possible, worst possible, and most probable sales results.

Next, decide, with the help of your controller or accountant, what portion of the increased profits or margins should pay for the contest costs. If a $100,000 sales increase produces a $20,000 pretax profit margin increase, you might budget 33 percent, or $6,600, for contest expenses. A more successful contest generates greater marginal sales and profits, but if you use an individual quota plan, it also results in greater prize expenses. You must also take into account that a contest affects both current and future sales and profits and that there are motivational benefits that cannot be measured in dollars.

Let's assume that the most probable result of your individual quota contest is a 5 percent, or $100,000, sales increase, resulting in a $20,000 pretax profit increase, which thus creates a $6,600 budget for the program. First, you deduct from the $6,600 the sum of $1,000 for out-of-pocket promotional costs. This covers extra phone calls, mailing expenses, and certain promotional literature and leaves you with $5,600 to purchase prizes for your six salespeople.

Now you work backward, assigning each salesperson a portion of the $100,000 increase, appropriate to the contest's objectives and to the potential of his or her territory. This portion, whether $10,000, $15,000, $20,000, or $30,000 becomes related to his or her quota, which might be an activity-driven result. If they all reach goal, the cost of their prizes would be $5,600 divided by six, or $933 each. If one, several, or all exceed quota, you change the $933 on a prorated basis. These numbers then become your budget. The procedure for budgeting a direct competition or team contest uses a similar process.

Some contests and incentive plans may involve objectives and activities that do not produce immediate sales or profit increases and are thus more difficult to budget. If the contest's objectives involve more prospecting, improved collections, reducing the sales cycle, or more trials, it is difficult to measure the immediate impact on sales or profits. In such instances you use the same technique, but you must place a value on the longer-range benefits and make certain assumptions.

TIME FRAME AND FREQUENCY

Sales contests that go on too long or are held too often lose their effectiveness because participants lose their enthusiasm and interest. Contests should be looked on as temporary schemes to elicit extra effort in a particular area. Sales contests lasting from one to two months usually prove most effective. Generally, one to three contests a year will provide enough extra motivation for a sales force.

Contests lasting less than a month do not allow salespeople sufficient time to become involved or to translate their enthusiasm into results. The minimum time span for a contest would be that required to perform the necessary tasks. For example, if a contest involves increasing dollar sales or closing ratios to achieve certain goals, you must allow enough time for the salespeople to contact all their important customers. If a contest involves opening new accounts or placing new systems, you must allow enough time for proper prospecting, appointment setting, and callbacks.

PRIZES

To maintain interest and enthusiasm, longer contests require more substantial prizes than those appropriate for shorter contests. You may obtain good results by offering a free dinner for two at a fine French restaurant to any salesperson who increases his or her number of demos by 20 percent, or who reduces his or her territory's overdue accounts receivable by 10 percent in the next 30 days. However, such a prize would not generate sufficient enthusiasm for a contest lasting 90 days that involved opening a substantial number of new accounts or reducing the sales cycle time by 20 percent. By comparison, to whip up enthusiasm for the 90-day contest, you might have to offer a free weekend on the town at a local hotel. One sales manager offers an annual sales contest where the top 10 percent of the sales force measured by exceeding revenue and margin goals receive an all-expense-paid trip to Hawaii.

You can best motivate salespeople by offering luxurious, exotic, fascinating prizes that they normally would not purchase for themselves—in other words, prizes that capture the imagination. Cash, therefore, is not the best contest award and would also interfere with your regular compensation plan. Prizes such as limo service, pamper centers, flowers, or fruits of the month work better than cash.

If your budget is $300, dinner for two at a fine restaurant along with theater or sporting event tickets might provide an appropriate prize. If your budget is $800, a weekend for two on the town or a high-definition flat-screen home entertainment system might prove an appropriate prize. If your budget is $2,000, a professional digital camera, computer, or a weekend for two in New York, San Francisco, or New Orleans might provide an appropriate prize.

Always offer a choice because one type of prize is seldom acceptable to all the participants, yet you want all participants motivated to win a prize. For example, some salespeople do enough traveling during the week and would prefer a prize for the house rather than another trip.

Prizes such as maid service, babysitting, days off, entertainment, travel, lottery tickets, golf tees, or tennis lessons that benefit both the participant and spouse work well. This produces a little extra pressure at home to perform well and a little extra prestige for winning. Also, prizes such as computers, free cellular phone time, car wash coupons, auto accessories, GPS devices, home digital voice mail services or devices, time management software, PDAs, or online service subscriptions that a salesperson can use on the job prove very appropriate. One sales manager offers an annual sales contest where the top 25 percent of the sales force as measured by exceeding goal can attend an off-site training program of their choice.

The Internal Revenue Service considers the cash value or cost of most prizes as taxable income to the recipient. However, some prizes valued under $400 might not be taxable to the employee if considered a gift. You should consult your company's financial officer for details and inform your sales force.

In addition to prizes, you might also consider issuing inexpensive certificates and plaques. These represent a lasting form of recognition, and recognition represents an important motivational force.

Prizes need not be expensive to be effective. One sales manager takes over each winner's territory during an extra day off or offers first choice of vacation dates. Another gives winners an upgrade on their hotel rooms at sales meetings or on leased company cars. Another awards golf lessons and green fees. Another cooks dinner for the winners and their spouses or significant others.

Think about buying prizes from or through your customers to obtain discounts and make friends. A refuse removal company services many hotels and restaurants. If you sell through retail stores, think about awarding gift certificates. Think about asking your firm's suppliers to pay for all or part of contest prizes. The more products or services or systems the sales force sells, the more your firm purchases from suppliers. Industrial paint manufacturers ask their chemical suppliers to pay for contest prizes.

The sales manager for a contract computer programming service ran out of new ideas for contest awards, so he established a mystery prize. All winners and their spouses or significant others attended the awards luncheon. The sales manager announced that the prize was a choice of gift certificates at several local stores, and winners had the afternoon off to go shopping. Ask your salespeople what prizes would motivate them most.

PROMOTIONS

Like the product or service you sell, a successful sales contest requires creativity, merchandising, and promotion. A sales contest must capture the salesperson's imagination by injecting some pizzazz, drama, and adventure into the everyday corporate routine. Make the sales contest fun.

If possible, announce the contest at a sales meeting where you can personally sell it to the group and answer questions. Prepare an innovative promotional piece, clearly explaining the rules and describing or picturing the prizes. If a sales meeting is not practical, e-mail or snail mail the promotional piece to each salesperson with a covering letter and follow up with a telephone or conference call. Sales contests require personal enthusiastic selling by the sales manager to excite the participants.

Create an appropriate name and theme for your sales contest, one that relates to the prizes or objective. If most prizes are home entertainment or consumer electronic devices, you might call it "Electronic Whirl." If most prizes are trips to Florida, you might call it "Sunny Skies." If the objective is to sell recycling, you might call it "Waste Reduction."

Even properly organized individual goal sales contests that start out well can begin losing salespeople's interest at midpoint. To maintain interest, issue weekly bulletins or e-mails on results, write personal congratulatory letters or e-mails to the leaders, and remind all salespeople of the prizes involved. Coach the salespeople on how to meet their goals and win a prize. For example, in order to open 11 new accounts, how many prospecting calls are required? In order to place the new product in 7 accounts, which customers should the salesperson target?

If possible, end the contest with a dinner or a teleconference announcing the results. If this is not possible, issue a bulletin or e-mail with the results. You and the president or vice president of sales or marketing should write congratulatory letters or e-mails to all prize recipients. Remember that a sales contest not only achieves certain specific company objectives and awards prizes to participants but also reinforces salespeople's need for recognition, achievement, fulfillment, status, and belonging. A good sales contest boosts personal morale and pride in the company.

RULES

Many contests fail because participants do not understand the rules. Therefore, keep the rules as simple as possible and ask for individual feedback to ensure that salespeople have a complete understanding. Make certain that everyone knows the opening and closing dates; which achievements are sought by the company; by what date products or services have to be sold or shipped; what products or services, activities, processes, customers, expenses, or accounts receivable are included; how closing ratios, presentations, sales expenses, or new accounts are reported and validated; the basis for awards; how and when prizes will be awarded; and what assistance the company will provide salespeople in the contest. For example, are contest results based on orders or shipments? What about a customer's credit? Will reactivated inactive accounts be counted as new accounts? Must orders be written on the company order form but signed by the customer? Will e-commerce orders count? One very successful contest lost its impact because winners expected their prizes in August but did not receive them until November.

Using this chapter as a guide, put together a sales contest or incentive program for your people. The results will please you.

Sales Managers' Major Mistakes or Weaknesses in Motivating Salespeople

- Having one motivation program for all salespeople.
- Using negative motivation more than positive.
- Not planning motivation, just letting it happen.
- Blaming other functions for sales-related problems.
- Having direct competition contests rather than teams or individual goals.
- Not appropriately mixing fear and love in motivating salespeople. Lack of empathy.
- Lack of personal motivation or inability to communicate it.

- Lack of consistent style.
- Not a leader. Lack of personal discipline.
- Doing salesperson's job.
- Not asking salespeople for input or sharing ideas.
- Using house accounts.
- Not delegating. Not developing successor. Micromanagement.

Questions and Exercises for Chapter 13

- How do you or would you communicate personal motivation to the sales force?
- Design a sales contest for your sales force or a sales force you are familiar with.
- How do you or would you create a sense of belonging in the sales force?

Quiz for Chapter 13

1. Which of these are *not* types of sales contests?
   a. Direct competition
   b. Teams
   c. Individual goals
   d. Goal-based bonus
   e. Commission

2. Which of the following are ways of creating a sense of salesperson belonging?
   a. Salary
   b. Commission
   c. Total dollar compensation
   d. Sales meetings
   e. Teleconferencing
   f. Company social events
   g. Company newsletters

3. True or false?
   Unpleasant relationships represent a negative motivational force, which reduces a salesperson's productivity.

4. Successful sales managers have which of the following in common?
    a. Autocratic style
    b. Democratic style
    c. Persuasive style
    d. Sales oriented
    e. Task oriented
    f. Consultative style

5. Successful sales managers have which of the following in common?
    a. They believe in what they are doing.
    b. They realize they are agents of change.
    c. They can manage a wide variety of salespeople.
    d. They execute and implement well.

6. True or false?
    Company policies and administration that promote an open, constructive, and relaxed environment and embody trust, faith, consistency, and fairness will promote job satisfaction and positive motivation.

7. True or false?
    A salesperson who feels underpaid or on the verge of termination will generally not put forth extra effort to reach his or her goals.

8. Sales contests prove most helpful in meeting specific short-term goals that would include which of the following?
    a. Smoothing out seasonal dips
    b. Launching a new product
    c. Reaching the annual bonus or quota
    d. Increasing the number of active accounts

9. True or false?
    To maintain interest and enthusiasm, longer contests require more substantial prizes than those for shorter contests.

10. Which of the following represent reasons why sales contests fail?
    a. Participants do not understand the rules.
    b. Participants do not have an equal opportunity to win.
    c. The contest is too long or too short.
    d. Prizes are not interesting.
    e. The purpose is to revive an unneeded product or service.
    f. The company already has a 70 percent market share.
    g. The company can't deliver the product or service in the contest.

PART EIGHT

Performance Management

Performance Evaluations

Each quarter a sales manager must not only formally evaluate his or her salespeople's and channel partners' results but also the activities, skills, knowledge, and personal characteristics that drive those results. Generally, you and the salespeople or channel partners informally review results on a continuous basis, possibly monthly or weekly. The performance evaluation and resulting development plan, along with the job description, candidate profile, training checklist, deployment, targeting, strategy, and sales forecast or plan, represent the key control points for sales force management.

Your job as a sales manager is to get work done through other people, to make salespeople successful. Your success depends on their success. To increase sales force productivity, this book recommends that sales managers spend more time dealing with people, process, and technology. Each quarter the sales manager must stop and ask, "How are my people doing?" "How am I doing?" "Is my extra effort

and time bearing results?" "Which of the new ideas, tools, and techniques work best?"

Performance evaluations are equally important for field salespeople, channel partners, inside salespeople, and telesales people. The channel partner's agreement should require quarterly participation in performance reviews. This participation would involve the principal company's evaluating the channel partner and also the channel partner's management's evaluating its salespeople. In evaluating the performance of channel partners, inside salespeople, and telesales people, you appraise the same items as for field salespeople plus a few customized items. For example, for telesales people you also might want to evaluate number of dials, number of contacts, and hours of telephone time. And for channel partners, you also might want to evaluate inventory levels, time training salespeople, and staffing levels.

Performance evaluations force sales managers to manage their salespeople. Many sales managers abdicate their responsibility to a performance-based compensation program and operate as little more than traffic managers. In some firms, human resources takes a major role in hiring and training salespeople, and compensation and deployment issues are decided at management levels above the sales manager. However, performance evaluations can still give such sales managers an important tool to increase sales force productivity. Performance evaluations force sales managers to set standards, be critical, and sit in judgment.

Why Sales Managers Dislike Performance Evaluations

Many sales managers would rather complain about a salesperson or a channel partner than analyze the underlying problems and attempt to solve them through a formal evaluation process. They dislike setting standards, being critical, and sitting in judgment, which are actions that separate the best from the not-so-best sales managers. When sales managers give a salesperson or a channel partner a poor appraisal, they are in effect evaluating their own performance as managers. After all, your job as a sales manager is to make the salespeople successful. When a salesperson fails, the sales manager has failed.

Many sales managers prefer being evaluated by their superior to evaluating the salespeople who work for them. Many sales managers dislike dealing with the possible confrontations that might occur when their evaluation of a salesperson falls below the salesperson's expectations. Successful sales managers deal with these confrontations by concentrating on a salesperson's goals or development plans and through the salesperson's self-evaluation process. When asked to formally evaluate their own results, activities, skills, knowledge, and personal characteristics, most salespeople will be more critical than their manager.

Many sales managers dislike performance evaluations because of the time involved. It takes at least an hour to properly prepare for a performance evaluation and 90 minutes for the actual meeting. Multiply two and one-half hours times seven salespeople, four times a year, and you realize this process requires 70 hours, or two weeks each year. However, because of the many benefits, which we will explain later, performance evaluations actually save the sales manager's time and make his or her job easier in the long run.

The two major complaints from salespeople concerning evaluations involve their boss's not understanding the job or not being qualified to evaluate their performance of the job and their boss's not doing the evaluation on a timely basis. With all the downsizings, right sizings, and corporate reorganizations, salespeople complain their constantly changing sales managers have not had the proper opportunity to observe their skills, knowledge, and personal characteristics. A typical salesperson complaint might be, "How can my sales manager evaluate my skills and knowledge when she has never worked with me in front of customers?"

Another typical salesperson complaint is, "By the time my sales manager evaluates last quarter, the next quarter has ended." If performance evaluations are not completed on a timely basis, they lose their impact.

Sources for Performance Evaluations

In order to obtain the information necessary to evaluate salespeople, the sales manager must ride-with them and read the call reports. Field coaching, as we discussed in Chapter 6, provides the sales manager necessary insights into a salesperson's activities, skills, knowledge, and personal characteristics. A sales manager must ride with salespeople to understand their selling skills and customer, product, and competitive knowledge.

As a sales manager, you are always evaluating your salespeople: in field visits, weekly sales results, sales forecasts, sales plans, 10/10/10 reports, call reports, phone calls, funnel reviews, or hallway conferences. The quarterly performance evaluation represents a summary of each of these less formal encounters. It also formalizes the process into some planned quiet time, when both parties can get their heads in front of their jobs. Planning makes good things happen; not planning can make not-so-good things happen. Because the formal quarterly performance evaluation is a summary of past discussions, it should seldom contain any surprises, which makes both participants more comfortable. The performance

review evaluates a salesperson's results, activities, skills, knowledge, and personal characteristics against the goals expressed in the sales forecast and sales plan.

To efficiently conduct these rather time-consuming quarterly performance evaluations, sales managers must keep a current hard copy or digital log on each salesperson. As suggested in Chapter 6, use the field coaching salesperson evaluation form for each ride-with, and review them before the quarterly performance evaluations. After you and a salesperson discuss a customer call or competitive knowledge over the phone or in the hallway, make a follow-up note for discussion at the next performance review. After you and the salesperson discuss quantifying benefits at a sales meeting, or after you send the salesperson an e-mail based on a call report, make a follow-up note for discussion at the next performance review. With this material at hand, preparation for the performance review is easier, and specific information to substantiate evaluations is readily available.

A sales manager also might use customers and peers as additional sources of information to evaluate the salesperson. How did the salesperson rate on customer satisfaction surveys and the 360-degree climate survey? Did any customers and fellow employees in sales or other departments openly praise or criticize this salesperson?

Benefits of Performance Evaluations

Salespeople have a need and a right to know what the sales manager expects from them, if those expectations are being met, and if not, what corrective action is necessary. They can't read your mind. The salesperson who started out well but has since gone downhill and now must be dismissed might well have been rehabilitated along the way through regular performance evaluations. Companies that regularly evaluate salespeople and hold them accountable outperform those that do not.

Regular performance evaluations motivate salespeople through recognizing positive action and results. Recognition of positive performance motivates a salesperson to do even better, and anticipation of such recognition stimulates self-motivation. Quarterly performance evaluations make salespeople feel useful, important, and worthwhile. Management cares about them.

From a legal standpoint, regular performance appraisals can document and justify termination, leave an audit trail, and prevent lawsuits by ex-employees. Terminations should never be a surprise. Too often, performance evaluations of recently terminated salespeople are not critical enough. The manager has not set standards and sat in judgment.

Most sales managers claim the major benefit of performance evaluations, as is true for sales forecasts or plans, lies in the meaningful dialogue generated between the sales manager and the salesperson. It forces the sales manager and the salesperson to discuss not only results but also the activities, skills, knowledge, and personal characteristics that drive results. It forces the sales manager and each salesperson to agree on individualized objectives, goals, corrective action, and a development plan. Both parties commit to a time frame for accomplishing these performance standards and set metrics for measuring them. Performance evaluations make the sales manager's job easier. You can't afford to waste your most important resource, people.

For these reasons, sales managers also use performance evaluations for channel partners, customer service people, and sales administrators. Just as you have channel partners submit a sales forecast or plan, you want to engage them in formal quarterly performance evaluations. The categories you review may differ, but the process remains powerful. Companies that contractually insist on performance reviews, forecasts, and plans from independent sales representatives, distributors, brokers, and other channel partners receive more of their time, energy, and commitment.

Quarterly versus Annual Reviews

Quarterly evaluations prove more beneficial than annual evaluations. Sales managers cannot realistically evaluate an entire year at one sitting, and salespeople know this. Rather than annual evaluations, I recommend no evaluation. In an annual review the last quarter receives most of the attention. Quarterly evaluations allow you and the salesperson to set quarterly goals and development plans, which are more meaningful than annual goals and annual development plans. Annual reviews place too much pressure on the salesperson and the sales manager. Quarterly reviews remove some of the emotion and allow room for disagreement because the next quarter can show improvement. On a quarterly basis you have a continuous process for improvement—a helpful dialogue rather than a dreaded event. Salespeople don't feel you are using the evaluation as an excuse for reducing their compensation.

Separating Performance Evaluations from Compensation Reviews

Most companies try to separate performance evaluations from compensation reviews even though one strongly influences the other. If salespeople feel the

purpose of a performance evaluation is to justify a change in compensation, they become very resistant to constructive criticism and development plans. Emotional issues overwhelm the process of continuous improvement. In companies with compensation programs heavily weighted by performance pay, these concerns remain less important. Quarterly evaluations help to disconnect this process from compensation. Many companies complete this task by having either a separate compensation review or replacing one of the quarterly performance evaluations with a compensation review. Then the compensation review topics, although related to, are different from the topics in the performance evaluation. Many companies have customized performance evaluations for each functional area including sales. These appraisals evaluate tasks specific to each function or position. However, these companies use a more general universal generic format for compensation reviews.

Some companies use an annual corporate generic performance evaluation for all employees including salespeople. In addition, they have quarterly customized performance evaluations for each function including sales.

What this book recommends is conducting quarterly salesperson performance evaluations with topics customized to salespeople's results, activities, skills, knowledge, and personal characteristics. These topics will vary from one company and sales function to another. This book also recommends asking salespeople to evaluate themselves and set their own goals and development plans. Then the salesperson and the sales manager compare their respective evaluations to reach a consensus on goals and plans.

The evaluation process then involves (1) deciding what you wish to appraise; (2) developing metrics and performance standards for these categories; (3) creating a rating system; and (4) holding an evaluation review meeting with each salesperson. Most important, using the appraisal form, ratings, and discussion, you agree on future objectives and obtain a commitment from each salesperson to a plan and time frame for achieving these goals.

What to Appraise

The evaluation process starts by deciding what you wish to appraise. Prepare a list of activities, actions, personal characteristics, knowledge, skills, and results critical to the successful performance of a salesperson, channel partner, or telesales person for your particular company. This will differ greatly from company to company and may even differ from salesperson to salesperson within the same organization. Performance appraisals are meant to be flexible. Start by reviewing the job description and candidate profile used to hire each salesperson. The job description lists a salesperson's anticipated duties, and the candidate profile lists his or her desired skills, knowledge, and personal characteristics. Next, review the format of your training program, which again lists the skills and knowledge necessary for success. Then add any other items not mentioned in the job description, candidate profile, or training format that contribute to effective performance.

Again you can see that each step in the sales management process relates to the other steps. We must evaluate each salesperson based on anticipated duties, the job description, candidate profile, and the training checklist. Without an accurate job description, candidate profile, and training checklist, it will be difficult to properly evaluate members of the sales team.

The appraisal list will contain quantitative issues such as sales results, quality of results and activities plus qualitative issues such as skills, knowledge, self-organization, time management, reporting, administrative, expense control, personal characteristics, company relations, and customer relations. You must prioritize topics based on their importance to a salesperson's success at your firm. Divide the appraisal list into 12 major categories: sales results, sales quality, sales activity, selling skills, job knowledge, self-organization and planning, participation, paperwork, expense control, customer relations, company relations, and personal characteristics. Whether your sales force sells soft goods or durables, products or services, to consumer, industrial, or government users, these 12 interrelated categories should prove helpful in deciding what to evaluate. These 12 interrelated categories apply to both long, complex sales cycles and modified rebuys, to both relationship and consultative sales, direct salespeople and channel partners, e-commerce, bakery products, motherboards, fiber optics, and telcos.

SALES RESULTS

Sales results should include such items as market share compared to forecast or goal and previous year or period; total dollar and unit sales volume; sales volume as a percentage of quota or forecast; sales volume compared with previous year or month; number of new accounts opened; number of new product placements, number of existing customers lost, and total number of active accounts. Did market share, total sales, total revenues, and total number of customers grow or decline, and how does that compare with the forecast? If a salesperson had responsibility for collections, then results would also include days of sales outstanding or accounts receivable aging.

For longer, more complex sales cycles, sales results also might include such items as movement from one step to the next in the sales funnel for each major

customer and prospect. For each major customer or prospect, has the salesperson moved from qualifying needs to finding a fox, to quantifying benefits or making a group presentation?

SALES QUALITY

The metrics for measuring sales quality would include such items as dollars and unit sales by product or service group, area coverage, pricing, credit losses, territory gross margin, average revenue per account or order, cost per call or cost per sale, and customer mix. Compare these sales quality results to the previous year and forecast or quota. Did the salesperson sell the entire range of products or services or just a few? Did he or she concentrate on selling the least expensive and/or the least profitable? Did he or she maintain list prices or sell-off prices? Did the Ohio salesperson saturate the Cleveland market but neglect Dayton, Columbus, and Cincinnati? Did the Illinois salesperson call on appliance companies but not on printed-circuit-board manufacturers? Did the California salesperson call on chain and discount stores but not pharmacies and garden shops? How many new and existing accounts pay slowly?

SALES ACTIVITIES

The metrics for evaluating sales activities would include such items as number of calls per day or week on present accounts versus prospects, on one market segment versus another, on targeted A accounts versus lower-potential C accounts. For longer, more complex sales cycles, sales activities also might include number of proposals, trials, demos, betas, plant visits, appointments with key decision makers, and contracts. The sales manager knows that certain activities lead to increased sales. As part of the performance evaluation, you need to measure these activities against predetermined standards or objectives.

SELLING SKILLS

Selling skills would include such items as the following:

- Finding prospects
- Qualifying leads
- Asking for referrals
- Lateral sales to different departments within the same firm
- Calling on inactive accounts

- Upgrading accounts
- Doing conversions
- Creating empathy
- Using probing questions to identify customer needs and problems
- Presenting features, benefits, and proof
- Quantifying benefits
- Answering objections
- Shortening the sales cycle
- Identifying decision makers and influencers
- Handling price increases
- Resolving conflicts
- Handling complaints
- Planning each call
- Closing
- Using sales aids
- Written and verbal presentation skills

You base your evaluation of selling skills on observations made during field visits. Part of each ride-with is spent observing the salesperson's selling skills and how he or she relates to customers and prospects. Part of each postcall critique and end-of-day summary involves a discussion of selling skills. The performance evaluation summarizes these postcall critiques.

JOB KNOWLEDGE

The metrics for measuring job knowledge would include knowledge of your company, its customers, the competition, competitive advantages, product or service features and applications, pricing, programs, market and industry information, and company policy. During a customer visit, could the salesperson answer questions on product performance, competitive pricing, industry sales trends, or new applications? Customer knowledge metrics would include knowledge of decision makers, the decision-making process, key drivers of the customer's business, and past history with your company. Information exchanged in e-mails, call reports, phone calls, sales forecasts or plans, sales meetings, and individual meetings would influence your evaluations along with actual observations in the field. Did the salesperson know all the decision makers' names and roles at each customer and understand the steps from search to purchase in the sales cycle? Did the salesperson make suggestions to increase the customer's sales or lower expenses? Some companies also use tests to measure job knowledge.

SELF-ORGANIZATION AND PLANNING

Self-organization and planning would include the following:

- Using time efficiently when traveling in the territory
- Allocating time correctly among different activities, functions, types of accounts, and different geographic areas
- Keeping accurate records and profiles on customers
- Setting up appointments
- Planning each day and week; planning each presentation
- Keeping samples and sales literature neat

Does the salesperson call on clusters of customers or spend many hours traveling between accounts? Does the salesperson use his or her cell phone and e-mail to communicate between customer visits and reduce unscheduled visits? On Monday morning does he or she call ahead for a week from Friday's appointments? Does the salesperson have an objective for each sales call and know what happened on the last visit? Does the salesperson spend too much time in his or her office or car rather than in front of customers? Again, you base your evaluations on observations made during field visits as well as on information obtained from call reports, phone calls, e-mails, sales meetings, and individual meetings.

PARTICIPATION

Participation would include attendance at and involvement in sales meetings, trade shows, seminars, outside workshops, advisory groups, and new product committees; as well as promptly responding to company questionnaires. A salesperson who continually misses or arrives late to training sessions or fails to return memos or e-mails on what new services received the best customer response would receive a poor rating in this category. A salesperson who does mentoring, interviews new candidates, and actively contributes to climate surveys would receive a superior rating.

ADMINISTRATIVE

Administrating, planning, and monitoring the sales effort include the prompt submission of accurate route sheets, call reports, orders, service agreements, expense accounts, customer credit information, requests for advertising material, requests for return permission, sales forecasts, sales plans, customer profiles and status reports, market assessment analysis, and any other required written material. A salesperson who submits call reports once a month when you require them once a week or who submits requests for advertising material after the customer has run an unauthorized ad would not rate well in this category. Does the salesperson properly update customer profiles and account files? Are orders or service agreements filled out correctly in legible handwriting? A salesperson who submits the required customer decision-making steps, names, and roles of decision makers and also tracks the monthly status would rate well in this category. This category also includes a salesperson's proper use of sales force automation and IT tools.

EXPENSE CONTROL

Expense control refers to maintaining reimbursable travel or entertainment costs, samples, betas, in-service training, customer terms, discounts, promotions, freight, and advertising allowances at an agreed-upon budgeted level. If a salesperson's reimbursed annual travel expense is budgeted at $20,000 but actually amounts to $30,000, or if annual territorial cooperative advertising and freight allowances are budgeted at $15,000 but actually amount to $20,000, the salesperson would probably receive a needs-improvement evaluation in this category.

You may wish to carry the sales quality and expense control evaluation one step further by evaluating territorial profits. Using the territorial profit-and-loss analysis discussed in Chapter 9, you can rate each salesperson's profitability in total dollars and as a percentage of sales.

CUSTOMER RELATIONS

Some firms use annual customer satisfaction surveys to measure a salesperson's customer relations. Other firms evaluate the salesperson's ability to solve customer problems and satisfy needs, timeliness in responding to complaints and service calls, conflict resolution, providing technical knowledge, merchandising or engineering skills, stock counting, order expediting, and postsale follow-up services. Does the salesperson call on different types of customers frequently enough, provide the necessary service and assistance, and develop positive relationships with correct customer personnel? A salesperson who avoids target customers that require conflict resolution would need improvement in this category.

COMPANY RELATIONS

Company relations involve abiding by company policies and procedures and cooperating with other company personnel. Proper cooperation with other company personnel or functions in engineering, design, credit, customer service, warehouse, distribution, operations, marketing, and billing create seamless service for

customers and improve employee morale. If it is company policy for salespeople to quote a four-week delivery date or not call the warehouse, and a salesperson continually quotes two-week dates and then calls the warehouse, this would affect his or her rating. The salesperson who annoys fellow workers as a know-it-all or yells at customer service about technical support, such as the Detroit auto after-market salesperson in Chapter 13, would not rate well in this category.

PERSONAL CHARACTERISTICS

Personal characteristics might include such items as enthusiasm, self-confidence, assertiveness, aggressiveness, follow-up, persistence, drive, flexibility, judgment, stability, dependability, sense of urgency, imagination, creativity, initiative, responsibility, team player, consistency, ethics, integrity, problem-solving, and appearance. The salesperson who fights any change in products, services, prices, procedures, or personnel would not be considered flexible. The salesperson you must remind for six months to call on a specific prospect would rank poorly in initiative. These qualitative soft issues, such as personal characteristics, are important to the success of your salespeople, but they are sensitive matters to discuss. Listing these qualities in your appraisal informs salespeople of their importance and forces a discussion of them. Listing these qualities in your appraisal could help control the supersalesperson with the superego whom we discussed in Chapter 13 on motivation.

Exhibit 14.1 at the end of this chapter lists a menu of topics you may wish to include on the salesperson's performance appraisal. Pick those topics most appropriate to the success of your sales organization. Topics can be altered or changed from year to year. The topics and categories contain considerable overlap. Ask salespeople for their input on topics to be added and deleted. In addition, Exhibit 14.1 outlines the major categories you will want to appraise and the measurable features or metrics relevant to each.

Evaluating salespeople quarterly based on these topics forces the sales manager to deal with potential problem areas while they are campfires not forest fires.

The Rating System

After the sales manager decides what to appraise and what metrics to use for each category, he or she must establish a meaningful rating system. The most recent trends in rating systems for salespeople's performance evaluations involve (1) removing middle ratings, (2) keeping it simple, and (3) eliminating overall ratings. This structure focuses you and your salespeople on each category's goals, objectives, and development plan. And it asks managers to set standards, be critical, and sit in judgment.

Rating systems that include good, average, and poor or 1, 2, and 3 encourage managers to select the safer middle ground. Most firms are changing rating systems that involve multiple choices but have middle ground such as those using poor, fair, expected, very good, or excellent or poor, consistently below average, average, consistently above average, or excellent. Many of these firms are adopting binary rating systems—that is, there are only two choices for ratings. Such systems use meets standard or below standard, acceptable or not acceptable, very satisfactory or less than very satisfactory, very satisfactory or needs improvement. Many company presidents insist on the use of such ratings to create continuous improvement of the sales force. They don't want salespeople with mediocre skills, knowledge, and personal characteristics.

Other firms offer more than two choices, but they also attempt to remove middle ratings. Regional sales managers for a software firm must choose between outstanding, very satisfactory, fair, and unsatisfactory. Fair and unsatisfactory ratings require immediate corrective action. Keep it simple and remove emotionally loaded words so that you and the salesperson can concentrate on goal setting and development plans.

In an attempt to eliminate emotionally loaded words, some firms use numbers— 1 through 4 or 1 through 10—and others use letters—A through D. However, at some point the manager must define what these numbers, letters, and words stand for. Salespeople need to know what proficiency level of skills and knowledge result in a rating of C or 3 or less than satisfactory or below standard. What constitutes satisfactory and standard? You need to clearly define whatever terms, letters, and numbers you choose.

The salesperson's or channel partner's appraisal will consist of quantitative issues such as sales results, quality of results and activities, and qualitative issues such as skills, knowledge, self-organization, time management, reporting, administrative responsibilities, expense control, personal characteristics, and company and customer relations. Rating the quantitative issues involves comparing current actual numbers to the goal or forecast and previous periods. Rating the qualitative issues involves using the terms, letters, and numbers mentioned above.

Most companies have eliminated overall or total ratings for each salesperson because such ratings take the emphasis off a meaningful discussion of individual goals for each category or topic. Overall or total ratings carry considerable emotional baggage and often are tied to compensation. Overall ratings create more arguments than meaningful discussions because salespeople obsess over their final score.

An example of a rating system is the following system used by the sales manager for an independent regional telephone firm:

Rating 1: Poor. Accomplishment is significantly below acceptable levels.
Rating 2: Fair. Performance is close to but not yet at an acceptable level. Some improvement has been made.
Rating 3: Expected. Performance is at an acceptable level, with accomplishment very satisfactory.
Rating 4: Very good. Performance is above acceptable level, and accomplishment is satisfactory.
Rating 5: Excellent. Performance and accomplishments are outstanding.

In contrast, the sales manager for an e-commerce B2B marketplace rates each salesperson's performance for each category and topic only as strong or weak, with a note explaining next quarter's objectives and any necessary corrective action. Both sales managers consider their evaluation methods to be successful tools, but the telephone company manager is considering eliminating overall scores and the middle ratings. The e-commerce sales manager will add arrows to indicate changes in ratings from the last evaluation.

Select a rating system that proves most appropriate for your particular sales organization—a rating system that accomplishes the desired results in the simplest, easiest, fairest way possible. Overly complicated rating systems prove hard to administer and understand.

The Evaluation Interview

The ultimate effectiveness of the appraisal process depends on how the sales manager prepares for, organizes, and conducts the salesperson appraisal interviews. Let us assume you currently conduct quarterly performance evaluations. You and the salespeople have some experience with the process. If this is not correct, you must vary the suggested procedure.

GROUP DISCUSSION OF PERFORMANCE EVALUATION

Thirty days before the evaluation date, send each salesperson by snail mail or e-mail a copy of the appraisal form and fully explain or re-explain the process. Some topics may have changed or another rating system added. Be sure to clearly define any new topics, their measurement metrics, and what each rating means. You may choose to do this in a comprehensive memo or e-mail, but you can also devote time at a sales meeting or during a conference call. Include information on the appraisal's goals, benefits, topics, metrics, definitions, rating system, interview process, time frame, changes, and each party's responsibilities. Also include a copy of the evaluation form noting any new topics, metrics, or ratings. Encourage questions so that your salespeople know what to expect and can express whatever concerns they may have. Remember, most salespeople have apprehensions concerning appraisals. Explain that your job involves helping the sales force to improve performance, which leads to greater compensation, and that the appraisal form and interview assist in that task. Exhibit 14.2 at the end of this chapter is an example of a performance evaluation format.

WHERE AND WHEN TO HOLD PERFORMANCE EVALUATION

If the sales force or channel partners reside locally, conduct performance reviews at your office. If the sales force or channel partners reside an airplane ride away, conduct the appraisal interview in your hotel room or at the channel partner's office at the end of a field visit. Set appointments at least a week in advance. The meeting should last one to two hours.

Do not hold appraisal interviews at sales meetings because you cannot devote the proper time and it detracts from the learning or social atmosphere necessary for a successful sales meeting. Combining them confuses and enervates participants. Often, sales managers use sales meetings for individual appraisals because of the convenience. Even though you are pressed for time, especially with an international sales force, don't hold appraisals over the phone. This negates the benefits, insults salespeople, and trivializes the process. Some managers and salespeople prefer to review performance over dinner. Keep in mind the importance of the process.

As stated earlier, schedule performance evaluations away from compensation reviews. Although appraisals certainly influence compensation decisions, the appraisal interview becomes too emotional if held as part of the compensation review. Salespeople may feel that the performance review is being used to justify lower compensation, and that attitude would make the appraisal much less effective.

SELF-EVALUATIONS

Several weeks before the interview, ask the salespeople and/or channel partners to review their past performance, future goals, and objectives. Using the performance evaluation format, ask them to rate themselves on each category and fill in the necessary information on results and data. Salespeople must have access to the results on which they are being evaluated. Ask them to review their previous evaluation and previous goals. Has anything changed? Did they accomplish goals agreed to on the last evaluation review?

At the same time, you should start rating the salespeople and channel partners for each item on the appraisal form, making written comments, noting any corrective action you feel is necessary and suggesting goals and objectives for the next 90 days. Do your homework. Don't wing it. Be prepared to discuss each topic. Review the past three quarterly appraisals for recurring problems, trends, and objectives. Review the notes, logs, and files you have prepared for each salesperson, including the field coaching ride-with evaluations. How does this information influence each salesperson's appraisal? What proof does this lend to ratings?

Some sales managers exchange performance appraisal ratings and goals with the salesperson several days before their meeting. This prevents surprises and gives the participants more time to prepare. Most salespeople download the performance evaluation format and fill it out manually.

At the appraisal meeting, whether in an office or elsewhere, create a relaxed positive atmosphere. Don't accept phone calls, do offer coffee, and sit away from your desk in a comfortable chair. If you give your total attention to the salesperson and the evaluation, you add an element of importance and recognition to both.

After some small talk to put the salesperson at ease, review the reasons for the appraisal process and state what you hope to achieve. Restate the agenda. Pose broad opening questions related to last quarter's evaluation and the salesperson's objectives for this quarter. Review the last period's goals and development plan. Stress this quarter's overall goal of mutually agreeing on guidelines, objectives, action, and a time frame to improve future performance. Remind the salesperson that you are not here to complain about any substandard performance and that another appraisal will be held in 90 days.

Next and most important, review each section of the appraisal form, asking for his or her assessment and then giving yours. You will be surprised how often salespeople rate themselves lower than you do, admitting the need for improvement and help. This makes your job easier and trains salespeople in self-evaluation. The appraisal form becomes a basis or agenda for discussion and thus provides a starting point for talking about the job. Deal not only with results but also with the knowledge, skills, activities, and personal characteristics that lead to results.

BEING POSITIVE, NOT ADVERSARIAL

Be positive, straightforward, and helpful. Ask probing questions that encourage talk. "How did you determine the decision maker, decision-making process, and budget?" Mix praise with criticism. *Appraisal* contains the word *praise*. Reward positive actions and results with recognition. "Your closing skills have improved." "A great job on new business."

Use positive, nonemotional language. Use "I statements" so that the salesperson knows you are expressing your opinion. Deal with issues and problems, not personalities. Don't criticize people; criticize their work. A salesperson may have an obnoxious personality, but the problem lies in being disruptive. A salesperson may be complacent, but the problem lies in loss of market share. A salesperson may be sloppy, but the issue is accuracy. When evaluating a friend, ask yourself, "Would the evaluation be similar if I did not like this person?"

AVOIDING COMMON PITFALLS

Avoid the following pitfalls: Don't overemphasize one or two skills, activities, or results that could lead to an unbalanced evaluation of the person's overall contribution. Alex has weak computer skills but top sales skills. Joan seldom submits required reports but leads the sales organization on new business. Corrective action is still necessary, but keep the larger picture in mind.

Sales managers often view salespeople as angels or devils, when in reality each person has positive and negative traits. One quarter, a salesperson performs well, and she is an angel. The next quarter, performance is below expectations, and the same person becomes a devil. This type of change confuses and demotivates salespeople and makes performance evaluations very emotional and less useful. Fairly evaluate each topic on the performance appraisal and try not to see the salesperson as totally weak or totally strong. This sales manager syndrome is closely related to the fear and love extremes discussed in Chapters 12 and 13 on motivation. Sales managers need to balance fear and love in motivating and evaluating salespeople.

Don't rely on impressions; rely on fact. When discussing weaknesses, have some examples, facts, and figures to offer as proof. "Do you remember the competitor questions you could not answer when we visited Intel on our June ride-with?" "Your closing ratio for this quarter is half of last quarter's." "Your customer profiles don't note the decision-making process." "The number of target account calls on your reports has halved this quarter."

Don't hold salespeople responsible for the impact of factors beyond their control. Don't compare one salesperson to another. Don't talk too much. Instead, listen to what salespeople tell you and search for important messages. Restate what the person says to make sure you have understood it. Summarize points along the way to confirm agreement.

As you and the salesperson move through the performance evaluation topics, explain your ratings and justify them, using supportive feedback, but don't argue, complain, threaten, or lose your temper. Where appropriate, commend strong performance, good points, or improvements first before discussing weaknesses. Stressing the positive reduces defensiveness. However, never ignore unsatisfactory performance. Discuss the salesperson's ideas for improvement. Ask how you can be helpful. Develop trust. Be tactful, frank, and fair but not adversarial. Avoid negative words such as *fail*, *neglect*, or *fault*. Be specific, not general. Be flexible. Ask salespeople to discuss their reasons for poor performance. Encourage open-ended answers, not simply yes or no answers.

Performance evaluations prove less productive when salespeople become overly defensive. If the techniques previously mentioned don't overcome defensiveness, think about how the salesperson "feels" concerning the discussion. What is causing the defensiveness? Share your feelings, experiences, and personal information. Rephrase statements that become too emotional. Skip over sensitive areas of the evaluation and return to them later. Be empathetic to the salesperson's feelings and concerns. Usually appropriate doses of empathy, concern, recognition, praise, and understanding will correct defensiveness.

AGREEING ON GOALS AND OBJECTIVES

Most important, using the appraisal form, ratings, and discussion, agree on future objectives and obtain a commitment from the salesperson to an action plan and a time frame for achieving these goals. The goals should correct weaknesses and build on strengths. Stress their benefits. The time frame should be long enough to achieve the desired goal but short enough to maintain motivation. At the next quarterly appraisal you will discuss whether these objectives were met.

Leave time at the end of the performance appraisals to discuss your salespeople's career paths. What are their short- and long-range goals, and how will you help them reach these goals? One salesperson might want to enter management, another marketing, yet another advance to the top tier of field sales.

At the end of the appraisal discussions, some managers ask salespeople and channel partners for feedback on how to improve their management skills. If you engage in this, be prepared for criticism, and be prepared to make personal changes.

The sales forecast has set the goals for results and the sales plan has set the goals for activities. Each quarter you break the appropriate forecasted revenue, margin, or market share goals into bite-sized pieces. Each quarter you break the appropriate sales plan goals for number of calls, prospecting, the sales cycle, and

marketing funnel into smaller time frames. The sales forecast and plan are integral parts of the performance evaluation.

The agreed-to goals for skills, knowledge, and personal characteristics become the salesperson's development plan for training. How does the salesperson improve specific areas of customer or competitor knowledge and sales skills? What training is needed? The performance evaluation pulls together many steps in the sales management process. You should use information gained from appraisals to improve sales force training and update job descriptions. If you find most salespeople are not selling benefits or are not calling on target customers or are not aware of competitive pricing, possibly your training program requires changing. If you find that most salespeople no longer service customers by counting stock or working with design engineers, possibly the job description requires a change.

ENDING THE PERFORMANCE EVALUATION

Close the performance evaluation session with an upbeat, supportive summary of strengths, weaknesses, and goals. Ask, "Is there anything else you would like to discuss?" Then you and the employee or channel partner sign the appraisal form, which makes it more of a mutual commitment. You both agree to the goals and objectives. The signature does not represent a legal commitment. The salesperson or channel partner may not wish to sign the appraisal because she or he disagrees with it. If that happens, accept it, but express the goal of mutually agreeing to and signing the next performance appraisal. In either case, place the jointly discussed and hopefully agreed to performance evaluation in the salesperson's or channel partner's file and give the salesperson or channel partner a copy. Most firms also ask the sales manager to send a copy of each salesperson's performance evaluation to the sales manager's boss. This represents an efficient means for the next level of management to monitor the salesperson's and sales manager's performance. How well has the salesperson performed, and is the sales manager setting standards, being critical, and sitting in judgment?

Once the performance appraisal discussion has concluded, the sales manager should review any personal commitments he or she has made that require specific action. If you agreed to give the salesperson training audios for the car or videos and CD-ROMs for use at home, make sure you do it. Also evaluate how effectively you conducted the session. Was it fair, realistic, and equitable? Did you set standards and sit in judgment? Were you critical? Would you do it differently next time? What did you learn about the salesperson, the channel partner, the job, and yourself? Did you learn that this salesperson would like to be manager or does not have the characteristics required of a salesperson?

Be sure and follow up on whatever operational and developmental plans were agreed to. The entire appraisal process loses its impact without follow-up because the salesperson or channel partner then assumes that no one really cares about his or her performance. Your follow-up in fact becomes the initial stage of the next appraisal. For example, after 30 and 60 days, review the call reports to see if the salesperson targets agreed-to key accounts or calls on agreed-to market segments.

Sales Force Productivity

This chapter discusses quarterly evaluations of individual salespeople. How should a sales manager evaluate overall performance of the sales force? This book discusses increasing sales force productivity through improved hiring, training, compensation, deployment, forecasting, motivation, and performance management. What metrics should a sales manager use to measure productivity improvements?

The activities and results that a sales manager uses to measure sales force productivity will vary from one company and industry to another, but generally they can be classified as input and output. Some of these activities, or inputs, and results, or outputs, aggregate individual salespeople's activities and results. The activities and results might be stated as averages per salesperson or account or in total for the entire sales force. Some are unique to sales force productivity. Choose the activities and results appropriate for your company, report them quarterly, and compare them to previous quarters and industry standards.

Results, or outputs, might include revenues per salesperson, per order, or per account; margins or profits per salesperson in dollars and as a percent of revenues; costs per salesperson in dollars and as a percent of revenues; and costs per order or per call. Aggregated salespeople's results might include closing ratios, market share, number of new accounts, total accounts sold, lost accounts, and product mix. Activities, or inputs, that create outputs or results might include number of calls per week on present and potential accounts; frequency of calls on A, B, and C accounts; identifying decision makers and the decision-making process; number of demos, tests, betas, and presentations; and hours per week spent in front of customers or prospects. Exhibit 14.3, at the end of this chapter, lists some typical activities, or inputs, and results, or outputs, for measuring sales force productivity.

Sales Managers' Major Mistakes or Weaknesses in Performance Management and Evaluation

- Conducting annual rather than quarterly performance evaluations.
- Not having salesperson do self-evaluations.
- Forgetting to use performance evaluations to set goals and standards.
- Neglecting meaningful dialogue.
- Viewing salespeople as either devils or angels rather than as both.
- Evaluating only (concentrating on) results, not the skills, knowledge, activity, and personal characteristics that drive results.
- Not realizing that weak sales force performance reflects weak management.
- Not being critical and sitting in judgment.
- Not monitoring results between evaluations.
- Not taking action based on evaluations.

(Exhibits start on next page.)

Exhibit 14.1.   The 12 Categories on Which Appraisal Are Based.

Sales Results
< Dollar sales volume
< Unit sales volume
< Percent of quota or forecast
< Compared to previous year or month
< New accounts opened
< Existing customers lost
< Total active accounts

Sales Quality
< Dollar sales by product line
< Unit sales by product line
< Area coverage
< Coverage by type of account
< Credit losses
< Gross margin
< Pricing

Sales Activity
< Number of calls per week on prospects versus present accounts
< Number of proposals
< Number of presentations
< Number of appointments

Selling Skills
< Prospecting
< Using referrals
< Calling on inactive accounts
< Upgrading accounts
< Doing conversions
< Using empathy
< Planning each call
< Presenting benefits
< Handling objections, price increases, and complaints
< Use of sales aids
< Closing
< Written proposals
< Use of IT

Knowledge Of
< Product features
< Company strengths and policy
< Applications
< Pricing
< Customers
< Prospects
< Market
< Industry
< Competition
< Competitive advantages
< Programs

Self-Organization and Planning
< Traveling efficiently
< Customer records
< Allocation of time among accounts and geographic areas
< Planning each day, week, and presentation
< Condition of samples and sales literature

Participation
< Sales meetings
< Trade shows
< Seminars
< Setups
< Questionnaires

Administrative
< Route sheets
< Call reports
< Expense reports
< Credit reports
< Return requests
< Advertising requests
< Orders
< Sales force automation

(Continued on next page.)

Exhibit 14.1. *(Continued from previous page.)*

Expenses
< Travel and entertainment
< Freight and advertising allowances
< Terms and discounts
< Promotions

Customer Relations
< Frequency of visits
< Service and assistance
< Personal relationships
< Handling complaints

Company Relations
< Policies and procedures
< Personal relationships

Personal Characteristics
< Attitude
< Enthusiasm
< Assertiveness
< Self-confidence
< Aggressiveness
< Follow-up
< Drive
< Flexibility
< Persistence
< Judgment
< Stability
< Dependability
< Sense of urgency
< Imagination
< Initiative
< Appearance

Exhibit 14.2.   Account Representative Quarterly Performance Evaluation and Planner.

Sales Results

Revenue

Product Line	Quarter			Year to Date		
	Actual	Quota Budget	Previous Year	Actual	Quota Budget	Previous Year
Private home health care						
Pediatrics						
IV						
Rehab						
Institutional staffing						
Total						

Gross Profit

Product Line	Quarter			Year to Date		
	Actual	Quota Budget	Previous Year	Actual	Quota Budget	Previous Year
Private home health care						
Pediatrics						
IV						
Rehab						
Institutional staffing						
Total						

Number of Referrals

Product Line	Quarter			Year to Date		
	Actual	Quota Budget	Previous Year	Actual	Quota Budget	Previous Year
Private home health care						
Pediatrics						
IV						
Rehab						
Institutional staffing						
Total						

New Contracts Signed

Product Line	Quarter			Year to Date		
	Actual	Quota Budget	Previous Year	Actual	Quota Budget	Previous Year
Private home health care						
Pediatrics						
IV						
Rehab						
Institutional staffing						
Total						

(Continued on next page.)

Exhibit 14.2.   *(Continued from previous page.)*

Fill Rate and/or Number of Admissions

Product Line	Quarter			Year to Date		
	Actual	Quota Budget	Previous Year	Actual	Quota Budget	Previous Year
Private home health care						
Pediatrics						
IV						
Rehab						
Institutional staffing						
Total						

Comments, goals, and objectives:

_____

_____

_____

_____

_____

Payors

	Quarter			Year to Date		
	Actual	Quota Budget	Previous Year	Actual	Quota Budget	Previous Year
Medicare						
Insurance						
HMO/PPOs						
Total						

Comments, goals, and objectives:

_____

_____

_____

_____

_____

Market Penetration

Number of active physicians:

- Beginning of quarter   _____
- End of quarter   _____
- Percentage increase or decrease _____

Comments, goals, and objectives:

_____

_____

_____

_____

_____

(Continued on next page.)

Exhibit 14.2. *(Continued from previous page.)*

Customer Satisfaction

- Number of survey respondents that gave overall rating of
  very satisfactory   _____

Comments, goals, and objectives:

_____
_____
_____
_____
_____

Sales Activities

	Goal	Actual	Previous Quarter
Number of referral-source in-person calls a week:			
o Existing	___	___	___
o Prospecting	___	___	___
Frequency of visits to A accounts	___	___	___
Frequency of visits to B and C accounts	___	___	___
Efficient coverage of managed care	Very satisfactory	Less than very satisfactory	
Effective targeting	Very satisfactory	Less than very satisfactory	

Comments, goals, and objectives:

_____
_____
_____
_____
_____

Working Knowledge Of

Physicians	Very satisfactory	Less than very satisfactory
Payors or managed care	Very satisfactory	Less than very satisfactory
Facilities		
o Hospitals	Very satisfactory	Less than very satisfactory
o Extended care	Very satisfactory	Less than very satisfactory
Products		
o Nursing services	Very satisfactory	Less than very satisfactory
o Infusion services (acute and chronic)	Very satisfactory	Less than very satisfactory

(Continued on next page.)

Exhibit 14.2. *(Continued from previous page.)*

- Competition   Very satisfactory   Less than very satisfactory
- Competitive advantages   Very satisfactory   Less than very satisfactory
- Disease management programs   Very satisfactory   Less than very satisfactory
- Technical terminology   Very satisfactory   Less than very satisfactory
- Territory management   Very satisfactory   Less than very satisfactory
- Time management   Very satisfactory   Less than very satisfactory
- Company policies   Very satisfactory   Less than very satisfactory

Comments, goals, and objectives:

_____
_____
_____
_____
_____

Selling Skills

- Making appointments   Very satisfactory   Less than very satisfactory
- Precall planning   Very satisfactory   Less than very satisfactory
- Research on each account   Very satisfactory   Less than very satisfactory
- Building rapport   Very satisfactory   Less than very satisfactory
- Probing questions to uncover   Very satisfactory   Less than very satisfactory
  needs or problems to solve
- Needs analysis   Very satisfactory   Less than very satisfactory
- Value-added propositions   Very satisfactory   Less than very satisfactory
- Benefits statements   Very satisfactory   Less than very satisfactory
- Using referrals   Very satisfactory   Less than very satisfactory
- Overcoming objections   Very satisfactory   Less than very satisfactory
  o   Pricing   Very satisfactory   Less than very satisfactory
  o   Happy with current   Very satisfactory   Less than very satisfactory
      provider
  o   Service limitations   Very satisfactory   Less than very satisfactory

- Closing   Very satisfactory   Less than very satisfactory
- Negotiating skills   Very satisfactory   Less than very satisfactory
- Postcall analysis   Very satisfactory   Less than very satisfactory

Comments, goals, and objectives:

_____
_____
_____
_____
_____
_____

(Continued on next page.)

Exhibit 14.2. *(Continued from previous page.)*

Planning and Monitoring Sales Effort

• Market assessment analysis	Very satisfactory	Less than very satisfactory
• Sales forecast	Very satisfactory	Less than very satisfactory
• Sales plan	Very satisfactory	Less than very satisfactory
• Weekly activity reports	Very satisfactory	Less than very satisfactory
• Daily call reports	Very satisfactory	Less than very satisfactory
• Key account notes	Very satisfactory	Less than very satisfactory
• Territory management system	Very satisfactory	Less than very satisfactory
• Expense reports	Very satisfactory	Less than very satisfactory

Comments, goals, and objectives:

_____

_____

_____

_____

_____

Participation

• Sales meetings	Very satisfactory	Less than very satisfactory
• Field training	Very satisfactory	Less than very satisfactory
• Trade shows	Very satisfactory	Less than very satisfactory
• Mentoring	Very satisfactory	Less than very satisfactory

Comments, goals, and objectives:

_____

_____

_____

_____

_____

Customer and/or Company Relations

• Use of updated customer files and profiles	Very satisfactory	Less than very satisfactory
• Use of CRM	Very satisfactory	Less than very satisfactory
• Customer satisfaction surveys	Very satisfactory	Less than very satisfactory
• Understanding and usage of company policies	Very satisfactory	Less than very satisfactory
• Expense control	Very satisfactory	Less than very satisfactory
• Positive relations with other company personnel	Very satisfactory	Less than very satisfactory

(Continued on next page.)

Exhibit 14.2.   *(Continued from previous page.)*

Comments, goals, and objectives:

_____
_____
_____
_____
_____

Personal Characteristics

• Appearance	Very satisfactory	Less than very satisfactory
• Enthusiasm	Very satisfactory	Less than very satisfactory
• Self-organization	Very satisfactory	Less than very satisfactory
• Follow-up	Very satisfactory	Less than very satisfactory
• Sense of urgency	Very satisfactory	Less than very satisfactory
• Team player	Very satisfactory	Less than very satisfactory
• Self-confidence	Very satisfactory	Less than very satisfactory
• Assertiveness	Very satisfactory	Less than very satisfactory
• Drive to succeed	Very satisfactory	Less than very satisfactory
• Persistence	Very satisfactory	Less than very satisfactory
• Business judgment	Very satisfactory	Less than Very satisfactory
• Consistency	Very satisfactory	Less than very satisfactory
• Creativity or ability to develop new ideas	Very satisfactory	Less than very satisfactory
• Ethics; integrity	Very satisfactory	Less than very satisfactory
• Self-starter	Very satisfactory	Less than very satisfactory
• Initiative in solving problems	Very satisfactory	Less than very satisfactory
• Written and verbal communications	Very satisfactory	Less than very satisfactory

Comments, goals, and objectives:

_____
_____
_____
_____

Summary Plan of Action

_____
_____
_____
_____
_____
_____
_____
_____
_____
_____

(Continued on next page.)

Exhibit 14.2. *(Continued from previous page.)*

I agree to these goals and objectives:

_____   _____
Manager   Salesperson

Salesperson's Career Objectives:

Salesperson's Comments about His or Her Manager:

Exhibit 14.3.   Measuring Sales Force Productivity.

Activities and/or Input

- Number of calls per week on present and potential accounts.
- Frequency of calls on A, B, and C accounts.
- Identify decision maker and decision-making process.
- Number of demos, tests, betas, and presentations.
- Hours per week spent in front of customers or prospects.
- Actual versus goals and objectives versus previous period.

Results and/or Output

- Revenues per salesperson, per account. Margins or profits per salesperson in dollars and as a percent of revenues
- Costs per salesperson in dollars and as a percent of revenues.
- Closing ratios. New accounts conversion ratio.
- Market share for territory and by customer share by account.
- Number of new accounts.
- Actual versus previous period and forecast.
- Margins and costs per call, per customer.
- Number of accounts sold versus total accounts in territory.
- Product mix.
- Lost accounts.
- Average order size.
- Sales expenses in dollars and as a percent of sales.
- Average cost of a call.

Questions and Exercises for Chapter 14

- Does your company use a customized quarterly performance evaluation for salespeople?
- What sales force results, activities, skills, knowledge, and personal characteristics important to the success of your firm or a firm you are familiar with should be evaluated?
- What rating system would you use?
- How would you conduct the appraisal interview?

Quiz for Chapter 14

1. Which of these statements are correct? Sales managers dislike performance evaluations because
   a. They are really evaluating themselves.
   b. It forces them to set standards, be critical, and sit in judgment.
   c. They are time–consuming.
   d. There may be confrontations.

2. Which of the following are benefits of performance evaluations?
   a. Motivation
   b. Meaningful dialogue
   c. Compensation
   d. Training
   e. Lawsuit prevention

3. True or false?
   Annual performance appraisals are more productive than quarterly performance appraisals.

4. True or false?
   It is efficient to combine the performance evaluation and compensation review.

5. Which of the following should *not* be a topic in a salesperson's performance review?
   a. Sales results
   b. Sales quality
   c. Compensation
   d. Skills
   e. Personal characteristics

6. True or false?
   The rating system for a performance evaluation should allow the sales manager plenty of middle ground.

7. True or false?
   Salespeople are either angels or devils.

8. True or false?
   To save time, it is best to hold performance reviews by phone.

9. True or false?
    Asking salespeople to evaluate themselves causes a lot of conflicts.

10. True or false?
    We ask salespeople to sign their performance evaluation to make them legally binding.

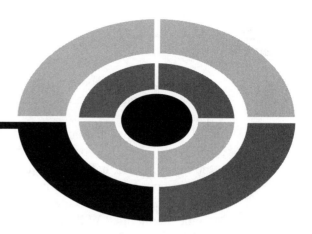

Final Thoughts

After reading this book, you now know what separates the best sales managers from the mediocre:

1. The will to manage—the will to set standards, be critical, and sit in judgment
2. The ability to manage change
3. Personal motivation
4. Proper delegation
5. Good communication with the sales force
6. The ability to execute and implement
7. Proper management of both rookies and veterans
8. The ability to train or terminate weak salespeople

The book contains hundreds of good sales management ideas on hiring, training, compensation, organization, deployment, forecasting, motivation, and performance management. To improve sales force productivity, you must choose those ideas most appropriate for your firm and then implement them. Execution and implementation make the difference between success and failure in sales force management.

I suggest you prepare a list of action items based on each chapter. Divide the action items into two groups: those that require management approval and those that do not.

Then prioritize the action items based on cost, ease of use, financial impact, or revenue benefits, or some other metric. Set a time frame for implementing the top 10 ideas that don't require management approval and the top 10 that do require approval. Consider how you will sell certain ideas to management. Will you emphasize that the ideas support the company vision of customer service or employee morale? Will you emphasize the expected revenue benefits?

I know you have gained many new ideas from this book, but knowledge is power only if we use it. So bridge the gap between ideas and action by deciding on priorities and time frames.

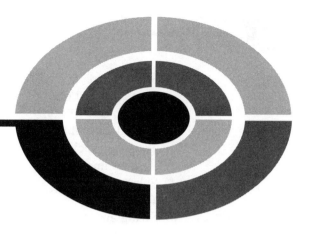

Final Exam

1. Which of these is not part of the sales management process?
   a. Strategies and objectives
   b. Hiring or recruitment
   c. Training or development
   d. Compensation
   e. Forecast or plans
   f. Product development
   g. Nonmonetary motivation
   h. Performance management and evaluations
   i. Market research

2. Which two of these do not separate the best sales managers from the not-so-best sales managers?
   a. Strong financial skills
   b. The will to manage
   c. Agent of change
   d. Strong communication skills
   e. The ability to execute and implement
   f. Strong selling skills

3. Select from this list the key control points.
   a. Strategies and objectives
   b. The job description
   c. Candidate profile
   d. Training checklist
   e. Product line P&L
   f. Sales contests
   g. Targeting
   h. Sizing and deployment

4. Which of these are parts of the changing landscape?
   a. Shorter product or service life cycles
   b. Longer, more complex sales cycles
   c. Group decision making
   d. Intense competition
   e. Less customer loyalty

5. True or false?
   Often the best salesperson does not have the skills, knowledge, experience, or personal characteristics appropriate for a sales manager.

6. Which of these strategic issues should be included in the job description and candidate profile?
   a. Target accounts, markets, and products
   b. Concentrating on new accounts versus further penetration of existing accounts
   c. Buyer behavior
   d. Negotiating price, delivery, or customization
   e. Channel choice

7. Which of the following salesperson's tactical duties should be included in a job description?
   a. Sales and servicing
   b. Planning
   c. Reporting
   d. Company relations
   e. Administrative chores

8. Which of these would be included under personal characteristics in a salesperson's candidate profile?
   a. Confidence
   b. Enthusiasm
   c. Persistence

    d. Team player

    e. Creative

    f. Appearance

9. Which of these is not a source for hiring salespeople?
   a. From within the firm
   b. Customers
   c. Referrals from employees
   d. Suppliers
   e. Competition
   f. Recruiters
   g. Media
   h. Internet
   i. Past employees

10. Which of these screening techniques should a sales manager use in hiring a salesperson?
    a. Telephone interviews
    b. Personal interviews
    c. Reference checking
    d. Testing
    e. Meeting the spouse

11. Which of these references can provide reliable information on the candidate?
    a. Customers
    b. Competitors
    c. Previous supervisors
    d. Peers

12. Which of these background investigations should be checked before hiring a candidate?
    a. Credit
    b. Criminal
    c. Education degrees
    d. Driver's license
    e. Drugs

13. Which of these are strategic training issues?
    a. Getting people from "0" to full productivity faster
    b. Reducing the sales cycle
    c. Increasing revenues
    d. Decreasing costs

14. Which topic should *not* be on the training checklist?
    a. Product knowledge
    b. Customer knowledge
    c. Salesperson motivation
    d. Selling skills

15. Which of these items should be on a customer profile?
    a. Decision maker
    b. Decision-making process
    c. Customer's markets
    d. Decision maker's hobbies
    e. Decision maker's favorite restaurant

16. To be successful, a firm must have a competitive advantage in which of the following categories?
    a. New product innovation
    b. Customer intimacy
    c. Operational efficiency
    d. Sales force organization

17. Strategic sales skills involve understanding which of the following?
    a. Decision-making process
    b. Obtaining an appointment
    c. Probing questions
    d. Value-added propositions
    e. Quantifying benefits

18. Tactical sales skills involve understanding which of the following?
    a. Qualifying customers
    b. Precall planning
    c. Obtaining an appointment
    d. Decision-making process
    e. Probing questions
    f. Overcoming objectives
    g. Closing

19. Quantifying benefits involves proving which of the following?
    a. How your product or service can increase customer revenues
    b. How your product or service can lower customer expenses
    c. How your product or service can lower customer working-capital and capital expenditure needs
    d. How your product or service can improve the customer's employee morale and the customer's company image

20. In training salespeople to overcome customer objections, the sales manager should use which of the following?
    a. Emphasize that objections show interest.
    b. Ask salespeople to restate the customer objections in front of the customer.
    c. At sales meetings, have salespeople present a list of their most common objections and how to overcome them.
    d. Have salespeople move on to another customer if the same objection surfaces twice.

21. Which of these are correct? After each customer visit on a ride-with, the sales manager should
    a. Ask the salesperson what went well and poorly.
    b. Tell the salesperson what went well and poorly.
    c. Review the objectives.
    d. Agree on follow-up.
    e. See if the salesperson adds new information to the customer profile.

22. Which of the following make sales meetings more interesting and productive?
    a. Salespeople's presenting certain topics
    b. Inviting a customer to present certain topics
    c. Inviting channel partners to attend
    d. Inviting sales support personnel to attend
    e. Presenting administrative issues and sales results

23. Which of these factors influence the level of sales force compensation?
    a. Complexity of sale
    b. Type salesperson you wish to attract
    c. Salesperson's influence on the sale
    d. Type product or service you sell

24. Which of these factors influence the mix between fixed and performance pay for salespeople?
    a. Complexity of sale
    b. Type of salesperson you wish to attract
    c. Salesperson's influence on the sale
    d. Type of product or service you sell

25. A salesperson's prominence in the sale is influenced by which of these factors?
    a. Team selling
    b. Closed bids

   c. Branding

   d. Selling skills

26. Which of these positive actions and results should be part of the salesperson's compensation reward?

   a. Revenue growth

   b. Profit growth

   c. Number of new accounts

   d. Customer satisfaction

   e. Teamwork

27. A bonus differs from a commission because

   a. A bonus is a deferred reward for exceeding a goal.

   b. A commission is expressed as a rate or percentage, and a bonus is expressed as a dollar amount.

   c. Sometimes a portion of a bonus is deferred until next year while commissions are paid immediately.

   d. Commissions reward positive action and results on the part of salespeople that are important to the company's success, but bonuses do not.

28. For commission plans to motivate salespeople, you require which of the following:

   a. Territories of unequal potential

   b. Territories of equal potential

   c. High salesperson influence on the sale

   d. Low salesperson influence on the sale

29. Goal-based bonus plans prove most effective when

   a. Territories have equal potential.

   b. When goal setting proves difficult.

   c. When businesses are just starting.

30. After altering sales force compensation, when should you measure whether changes produced desired results?

   a. After one month

   b. After one quarter

   c. After one year

   d. After one sales cycle

31. In arriving at a salesperson's breakeven point, you must consider which of the following factors?

   a. Gross margin after costs of goods sold

   b. Cost to put salesperson on road

c. Operating profit before cost of putting salesperson on road

d. Allocated overhead expenses

32. In arriving at a salesperson's contribution margin, you must consider which of the following factors?
   a. Net revenue
   b. Cost of putting the salesperson on road
   c. Bad debts
   d. Local advertising
   e. Allocated general and administrative expenses

33. In choosing between various sales channels (channel choice), you should *not* consider which of the following factors?
   a. Type of customers
   b. Type of selling
   c. Operating issues
   d. Type of product or service
   e. Sizing and deployment
   f. Channel conflicts
   g. Performance pay
   h. Dollars of contribution margin

34. In choosing whether to organize by major product line, major customer, geography, or function, you should consider which of the following factors?
   a. Type of customer
   b. Type of product
   c. Type of salesperson
   d. Job description
   e. Candidate profile
   f. Costs

35. True or false?
   Sales force sizing and deployment depends on creating territories of equal potential, a salesperson's workload, and a salesperson's call capacity.

36. A salesperson's time allocation planner contains which of the following items?
   a. The number of A, B, and C accounts in the territory
   b. The frequency of A, B, and C account calls
   c. The number of prospecting and service calls per period
   d. The number of calls a salesperson can make a year
   e. The salesperson's breakeven point

37. Items appearing on a salesperson's time log include which of the following? Time spent
    a. With customers.
    b. Traveling to see customers.
    c. Preparing bids or proposals.
    d. In conflict resolution.
    e. On personal matters.
    f. Playing golf with customers.

38. Items appearing on a sales manager's time log include which of the following? Time spent on
    a. Sales meetings.
    b. Field coaching.
    c. Lunch with salespeople.
    d. Performance management.
    e. Conflict resolution.

39. Which of these statements are correct? Preparing a sales forecast involves discussing
    a. Past and present sales trends.
    b. Changes at customers.
    c. Changes at competition.
    d. Changes in demand trends and business conditions.
    e. Changes within your company.

40. Which of the following are possible problems with a salesperson's bubble-up sales forecast?
    a. Salespeople may intentionally underestimate their sales.
    b. Salespeople may not take the forecast seriously.
    c. Salespeople may not have enough data to prepare an accurate forecast.
    d. Management may ask for numbers higher than the salesperson's forecast.

41. In preparing a sales forecast, the salesperson and sales manager must look at which of the following changes within the company?
    a. Competitors
    b. Past and present sales trends
    c. Market changes
    d. Capacity
    e. Prices
    f. Technology
    g. Strategy

   h. Promotion

   i. Territory boundaries

42. The 10/10/10 forecasting and time management tool involves which of the following?
    a. Top 10 competitors
    b. Top 10 growth accounts
    c. Top 10 products or services
    d. Top 10 prospects
    e. Top 10 accounts in dollars of revenue

43. Which of these is *not* a salesperson motivational need?
    a. Praise and recognition
    b. Feeling useful
    c. Challenge and achievement
    d. Sales meetings
    e. Authority and freedom
    f. Personal growth
    g. Belonging
    h. Competent leadership

44. From the following list, rank the top drivers of salesperson engagement.
    a. Competitive health benefits
    b. Competitive base pay
    c. Career advancement opportunities
    d. Work and life balance
    e. Challenging work
    f. Reputation of company
    g. Customer satisfaction
    h. Input in decision making

45. Which of the following represent ways to recognize salespeople?
    a. Salesperson of the month
    b. Top management involvement
    c. Honor societies
    d. Ranking salespeople
    e. Career ladder of titles

46. Which of the following represent ways to make salespeople feel useful, important, and worthwhile?
    a. Not returning their phone calls or e-mails
    b. Field coaching
    c. Performance evaluations

d. Bubble-up sales forecasts
    e. Centralizing decision-making authority

47. Which of the following are ways of creating a sense of salesperson belonging?
    a. Salary
    b. Commission
    c. Total dollar compensation
    d. Sales meetings
    e. Teleconferencing
    f. Company social events
    g. Company newsletters

48. Successful sales managers have which of the following management styles in common?
    a. Autocratic style
    b. Democratic style
    c. Persuasive style
    d. Sales-oriented style
    e. Task-oriented style
    f. Consultative style

49. Successful sales managers have which of the following in common?
    a. They believe in what they are doing.
    b. They realize they are agents of change.
    c. They can manage a wide variety of salespeople.
    d. They execute and implement well.

50. Which of the following represent reasons why sales contests fail?
    a. Participants do not understand the rules.
    b. Participants do not have an equal opportunity to win.
    c. The contest is too long or too short.
    d. Prizes are not interesting.
    e. The purpose is to revive an unneeded product or service.
    f. The company already has a 70 percent market share.
    g. The company can't deliver the product or service in the contest.

51. Which of the following are the benefits of performance evaluations?
    a. Motivation
    b. Meaningful dialogue
    c. Compensation
    d. Training
    e. Might prevent lawsuits

52. Which of the following should *not* be a topic in a salesperson's performance review?
    a. Sales results
    b. Sales quality
    c. Compensation
    d. Skills
    e. Personal characteristics

53. True or false?
    Asking salespeople to evaluate themselves causes a lot of conflicts.

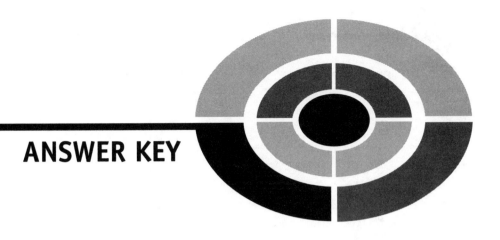

ANSWER KEY

Chapter 1

1. i
2. a f
3. a b c d g h
4. a b c d e
5. True
6. True
7. True
8. a c d
9. True
10. True

Chapter 2

1. a b c d e
2. a b c d e
3. True
4. True
5. a b c d e
6. True
7. e
8. a b c d e f
9. i
10. False

Chapter 3

1. a b c d
2. a c d e
3. True
4. True
5. True
6. False
7. a b c
8. True
9. a b c d e
10. False

Chapter 4

1. a b
2. c
3. a b c d e
4. a c b e
5. False
6. b c d
7. a b c d e
8. a b c
9. a b c d
10. a b c d

Chapter 5

1. True
2. a d e
3. b c e f g
4. False
5. False
6. a b c
7. b c d
8. False
9. a b c
10. a b c d

Chapter 6

1. None
2. a d
3. True
4. True
5. True
6. a b c d e
7. a b d
8. a b c d e
9. a b c d
10. True

Answer Key

Chapter 7

1. a
2. b c d
3. True
4. True
5. a b c
6. a b c
7. a b c d e
8. True
9. a b c
10. a b c d

Chapter 8

1. a b c
2. c
3. b c
4. None
5. a b c d
6. b d
7. True
8. b d e
9. a b c
10. d

Chapter 9

1. True
2. a b c
3. a b c d
4. e g
5. a b f
6. a b c d
7. a b c d e
8. True
9. True
10. True

Chapter 10

1. True
2. True
3. True
4. True
5. True
6. a b c d
7. a b c d
8. a b d e
9. a b c d e
10. a b c d

Chapter 11

1. a b c d
2. a b
3. True
4. a b c d
5. True
6. All
7. False
8. b d e
9. True
10. b

Chapter 12

1. False
2. d
3. b c e
4. a e f h g
5. All
6. b c d
7. a b c d e
8. a b c d
9. True
10. True

Chapter 13

1. d e
2. d e f g
3. True
4. None
5. All
6. True
7. True
8. a b d
9. True
10. All

Chapter 14

1. a b
2. a b e
3. False
4. False
5. c
6. False
7. False
8. False
9. False
10. False

Answer Key

Final Exam

1. i
2. a f
3. a b c d g h
4. a b c d e
5. True
6. a b c d e
7. a b c d e
8. a b c d e f
9. i
10. a b c d
11. a b c
12. a b c d e
13. a b
14. c
15. a b c d e
16. a b c
17. a d e
18. b c e f g
19. a b c
20. a b c
21. a b c d e
22. a b c d
23. a
24. b c d
25. a b c
26. a b c d e
27. a b c

28. b c
29. None
30. d
31. a b c
32. a b c d
33. e g
34. a b c f
35. True
36. a b c d
37. a b c d
38. a b d e
39. a b c d e
40. a b c d
41. All
42. b d e
43. d
44. a e f h g
45. All
46. b c d
47. d e f g
48. None
49. All
50. All
51. a b e
52. c
53. False

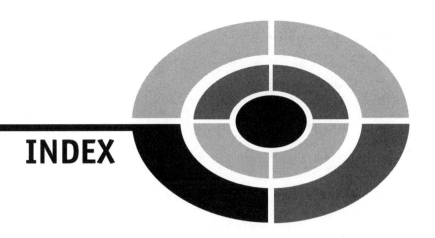

INDEX

Index

Index

About the Author

Robert Calvin is an adjunct professor of marketing and entrepreneurship at the Graduate School of Business at the University of Chicago, where he teaches Sales Force Management and New Enterprise and Small Business Management in the MBA and executive education programs. He is a visiting professor at Xiamen University School of Management in China, where he teaches in the IMBA and EMBA programs. In addition, Professor Calvin teaches sales force management in the executive education program at the Bank of China's International Institute of Finance in Shanghai and in the executive education program at the Chinese European International Business School [CEIBS] in Pudon, China.

Professor Calvin has spent the last 40 years combining his academic and business experiences to create a step-by-step proven formula for success in sales force management. As a salesperson, sales manager, vice president of sales, and company president, he has used this expertise to rebuild many sales forces. As president of Management Dimensions, Inc., he has built an international consulting firm specializing in marketing, sales, and sales management training.

During the last 30 years, in addition to consulting, teaching, and writing, Professor Calvin has bought several medium-sized businesses that were losing money, managed them back to profitability, and resold them to larger concerns. He has also founded several successful new enterprises. His consulting clients range from the Fortune 500 to the Inc. 100, from the new to the old economy, including such industries as financial services, medical devices, navigational equipment, consumer electronics, clothing, and building materials. As a consultant and company owner, he has found new profitable opportunities for many firms.

Professor Calvin has written numerous books, including *Managing Sales for Business Growth* and *Profitable Sales Management and Marketing for Growing Businesses*. He is the author of the McGraw-Hill Executive MBA Series titles *Entrepreneurial Management* and *Sales Management*, the latter of which was the winner of the Soundview Award as one of the 30 best business books in 2001. Both titles have been translated into Chinese.